Published by ROM with the generous support
of the Louise Hawley Stone Charitable Trust

Cisco

FRESHWATER FISHES of ONTARIO

A FIELD GUIDE TO

FRESHWATER FISHES of ONTARIO

ERLING HOLM
NICHOLAS E. MANDRAK
MARY E. BURRIDGE

SECOND EDITION

ROM

Published by the Royal Ontario Museum with the generous support of the Louise Hawley Stone Charitable Trust. The Stone Trust generates significant annual funding for the Museum, providing a steady stream of support that is used to purchase new acquisitions and to produce publications related to the ROM's collection. The Louise Hawley Stone Charitable Trust was established in 1998 when the ROM received a charitable trust of nearly $50 million—the largest cash bequest ever received by the Museum—by its long-time friend and supporter, the late Louise Hawley Stone (1904–1997).

Royal Ontario Museum | 100 Queen's Park | Toronto, Ontario | M5S 2C6
www.rom.on.ca

Manager, Publishing: Sheeza Sarfraz
Publication Editor: Dina Theleritis
Designers: Tara Winterhalt, Virginia Morin
Production Design: Claire Milne
Designer (Cover): Tara Winterhalt

Library and Archives Canada Cataloguing in Publication
Title: A field guide to freshwater fishes of Ontario / Erling Holm, Nicholas E. Mandrak, Mary E. Burridge. Other titles: ROM field guide to freshwater fishes of Ontario | Freshwater fishes of Ontario. Names: Holm, Erling, author. Mandrak, Nicholas Edward, author. Burridge, Mary E., author. Royal Ontario Museum, publisher. Description: Previously published under title: The ROM field guide to freshwater fishes of Ontario. Toronto: ROM © 2009. Includes indexes. Identifiers: Canadiana 20210289570 | ISBN 9780888545282 (softcover) Subjects: LCSH: Freshwater fishes—Ontario—Identification. | LCGFT: Field guides. Classification: LCC QL626.5.O6 H65 2021 | DDC 597.17609713—dc23

The Royal Ontario Museum is an agency of the Ontario Ministry of Culture.

Cover Illustration by Emily Damstra.

DEDICATION

Dr. E. J. Crossman
1930–2003

Dr. E. J. Crossman was Curator of Ichthyology at ROM between 1957 and 1995. Throughout his career, E. J. pursued research on the freshwater fishes of Canada with emphasis on Ontario fishes and the pike family in particular. He published more than 200 articles and books, including the seminal *Freshwater Fishes of Canada*, which he co-authored with Dr. W. B. Scott. *A Field Guide to Freshwater Fishes of Ontario* was to be another highlight of an extensive and illustrious career. We thank E. J. for inviting us to share in his vision of this book.

WHAT ARE FIELD GUIDES

ROM Field Guides are beautiful pocketbooks that connect readers with nature and wildlife across the province of Ontario. Packed with information on the biology, habitat, and conservation of the featured species, the books provide quick and easy access to amateur and professional naturalists alike. Lavishly illustrated with hundreds of colour photographs and distribution range maps, these publications are the definitive guides to the diversity of life found in Ontario.

CONTENTS

INTRODUCTION

Fishes are the most diverse group of vertebrates in the world, representing more than half, or 35,000, of the total number of vertebrate species. Of the recognized fish species worldwide, 43% (about 18,000) are found in fresh waters, although only 3% of the world's water is fresh. Canada is fortunate in having close to one-quarter of the world's fresh water, and close to 220 species are found in our lakes and streams.

Ontario is home to the highest diversity of freshwater fishes of any province in Canada. There are 131 native fish species in 25 families to Ontario. In addition, 22 species have been introduced and have **established** reproducing populations. This diversity is the result of events following the last Ice Age (approximately 10,000 years ago), the wide variety of habitats currently found in lakes and streams across Ontario, and the recent actions of humans. Ontario's native fishes range in size from the Least Darter, Canada's smallest vertebrate, measuring only a few centimetres in length, to the ancient Lake Sturgeon, which can be more than 2 m long. Some of Ontario's fishes are threatened with extinction, while others are abundant and the target of recreational and commercial fisheries.

The purpose of this book is to provide the reader with a deeper understanding and appreciation of the diversity of Ontario's freshwater fishes, and to assist the reader in identifying these fishes in the field. Such identifications may be done with fish in hand or caught by angling or other legal means, or by viewing fishes in their natural habitat. The reader will learn how best to view fishes, how to identify every species in Ontario, and how to distinguish them from similar-looking species. For each species, colour photographs, an interesting biological fact, important identification characteristics, biology (size, feeding, reproduction, and habitat), and a distribution map are provided. This book is the fourth in a series of Royal Ontario Museum (ROM) field guides to Ontario's flora and fauna. *A Field Guide to Freshwater Fishes of Ontario* will provide the naturalist, cottager, angler, boater, and biologist alike with the only modern, comprehensive reference to one of Ontario's most important resources.

FACTORS INFLUENCING DISTRIBUTIONS OF FISHES IN ONTARIO

The current distributions of fishes in Ontario were shaped by two main factors: events immediately following the last Ice Age, and the present-day climate.

GLACIATION

Between 100,000 and 18,000 years ago, all of Ontario was under a sheet of ice that was up to 1 km thick. In fact, this ice sheet covered much of northern North America, including most of Canada. During this time, freshwater fishes, which had previously occupied Ontario, were pushed along the edge of the advancing glaciers and survived the Ice Age in the Mississippi and Missouri River basins, and along the Atlantic coast. Some species also survived in areas of Alaska that were not covered by ice. Toward the end of the last Ice Age, the massive ice sheets started to melt and retreat northward. As they retreated, their meltwaters pooled in depressions along the margins of the ice sheets. Among the larger of the depressions were the Great Lakes. The Great Lakes filled and overflowed with meltwaters, at times being much larger than they are today. The overflow from the Great Lakes spilled over into the Atlantic coastal and Mississippi basins. The meltwaters also caused the sea levels to rise, resulting in the flooding of lowland areas by sea water. The largest of these areas in Canada was the St. Lawrence Lowlands, which was largely flooded by the Champlain Sea. These meltwater connections acted as corridors for the movement of fishes and other aquatic organisms into Ontario. As the ice sheets continued to melt, very large meltwater lakes formed in northern Ontario and central Canada, allowing species to move southward from Alaska and farther northward from southern locations. By about 6,000 years ago, the continental ice sheets were gone, and the land had rebounded upwards following its release from under the weight of the ice, forming the watersheds that are still present today. These watersheds prevented further movement of fishes between river basins. During the colonization of Ontario by fishes following the last Ice Age, the coldwater species (e.g., Lake Trout) arrived first, followed by the coolwater species (e.g., Yellow Perch), and finally the warmwater species (e.g., Northern Sunfish).

CLIMATE

Although watersheds currently provide physical barriers to the movement of fishes, climate provides a thermal barrier for many species where physical barriers are absent. Fishes rely on their environment to regulate their body temperatures. Different species prefer, and can survive in, different ranges of temperature. As a result of decreasing air temperatures with increasing latitude in Ontario, many species are at their northern range limits here. This northern limit is determined by the ability of individuals in the population of a species to survive their first year of life, in particular their first winter. To survive the cold, harsh winters of Ontario, newly hatched fishes need to grow enough during their first summer of life to survive starvation during the winter. The amount of growth that a fish can undergo during its first summer is dependent on summer temperatures, which influence the amount of food that can be produced by its environment. If a fish does not grow enough during its first summer, it will starve and die during the winter. Warmer temperatures associated with climate change are currently moving these range limits farther northward as species, such as the Smallmouth Bass, move naturally or with the help of humans.

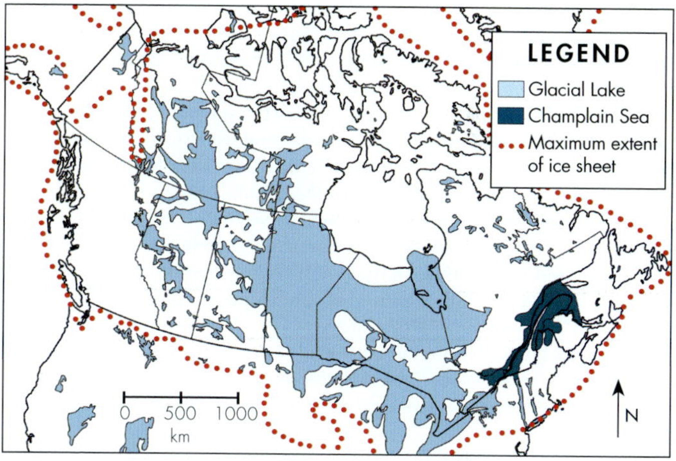

Maximum extent of ice sheet, glacial lakes, and Champlain Sea at the end of the last Ice Age

FISH HABITATS IN ONTARIO

The high diversity of fishes in Ontario is supported by a wide variety of aquatic habitats—from the smallest headwater stream to the largest of the Great Lakes.

Southern Ontario south of the Canadian Shield is underlaid by sedimentary bedrock, and its waterbodies consist mostly of streams. These streams begin in cold headwaters emerging from the ground as springs. These cold, clear waters become warmer, wider, and deeper as they flow downstream and join other headwaters to form larger streams until they end at one of the Great Lakes.

The Great Lakes straddle the Canadian Shield to the north and sedimentary bedrock, as exemplified by the Niagara Escarpment, to the south. There are many habitats in the Great Lakes themselves, including the deepest cold and vast, open waters; warm, shallow, rocky, and sandy shores; coastal wetlands overgrown with aquatic plants; and wide channels that connect and drain the lakes.

The Canadian Shield of central and northern Ontario is dotted with thousands and thousands of lakes and interconnecting streams, ranging from shallow, warm bogs to very large, cold, deep lakes. Some areas of the Canadian Shield are overlaid with the muddy remains of the bottoms of ancestral lakes (see FACTORS INFLUENCING DISTRIBUTIONS OF FISHES IN ONTARIO). Lakes and streams in these areas tend to be warmer and more **turbid**. In the HABITAT section of each species account, fishes are classified as to their preference for cold (<19°C), cool (19°C–25°C), or warm (>25°C) waters.

In the far north of Ontario, widespread wetlands are found in the Hudson Bay Lowlands, an area once flooded by the ocean after the last Ice Age. The wetlands are intersected by very large rivers that drain into Hudson Bay.

Headwater stream

Middle reach of stream

Mouth of stream

Great Lakes – open water

Great Lakes – beach

Great Lakes – wetland

Great Lakes – interconnecting river

Canadian Shield – bog

Canadian Shield – large lake

Hudson Bay Lowlands – larger river

Hudson Bay Lowlands – bog

OBSERVING FISHES

Fishes may be viewed in many ways—in captivity, in the wild from shore or a boat, underwater by snorkelling or scuba diving, or while angling. Fish watching is enhanced by knowledge of how to tell species apart, which habitats individual species prefer, and what time of year is best to look for certain species.

Beyond that, you may encounter other difficulties as a result of the colouration and behaviour of the fishes themselves. Most fishes are countershaded—dark on top and light underneath. This makes them difficult to see from above against a dark bottom and from below against a sunlit surface of the water. Many fishes also camouflage themselves by remaining motionless for long periods of time. It is much easier to view a fish when it is moving than when it is still. Look for dark, moving objects or flashes of silver in deeper water, or the surface wakes and splashes of feeding or spawning individuals.

The very nature of water itself often makes it difficult to view fishes. Water acts as a mirror as it readily reflects, refracts, and absorbs sunlight. The biggest problem facing fish watchers—who wish to remain dry—is glare on the surface of the water. To minimize glare, wear polarized sunglasses, use binoculars, position yourself with your back to the sun, and view at midday on clear, sunny days. Viewing from high vantage points, such as dams, bridges, high banks, or trees, also reduces glare. Fish viewing is often made more difficult by surface disturbances caused by wind or water movement. Plan to view on calm, sunny days and, if viewing in running water, look for smooth water surfaces downstream from obstacles and over deeper pools.

Surface glare and turbulence can be overcome by an underwater viewer. This device can take any number of forms and can be homemade or bought at science specialty stores. The basic idea is that a piece of glass forms the bottom of an open-ended, box-like structure. The glass bottom is submerged while the open end remains above the surface and forms a "window" through which you can see into the water below.

Another way to overcome glare is to view fishes at night. Many fishes are more active at night than during the day. The nocturnal behaviour of fishes often involves feeding forays into shallow nearshore waters. These fishes may be readily seen by shining a flashlight into the calm, shallow waters of lakes and rivers. Nocturnal viewing is enhanced by not only the lack of glare, but also by the observer being camouflaged in darkness.

Spawning season is an excellent time to view fishes from shore. Movements and aggregations of large numbers of individuals often occur prior to, and at, spawning time in streams and in the nearshore shallows of lakes. Spawning adults often have enhanced colouration and anatomical features (e.g., **nuptial tubercles** in suckers) that are absent during most of the year. Some species build nests (e.g., minnows), carry out interesting mating rituals (e.g., sticklebacks), and defend nests and newly hatched young against predators (e.g., basses).

Snorkelling and scuba diving are ideal ways to observe fishes. These activities can be pursued in any lake or stream deep enough to swim in.

Fishes can be photographed with an underwater camera or from shore using a camera with a polarized lens. Keep in mind that water absorbs sunlight and colours across the spectrum are lost with increasing depth. Even photographs taken in shallow water will lose some colour. Caution should be exercised when carrying out these activities in fast-flowing water, and only certified individuals should participate in scuba diving.

Angling makes possible the close examination of captured fish, but anglers will likely encounter only a small number of species found in Ontario. In addition to sport fishes, several of the larger minnows may be incidentally caught. Anglers should examine closely any catch they intend to keep, whereas any individuals to be released alive should be returned to the water as quickly as possible with a minimum of handling. Fish can also be placed in a small aquarium or fish viewer, a specially designed narrow, clear tank used to view fish while keeping them in water.

With patience and experience, fish watching can be an exciting and pleasurable pastime. Please remember, however, that you should do your viewing in ways that will not disrupt the lives of the fishes.

Brook Trout photographed using a GoPro camera

Fish viewer used to take photos of live fishes

Spotted Gar photographed using a polarized lens

USING THIS BOOK

This field guide includes descriptions for all 131 native and 22 introduced species of Ontario fishes. It is designed to be used in the field to identify most adult fishes in Ontario. Juveniles and the adults of some species may not be readily identified in the field. Positive identification of these individuals may require preservation (such as freezing), examination using more technical taxonomic keys (see FURTHER INFORMATION), and a dissecting microscope.

MAKING AN IDENTIFICATION

To keep your fish alive, it is important to minimize the time out of water. Fishes should be transferred using a knotless dip net to a small container for short-term viewing or a larger, well-aerated tank for longer-term holding. Knotted nets can damage scales and remove protective slime, which may lead to infection and possible death. Ensure that the water in the container stays cool. Do not overcrowd your catch, and keep fishes in the dark by covering the container. If you intend to keep your fish for eating, it can be euthanized by a sharp blow to the top of the head. It is important to remember that if a fish is being released back to the wild, it should be returned to the waterbody from which it was removed.

Before attempting identification, familiarize yourself with basic fish anatomy as illustrated in the ANATOMICAL FIGURES. You will need to know the features in these figures to determine the family and species to which your fish belongs.

Turn to the PICTORIAL KEY TO FAMILIES, and identify your fish to family. Look at the general body shape (e.g., eel-like, elongate, or deep-bodied), and check for unique features, such as whisker-like, fleshy structures (**barbels**) on the head. If you are unsure of the meaning of terms, check the anatomical figures or refer to the glossary at the back of the book; words in bold type are defined in the glossary.

The PICTORIAL KEY TO FAMILIES, will direct you to a plate, or series of plates, in the COMPARATIVE PHOTOGRAPHS section. To facilitate identification by comparison, these plates include photographs of all species grouped by similar appearance. In the COMPARATIVE PHOTOGRAPHS section, select one or more species that appear to match your unknown fish, and then go to the appropriate SPECIES ACCOUNTS.

The species accounts are arranged by family, each of which is represented by a different coloured page edge. Families are arranged by the length of time that they are believed to have been on Earth; earlier families (those that have been on Earth for the longest time) precede more recent families and, within each family, species are arranged alphabetically by their common names.

In the SPECIES ACCOUNTS, determine if your fish matches the Description and check Similar Species for possible alternatives. Individuals of the same species can vary greatly in appearance. Counts (e.g., scales, fin rays) and other features (e.g., fin shape, colouration) presented in the Description represent the normal range of variation and do not necessarily include the extremes. Fishes also vary in their colour. For example, fishes from **turbid** waters tend to be pale, whereas fishes from clear water are generally darker. A fish in distress, such as one that has been taken out of water, also tends to lose its colour and become paler.

Once you have identified your fish, check the distribution map to determine if the location where you found it is within its known range. If it is outside the range, it is likely an incorrect identification. There is a small possibility, however, that you have found an individual outside of its known range. In this case, it is important to report it to ROM or an Ontario Ministry of Natural Resources office. A frozen specimen or a series of clear photographs is required to verify a report of a species outside its known range. Some species and most non-gamefish juveniles are impossible to identify in the field and must be taken to a lab for verification.

SPECIES ACCOUNTS

All species are known by a single scientific name and one or more common names. Scientific names are made up of two parts—a **genus** name (pl. genera) and a specific name—and are usually based on Latin or Greek words. The **genus** name is shared among closely related species; however, together, a **genus** name and specific name can be used for only a single species. No two species can have the same scientific name. The first letter is always capitalized in the **genus** name and is always lower case in the specific name. Scientific names should always be italicized. Common names often describe prominent characteristics of the species (e.g., Walleye). However, they frequently cause problems as one species may have several common names depending on regional preferences (e.g., Walleye vs. pickerel for *Sander vitreus*) and language (Walleye vs. doré jaune for *Sander vitreus*). Species in different, but closely related, genera are further grouped into families. Except for Grass Pickerel, the scientific and common names for families and species used in this book are based on the official list published by the American Fisheries Society (AFS) (Page et al., 2023, see BOOKS on p. 474). Based on the 2013 AFS list and changes to be made to the 2022 AFS list, we split the family Cyprinidae into four families that occur in Ontario and merge Umbridae into the Esocidae family. We use the new common name for the Longear Sunfish (Northern Sunfish), and new scientific names for the American Brook Lamprey and Northern Sunfish.

SPECIES ACCOUNTS provide information on the origin of the scientific name and an interesting fact about the species. Food and feeding behaviour are identified in the Feeding section. The nature and timing of spawning behaviour is outlined in the Reproduction section. The preferred location and conditions within lakes and streams are in the Habitat section. A distribution map provides the general range of the species in Ontario. A table summarizes average size, maximum size, and age in years, where known. For recreational species, these values are based on records from the International Game Fish Association and the Ontario Federation of Anglers and Hunters. For all other species, these values are based on records in FishBase (an online resource), ROM collections, and literature sources. For some recreational species, both overall maximum size and angling records are provided. The conservation status of each species in Ontario is summarized in the Status section. Conservation status rankings are provided as of publication date and subject to change, and the appropriate websites should be consulted for current rankings (see INTERNET SOURCES on p. 474). The conservation status of each species in Ontario is assessed by NatureServe at global, national, and provincial levels as follows:

G—Global status, with G5 secure to G1 critically imperilled.
N—Canada status, with N5 secure to N1 critically imperilled.
S—Ontario status, with S5 secure to S1 critically imperilled.
Format: G1-5x/N1-5x/S1-5x, where x is one or more of:

- H—historical, known only from historical occurrences;
- NA—not applicable, not a suitable target for conservation activities (e.g., not native).
- NR—not ranked, has not yet been assessed.
- Q—questionable taxonomy.
- T—infraspecific taxon.
- U—unrankable, cannot be assessed, due to lack of, or conflicting, information.
- X—extinct (G), no longer found anywhere on Earth.
- X—**extirpated** (N, S), no longer present in Canada or the province, respectively.
- ?—inexact, indicates uncertainty in rank.

Two numbers are provided (e.g., G4G5) if there is a range of possible status, indicating uncertainty.

The conservation status of select species and populations in Ontario is assessed by the federal Committee on the Status of Endangered Wildlife in Canada (COSEWIC) and the provincial Committee on the Status of Species at Risk in Ontario (COSSARO) (see INTERNET SOURCES). Although the federal and provincial rankings are consistent for most species, they differ for some. Where they differ between the jurisdictions, rankings are given for both jurisdictions (i.e., T^F, E^P; where F—federal and P—provincial). When a wildlife species has been evaluated for placement in a risk category by COSEWIC or COSSARO, the following status categories are given:

Not at Risk (NAR)—a wildlife species that has been evaluated and found to be not at risk of extinction given the current circumstances.
Special Concern (SC)—a wildlife species that may become a threatened or an endangered species because of a combination of biological characteristics and identified threats.
Threatened (T)—a wildlife species likely to become endangered if

limiting factors are not reversed.

Endangered (E)—a wildlife species facing imminent extirpation or extinction.

Extirpated (XP)—a wildlife species no longer existing in the wild in Canada, but occurring elsewhere.

Extinct (X)—a wildlife species that no longer exists.

Data Deficient (DD)—a wildlife species for which there is insufficient information available to make an assessment.

See INTERNET SOURCES (p. 474) for further information on Ontario species at risk.

DISTRIBUTION MAPS

A distribution map provides the general range of the species in Ontario, based largely on Mandrak et al. 2022 (see BOOKS on p. 474) and more recent collection records. The coloured areas show the known range of each species:

- represents the range in which it is **native**
- represents the native range from which it has been **extirpated**
- represents the range in which it has been **introduced**

LEGAL ISSUES

Several provincial and federal regulations and acts are relevant to the use of fishes and their habitats in Ontario. In Ontario, both recreational and commercial fishing are managed by the province on behalf of the Canadian government. The federal *Fisheries Act* is the basis for regulations covering many aspects of fishes, fishing, and fisheries. The Ontario Fishing Regulations govern all aspects of recreational angling, including open seasons, possession limits, and bait restrictions. The current regulations must be referred to before angling and can be obtained from the Ontario Ministry of Natural Resources and Forestry.

Seasons, quotas, and gear restrictions for commercial fisheries are regulated by the province and, when Indigenous fisheries are involved, co-managed by Indigenous Peoples. The federal *Fisheries Act* also protects fish habitats from harmful alteration and destruction. In Ontario, all proposed projects in or around water must be approved by the federal Department of Fisheries and Oceans, and this protection is enforced by federal Fishery Officers. The provincial *Endangered Species Act* and the federal *Species at Risk Act* protect species and habitats considered to be at risk of extinction. See INTERNET SOURCES (p. 474) for further information.

ANATOMICAL FIGURES

General anatomical characteristics of a soft-rayed fish

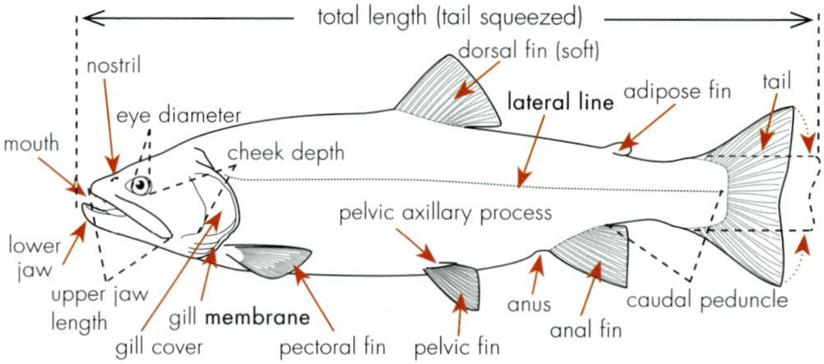

(e.g., Brook Trout)

General anatomical characteristics of a spiny-rayed fish

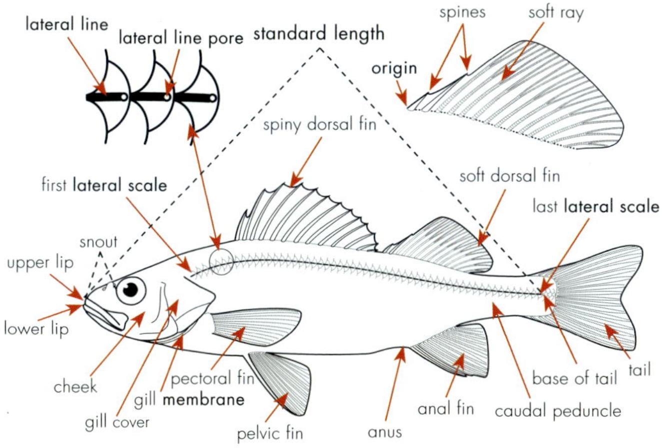

(e.g., Yellow Perch)

Joined dorsal fin—unnotched

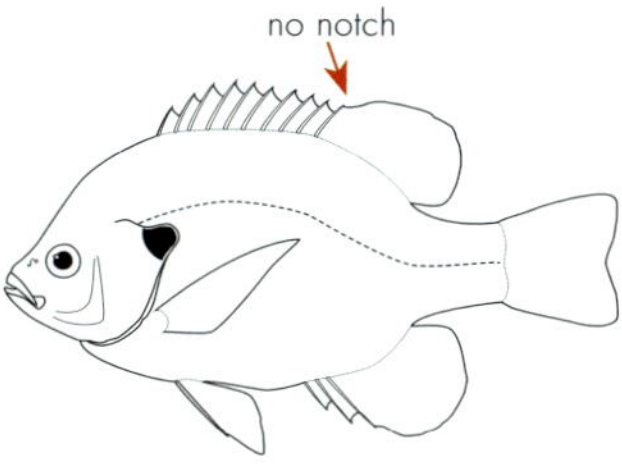

(e.g., Bluegill)

Joined dorsal fin—notched

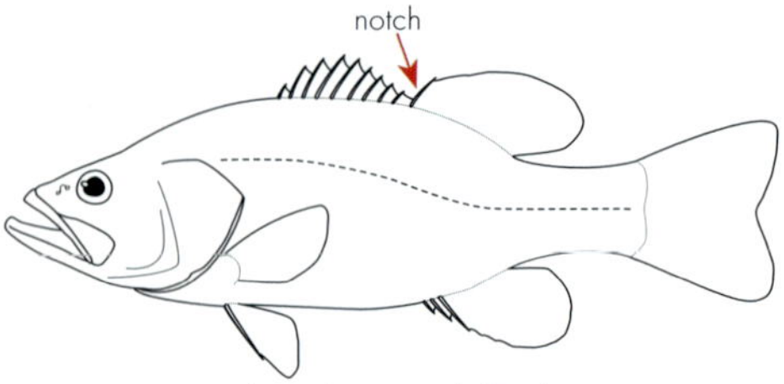

(e.g., Largemouth Bass)

Lateral body shapes

very elongate (e.g., American Eel)

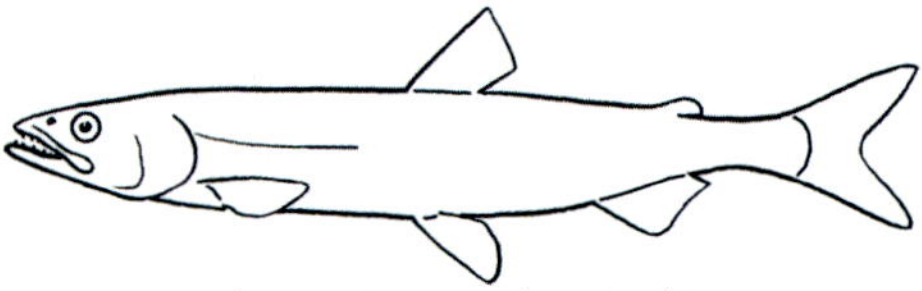

elongate (e.g., Rainbow Smelt)

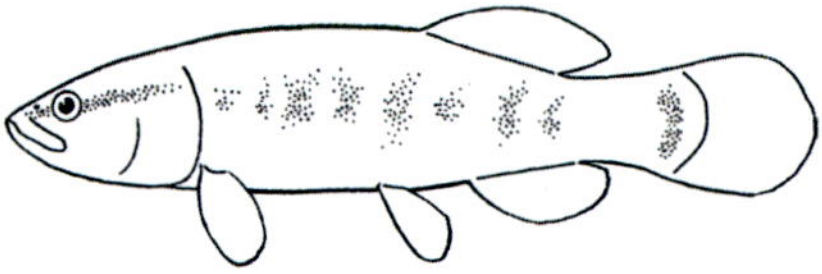

slightly deep-bodied (e.g., Central Mudminnow)

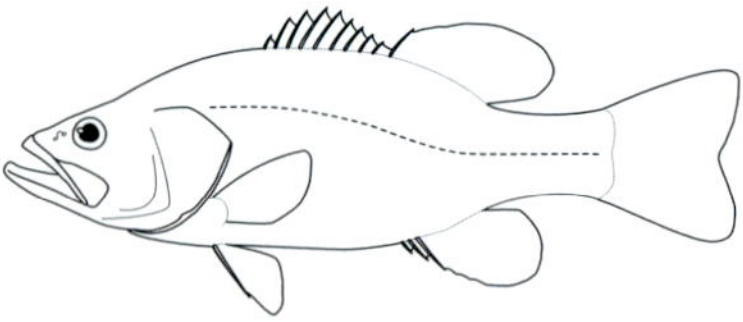

deep-bodied (e.g., Largemouth Bass)

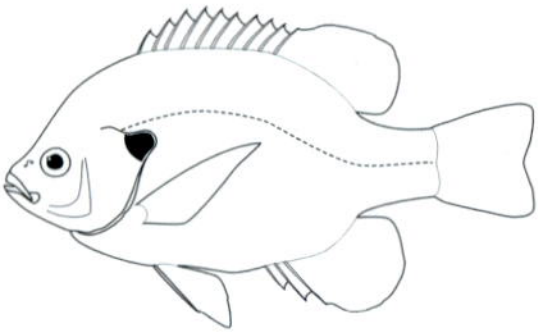

very deep-bodied (e.g., Bluegill)

Cross-sectional body shapes

very thin from side to side (e.g., sunfish)

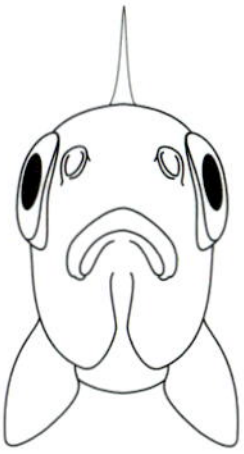

oval (e.g., minnow)

Fins

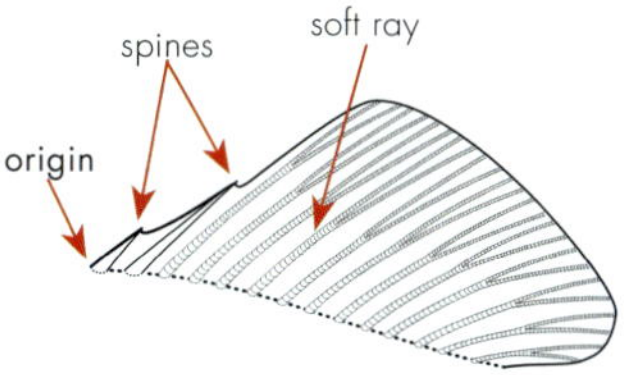

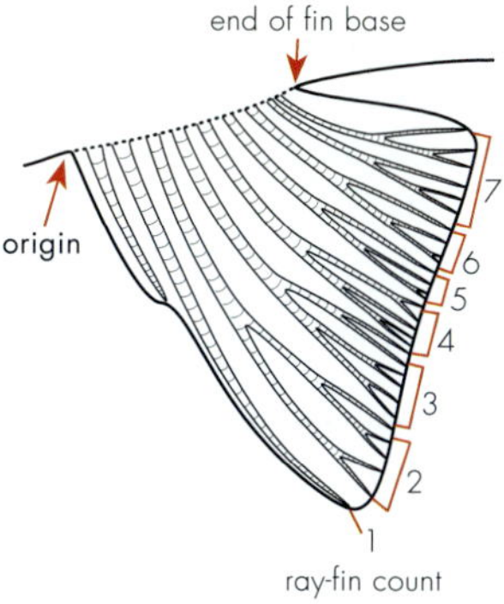

Shapes of fin edges

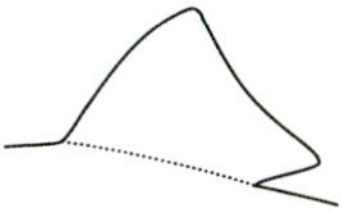

concave

straight

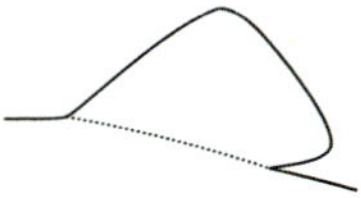

rounded

Scales

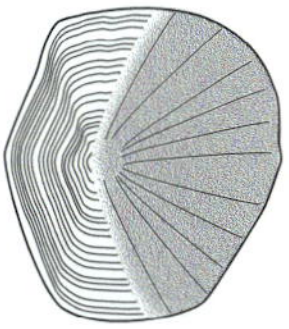

cycloid scale

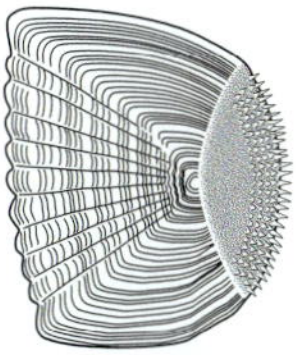

ctenoid scale

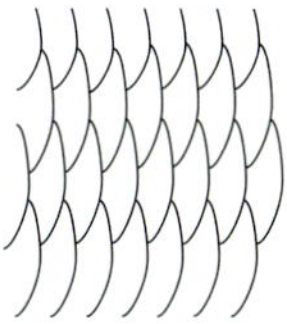

scales more than twice as high as wide

Lateral lines

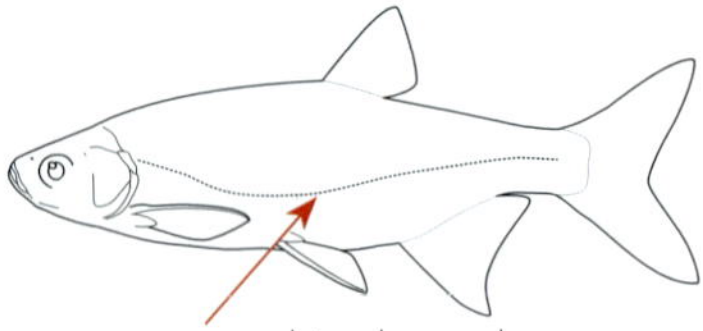

complete, decurved

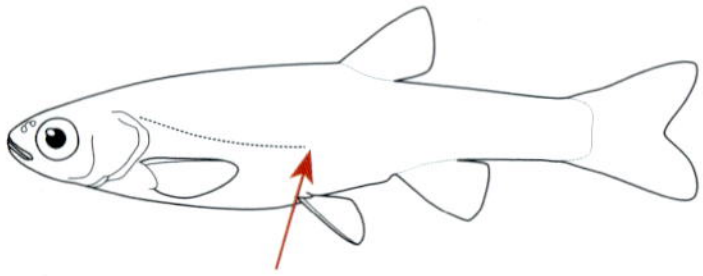

incomplete

Gill rakers

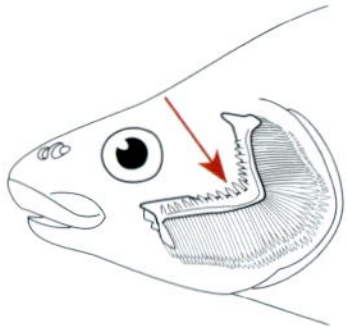

short

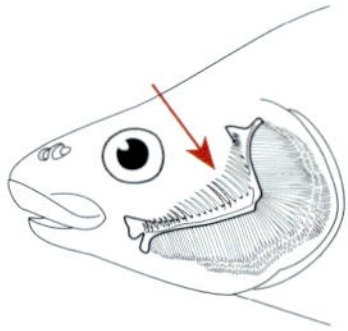

medium

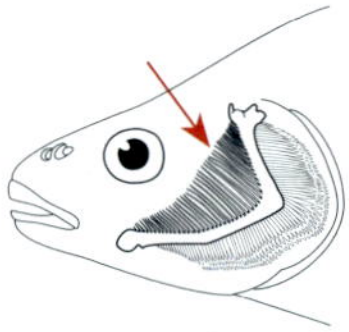

long

Mouths and snouts

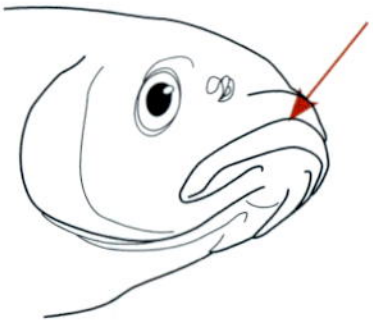

groove between the upper lip and snout is continuous

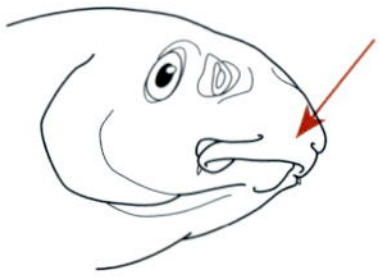

groove between the upper lip and snout is not continuous

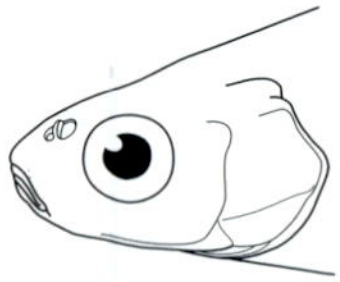

mouth upturned

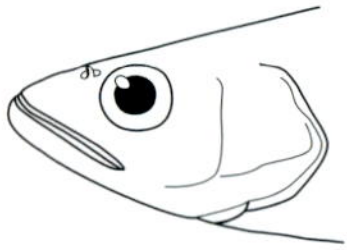

lower jaw protruding

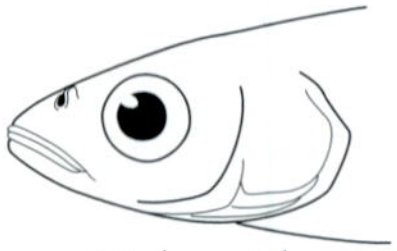

pointed snout does not overhang mouth

rounded snout overhangs mouth

snout greatly overhangs mouth

Pharyngeal teeth

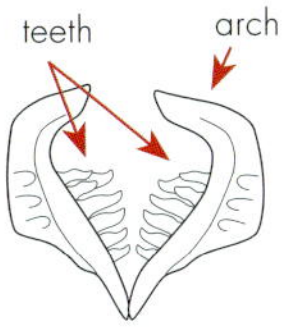

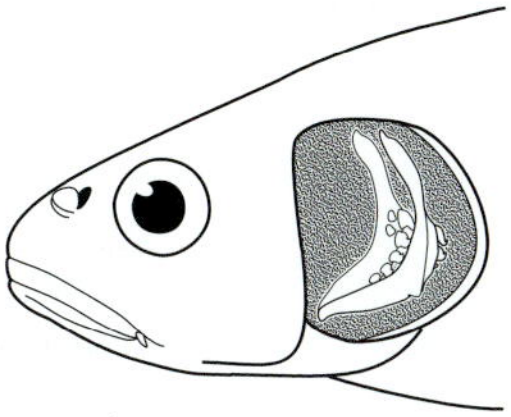

minnow

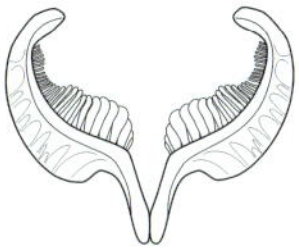

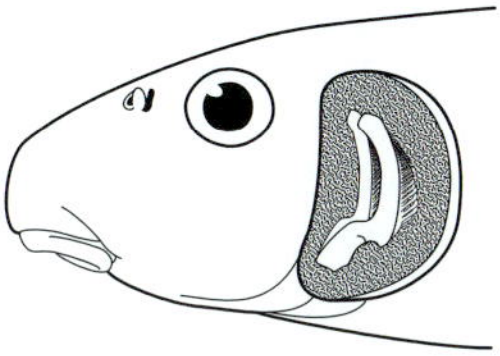

sucker

Gill membranes

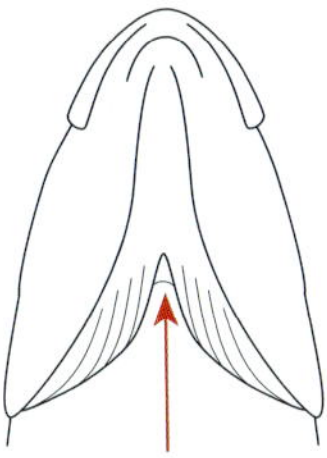

gill **membranes** not attached to body but narrowly attached to each other

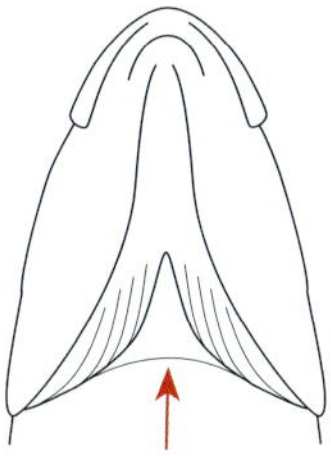

gill **membranes** not attached to body but broadly attached to each other

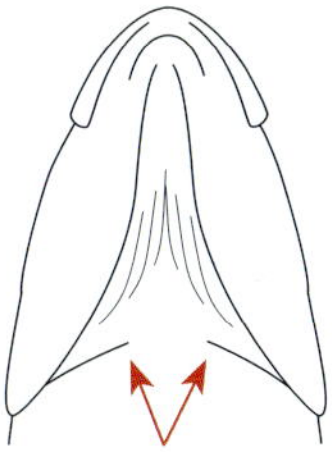

gill **membranes** attached to body

Barbels

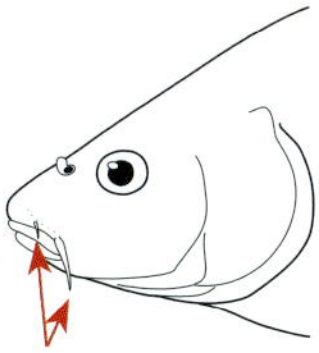

2 **barbels** on each side of upper lip (e.g., Common Carp)

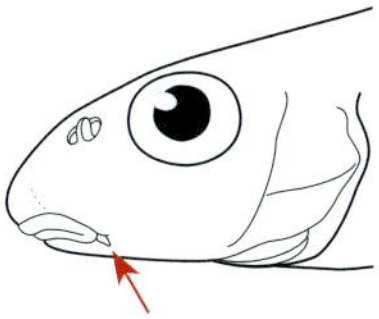

barbel at corner of mouth (e.g., Gravel Chub)

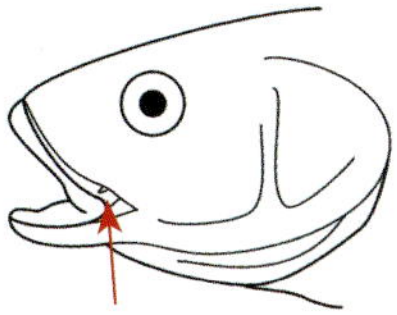

barbel in front of corner of mouth (e.g., Fallfish)

PICTORIAL KEY TO FAMILIES OF ONTARIO FISHES

In this Key, all families of Ontario fishes are divided into five main numbered categories. Categories 1–3 are not divided into subcategories. Category 4 is subdivided into three subcategories, and category 5 is subdivided into seven subcategories. Each category or subcategory includes one to five families, or parts of families, illustrated with a line drawing (used with permission from C. L. Hubbs, K. F. Lagler, and G. R. Smith, 2004). Important features for identifying each family or group are indicated by labelled arrows. **It is important to start at the beginning of the Key because some fishes will fall into more than one category (e.g., North American Catfishes fall into Category 2 [have barbels] as well as Category 3 [adipose fin present]).**

1. Eel-like body

LAMPREYS, p. 83 Comparative Photographs, p. 36

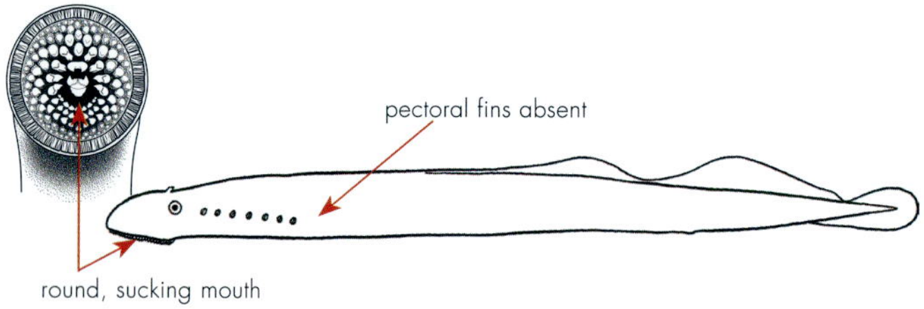

FRESHWATER EELS, p. 115 Comparative Photographs, p. 36

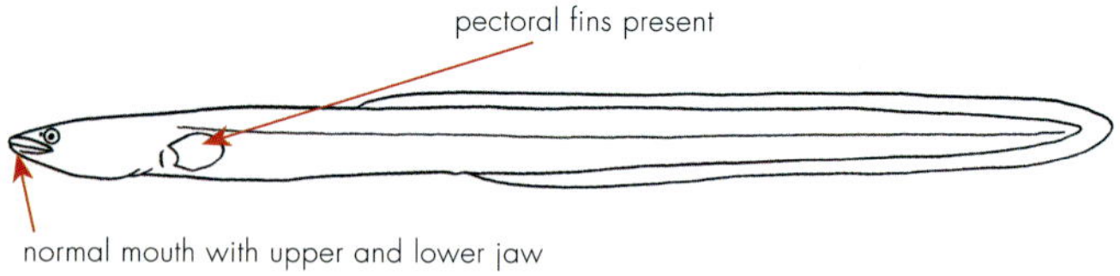

2. Head with distinct whisker-like, fleshy barbels

STURGEONS, p. 97 Comparative Photographs, p. 37

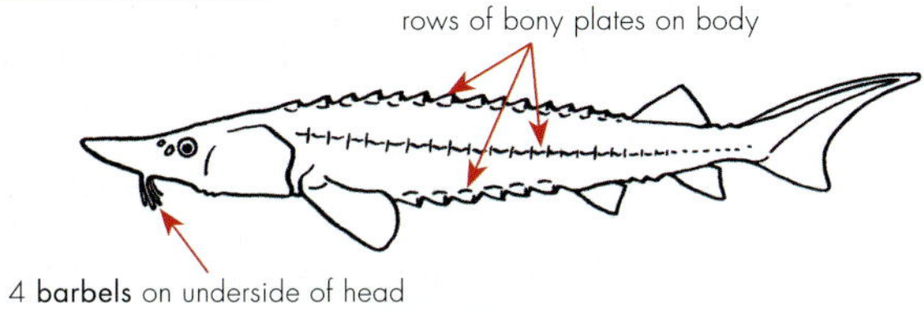

NORTH AMERICAN CATFISHES, p. 255 Comparative Photographs, pp. 64–65

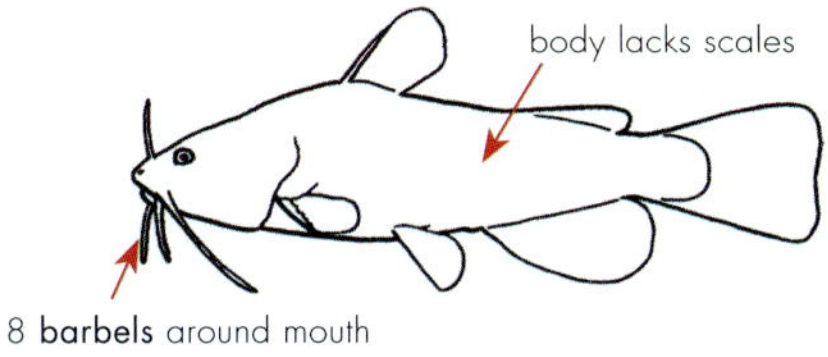

BURBOT, p. 339 Comparative Photographs, p. 37

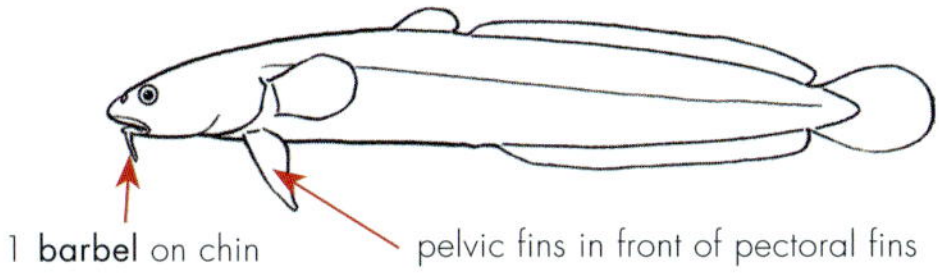

COMMON CARP, p. 130 Comparative Photographs, p. 52

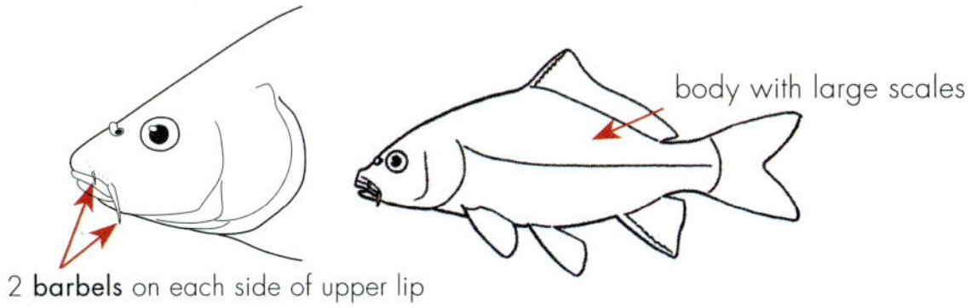

TENCH, p. 216 Comparative Photographs, pp. 53

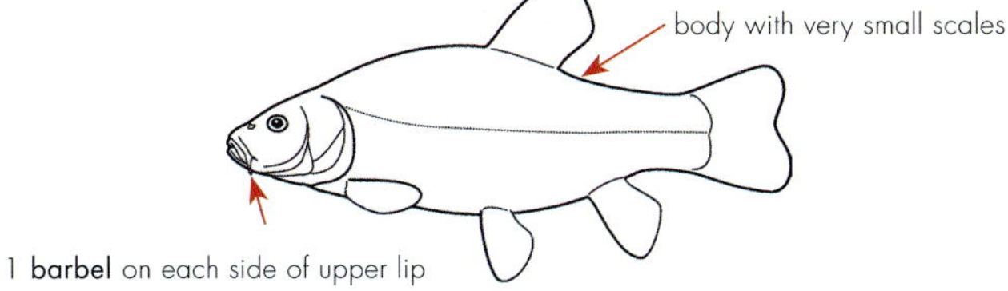

3. Small, fleshy adipose fin on back

TROUTS and SALMONS, p. 299 Comparative Photographs, pp. 38–41

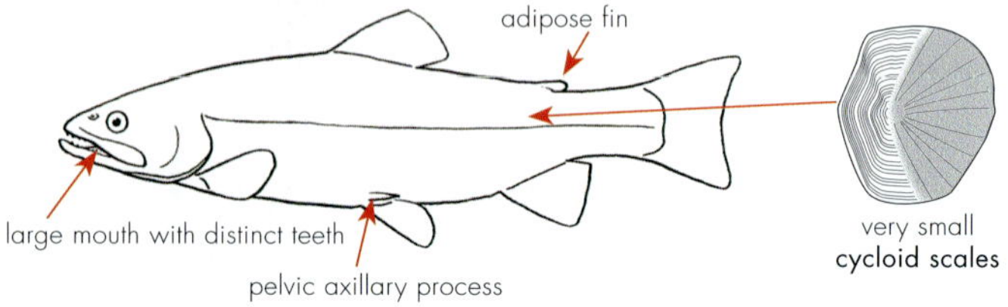

TROUTS and SALMONS (WHITEFISHES), p. 299 Comparative Photographs, pp. 42–43

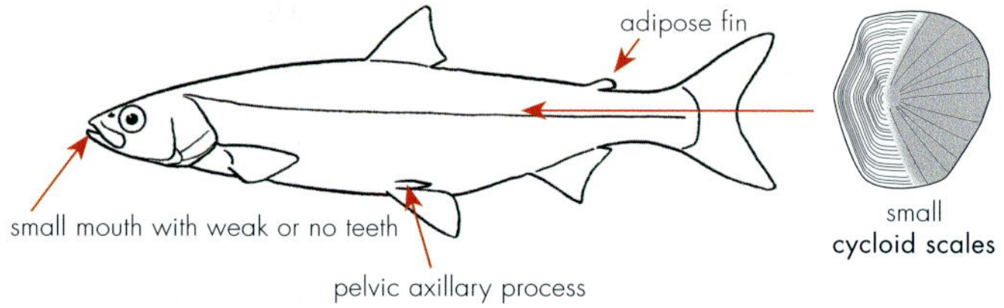

SMELTS, p. 295 Comparative Photographs, p. 42

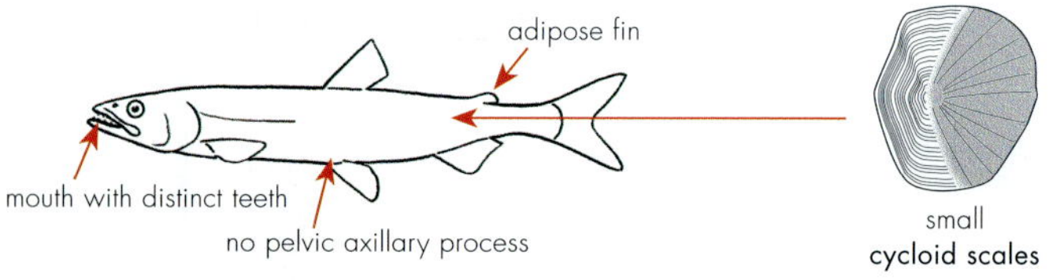

TROUT-PERCHES, p. 333 Comparative Photographs, pp. 43 and 73

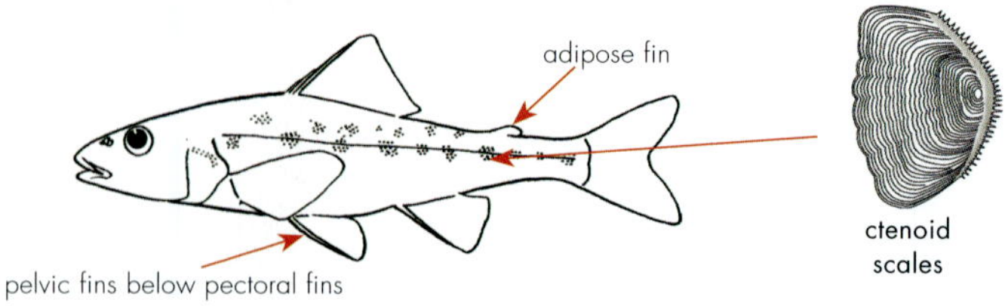

4. Single soft dorsal fin without spines

a. Square/rounded tail

GARS, p. 101 Comparative Photographs, p. 37

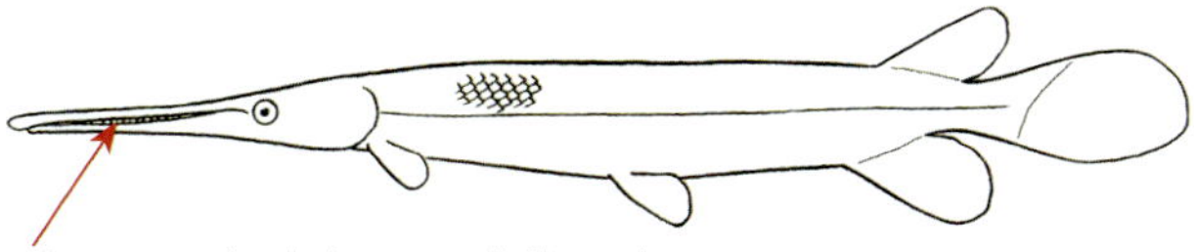

BOWFINS, p. 107 Comparative Photographs, p. 37

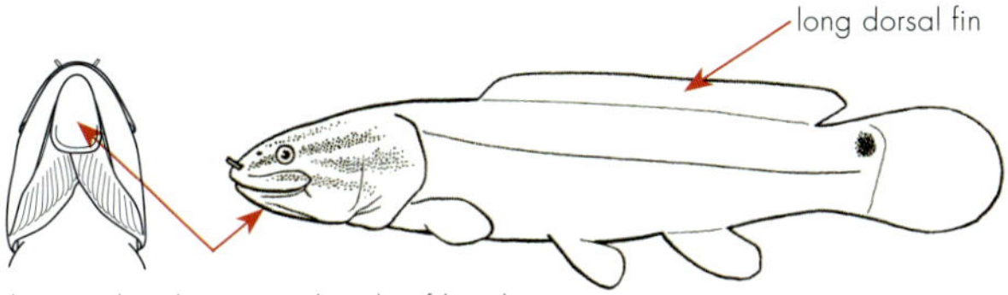

CENTRAL MUDMINNOW, p. 282 Comparative Photographs, p. 66

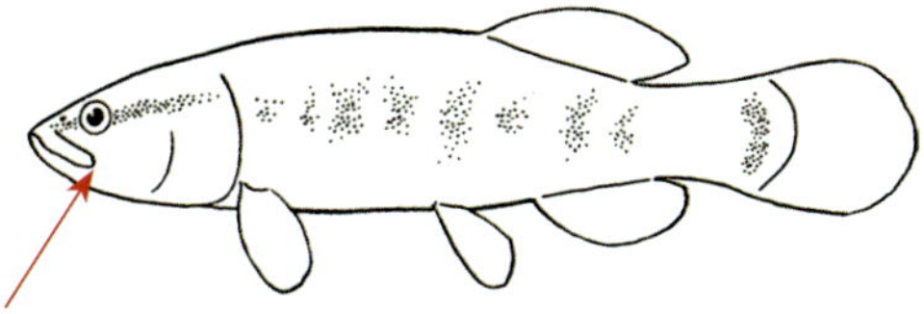

TOPMINNOWS, p. 345 Comparative Photographs, p. 66

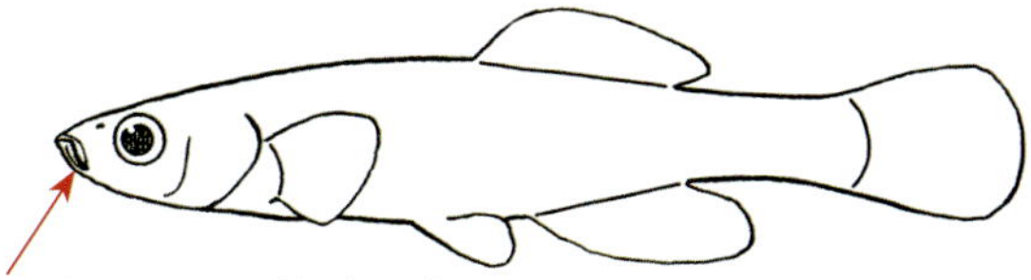

4. Single soft dorsal fin without spines (continued)
b. Forked tail (keel in front of anal fin)

MOONEYES, p. 111 Comparative Photographs, p. 44

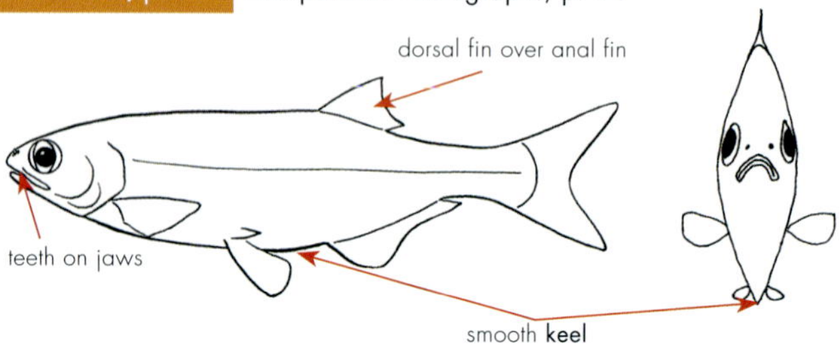

SHADS, p. 119, **THREAD HERRINGS,** p. 125

Comparative Photographs, p. 44

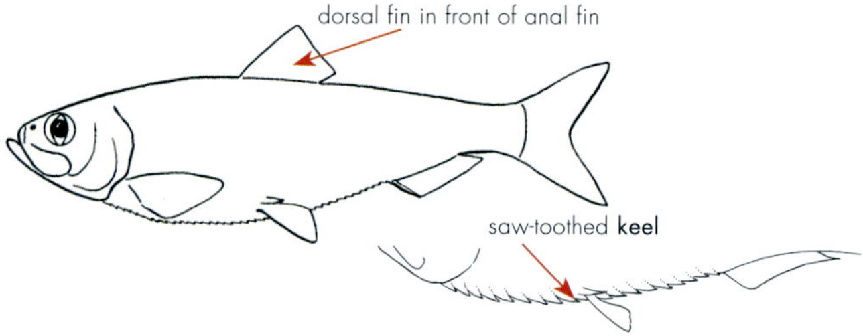

GOLDEN SHINER, p. 168, **RUDD,** p. 198, **GOLDFISH,** p. 132
BIGHEAD CARP, p. 457 **and SILVER CARP,** p. 467

Comparative Photographs, Goldfish, p. 52; Bighead Carp and Silver Carp, p. 53; and Golden Shiner and Rudd, p. 61

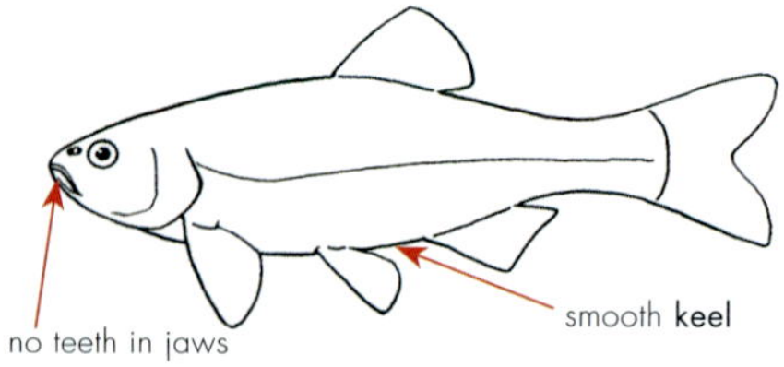

c. Forked tail (no keel in front of anal fin)

PIKES AND MUDMINNOWS (PIKES) p. 279 Comparative Photographs, pp. 46–47

long- duck-like snout

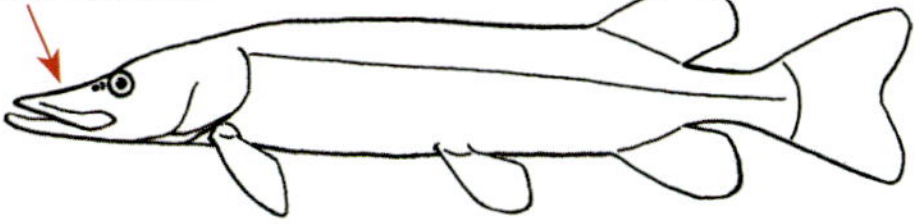

GRASS CARP, p. 220 **and BLACK CARP,** p. 467 Comparative Photographs, pp. 53

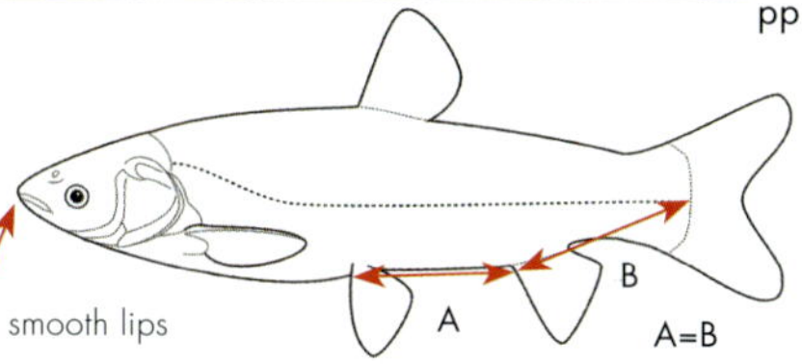

thin, smooth lips

MINNOWS, p. 135 Comparative Photographs, pp. 54–63

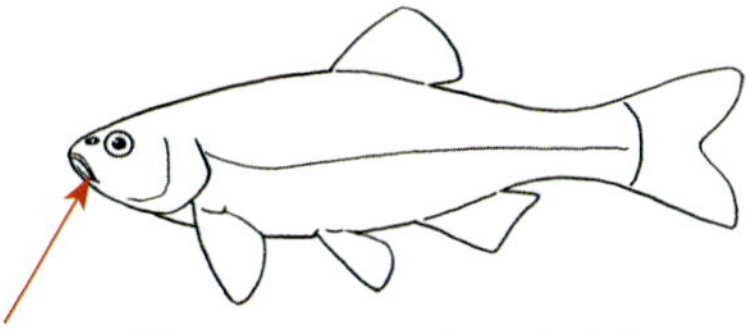

thin, smooth lips, sometimes with tiny barbels

SUCKERS, p. 223 Comparative Photographs, pp. 48–52, 56

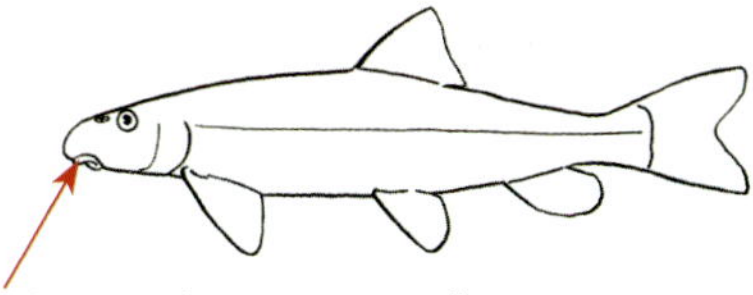

thick lips with **plicae** and/or **papillae**

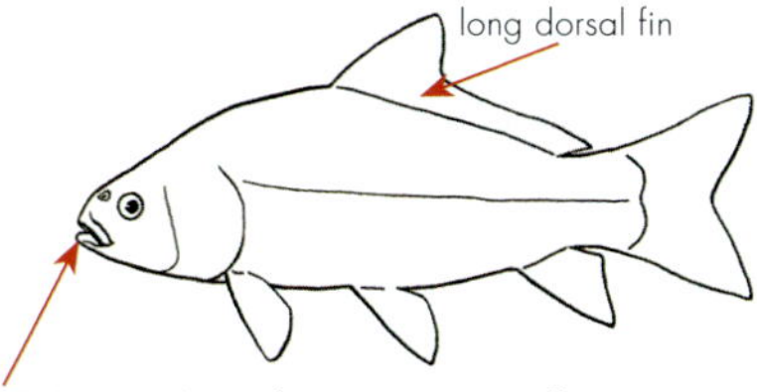

thick lips with faint **plicae** and/or **papillae** (Bigmouth Buffalo)

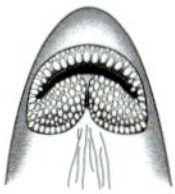

lips with **papillae**

lips with **plicae**

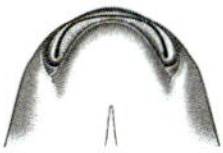

Bigmouth Buffalo lips

5. Dorsal fin with one or more spines

a. Dorsal spines isolated

STICKLEBACKS, p. 351 Comparative Photographs, p. 67

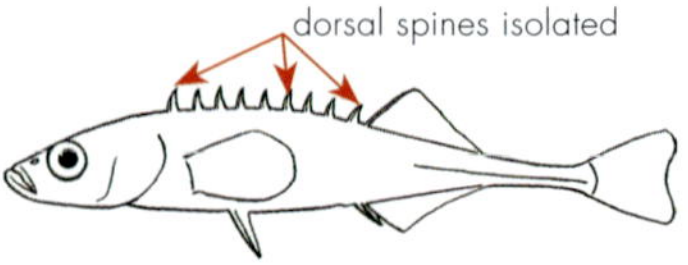

b. Single serrated dorsal spine

COMMON CARP, p. 130 **and GOLDFISH,** p. 132 Comparative Photographs, p. 52

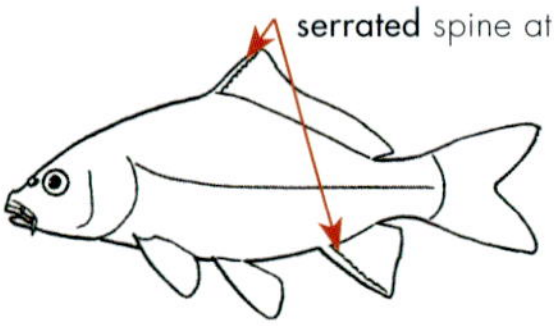

c. Four inconspicuous dorsal spines

NEW WORLD SILVERSIDES, p. 341 Comparative Photographs, p. 42

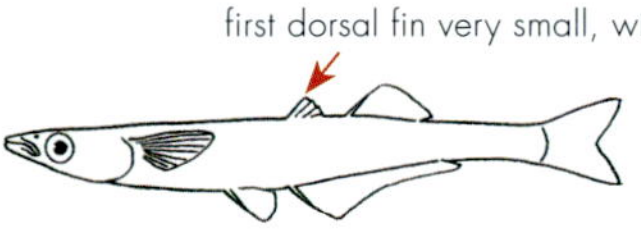

d. Pelvic fins united

GOBIES, p. 451 Comparative Photographs, p. 78

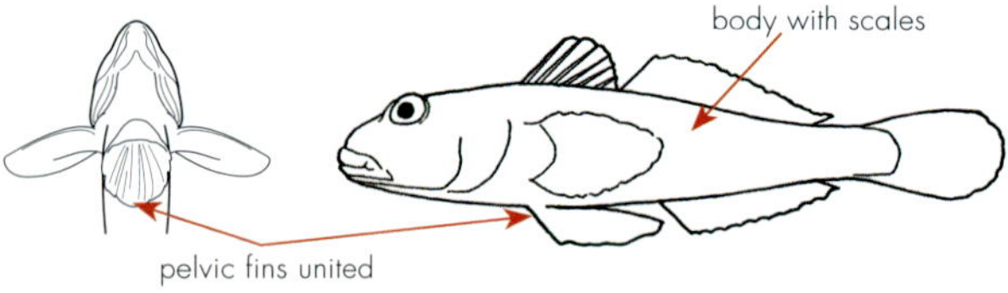

e. Body naked or with prickles

SCULPINS, p. 361, **and FATHEAD SCULPINS,** p. 369

Comparative Photographs, pp. 77–78

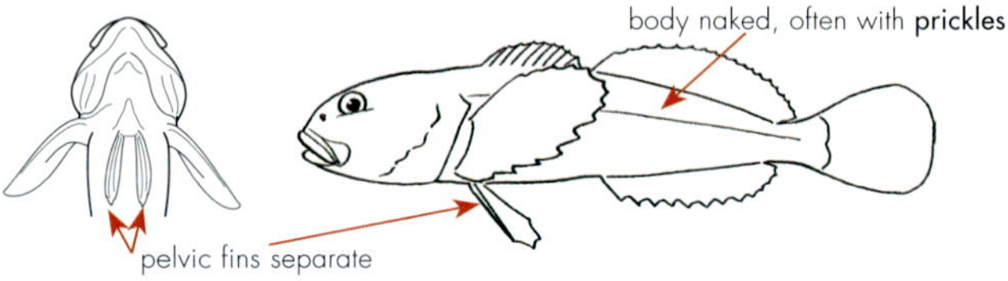

f. 1–2 anal spines

DRUMS, p. 447 Comparative Photographs, p.45

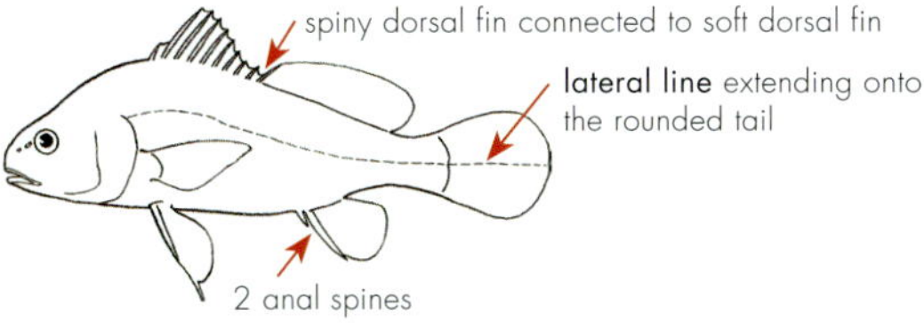

PERCHES and DARTERS, p. 413 Comparative Photographs, pp. 45, 73, 74–76

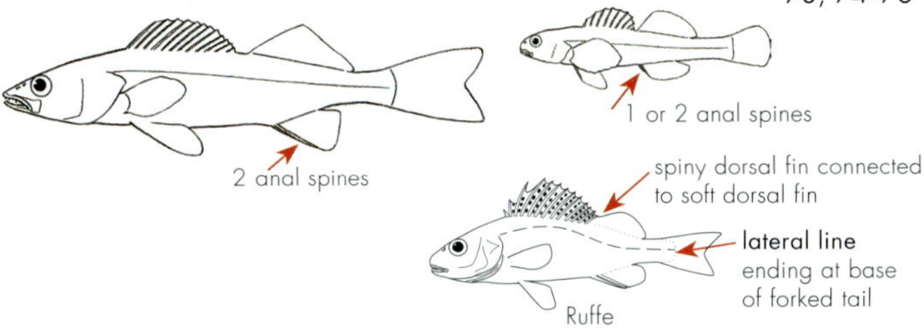

g. 3–7 anal spines

SUNFISHES and BASSES, p. 379 Comparative Photographs, pp. 68–72

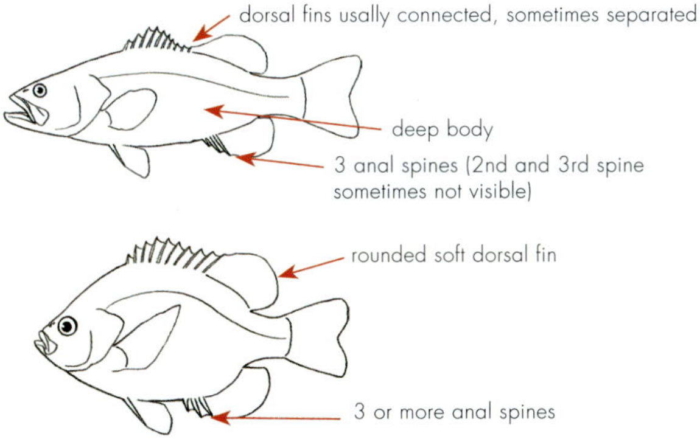

TEMPERATE BASSES, p. 373 Comparative Photographs, p. 45

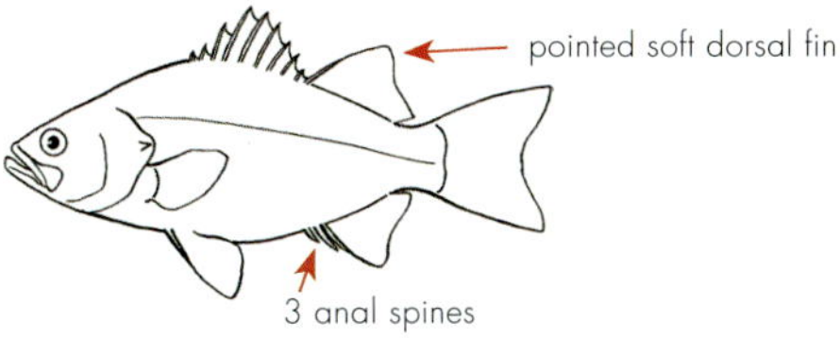

COMPARATIVE PHOTOGRAPHS

Eel-like fishes

Chestnut Lamprey

single 2-lobed dorsal fin

large circular mouth with sharp teeth

3 or more **bicuspid** lateral **circumoral** teeth

Silver Lamprey

single 2-lobed dorsal fin

large circular mouth with sharp teeth

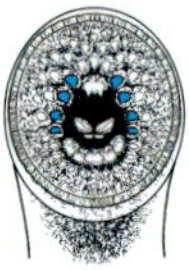

No (rarely 1–2) **bicuspid** lateral **circumoral** teeth

Northern Brook Lamprey

single 2-lobed dorsal fin

small mouth with few blunt teeth

American Brook Lamprey

2 joined dorsal fins

small mouth with few blunt teeth

Sea Lamprey

2 dorsal fins

large mouth with sharp teeth

American Eel

1 gill opening

mouth with upper and lower jaws

Distinctive fishes

Lake Sturgeon

Longnose Gar

Spotted Gar

Emerald Bowfin

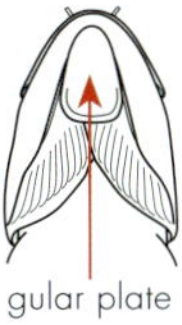

Burbot

Trouts and salmons (adults)

Brook Trout

Lake Trout

Atlantic Salmon

Brown Trout

Trouts and salmons (juveniles)

Brook Trout

Lake Trout

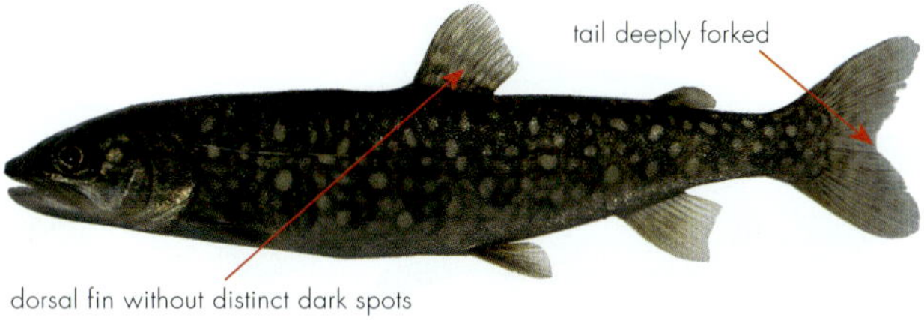

Atlantic Salmon

Brown Trout

Trouts and salmons (adults)

Rainbow Trout

Chinook Salmon

Coho Salmon

Pink Salmon

Trouts and salmons (juveniles)

Rainbow Trout

Chinook Salmon

Coho Salmon

Pink Salmon

Silvery fishes with a soft dorsal fin, no overhanging snout, and no keel

Cisco

Rainbow Smelt

Brook Silverside

Silvery fishes with a soft dorsal fin, an adipose fin, an overhanging snout and no keel

Lake Whitefish

Pygmy Whitefish

Round Whitefish

Trout-perch

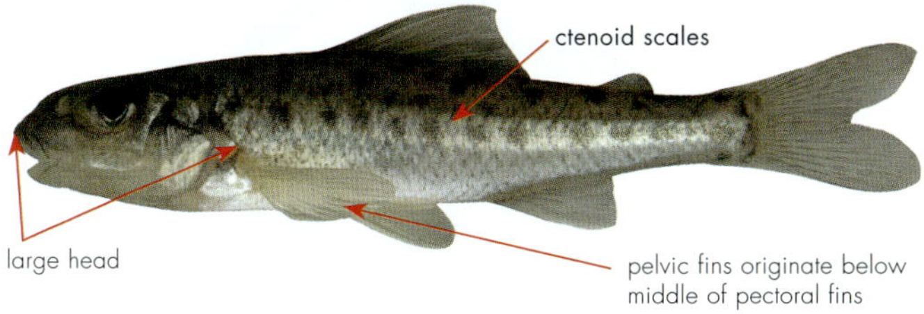

Silvery fishes with a soft dorsal fin and keel

Alewife

Blueback Herring (potential invader)

American Shad

Gizzard Shad

Mooneye

Goldeye

Silvery fishes with spines in dorsal fins

White Perch

White Bass

Wiper (occasionally caught)

Freshwater Drum

Ruffe

Pikes (adults)

Chain Pickerel

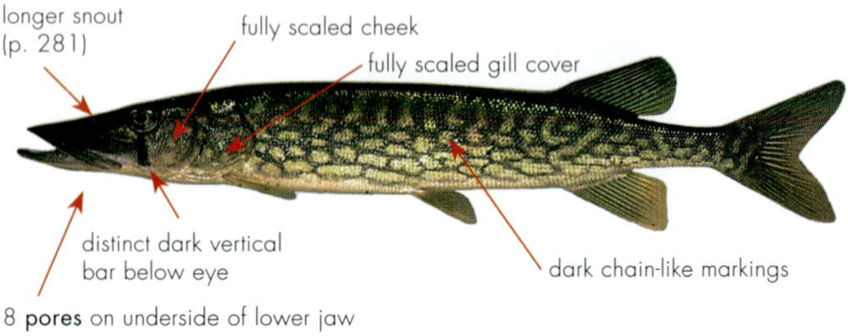

Grass Pickerel

Muskellunge

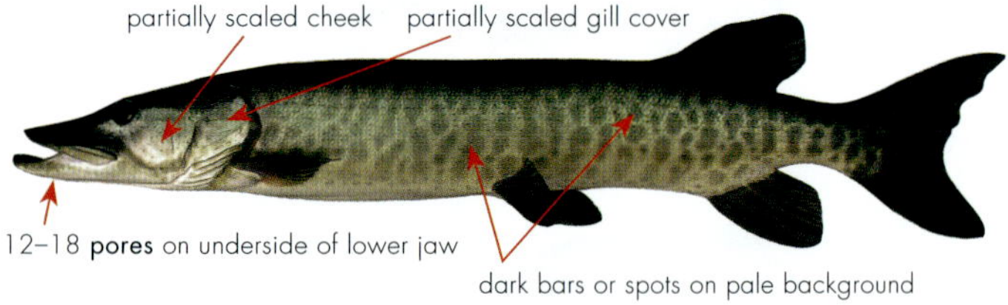

Northern Pike

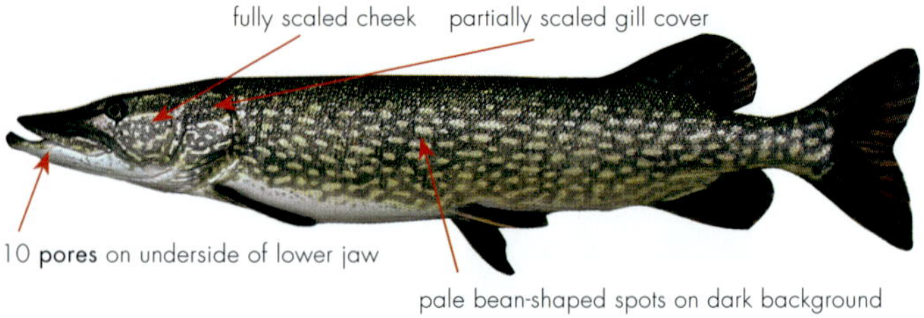

Pikes (juveniles)

Chain Pickerel

Grass Pickerel

Muskellunge

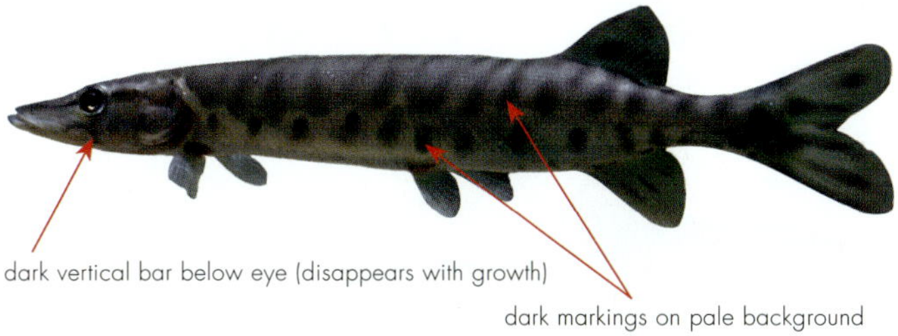

Northern Pike

Suckers (adults)

White Sucker

Longnose Sucker

Northern Hog Sucker

Spotted Sucker

Lake Chubsucker

Suckers (juveniles)

White Sucker

Longnose Sucker

Northern Hog Sucker

Spotted Sucker

Lake Chubsucker

Redhorses with grey tails

Silver Redhorse

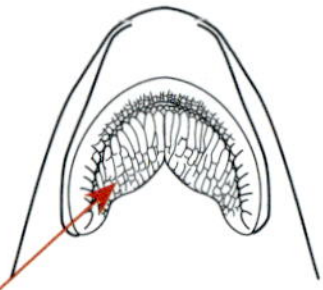

Golden Redhorse

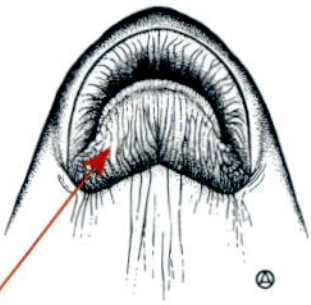

Black Redhorse

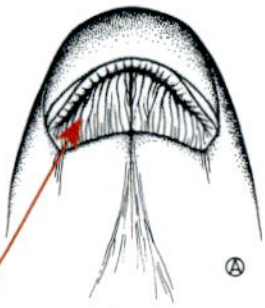

Redhorses with red tails

Shorthead Redhorse

Greater Redhorse

River Redhorse

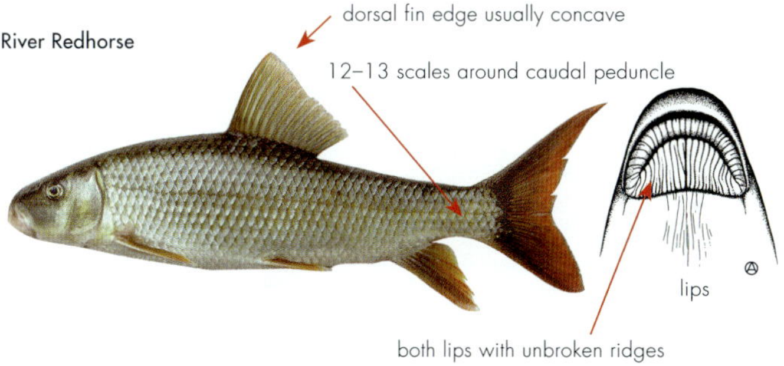

Suckers with long dorsal fins (15–31 rays)

Quillback

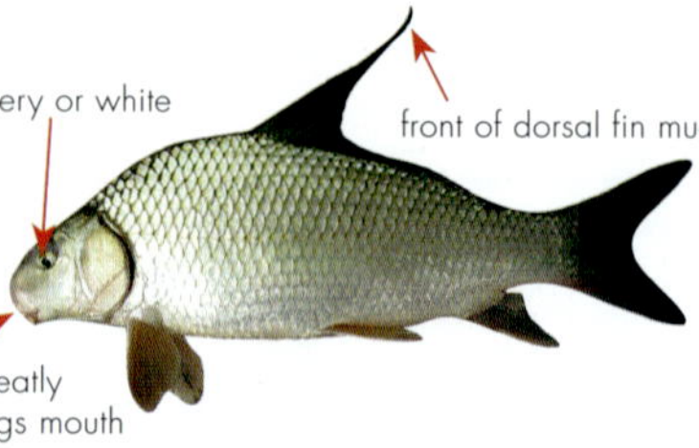

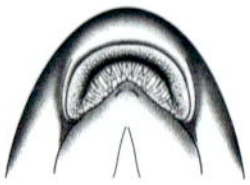

Bigmouth Buffalo

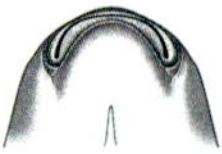

Black/Smallmouth Buffaloes or Hybrid

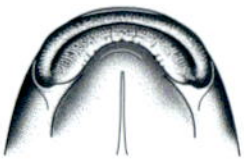

Goldfish and Common Carp

Goldfish

Common Carp

Tench and Xenocarps

Tench

Grass Carp

Black Carp (potential invader)

Bighead Carp (occasionally caught)

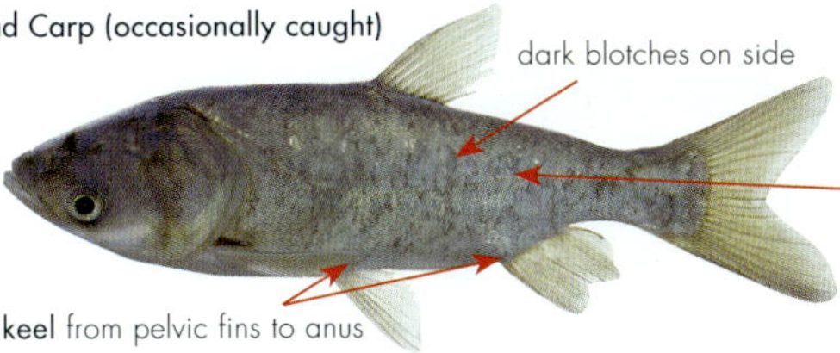

Silver Carp (potential invader)

Shiners with overhanging snout and faint lateral stripe

Spottail Shiner

Silver Chub

River Shiner

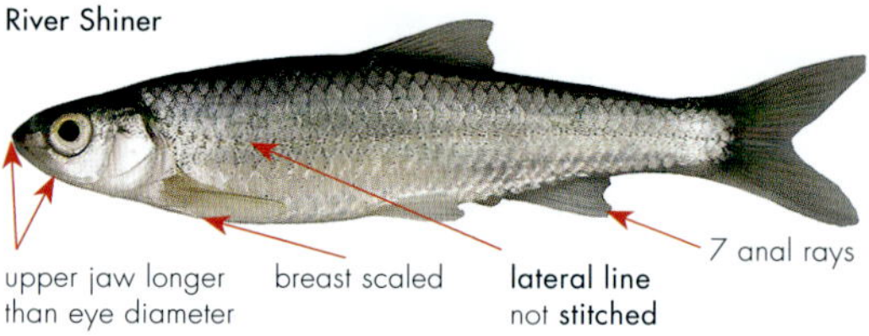

Sand Shiner

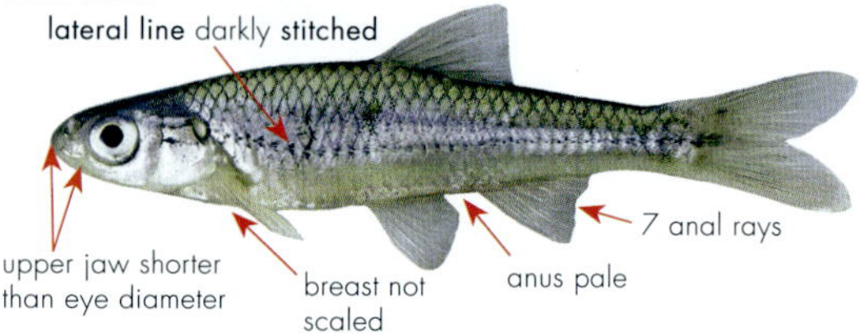

Mimic Shiner

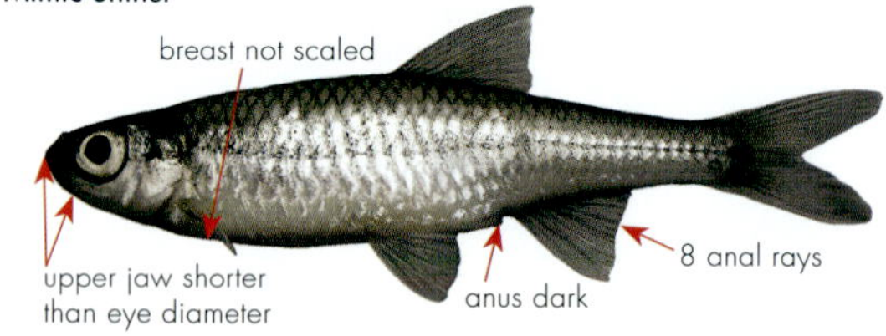

Ghost Shiner

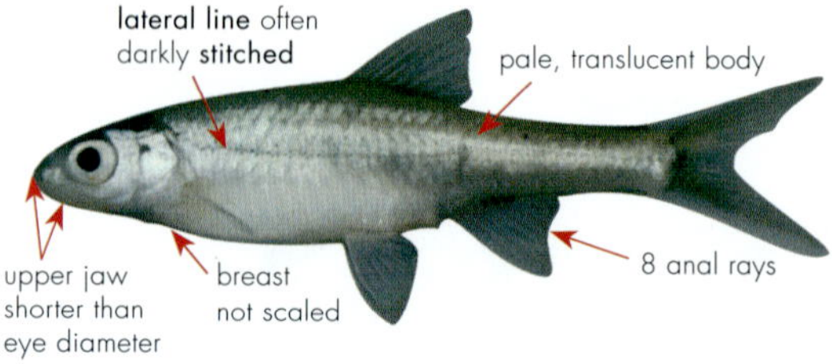

Elongate shiners without overhanging snout, and more than 8 anal rays

Emerald Shiner

Rosyface Shiner

Silver Shiner

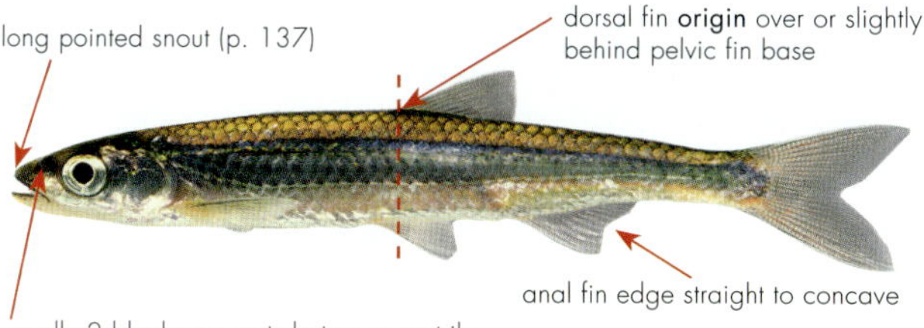

Blackline shiners, Pugnose Minnow, and juvenile Lake Chubsucker

Blacknose Shiner

Bridle Shiner

Pugnose Minnow

Lake Chubsucker

Blackchin Shiner

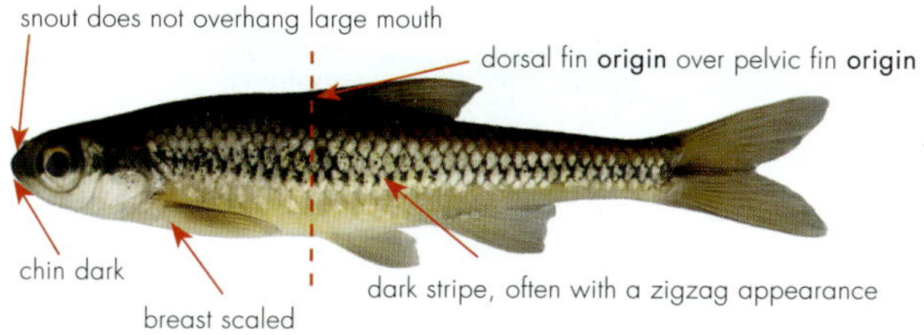

Weed Shiner (potential invader)

Pugnose Shiner

Minnows with small scales (> 48 lateral scales)

Western Blacknose Dace

Longnose Dace

Central Stoneroller

Cutlip Minnow

Redside Dace

Northern Redbelly Dace

Finescale Dace

Northern Pearl Dace

Lake Chub

Creek Chub

Deep-bodied minnows without overhanging snout

Common Shiner

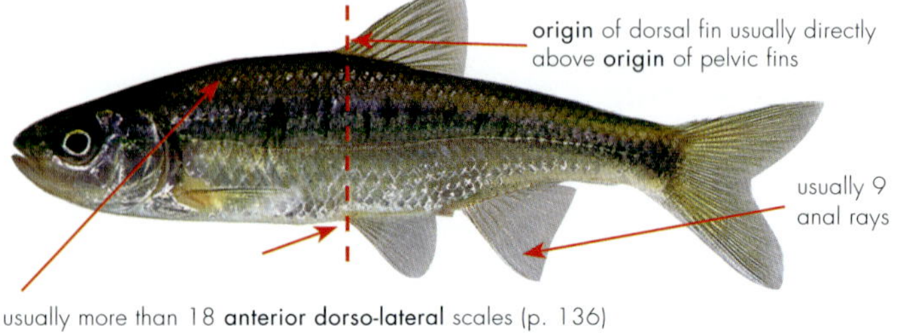

Striped Shiner

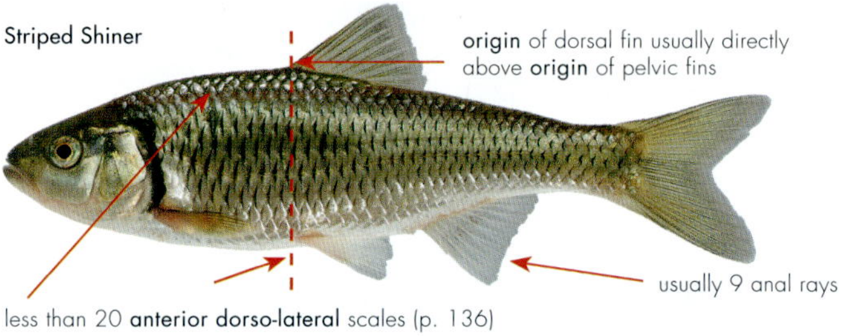

Spotfin Shiner

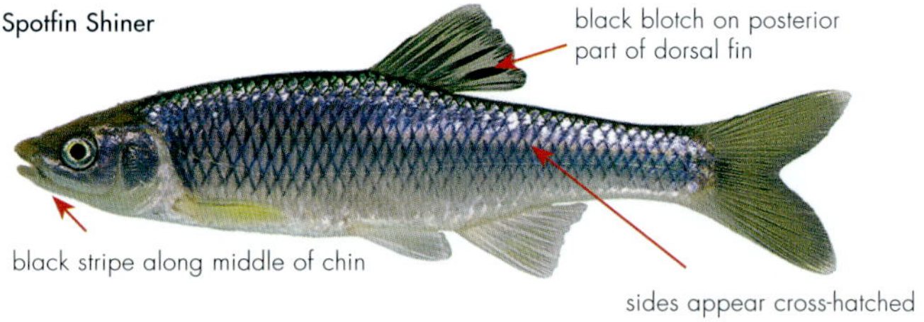

Redfin Shiner

Golden Shiner

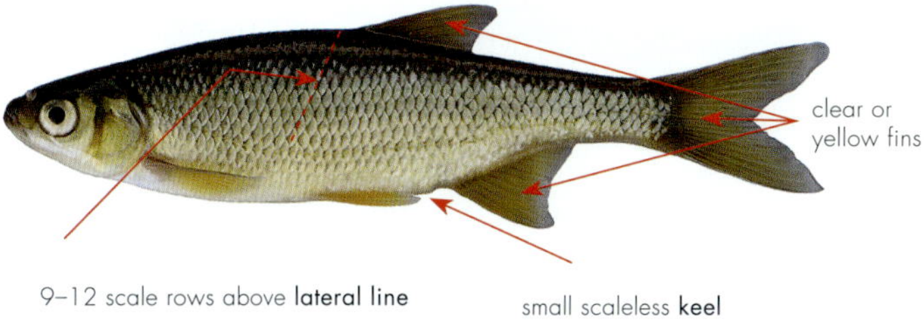

Rudd

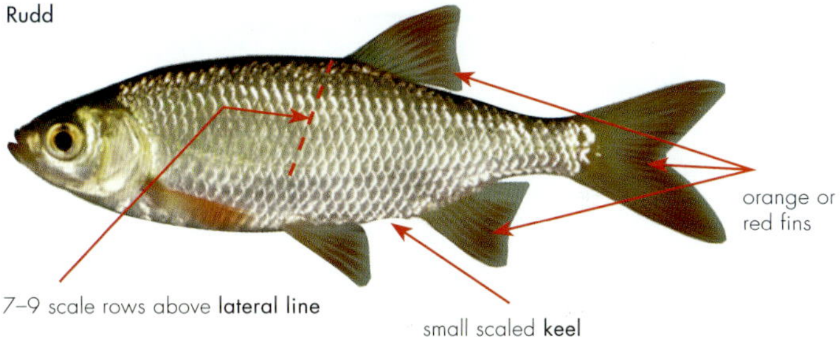

Minnows and xenocarps with medium to large scales (36–54 lateral scales)

Bluntnose Minnow

Fathead Minnow

Brassy Minnow

Eastern Silvery Minnow

River Chub

Hornyhead Chub

Gravel Chub

Fallfish

Grass Carp

Catfishes and Bullheads

Channel Catfish

Flathead Catfish

Brown Bullhead

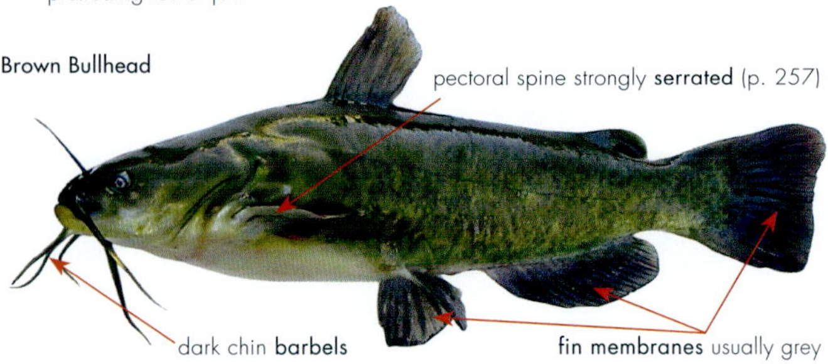

Black Bullhead

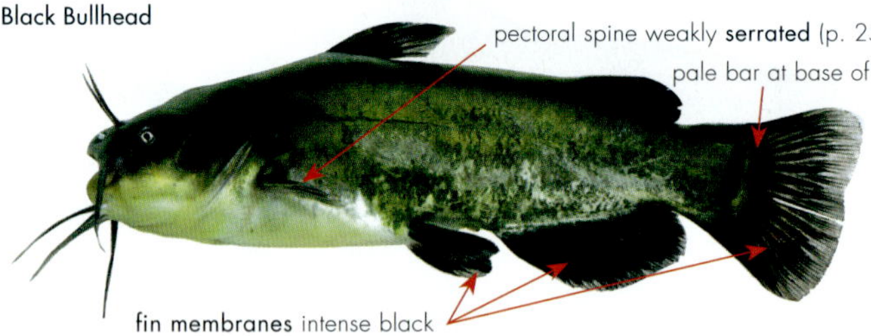

Yellow Bullhead

Madtoms

Tadpole Madtom

Stonecat

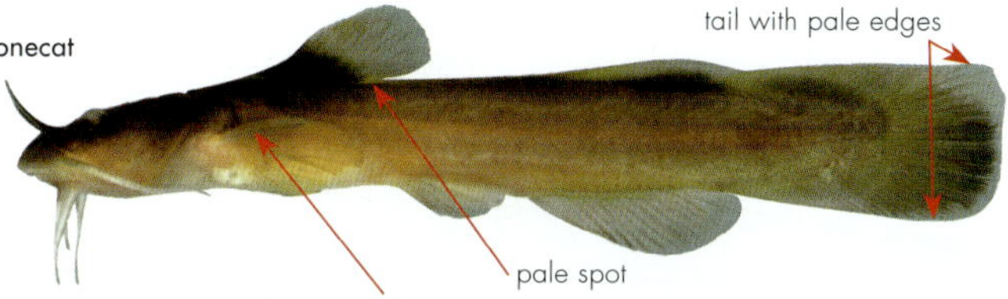

Margined Madtom

Brindled Madtom

Northern Madtom

Central Mudminnow and Topminnows

Central Mudminnow

Banded Killifish

Blackstripe Topminnow

Sticklebacks

Brook Stickleback

Ninespine Stickleback

Threespine Stickleback

Fourspine Stickleback

Basses (adults)

Smallmouth Bass

Largemouth Bass

Sunfishes with small mouths and large pectoral fins (adults)

Pumpkinseed

Bluegill

Basses (juveniles)

Smallmouth Bass

Largemouth Bass

Sunfishes with small mouths and large pectoral fins (juveniles)

Pumpkinseed

Bluegill

Sunfishes with medium-sized mouths and pectoral fins (adults)

Northern Sunfish

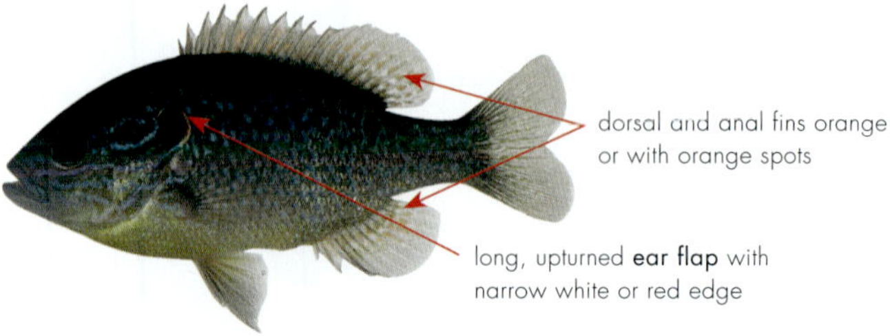

Orangespotted Sunfish

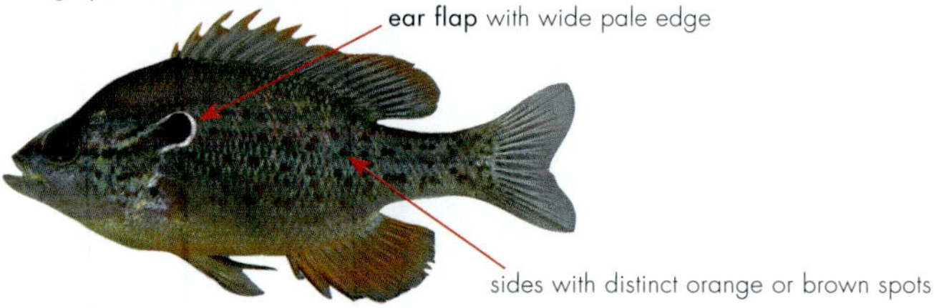

Sunfishes with large mouths and small pectoral fins (adults)

Green Sunfish

Warmouth

Sunfishes with medium-sized mouths and pectoral fins (juveniles)

Northern Sunfish

Orangespotted Sunfish

Sunfishes with large mouths and small pectoral fins (juveniles)

Green Sunfish

Warmouth

Sunfishes with more than 4 anal spines

Rock Bass (adult)

Rock Bass (juvenile)

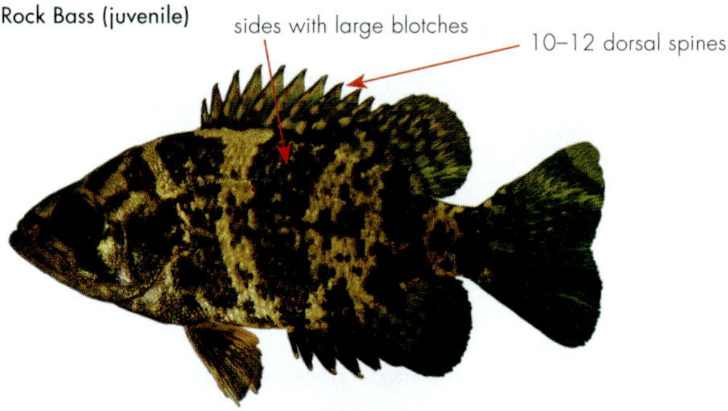

Black Crappie

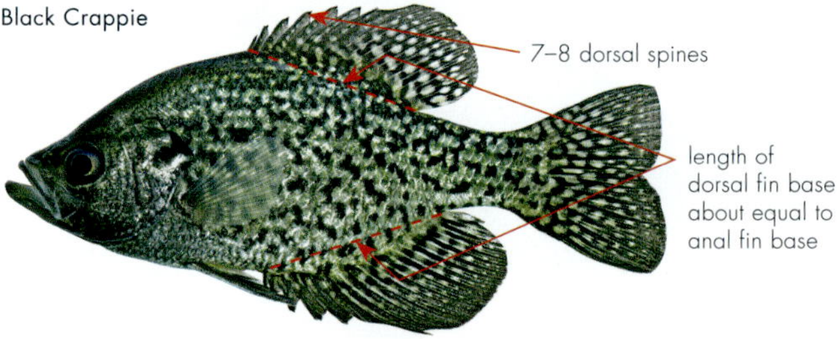

White Crappie

Large perches and Trout-perch

Yellow Perch

Walleye

Sauger

Ruffe

Trout-perch

Darters

Johnny Darter

Tessellated Darter

Channel Darter

River Darter

Rainbow Darter

Least Darter

Iowa Darter

Fantail Darter

Darters (continued)

Eastern Sand Darter

Greenside Darter

Logperch

Blackside Darter

Sculpins and gobies

Mottled Sculpin

Slimy Sculpin

Spoonhead Sculpin

Fathead Sculpins and gobies

Deepwater Sculpin

Round Goby

Tubenose Goby

SPECIES ACCOUNTS

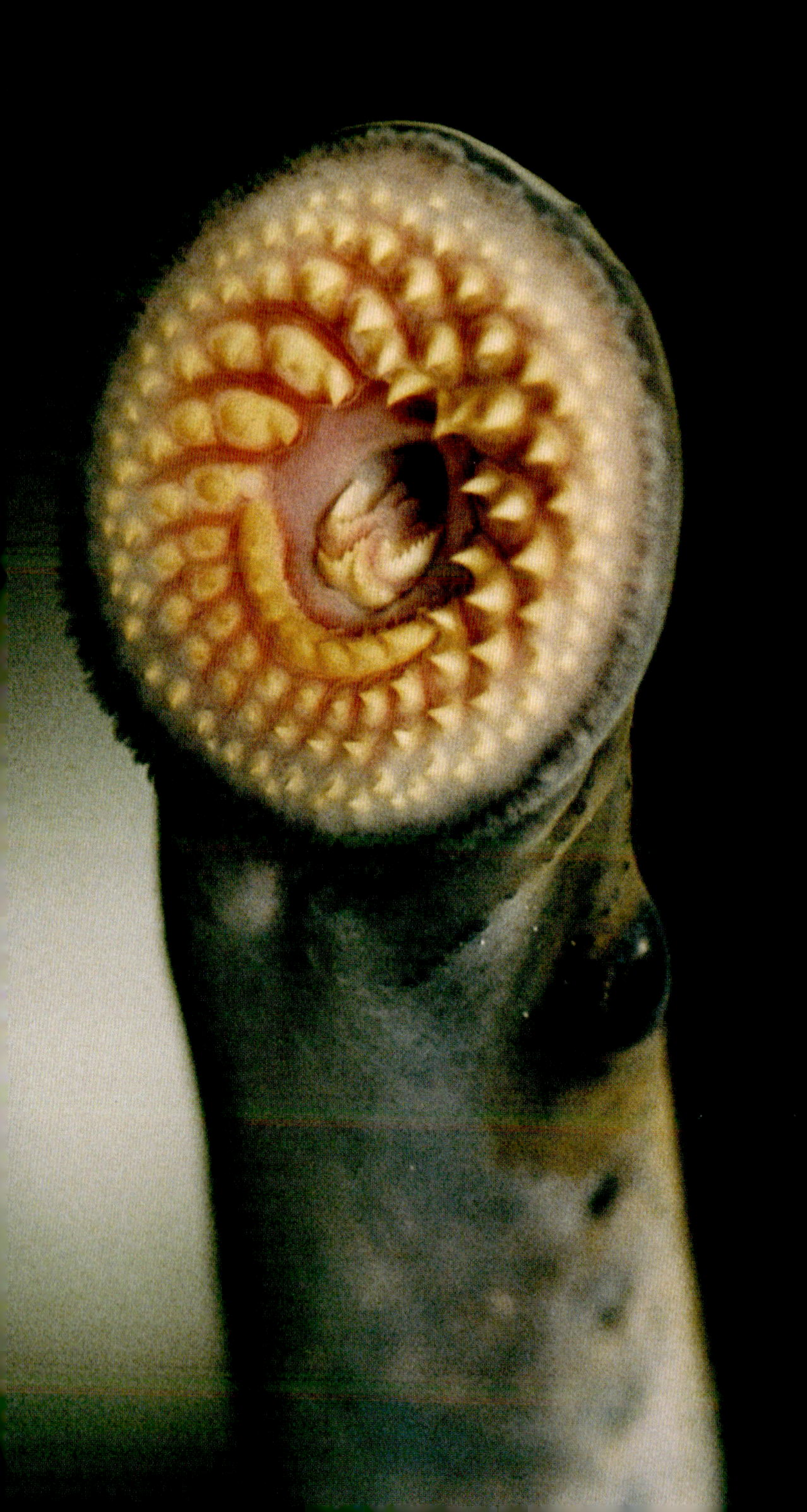

PETROMYZONTIDAE
Lampreys

Lampreys are considered to be one of the most ancient vertebrates alive today, with fossils dating back to the Devonian period, 360 million years ago. They are found throughout the fresh and marine waters of **anti-tropical** areas of the northern and southern hemispheres. These jawless fishes have a cartilaginous skeleton, and lack scales and pectoral and pelvic fins. Adult lampreys have a round, sucking mouth with rows of horny teeth and a toothed tongue. Some species are parasitic, attaching themselves to other fishes, rasping through their skin and sucking their body fluids. **Larval** lampreys, known as **ammocoetes**, are usually found burrowed in stream bottoms. They lack the sucking mouth of the adult and **filter feed** on **plankton** instead. **Ammocoetes** may live up to 12 years before undergoing **metamorphosis** into adults.

There are 44 species worldwide. Five species are found in Ontario, three of which are parasitic as adults.

< Sea Lamprey

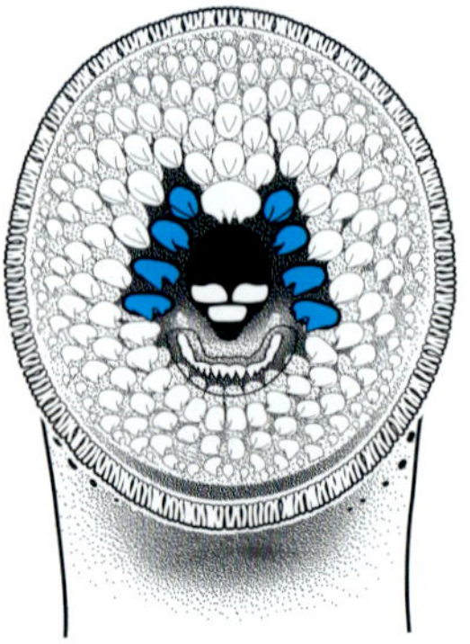

Chestnut Lamprey
(**bicuspid** lateral **circumoral** teeth
shaded blue)

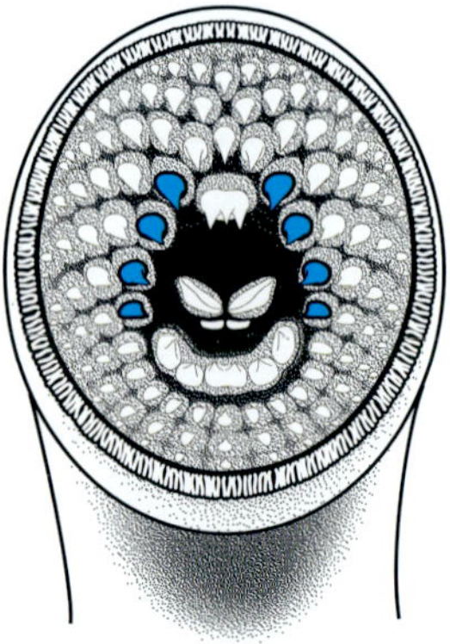

Silver Lamprey
(**unicuspid** lateral **circumoral** teeth
shaded blue)

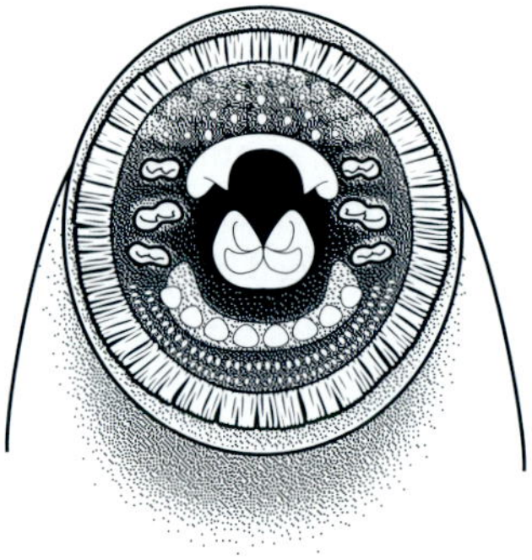

American Brook Lamprey

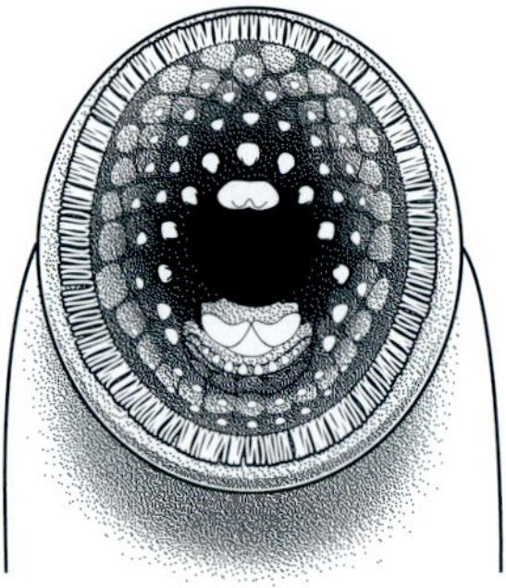

Northern Brook Lamprey

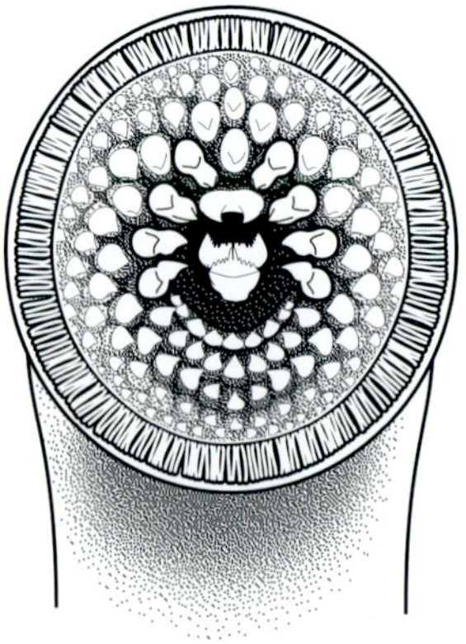

Sea Lamprey

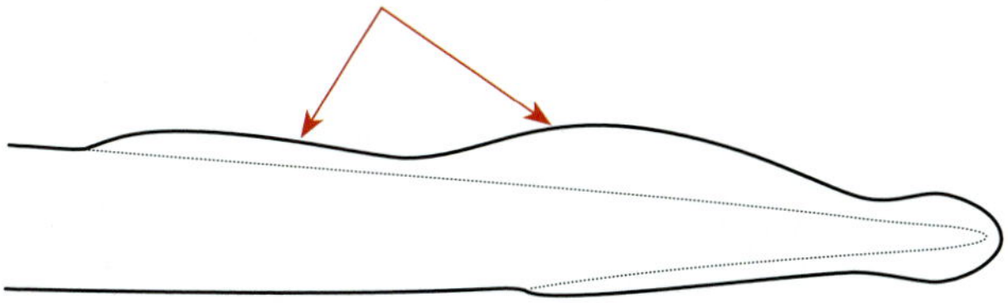

1 dorsal fin with 2 lobes (Chestnut, Northern Brook, Silver lampreys)

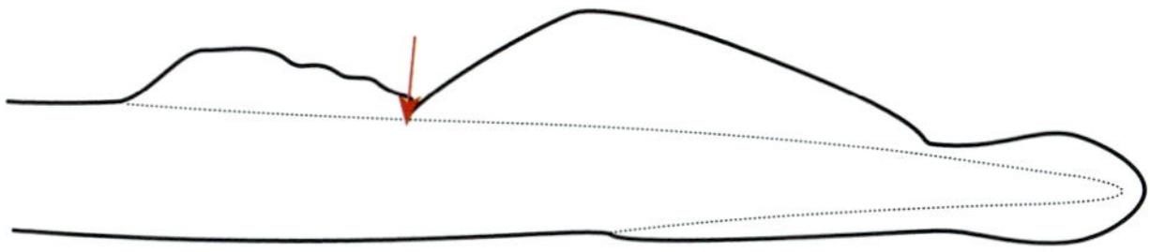

2 dorsal fins joined by narrow **membrane** (American Brook Lamprey)

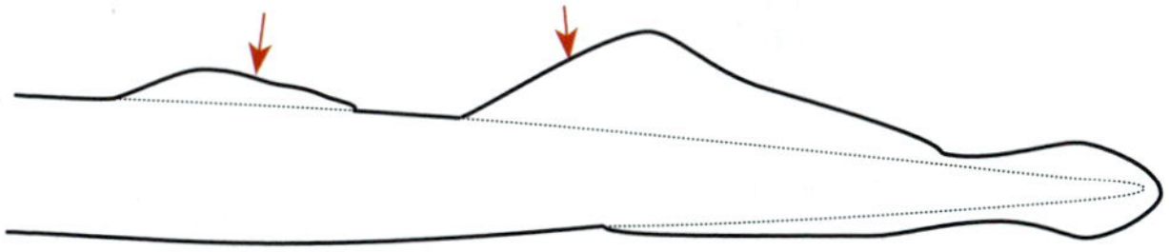

2 separate dorsal fins (Sea Lamprey)

AMERICAN BROOK LAMPREY *Lethenteron appendix*

Lethenteron—lethe: oblivion; *enteron*: intestine; refers to the deterioration of the intestine from **ammocoete** to adult.
appendix: appendage; spawning males have a thread-like **urogenital papilla**.

This small species is Ontario's most common native lamprey. It is found in small streams and does not harm other fishes.

DESCRIPTION: This fish is very elongate. The round, jawless mouth is small with a few blunt teeth (p. 84). The body is scaleless and slimy, with 7 **pore**-like gill openings behind each eye. There are 2 dorsal fins joined by a very narrow **membrane** (p. 85). There are no pectoral or pelvic fins. It has a grey to brown back and a silver or white belly. The fins are faint yellow to orange, with greyish smudges. There is a dark blotch at the end of the tail.

SIMILAR SPECIES: The American Eel has a jaw with many small teeth, a single gill opening behind each eye, and pectoral fins. Silver, Chestnut, and Northern Brook lampreys have 1 dorsal fin with 2 lobes joined by a wide **membrane**. The Sea Lamprey has a large mouth with sharp teeth and dorsal fins sometimes joined by a very low ridge.

FEEDING: The **ammocoete filter feeds** on microscopic plant and animal material, such as algae and pollen. The short-lived adult does not feed.

REPRODUCTION: In spring, males construct saucer-shaped nests on sand and gravel bottoms in shallow streams. Females arrive and attach to stones with their sucker mouths. Spawning occurs in water temperatures between 12°C and 17°C. Males wrap around the females, spawning occurs, and the adhesive eggs stick to the bottom. Adults die after spawning.

HABITAT: This lamprey lives its entire life in coldwater streams, mostly as an **ammocoete** buried in soft bottoms of silt and sand.

STATUS: G4; N4; S3.

Spawning

Maximum Age: 5	Ontario Average	Ontario Record	World Record
Length:	18.7 cm (7.4 in)	24.0 cm (9.4 in)	35.0 cm (13.8 in)

CHESTNUT LAMPREY *Ichthyomyzon castaneus*

Ichthyomyzon—*ichthys*: fish; *myzo*: to suck; refers to its parasitic nature.
castaneus: the colour of chestnuts.

Very similar in appearance and size to the Silver Lamprey, the Chestnut Lamprey was first discovered in Ontario in 1994 in the St. Lawrence River. A subsequent examination of preserved museum specimens revealed several caught since 1966 that had been misidentified as Silver Lamprey.

DESCRIPTION: The Chestnut Lamprey is very elongate. The large, round, jawless mouth has sharp teeth; at least 3 of the 8 lateral **circumoral** teeth are **bicuspid** (p. 84). The body is scaleless and slimy, with 7 **pore**-like gill openings behind each eye. The dorsal fin has 2 lobes joined by a wide **membrane** (p. 85). There are no pectoral or pelvic fins. The back is dark grey to olive or yellow-brown. The belly is lighter in colour. The sides are sometimes mottled and the **pores** of the **lateral line** are black. The fins are olive-yellow.

SIMILAR SPECIES: The American Eel has a jaw with many small teeth, a single gill opening behind each eye, and pectoral fins. The Sea Lamprey usually has 2 separate dorsal fins, and the American Brook Lamprey has 2 dorsal fins joined by a very narrow **membrane**. The Northern Brook Lamprey has a small mouth and blunt teeth. The Silver Lamprey has lateral **circumoral** teeth that are **unicuspid**.

FEEDING: The **ammocoete** filters microscopic algae and animal material from the surrounding water and the bottom. The adult parasitizes other fishes with its sucking mouth by breaking through their skin with its tongue and feeding on their blood.

REPRODUCTION: Adults migrate in spring to small tributary streams and build nests in gravel **riffles**. Females attach to stones, and males attach to the female's head, wrapping themselves around her. Spawning with random pairings occurs multiple times within a spawning season, when water temperatures are between 16°C and 22°C. Adults die shortly after spawning.

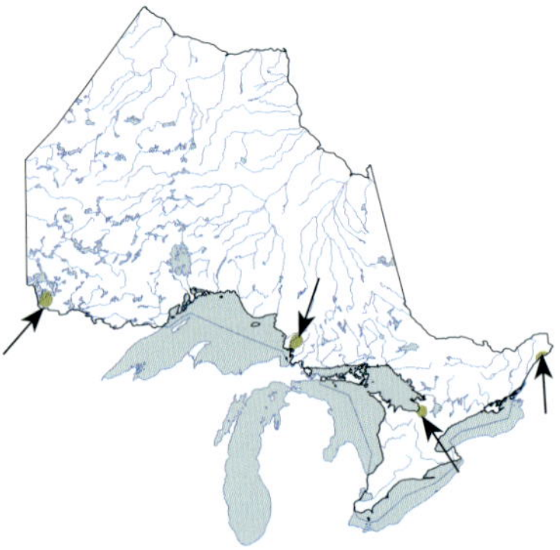

Feeding on a minnow

Ammocoete

Ammocoete mouth

HABITAT: The Chestnut Lamprey lives its entire life in coolwater streams, mostly as an **ammocoete** buried in soft bottoms of silt and sand.

STATUS: G4TUQ; NU; SU; DD (Great Lakes–Upper St. Lawrence populations).

Maximum Age: 8	Ontario Average	Ontario Record	World Record
Length:	22.4 cm (8.8 in)	22.4 cm (8.8 in)	38.0 cm (15.0 in)

NORTHERN BROOK LAMPREY *Ichthyomyzon fossor*

Ichthyomyzon—ichthys: fish; *myzo*: to suck. Despite the name, this species is non-parasitic.
fossor: digger; refers to its digging habits.

Scientists believe that lampreys evolved as pairs of species, one parasitic on fishes and the other strictly non-parasitic. The Northern Brook Lamprey is thought to be the non-parasitic **sister species** to the parasitic Silver Lamprey.

DESCRIPTION: This species is very elongate. The small, round, jawless mouth has a few blunt teeth (p. 84). The body is scaleless and slimy, with 7 **pore**-like gill openings behind each eye. The single dorsal fin has 2 lobes joined by a wide **membrane** (p. 85). There are no pectoral or pelvic fins. This lamprey has a dark grey to brown back with a pale median stripe. The belly is grey, yellow, or silvery white. The throat may be orange. The tail is dark grey or black, and the fins are grey, yellow, or tan.

SIMILAR SPECIES: The American Eel has a jaw with many small teeth, a single gill opening behind each eye, and pectoral fins. The Sea Lamprey has 2, usually separate, dorsal fins sometimes joined by a very low ridge. The American Brook Lamprey has 2 dorsal fins joined by a very narrow **membrane**. Chestnut and Silver lampreys have a large mouth with many sharp teeth.

FEEDING: **Larval ammocoetes filter feed** on **plankton** from the surrounding water and the bottom. Adults do not feed.

REPRODUCTION: Using its mouth to move gravel and small stones, the Northern Brook Lamprey prepares its nest in streams. Spawning occurs in spring when water temperatures are between 13°C and 15°C. Mating pairs swim together in a vertical position and vigorously vibrate, causing eggs and sperm to drop over the nest. Adults die shortly thereafter.

HABITAT: This lamprey lives its entire life in coolwater streams, and most of that time as an **ammocoete** buried in soft bottoms of silt and sand.

STATUS: G4; N3; S3; SC (Great Lakes–Upper St. Lawrence populations).

Spawning

Maximum Age: 8	Ontario Average	Ontario Record	World Record
Length:	15.0 cm (5.9 in)	16.4 cm (6.5 in)	17.0 cm (6.7 in)

SEA LAMPREY *Petromyzon marinus*

Petromyzon—*petra*: rock; *myzo*: to suck; refers to its ability to move stones with its mouth.
marinus: of the sea.

Native to the Atlantic Ocean, the Sea Lamprey gained access to Lake Ontario through the Erie Canal and, subsequently, to the remaining Great Lakes through the Welland Canal. Its devastating effect on Lake Trout and other native fishes led to the formation of the international Great Lakes Fishery Commission in 1955 to coordinate the control of this **invasive species**.

DESCRIPTION: This lamprey is very elongate. The large, round, jawless mouth has sharp teeth (p. 84). The body is scaleless and slimy, with 7 **pore**-like gill openings behind each eye. There are 2 dorsal fins, sometimes joined by a very low ridge (p. 85). There are no pectoral or pelvic fins. The Sea Lamprey is greyish blue to dark brown. Large adults are marbled. They have dark brown or black backs and silver, light yellow, light brown, or white bellies.

SIMILAR SPECIES: The American Eel has a jaw with many small teeth, a single gill opening behind each eye, and pectoral fins. Silver, Chestnut, and Northern Brook lampreys have 1 dorsal fin joined by a wide **membrane**. The American Brook Lamprey has a small mouth with a few blunt teeth.

FEEDING: The **ammocoete** burrows into the mud and feeds on drifting microscopic plant and animal material. The adult is parasitic on other fishes, such as trouts and salmons. It uses its sucker mouth to attach to the host fish then its tongue teeth to rasp through skin to suck blood.

REPRODUCTION: Sea Lamprey are attracted to spawning streams by chemicals released by all lamprey species. Adults migrate into streams in spring and choose nesting sites in swift water. Males excavate the nest using their mouths and tails to move stones and sweep away sand. Females appear on the nests; males then attach themselves to, and coil around, the females. Spawning occurs over several weeks at water temperatures between 11°C and 24°C, after which the adults drift downstream and die.

Spawning

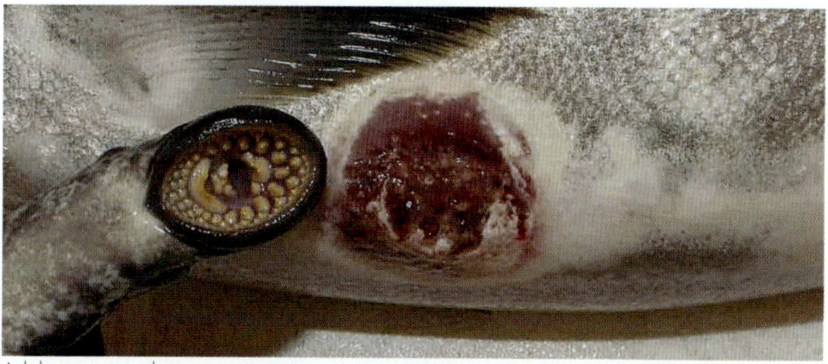

Adult scar on salmon

HABITAT: In Ontario, adults live in the cold **pelagic** areas of the Great Lakes and their connecting channels. **Ammocoetes** spend most of their lives in streams, buried in soft bottoms of primarily silt and sand.

STATUS: G5; N5; SNA.

Maximum Age: 12	Ontario Average	Ontario Record	World Record
Length:	43.9 cm (17.3 in)	58.3 cm (23.0 in)	120.0 cm (47.2 in)
Weight:	–	–	2.5 kg (5.5 lbs)

SILVER LAMPREY *Ichthyomyzon unicuspis*

Ichthyomyzon—*ichthys*: fish; *myzo*: to suck; refers to its parasitic nature.
unicuspis—*uni*: one; *cuspis*: pointed; refers to having single, pointed teeth.

A Canadian study found that the Silver Lamprey is genetically indistinguishable from its **sister species**, the Northern Brook Lamprey. Therefore, these two species may actually be a single species with two very different feeding behaviours.

DESCRIPTION: The Silver Lamprey is very elongate. The large, round, jawless mouth has sharp teeth. The lateral **circumoral** teeth are usually **unicuspid** (p. 84); rarely, 1 or 2 teeth may be **bicuspid**. The body is scaleless and slimy, with 7 **pore**-like gill openings behind each eye. There is 1 dorsal fin with 2 lobes joined by a wide **membrane** (p. 85). There are no pectoral or pelvic fins. The back is yellow to tan in young adults and brown, silver-grey or blue-grey in large adults. The belly is lighter blue-grey or silver. The sides are sometimes mottled, and the **pores** of the **lateral line** are slightly darkened in large individuals. The tail is dark grey or black, and the fins are yellow.

SIMILAR SPECIES: The American Eel has a jaw with many small teeth, a single gill opening behind each eye, and pectoral fins. The Sea Lamprey has 2 dorsal fins, sometimes joined by a very low ridge, and the American Brook Lamprey has 2 dorsal fins joined by a narrow **membrane**. The Northern Brook Lamprey has a small mouth and blunt teeth. The Chestnut Lamprey has at least 3 lateral **circumoral** teeth that are **bicuspid**.

FEEDING: Ammocoetes feed on drifting **plankton** and **detritus**. Adults use their rasping tongue teeth and sucking mouth to parasitize a variety of fishes, feeding on their blood.

REPRODUCTION: Adults migrate into streams in spring and construct shallow nests in gravel **riffles**, moving stones with their mouths and sweeping sand away with their tails. Spawning occurs over several weeks when the water

Feeding on a Walleye

Spawning

temperature is near 18°C. Nest building continues throughout the spawning period. The male attaches to the female's head, coils around her, and the pair vibrates rapidly, releasing eggs and sperm. Adults die after spawning.

HABITAT: Adults live primarily in the cool waters of lakes. **Ammocoetes** spend most of their lives in streams, buried in the soft bottoms of silt and sand.

STATUS: G5TNRQ; N3; S3; SC (Great Lakes–Upper St. Lawrence populations).
G5TNRQ; N3?; S1; SC^{F}; DD^{P} (Saskatchewan–Nelson River populations).

Maximum Age: 8	Ontario Average	Ontario Record	World Record
Length:	25.5 cm (10.0 in)	30.6 cm (12.0 in)	39.0 cm (15.4 in)

ACIPENSERIDAE
Sturgeons

Sturgeons are the largest freshwater fishes in the world—the Beluga Sturgeon in Europe reaches 6 m in length and more than 2,000 kg in weight. Sturgeons are long-lived, sometimes living more than a hundred years. They occur in the coastal and fresh waters of the northern hemisphere, with some species being **anadromous**. They have a skeleton made of **cartilage** and an upturned **asymmetric** tail. Their heads are covered with bony plates, and there are five rows of bony **scutes** running along the body that disappear in large adults. Sturgeons are bottom feeders and have four **barbels** in front of the mouth, which aid in finding food. Their flesh is flavourful, and their eggs are used for caviar. Overfishing and dams that block their spawning migration, combined with a slow maturation (around 25 years) and infrequent spawning (once every seven to nine years) in females, have led to their dramatic decline. As a result, all 25 species are considered at risk, with more than half being ranked as critically endangered. Sturgeons are regulated by the Convention on International Trade in Endangered Species (CITES). Global conservation initiatives have been established in an attempt to regulate and maintain sturgeon stocks to ensure sustainability.

There are 27 species worldwide, one of which is found in Ontario.

< Lake Sturgeon

LAKE STURGEON *Acipenser fulvescens*

Acipenser: ancient Greek word for sturgeon.
fulvescens: reddish-yellow colour.

The Lake Sturgeon is Ontario's largest and longest-lived freshwater fish. A huge commercial fishery in the Great Lakes caught millions of kilograms of sturgeon between the mid-1800s and early 1900s. Shortly thereafter, Lake Sturgeon virtually disappeared from the Great Lakes, and only after a century are populations starting to show signs of recovery.

DESCRIPTION: This distinctive species is very elongate and has a triangular snout with 4 **barbels** on the ventral surface. The mouth is on the bottom of the head behind the **barbels**. Its head is covered with bony plates, and 5 rows of bony **scutes**, which disappear in large adults, are found along the body. The tail is **asymmetric** and upturned. Young are grey or brown, with scattered black blotches disappearing when the fish achieves a length of about 60 cm. Adults are grey or olive-brown on the back, sides, and fins, and white on the belly.

SIMILAR SPECIES: None.

FEEDING: The Lake Sturgeon uses its **protrusible** mouth to suck in prey, such as insect **larvae**, crayfishes, and molluscs, off the bottom. The 4 fleshy **barbels** are touch and taste sensitive and are dragged along the bottom when searching for food.

REPRODUCTION: In spring, adults migrate up to 400 km to spawn in fast-flowing streams. Spawning occurs when water temperatures are between 13°C and 21°C. Nests are not built, but rather, the fertilized adhesive eggs attach to rocks and logs. The Lake Sturgeon is slow to mature, with males first spawning at 20 and females at 25 years of age. Females spawn only every 4–6 years and may release more than 500,000 eggs depending on their age and size.

HABITAT: The Lake Sturgeon lives primarily in the cool waters of the bottoms of lakes and large streams. It prefers sand and silt bottoms but is also found over rubble and gravel.

STATUS: T^F, E^P Great Lakes–Upper St. Lawrence River populations; E^F,T^P Lake of the Woods-Rainy River populations; SC Southern Hudson Bay-James Bay populations.

Juvenile

Protrusible mouth

Egg

Maximum Age: 154	Ontario Average	Ontario Record	World Record
Length:	117.0 cm (46.1 in)	241.5 cm (95.0 in)	274.0 cm (107.9 in)
Weight: Overall	10.0 kg (22.0 lbs)	140.6 kg (31.0 lbs)	140.6 kg (310.0 lbs)
Angling	–	76.2 kg (168.0 lbs)	76.2 kg (168.0 lbs)

LEPISOSTEIDAE
Gars

This ancient group of large predatory fishes is found in eastern North America, Central America south to Costa Rica, and Cuba. They have elongated jaws armed with sharp, needle-like teeth, slightly **asymmetric** tails, and heavily armoured bodies with non-overlapping, bony **ganoid scales**.

Gars often live in warm, shallow waters with low-oxygen conditions. To do this, they are able to breathe air by gulping it at the surface. The air passes through a connection from the **esophagus** to the **swim bladder**, which acts like a lung and absorbs oxygen. Young gar have an adhesive disc on their snouts used to attach themselves to vegetation until they are fully developed.

There are seven species worldwide, two of which are found in Ontario.

Side view of head of Longnose Gar

Top view of heads of Longnose Gar (top) and Spotted Gar (bottom)

Side view of head of Spotted Gar

Ganoid scales

< Spotted Gar

LONGNOSE GAR *Lepisosteus osseus*

Lepisosteus—lepis: scale; *osteo*: bone; refers to the thick, bony scales.
osseus: bony.

This is the more common of the two gar species found in Ontario. Although it has spots, it should not be confused with the much rarer Spotted Gar. Gars should not be called gar-pike, as they are not members of the pike family.

DESCRIPTION: This species is very elongate and covered with hard, diamond-shaped scales. The snout and jaws are elongated into a beak with sharp teeth. The length of the beak from its tip to the eye is greater than 12 times its narrowest width (p. 101), except in fish less than 10 cm in length. Adults are olive-brown to dark green on back. The back and sides of the body are often spotted, particularly in smaller adults and individuals from clear waters. The fins are yellow, orange, or brown, and the tail and dorsal and anal fins have large black spots. The juvenile has a fleshy extension of the spine above the upper edge of the tail, a brown or black lateral stripe from snout to tail, and a dark belly bordered above by a white stripe.

SIMILAR SPECIES: Other gars have a shorter and wider beak; length of the beaks from the tip to the eye is less than 10 times their narrowest width. Gars less than 10 cm in length are difficult to distinguish.

FEEDING: The Longnose Gar lies in wait near the surface, then darts out and impales nearby prey fishes with its needle-sharp teeth. It is **piscivorous**, feeding almost exclusively on fishes, including bass, sunfish, perch, and minnow species. Food of the very young consists of **invertebrates**, such as aquatic insect **larvae**.

REPRODUCTION: Adults appear in shallow waters of lakes and streams in late spring. Nests are not made. Spawning occurs over several weeks when the water temperature is around 19°C. The female swims side by side with several males over weedy beds and deposits her eggs in numerous locations. The large adhesive eggs become attached to vegetation and hatch in about a week.

Longnose Gar

Juvenile

HABITAT: The Longnose Gar lives in warmwater lakes and slow-moving streams with abundant aquatic vegetation of all types.

STATUS: G5; N4; S4.

Maximum Age: 36	Ontario Average	Ontario Record	World Record
Length:	76.0 cm (29.9 in)	137.2 cm (54.0 in)	200.0 cm (78.7 in)
Weight: Overall	1.1 kg (2.5 lbs)	9.6 kg (21.2 lbs)	22.8 kg (50.3 lbs)
Angling	–	9.6 kg (21.2 lbs)	22.8 kg (50.3 lbs)

SPOTTED GAR *Lepisosteus oculatus*

Lepisosteus—lepis: scale; *osteo*: bone; refers to the thick, bony scales.
oculatus: having eyes; refers to the spots on the body.

This is one of the rarest fishes in Canada and is found only in Ontario, where fewer than 500 individuals have ever been caught. This species is protected by the federal *Species at Risk Act*.

DESCRIPTION: The Spotted Gar is very elongate and covered with hard, diamond-shaped scales. The snout and jaws are elongated into a beak with sharp teeth. The length of the beak from the tip to the eye is less than 10 times its narrowest width (p. 101). It has bony plates on the underside of the head, which are mostly covered by the gill **membrane**. Young fish have a fleshy extension of the spine above the upper edge of the tail, are brightly coloured, and have wide dark brown stripes on the back, sides, and belly. The adults are brown to olive-green, with large darker brown spots on snout, head, body, and fins.

SIMILAR SPECIES: The introduced Florida Gar lacks bony plates on the underside of the head. Longnose Gar that are greater than 10 cm in length have a longer, narrower beak; the length of the beak from its tip to the eye is greater than 12 times its narrowest width. Gars less than 10 cm are difficult to distinguish.

FEEDING: Called an **ambush predator**, the Spotted Gar waits motionless near the surface in heavy vegetation until a prey fish approaches. Adults are **piscivorous**, feeding almost exclusively on small fishes. The very young prefer small crustaceans.

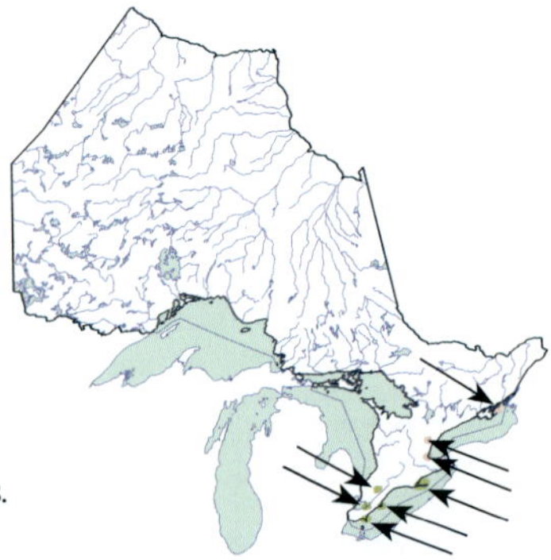

REPRODUCTION: Spawning occurs in spring in shallow, warm, heavily vegetated wetlands when the water temperature is between 21°C and 26°C. Several males swim side by side with a single, usually larger, female, and eggs and sperm are deposited over weedy beds. The adhesive eggs stick to submerged plants and hatch in one or two weeks.

Juvenile

Leucistic colour pattern

HABITAT: The Spotted Gar is found in the shallow, warm waters of nearshore wetlands with abundant vegetation.

STATUS: G5; N1; S1; E.

Maximum Age: 18	Ontario Average	Ontario Record	World Record
Length:	51.0 cm (20.1 in)	79.0 cm (31.1 in)	150 cm (59.1 in)
Weight: Overall	–	1.94 kg (4.3 lbs)	4.4 kg (9.8 lbs)
Angling	–	–	4.4 kg (9.8 lbs)

AMIIDAE
Bowfins

Sometimes known as a living fossil, the Emerald Bowfin is one of two survivors of a larger group of fishes that evolved more than 200 million years ago. Found only in eastern North America, the Emerald Bowfin has a bony gular plate on the underside of the head, **cartilage** in much of the skeleton, and a thick, bony skull. Its head is scaleless, its mouth has many sharp teeth, and its body is covered in **cycloid scales**.

Usually found in swampy, vegetated lakes and streams, the Emerald Bowfin can tolerate high temperatures with stagnant conditions that are unsuitable for most fishes. To avoid these extreme conditions, the Emerald Bowfin is known to burrow into the bottom and **aestivate**. Like gars, the Emerald Bowfin is able to breathe air by gulping it at the surface. The air then enters the **swim bladder**, which acts like a lung by absorbing oxygen. The Emerald Bowfin is an aggressive predator that sucks prey into its mouth by rapidly gulping water. Females are larger and live much longer than males.

There are two species worldwide, one of which is found in Ontario.

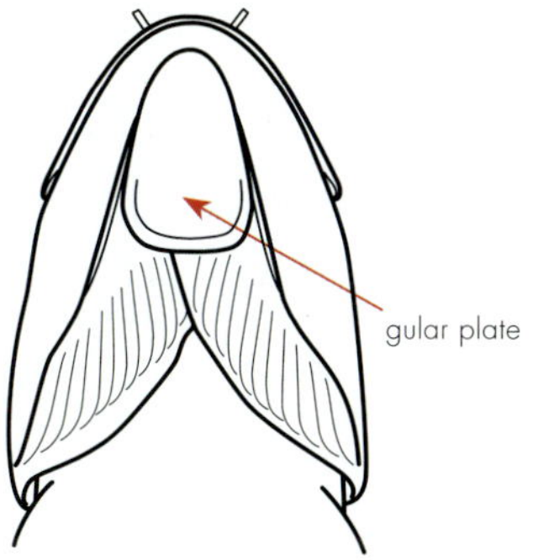

< Emerald Bowfin

EMERALD BOWFIN *Amia ocellicauda*

Amia: ancient Greek name for a perch-like fish.
ocellicauda-ocelli: little eye; *cauda*: tail; refers to the spot at the upper base of the caudal fin.

♀

♂

This fish is also commonly known as "dogfish" in Ontario, not to be confused with small species of sharks also known as "dogfish." We highly recommend that the accepted common name "Emerald Bowfin" be used when referring to this species.

DESCRIPTION: The Emerald Bowfin has a large head and elongated body. There is a bony gular plate on the underside of the head (p. 107). The dorsal fin is long, extending along most of the back. The tail is rounded. The juvenile is strongly marbled, becoming less so with age. The back and sides are dark olive, and the belly is white or cream. All young, and adult males, have a black spot with a yellow to orange edge at the upper base of the tail. The spot is absent, or faint without a yellow or orange edge, in adult females. The spawning male has a bright green belly and lower fins.

SIMILAR SPECIES: No other species in Ontario has a gular plate (p. 107).

FEEDING: The Emerald Bowfin is an **opportunist**, feeding on whatever is available, including aquatic insects, fishes, crayfishes, frogs, and snakes. It uses scent as much as sight to find its prey and is most active at night.

REPRODUCTION: The Emerald Bowfin spawns in shallow, vegetated waters in spring when the water temperature is between 16°C and 19°C. In communities with

Juvenile

other male Emerald Bowfin, the male prepares a nest by clearing out sticks and leaves or finding protected spots under logs. He then attracts a female into the nest, circles around her, and spawning occurs. Males aggressively defend the nest and guard the young for several weeks until they leave the nest.

HABITAT: The Emerald Bowfin lives in the warm waters of wetlands and slow-moving streams with abundant vegetation.

STATUS: G5; NNR; S4.

Maximum Age: 30	Ontario Average	Ontario Record	World Record
Length:	54.0 cm (21.3 in)	83.5 cm (32.9 in)	109.0 cm (42.9 in)
Weight: Overall	1.2 kg (2.7 lbs)	6.8 kg (15.1 lbs)	9.8 kg (21.5 lbs)
Angling	–	6.8 kg (15.1 lbs)	9.8 kg (21.5 lbs)

HIODONTIDAE
Mooneyes

This family belongs to a group of fishes known as the bony-tongues. Other members of this group include the large Arapaima and arawanas. The mooneyes occur in the fresh waters of central North America. Their shiny silver or gold eyes are large and reflective (hence the name), allowing them to see in the dim, **turbid** waters in which they live. Their bodies are covered in large, silvery **cycloid scales** and end in a strongly forked tail. They lack an adipose fin. Mooneyes give a fierce battle when angled with flies and live bait, earning them the nickname "freshwater tarpon."

The only two living species in this family are found in Ontario.

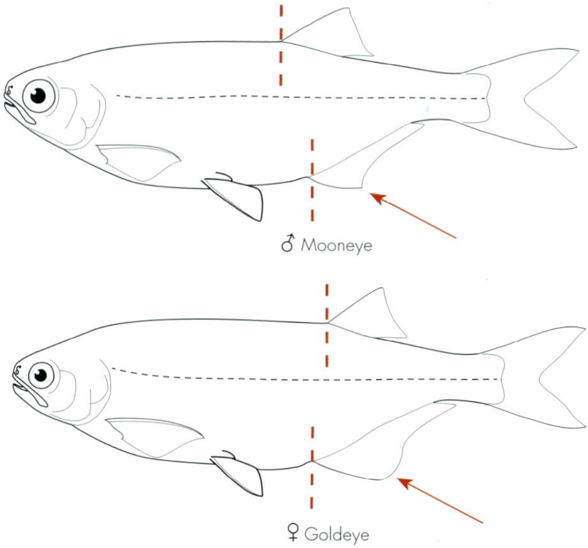

Location of the dorsal fin in relation to the anal fin.
Note the difference in the shape of the anal fin between the male and female.

< Goldeye

GOLDEYE *Hiodon alosoides*

Hiodon—*hyoid*: bone on floor of mouth; *dont*: toothed; refers to the toothed hyoid bone.
alosoides: shad-like; resembles the herrings or shads.

Smoked "Winnipeg Goldeye" became famous by being served on the Canadian National Railway. No longer abundant in Lake Winnipeg (Manitoba), they are still caught in other northern lakes, smoked, and marketed as "Winnipeg Goldeye."

DESCRIPTION: This silvery fish is very deep-bodied and very thin from side to side. The mouth is large, the upper jaw ending below the back half of the large eye, and there are many fine teeth. The belly has scales forming a smooth **keel** from the head to the anal fin. The **origin** of the dorsal fin is behind the **origin** of the anal fin (p. 111). The front of the anal fin is rounded in the male and pointed in the female (p. 111). Goldeye have a dark blue or blue-green back. The sides are silvery with a golden lustre, and the belly is white. The eye is bright yellow.

SIMILAR SPECIES: The Alewife and Gizzard Shad have sharp scales forming a saw-toothed **keel**. Whitefishes, ciscoes, and Rainbow Smelt have an adipose fin. The Mooneye has a smaller mouth, and the **origin** of its dorsal fin is in front of the **origin** of the anal fin.

FEEDING: The Goldeye is **opportunistic**, eating crustaceans, molluscs, frogs, small fishes, and aquatic insects.

REPRODUCTION: The Goldeye spawns in early spring over a 3–6 week period. A spawning migration occurs from deeper overwintering grounds to shallows in lakes and into streams. No nest is built. Spawning usually occurs at night. Fertilized eggs are buoyant and hatch after two weeks.

HABITAT: The Goldeye prefers the warm, **pelagic** waters of large streams and shallow, **turbid** lakes in northern Ontario.

STATUS: G5; N5; S3.

Maximum Age: 14	Ontario Average	Ontario Record	World Record
Length:	34.3 cm (13.5 in)	42.6 cm (16.8 in)	53.0 cm (20.9 in)
Weight: Overall	0.3 kg (0.7 lbs)	1.0 kg (2.2 lbs)	1.7 kg (3.8 lbs)
Angling	–	1.0 kg (2.2 lbs)	1.7 kg (3.8 lbs)

MOONEYE *Hiodon tergisus*

Hiodon—hyoid: bone on floor of mouth; *dont*: toothed; refers to the toothed hyoid bone.
tergisus: polished; refers to its shiny, silvery appearance.

Although not as tasty as the Goldeye, the Mooneye provides good angling opportunities. Excellent spring fly-fishing can be found in the lower Grand River (Lake Erie drainage).

DESCRIPTION: This silvery fish is deep-bodied and very thin from side to side. The mouth is medium-sized, the upper jaw ending below the front half of the large eye, and there are many fine teeth. Scales along the belly form a smooth **keel** that does not extend forward to the head. The **origin** of the dorsal fin is in front of the **origin** of the anal fin (p. 111). The front of the anal fin is rounded in the male and pointed in the female (p. 111). The back is olive to brown, the sides are silvery blue, and the belly is white. The eye is golden.

SIMILAR SPECIES: The Alewife and Gizzard Shad have sharp scales forming a saw-toothed **keel**. Whitefishes, ciscoes, and Rainbow Smelt have an adipose fin. The Goldeye has a larger mouth, and its dorsal fin **origin** is behind the **origin** of the anal fin.

FEEDING: Young Mooneye eat a variety of aquatic insect **larvae**. The adult feeds on insects, small fishes, molluscs, and crayfishes.

REPRODUCTION: Spawning occurs in spring when large numbers of Mooneye migrate into streams to spawn. Nests are not built, and eggs are deposited over a gravel bottom.

HABITAT: The Mooneye is found in warm waters of large **turbid** streams in southern Ontario and large, shallow, **turbid** lakes and streams in northern Ontario. It is also found in the **pelagic** waters of the Great Lakes.

STATUS: G4; N4; S4.

Maximum Age: 10	Ontario Average	Ontario Record	World Record
Length:	28.0 cm (11.0 in)	43.2 cm (17.0 in)	47.0 cm (18.5 in)
Weight: Overall	0.2 kg (0.4 lbs)	0.9 kg (2.0 lbs)	0.9 kg (2.0 lbs)
Angling	–	0.9 kg (2.0 lbs)	0.9 kg (2.0 lbs)

ANGUILLIDAE
Freshwater Eels

Although called freshwater eels, members of this family are **catadromous**. After hatching in salt water, they spend most of their lives in fresh water and then return to salt water to spawn. They occur in tributaries of the Atlantic, western Pacific, and Indian oceans. Their very elongate body allows them to hide in crevices and burrow in the bottom. This gives them an advantage over other fishes, both in hunting prey and seeking shelter from predators. They have long dorsal and anal fins, and lack pelvic fins. Their **cycloid scales** are small and embedded in the skin, giving eels the appearance of being scaleless.

Freshwater eels have always been important food fishes. Once a staple for North American Indigenous Peoples, the eel is also considered a delicacy in Asian cuisine. The demand for freshwater eels was once supplied by the European Eel, *Anguilla anguilla*; however, with the crash of these eel populations by over 90% in the 1980s, the American Eel is now highly sought. Asian markets now depend on wild-caught North American **elvers** to feed the demand. **Elvers** are harvested on the east coast of Canada and the USA and grown to market size in Asia. In 2015, high market demand for North American **elvers** caused prices to skyrocket from $53 per kg to $4,500 per kg, making **elvers** the most valuable marine resource in North America. Despite poaching and black-market trade for **elvers**, harvest quotas are strictly enforced by Fisheries and Oceans Canada in an attempt to protect the American Eel population.

There are 18 species recognized worldwide, one of which is found in Ontario.

< American Eel **elvers**

AMERICAN EEL *Anguilla rostrata*

Anguilla: eel.
rostrata: beaked.

In Ontario and elsewhere, American Eel populations have declined dramatically in recent years, likely as a result of commercial overharvesting and dams that block migration.

DESCRIPTION: This fish is very elongate and has a small pointed head. The jaws have many small teeth. The lower jaw protrudes past the upper jaw. The scales are tiny and inconspicuous. A single gill opening is located just in front of each pectoral fin. Pelvic fins are absent. The long dorsal and anal fins are continuous with the tail. Immature adults range in colour from yellow to green to olive-brown. While transforming from immature to mature adults, eels are silvery. Once sexually mature, adults have a metallic bronze or black back. The American Eel alters its colouration within hours in response to light conditions.

SIMILAR SPECIES: Lampreys resemble the American Eel, but have 7 **pore**-like gill openings behind each eye, a single nostril, no pectoral fins, no scales, and a mouth consisting of a sucking disc with or without teeth.

FEEDING: The American Eel is **carnivorous**, feeding at night on a wide variety of fishes, **invertebrates**, and frogs.

REPRODUCTION: The American Eel is **catadromous**. On reaching maturity at 10–20 years of age in fresh water, adults migrate downstream to the Atlantic Ocean and follow the coast south to spawn in the Sargasso Sea, a sea bounded by Bermuda to the north and the Greater Antilles to the south. Adults die after spawning. Once hatched, the young, transparent, leaf-shaped **larva** (called a **leptocephalus**) drifts back up the eastern seaboard. It then undergoes **metamorphosis**, first into a transparent juvenile (called a **glass eel**), and then into a pigmented juvenile (called an **elver**). It then enters fresh water, where it lives until it reaches sexual maturity. Only females migrate as far as Ontario waters.

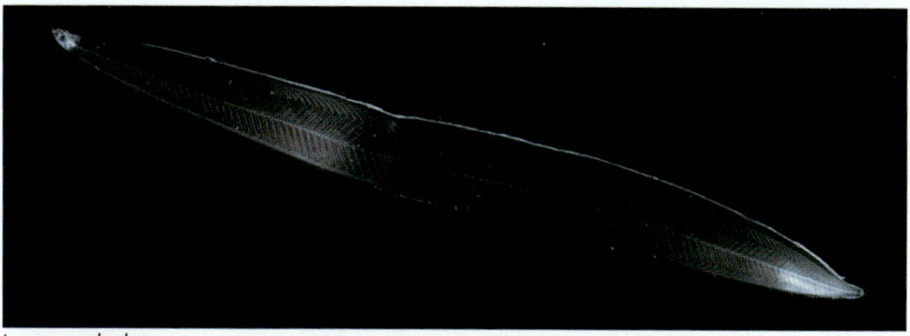

Leptocephalus

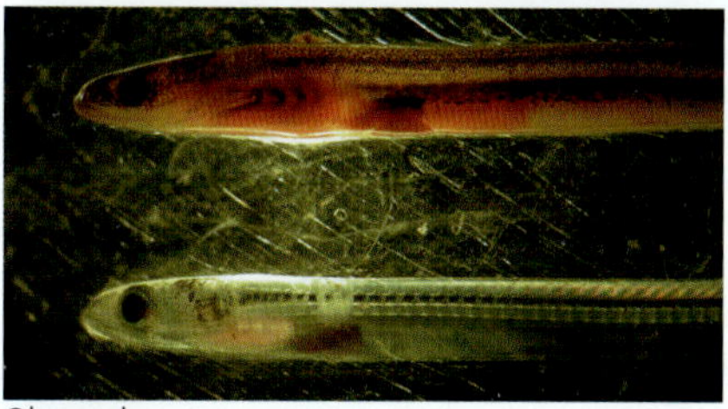

Glass eels

HABITAT: Historically, the American Eel was present only in the cool waters of the St. Lawrence and Ottawa rivers, Lake Ontario, and their tributaries. In 1829, when the Welland Canal was completed, the American Eel dispersed into lakes Erie, Huron, and Superior, and their tributaries. Since then, it has disappeared from many of the tributaries due to dam construction. The American Eel prefers bottoms of gravel, sand, and silt.

STATUS: G4; N2N4; S1S2; T^F; E^P.

Maximum Age: 43	Ontario Average	Ontario Record	World Record
Length:	90.0 cm (35.4 in)	120.0 cm (47.2 in)	152.0 cm (59.8 in)
Weight: Overall	1.4 kg (3.0 lbs)	2.3 kg (5.1 lbs)	7.3 kg (16.1 lbs)
Angling	–	2.3 kg (5.1 lbs)	4.2 kg (9.3 lbs)

ALOSIDAE
Shads

Shads were part of the large family, Clupeidae, but recent studies indicate that they are in a distinct family. They include shads, menhadens, sardines, and pilchards. Shads are most closely related to the Thread Herrings and, like them, they are silvery fishes with a single dorsal fin, cycloid scales, a saw-toothed ventral keel, and no adipose fin. They are distinct from other herring-like fishes by having gill covers marked with fine, parallel grooves or ridges.

Shads are found globally in marine, brackish, and fresh waters, and many of them are anadromous, migrating from the ocean to freshwater rivers to spawn and playing a key role, similar to salmons, in transporting nutrients between marine and freshwater ecosystems. Some shads have adapted to freshwater lakes, such as Lake Ontario, forming non-migratory populations.

There are 34 species worldwide, two of which occur in Ontario.

American Shad showing fine ridges and grooves on gill cover

< School of Alewife

ALEWIFE *Alosa pseudoharengus*

Alosa: old name for European shad.
pseudoharengus—pseudo: false; *harengus*: herring; similar to a herring.

The Alewife is not native to Ontario, but it colonized the Great Lakes from the Atlantic coast after construction of the Erie and Welland canals. This **invasive species** has become the most important prey species in the Great Lakes and is eaten by many sport fishes, but it has also contributed to the decline of many native fishes through **competition** and **predation**.

DESCRIPTION: This silvery fish is deep-bodied and very thin from side to side. It has a pointed snout with a lower jaw that protrudes beyond the upper jaw. The eye diameter is usually longer than the snout length and equal to or longer than the cheek depth (p. 23). The mouth is small, the upper jaw ending below the front half of the eye. Teeth are weak or absent. Along the belly, sharp scales form a saw-toothed **keel** (p. 125). There is no adipose fin. The dorsal fin is entirely in front of the anal fin. The last dorsal fin ray is shorter than the others. The anal fin is short with 15–19 rays. The back is greyish green and the upper side sometimes possesses dark stripes. There is usually a black spot immediately behind the head.

SIMILAR SPECIES: Whitefishes, ciscoes, and Rainbow Smelt have an adipose fin. Mooneye and Goldeye have teeth, a rounded snout, a dorsal fin mostly over the anal fin, and a smooth **keel**. The American Shad has a larger mouth, and its eye diameter is usually less than its cheek depth. The Gizzard Shad has a rounded snout, a noticeably longer last dorsal fin ray, and a long anal fin with 27–34 rays. The Blueback Herring, a potential invader, has a blue back and eye diameter usually less than the snout length.

FEEDING: Young Alewife **filter feed** on tiny crustaceans. The adult also consumes **larval** insects and fishes. Since

its introduction in the 1980s, the invasive spiny water flea constitutes a significant portion of the Alewife's diet.

REPRODUCTION: The Alewife on the Atlantic coast is **anadromous**, migrating into fresh water to spawn. In Ontario, it is **landlocked**, and large schools of Alewife move in early spring from open lakes to nearshore areas to spawn. No nests are built. Spawning takes place at night in pairs or threes, with eggs broadcast randomly over gravel or sand bottoms. The young remain on the spawning grounds for most of the summer before moving into deeper water.

HABITAT: Alewives form large schools in the cool, open waters near the **thermocline** throughout the Great Lakes (except Lake Superior). They often congregate in warmwater outflows of power plants in winter and, in cases of plant shutdowns, thermal shock may cause massive die-offs.

STATUS: G5; N5; SNA.

Maximum Age: 9	Ontario Average	Ontario Record	World Record
Length:	15.0 cm (5.9 in)	30.9 cm (12.2 in)	40.0 cm (15.7 in)
Weight:	0.03 kg (0.07 lbs)	–	0.2 kg (0.4 lbs)

AMERICAN SHAD *Alosa sapidissima*

Alosa: old name for European shad.
sapidissima: most tasty.

The American Shad is rare in Ontario, as it historically entered the upper St. Lawrence and lower Ottawa rivers only during spawning migrations. Dams now limit migration into the lower Ottawa River and the upper St. Lawrence River.

DESCRIPTION: This silvery fish is deep-bodied and thin from side to side. It has a pointed snout. The lower jaw is nearly equal in length to the upper jaw and fits into a notch in the upper jaw. The eye diameter is less than the cheek depth (p. 23). The mouth is large, the upper jaw ending below or beyond the back half of the eye. The teeth are weak or absent. Sharp scales form a saw-toothed **keel** along the belly (p. 125). There is no adipose fin. The dorsal fin is entirely in front of the anal fin. The last dorsal fin ray is shorter than the others. The anal fin is short with 18–24 rays. The back is metallic blue or blue-green, and the upper side usually has a row (sometimes 2 or 3 rows) of 4–27 black spots.

SIMILAR SPECIES: Whitefishes, ciscoes, and Rainbow Smelt have an adipose fin. Mooneye and Goldeye have teeth, a rounded snout, a dorsal fin mostly over the anal fin, and a smooth **keel**. The Gizzard Shad has a rounded snout, a noticeably longer last dorsal fin ray, and a long anal fin with 27–34 rays. The Alewife has a smaller mouth, and its eye diameter is equal to or greater than its cheek depth.

FEEDING: The American Shad feeds mainly on **plankton**, such as copepods and insect **larvae**. Feeding ceases during the upstream spawning migration and resumes again for the downstream post-spawning migration.

REPRODUCTION: American Shad are **anadromous**, entering fresh water to spawn. Many undertake long journeys to their favoured spawning grounds. Spawning occurs in spring. At

Carillon Dam. A major barrier preventing American Shad and other migrating species from moving farther up the Ottawa River.

sundown, males and females pair and swim close together, releasing eggs and sperm. Adults return to the ocean shortly after spawning, while the young spend their first summer in fresh water before entering the ocean.

HABITAT: This species is present in Ontario only during the spawning run, when it enters the Ottawa River and is found below the Carillon Dam in southeastern Ontario.

STATUS: G5; N4; SNA.

Maximum Age: 13	Ontario Average	Ontario Record	World Record
Length:	38.0 cm (15.0 in)	54.0 cm (21.3 in)	76.0 cm (29.9 in)
Weight: Overall	0.5 kg (1.1 lbs)	–	5.5 kg (12.1 lbs)
Angling	–	–	5.1 kg (11.2 lbs)

DOROSOMATIDAE
Thread Herrings

Originally a subfamily within the large family Clupeidae, the Dorosomatidae has been elevated to full family status. Thread Herrings are deep-bodied silvery fishes with a single dorsal fin, cycloid scales, belly scales that form a saw-toothed keel, and no adipose fin. Many have the last ray of the dorsal fin elongated into a thread-like filament, referred to in their common name. They are found globally in marine, brackish, and freshwater habitats and filter feed on plankton. Many are commercially important and serve as forage for larger fishes, birds, and marine mammals.

Thread herrings are usually found in schools, and some of the largest schools (tens of thousands) occur in the Gizzard Shad. Because of their immense size and rapidly shifting shapes, these schools confuse predators and make it difficult for them to single out one individual. Schooling fish synchronize their movements using visual cues to maintain spacing between their neighbours. When predators approach, the school shrinks and becomes more dense as the fish move closer together in an attempt to seek refuge behind one another.

There are 116 species worldwide, one of which occurs in Ontario.

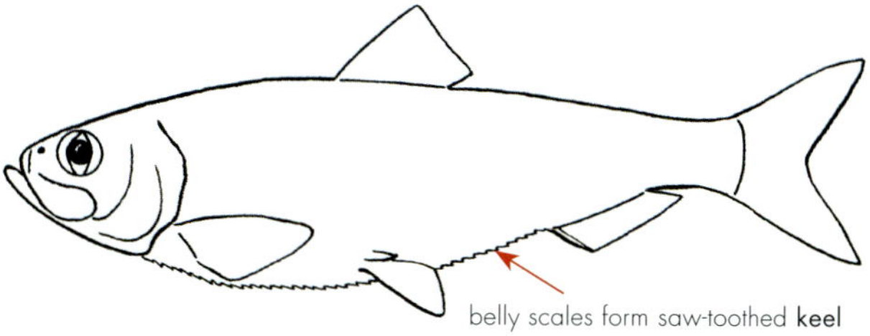

< School of Gizzard Shad

GIZZARD SHAD *Dorosoma cepedianum*

Dorosoma: lance-shaped; refers to the body shape of the young.
cepedianum: named after Bernard-Germain-Étienne de Lacépède, French naturalist and author of *Histoire Naturelle des Poissons*.

Young Gizzard Shad are often eaten by larger fishes, but those that survive grow rapidly and soon become too large to be eaten by most species. Populations can become very large and suffer heavy mortalities from **competition** with each other and diseases.

DESCRIPTION: This silvery fish is very deep-bodied and very thin from side to side. It has a rounded snout. The teeth are weak or absent. Sharp scales form a saw-toothed **keel** along the belly (p. 125). There is no adipose fin. The dorsal fin is entirely in front of the anal fin. The last dorsal fin ray is noticeably longer than the others. The anal fin is long with 27–34 rays. The back is silvery blue, the silvery sides often have a brassy tinge, and the belly is white. Fish up to 20 cm long usually have a dark spot on the side behind the head.

SIMILAR SPECIES: Whitefishes, ciscoes, and Rainbow Smelt have an adipose fin. Mooneye and Goldeye have distinct teeth, a dorsal fin mostly over the anal fin, and a smooth **keel**. The American Shad and Alewife have a pointed snout, a last dorsal fin ray that is not noticeably long, and a short anal fin with fewer than 27 rays.

FEEDING: Young Gizzard Shad feed on minute **zooplankton**. As adults, Gizzard Shad become **herbivorous**, feeding on **phytoplankton**. This species is one of few in Ontario that can exist solely on plant material because it has a specialized, long, convoluted gut for digesting vegetation.

REPRODUCTION: Spawning occurs from early spring to mid-August in shallow water. Males and females swim together in a mass near the surface, releasing eggs and sperm. The adhesive eggs drift in the current and sink to the bottom, becoming attached to whatever they contact. Eggs hatch in about one week.

Herring Gull taking advantage of a Gizzard Shad die-off in Lake Erie

Juveniles

HABITAT: The Gizzard Shad prefers cool nearshore and **pelagic** waters of the Great Lakes and **turbid**, vegetated tributaries.

STATUS: G5; N5; S4.

Maximum Age: 10	Ontario Average	Ontario Record	World Record
Length:	25.0 cm (9.8 in)	52.5 cm (20.7 in)	57.0 cm (22.4 in)
Weight: Overall	0.5 kg (1.1 lbs)	1.6 kg (3.6 lbs)	2.0 kg (4.4 lbs)
Angling	–	–	2.0 kg (4.4 lbs)

CYPRINIDAE
Carps

In the past 10 years, a flurry of scientific papers have been published on the large group of fishes in the **Order** Cypriniformes, which includes the carps, minnows, and suckers. Cypriniformes has well over 4,000 species that occur in Europe, Asia, and North America, and has nearly as many species as the **Class** Mammalia! These published studies used characters including body shape, bones, and genetics to determine which species are closely related. Dynamic relationships within Cypriniformes, such as **hybridization** and invasions of North America from Eurasia over several geological time periods, have created unique lineages and some very confusing results. But something did become clear: one of the larger families, once called carps and minnows (Cyprinidae), needed to be split into several smaller families. In addition to Cyprinidae, species in three new families (Leuciscidae, Tincidae, Xenocyprididae) also occur in Ontario. The new family Leuciscidae is now the dominant minnow family in North America and includes all native Ontario minnows.

The family Cyprinidae now includes the Goldfish and Common Carp, both of which were introduced to Ontario in the 1800s and originally came from Asia.

There are over 1801 species worldwide, two of which occur in Ontario.

< Common Carp

COMMON CARP *Cyprinus carpio*

Cyprinus: ancient Greek name for carp.
carpio: **carp**.

The Common Carp was the first **invasive species** of fish in North America, having been introduced as early as the 1600s. Wherever the Common Carp was introduced, it wreaked havoc by destroying large amounts of aquatic vegetation essential to native fishes and waterfowl for food and shelter.

DESCRIPTION: The Common Carp is a large deep-bodied fish. It is the only fish in Ontario that has 2 **barbels** on each side of the mouth (p. 27). It has large scales (35–39 **lateral scales**) and a long dorsal fin with 15–23 rays. There is a spine with **serrations** at the front of both the dorsal and anal fins. Colour varies from silver to olive-green, brassy, or grey on the back and sides. The belly is yellowish. Lower fins are orange-red. The Common Carp has distinct varieties known as the Mirror and Leather carps, which have naked bodies with scattered large scales. Koi, a special type of captive carp, are selectively bred for colour and are often multicoloured with patches of red, yellow, black, and/or white on the head and body.

SIMILAR SPECIES: The Quillback and buffaloes from the sucker family lack **barbels** and a **serrated** spine at the front of the dorsal and anal fins. Other members of the minnow family, except Goldfish, have a short dorsal fin with fewer than 10 rays. The Goldfish lacks **barbels** and has larger scales (fewer than 32 **lateral scales**). **Hybrids** of the Goldfish and Common Carp are common and show characteristics that are intermediate between the two species (e.g., usually only 1 pair of **barbels**).

FEEDING: The Common Carp is **omnivorous**, eating a variety of aquatic plants, algae, crustaceans, and molluscs by slurping up the bottom sediment.

Juvenile

Spawning

Mirror variety of Common Carp

Feeding

REPRODUCTION: The Common Carp spawns in shallow, weedy areas in late spring when the water temperature is between 17°C and 26°C. No nest is built. One female is accompanied by three or four males during spawning, and much splashing can be observed. This is a prolific species, and a large female may lay up to 100,000 eggs per season. No care is given to eggs or young.

HABITAT: The Common Carp lives in the warm, vegetated areas of slow-moving rivers and lakes, including nearshore areas of the Great Lakes.

STATUS: G5; NNA; SNA.

Maximum Age: 38	Ontario Average	Ontario Record	World Record
Length:	37.0 cm (14.6 in)	104.1 cm (41.0 in)	120.0 cm (47.2 in)
Weight: Overall	0.7 kg (1.5 lbs)	19.0 kg (41.9 lbs)	40.1 kg (88.2 lbs)
Angling	–	19.0 kg (41.9 lbs)	34.4 kg (75.7 lbs)

GOLDFISH *Carassius auratus*

Carassius: from "karass," the common name for the Crucian Carp of Europe.
auritus: golden; refers to the colour of the body.

This is the same species that is in your goldfish bowl and is now found in the wild because of the dumping of unwanted pets. This practice is harmful to our native ecosystems, is illegal, and should not be done under any circumstance.

DESCRIPTION: This deep-bodied fish ranges in colour from black to orange to white. The mouth lacks **barbels**. The scales are very large (25–32 **lateral scales**). There is a strong **serrated** spine at the front of the dorsal and anal fins. The dorsal fin is long with 15–18 rays. Wild fish are olive-green. The spawning male develops very small **nuptial tubercles** on the gill cover, back, and pectoral fins.

SIMILAR SPECIES: The Quillback and buffaloes from the sucker family lack a **serrated** spine at the front of the dorsal and anal fins, and have smaller scales (more than 34 **lateral scales**). Other members of the minnow family, except the Common Carp, have a short dorsal fin with fewer than 10 rays. The Common Carp has smaller scales (more than 34 **lateral scales**) and a pair of **barbels** on each side of the upper jaw. **Hybrids** of the Goldfish and Common Carp are common and show characteristics that are intermediate between the two species (e.g., usually only 1 pair of **barbels**).

FEEDING: The Goldfish is **omnivorous**, consuming plant material as well as a variety of aquatic worms, insects, and molluscs.

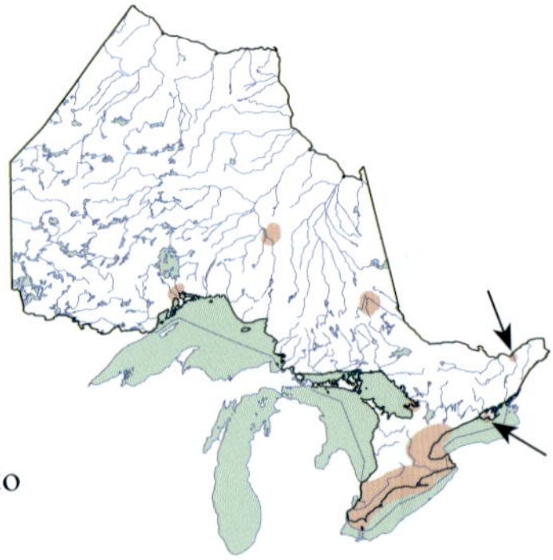

REPRODUCTION: Spawning occurs from May to July in shallows, over submerged vegetation. The female is accompanied by two or more males, and eggs and sperm are scattered over roots and aquatic plants. The eggs are adhesive and hatch in three to four days.

Osprey capturing a Goldfish, Burlington, ON

HABITAT: The Goldfish prefers the warm, vegetated areas of lakes, ponds, and slow-moving streams, including nearshore wetlands of lakes Ontario and Erie, where Goldfish may be locally abundant.

STATUS: G5; NNA; SNA.

Maximum Age: 41	Ontario Average	Ontario Record	World Record
Length:	19.0 cm (7.5 in)	38.0 cm (12.8 in)	48.0 cm (18.9 in)
Weight: Overall	0.1 kg (0.2 lbs)	1.8 kg (1.5 lbs)	4.3 kg (9.4 lbs)
Angling	–	–	4.3 kg (9.4 lbs)

LEUCISCIDAE
Minnows

This family includes all native minnows in Ontario and the vast majority of minnows in North America. Although the word "minnow" is often used for any small fish, the term is correctly used to identify only members of this family. Minnows lack teeth in their mouths, but have **pharyngeal teeth** (fewer than ten) on each side of the throat. They have a single dorsal fin and lack an adipose fin. They have a scaleless head, a body with **cycloid scales,** and an upper jaw that can usually protrude when feeding. There is a **Weberian apparatus** that transmits sound between the **swim bladder**, which amplifies the sound, and the **inner ear**. This apparatus is also found in carps, catfishes, and suckers, all close relatives of minnows.

Minnows are one of the few groups of fishes known to have an alarm substance. When injured, minnows release a chemical that causes other minnows in the vicinity to form tight schools to protect themselves from predators. Until recently, fishes in this family belonged to the family Cyprinidae. Scientific studies indicated that Cyprinidae actually contained several smaller families, based on differing genetic makeup and a diverse past between Eurasian and American lineages. The Common Carp and Goldfish (family Cyprinidae) and the Black Carp, Bighead Carp, Grass Carp, and Silver Carp (family Xenocyprididae) can be found elsewhere (pp. 129–33 and 219) in this field guide.

There are 705 species worldwide.

< Redside Dace

Mouth shapes and features

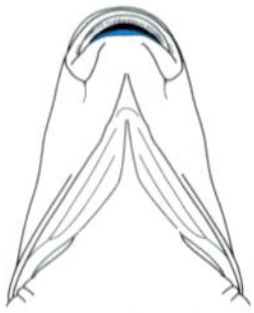

cartilaginous ridge (highlighted) and crescent-shaped mouth

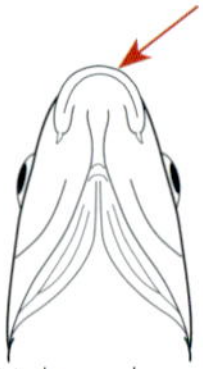

U-shaped mouth

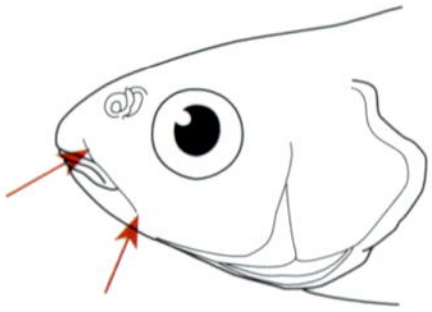

deep groove at the end of the upper jaw

Stripes on back in Common and Striped shiners

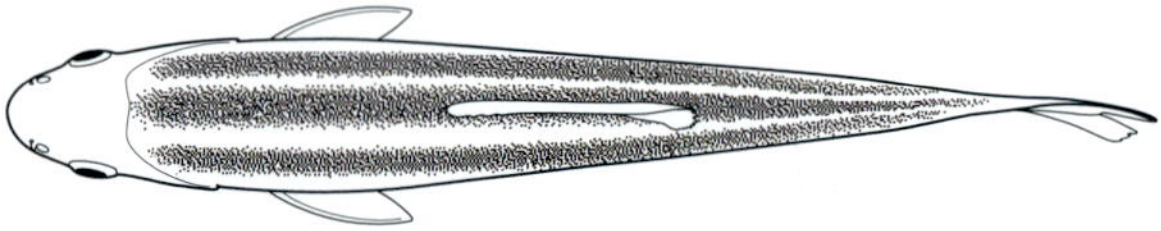

parallel stripes on the back (Common Shiner)

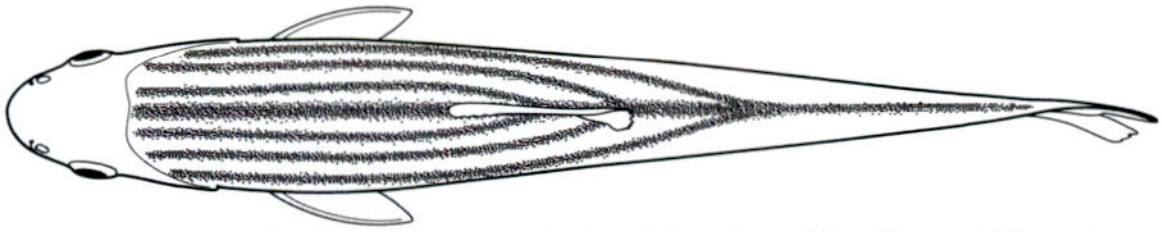

stripes on the back converge behind the dorsal fin (Striped Shiner)

Different scale sizes on back

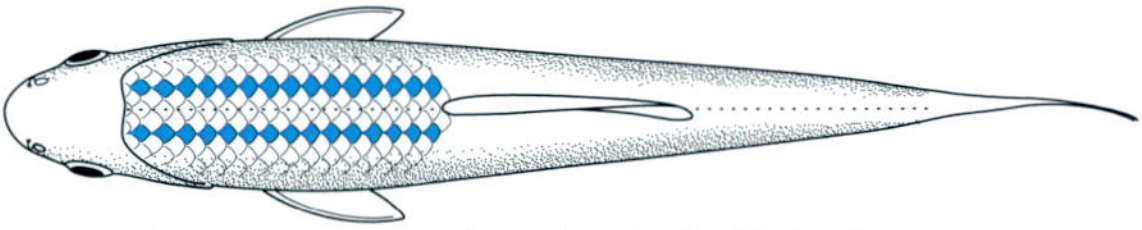

large **anterior dorso-lateral** scales (highlighted)

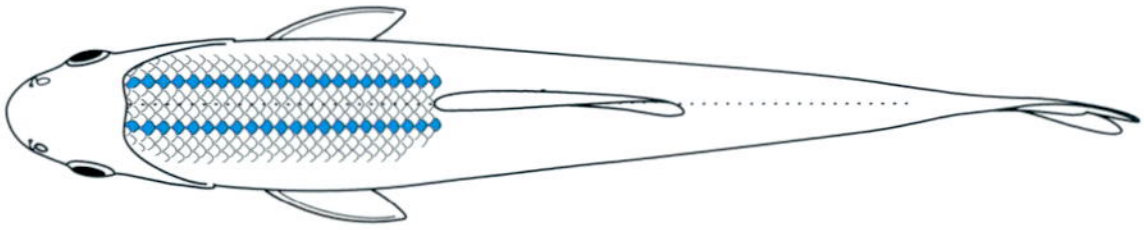

small **anterior dorso-lateral** scales (highlighted)

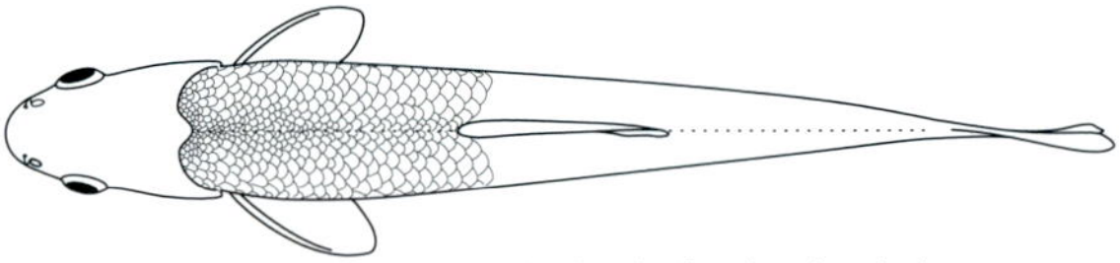

small crowded scales on the back of Fathead and Bluntnose minnows

Chin colouration of Common and Striped shiners

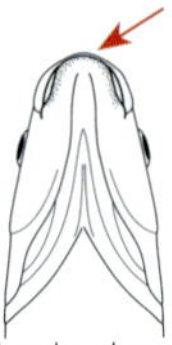

chin pigmented only along the outer edge (Common Shiner)

chin pigmented evenly (Striped Shiner)

Blackline shiners

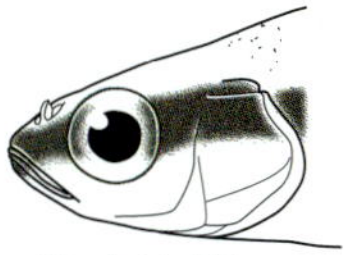

Blackchin Shiner

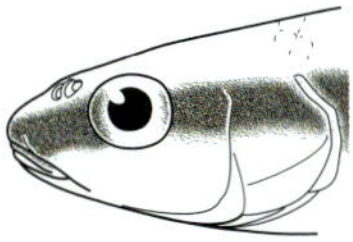

Blacknose Shiner

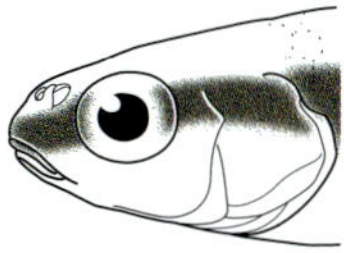

Bridle Shiner

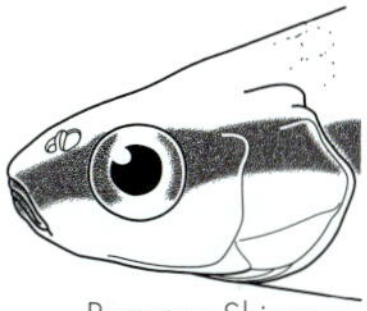

Pugnose Shiner

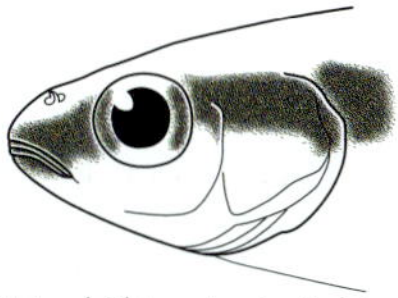

Weed Shiner (potential invader)

Heads of Hornyhead and River chubs

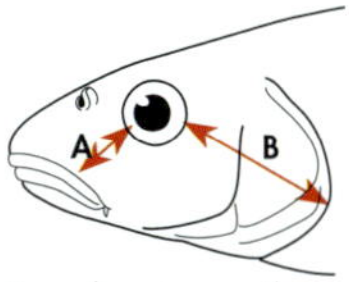

Eye close to mouth.
Distance **A** is less than ½ distance **B**
(Hornyhead Chub).

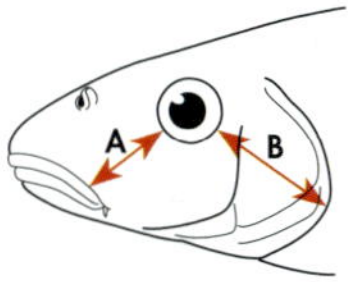

Eye far from mouth.
Distance **A** is more than ½ distance **B**
(River Chub).

Dorsal fin location

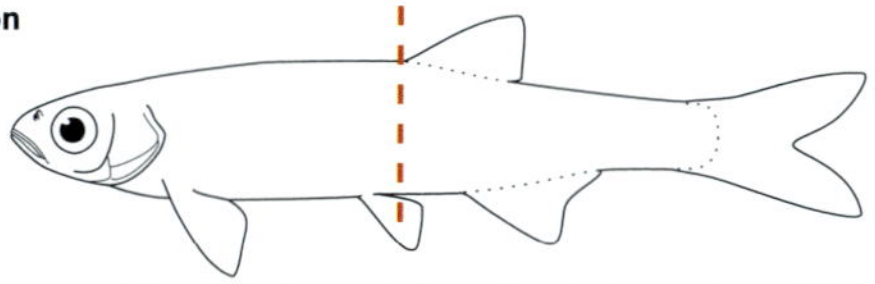

dorsal fin **origin** behind the base of the pelvic fin (e.g., Emerald Shiner)

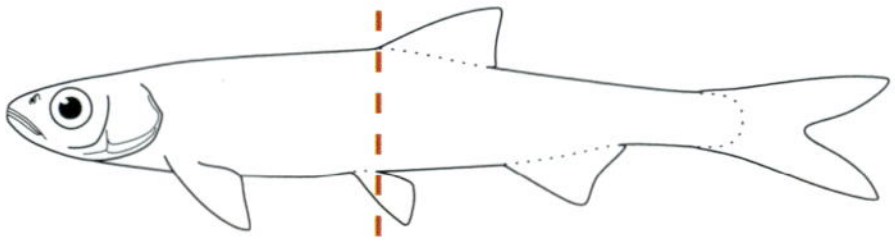

dorsal fin **origin** above the base of the pelvic fin (e.g., Silver Shiner)

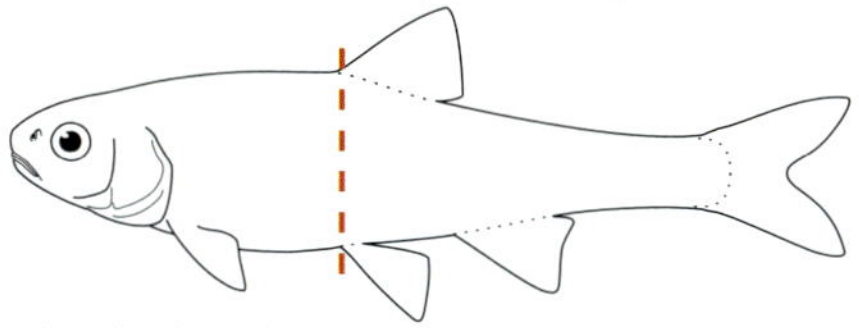

dorsal fin **origin** directly above the pelvic fin **origin** (e.g., Common Shiner)

Snouts of Emerald and Rosyface shiners

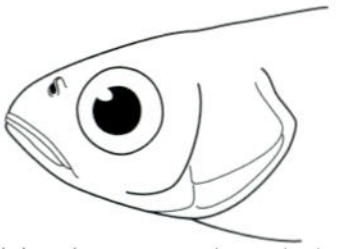

snout bluntly pointed and short
(Emerald Shiner)

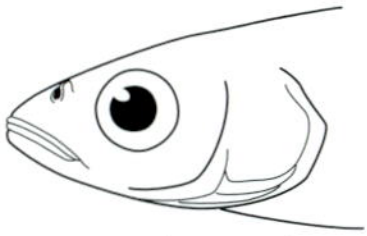

snout long and pointed
(Rosyface Shiner)

BLACKCHIN SHINER *Miniellus heterodon*

Miniellus-mini: small; ellus-smaller form, refers to their small size among North American minnows.
heterodon—hetero: different; *dont*: teeth; probably refers to the variation in number of teeth.

The Blackchin Shiner is one of the four **blackline shiners** (Blacknose, Bridle, and Pugnose are the others) in Ontario named for their dark lateral stripes. As they have a low tolerance for poor water quality, particularly high **turbidity**, they are found only in clear water.

DESCRIPTION: The Blackchin Shiner is a small, slightly deep-bodied, silvery fish with a dark lateral stripe. The snout is short and bluntly pointed. The mouth extends backwards to below the back part of the nostril or to below the front edge of the eye. The scales are large (31–38 **lateral scales**). It has 8, sometimes 7, anal rays. The lips and chin are black. The back is yellow or straw-coloured with large, darkly outlined scales. It has a black stripe, often having a zigzag appearance, extending from the tip of the snout to the tail. This stripe may not be obvious on silvery fish. There is a pale stripe just above the dark lateral stripe, and usually a small dark spot at the base of the tail. Spawning fish may have a pale yellow tinge on the belly. Spawning males develop minute **nuptial tubercles** on the head and pectoral fins.

SIMILAR SPECIES: The Blackchin Shiner is often difficult to distinguish from other **blackline shiners** (Blacknose, Bridle, and Pugnose). The Bridle Shiner and Blacknose Shiner differ in having a pale chin. The Weed Shiner, suspected to be present in northwestern Ontario, usually has a large spot at the base of the tail, and the **dorsal** fin **origin** is in front of the pelvic fin **origin**. The Blackchin Shiner is closest in appearance to the Pugnose Shiner, which differs in having a smaller, more upturned mouth.

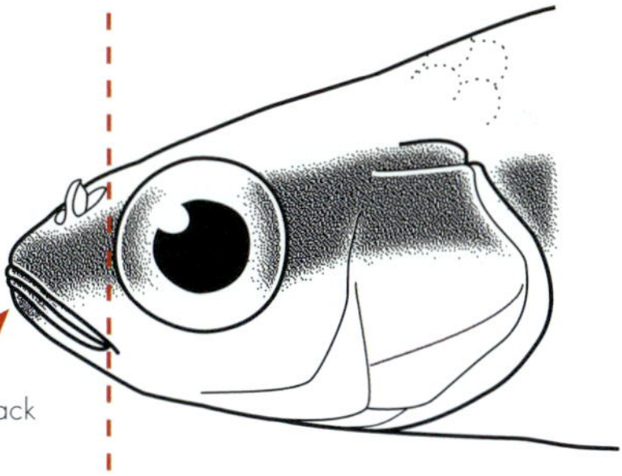

FEEDING: Food consists primarily of tiny crustaceans and small insects often taken at the surface.

REPRODUCTION: Little is known of the spawning habits of this species. It spawns in spring and deposits adhesive eggs over aquatic plants.

HABITAT: The Blackchin Shiner is found in clear, cool waters of shallow, vegetated areas of lakes and slow-moving areas of streams, over bottoms of sand, gravel, and **detritus**.

STATUS: G5; N4N5; S4; NAR.

Maximum Age: 3	Ontario Average	Ontario Record	World Record
Length:	5.6 cm (2.2 in)	7.3 cm (2.9 in)	7.3 cm (2.9 in)

BLACKNOSE SHINER *Notropis heterolepis*

Notropis—noto: back; *tropis*: **keel**. The **genus** was described from a specimen with a keeled back—likely due to the method of preservation.

heterolepis—hetero: different; *lepis*: scale; refers to the variation in the shapes of the scales.

Although abundant in clear, weedy waters of northern Ontario, the Blacknose Shiner is disappearing from much of southwestern Ontario, where this habitat is being degraded by human activities that destroy plant life and reduce water quality.

DESCRIPTION: The Blacknose Shiner is a small, elongate, silvery minnow with a dark lateral stripe. The rounded snout is long and usually overhangs the mouth. The upper jaw extends backwards to below the posterior half of the nostril. The scales are large (32–40 **lateral scales**). The lower lip and chin are pale. There is a dark lateral stripe extending from the upper lip and snout to the tail. This stripe may not be obvious on silvery fish, but a row of dark crescent-shaped markings is usually visible. There is a pale stripe just above the dark lateral stripe. The back is yellow or straw-coloured with large, darkly outlined scales. Spawning males develop minute **nuptial tubercles** on the head.

SIMILAR SPECIES: The Blacknose Shiner is often difficult to distinguish from other **blackline shiners** (Blackchin, Bridle, and Pugnose). The Blackchin Shiner differs in having a black chin and a dark lateral stripe, often with a zigzag appearance. The Pugnose Shiner has a smaller, more upturned mouth and a dark chin, and lacks crescent-shaped markings along the lateral stripe. The Bridle Shiner has a row of crescent-shaped markings along the lateral stripe and a shorter snout that usually does not overhang the mouth.

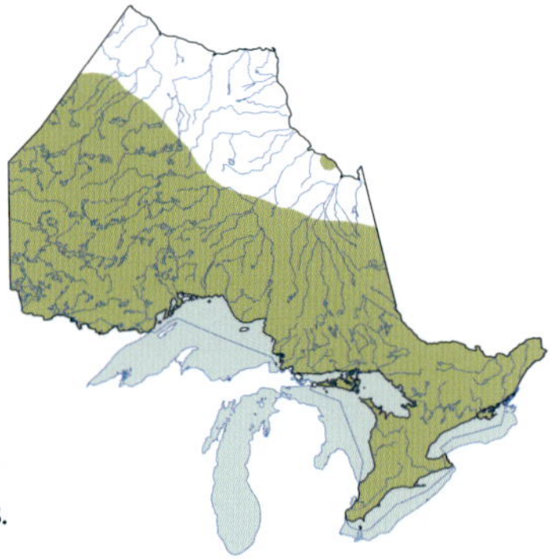

FEEDING: The diet consists primarily of tiny crustaceans and small insects.

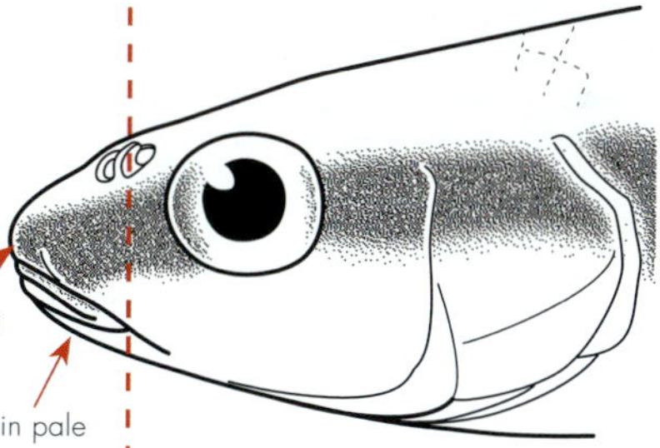

REPRODUCTION: The spawning habits of the Blacknose Shiner are unknown, but they are thought to spawn in summer. Adhesive eggs are scattered over sand or aquatic vegetation.

HABITAT: The Blacknose Shiner is found in clear, cool waters of shallow, vegetated areas of lakes and slow-moving areas of streams, over silt, sand, or gravel bottoms.

STATUS: G4; N5; S5.

Maximum Age: 2	Ontario Average	Ontario Record	World Record
Length:	7.4 cm (2.9 in)	9.5 cm (3.7 in)	9.8 cm (3.8 in)

BLUNTNOSE MINNOW *Pimephales notatus*

Pimephales—pime: fat; *phales*: head; refers to the swollen head in spawning males (likely based on the Fathead Minnow).
notatus: marked with spots.

♂

♀

The Bluntnose Minnow is arguably the most abundant minnow species where it occurs in Ontario, likely as a result of its tolerance of a wide range of environmental conditions and protracted spawning season.

DESCRIPTION: The Bluntnose Minnow is a small elongate fish. It has a rounded snout overhanging the small, almost horizontal, mouth, which is low on the head. The scales on the side are large (42–50 **lateral scales**) and have a cross-hatched appearance. The scales on the back are small and particularly crowded just behind the head (p. 136). Adults have a rounded dorsal fin with a small dark spot. The anal fin is small and rounded with 7 rays. There is a dark lateral stripe (faint in silvery fish) running from the snout to the base of the tail, where it often ends in a prominent spot (more obvious in young). Spawning males become black, and develop large **nuptial tubercles** on the snout and small ones on the pectoral fins.

SIMILAR SPECIES: The Fathead Minnow has a deeper body, its mouth is more upturned and opens higher on the head, and it lacks a caudal spot. The Mimic and Spottail shiners have larger scales on the back in front of the dorsal fin, much fainter lateral stripes (particularly faint in the front half of the body), and more pointed anal fins with 8 rays.

♂ preparing nest for egg laying

FEEDING: The Bluntnose Minnow feeds on crustaceans, worms, insects, and algae from the bottom.

REPRODUCTION: In spring, the male prepares a spawning site using his **nuptial tubercles** and tail to clear the underside of a large stone or piece of wood. Once the site is prepared, the female enters and deposits adhesive eggs with her **ovipositor** on the underside of the stone or wood. Spawning occurs from June through to August when water temperatures are between 20°C and 28°C. During this time, the male continuously guards the nest and fans the eggs. Eggs hatch in one to two weeks.

HABITAT: The Bluntnose Minnow is found in a wide range of shallow habitats in the warm waters of lakes and streams.

STATUS: G5; N5; S5; NAR.

Maximum Age: 5	Ontario Average	Ontario Record	World Record
Length:	6.5 cm (2.6 in)	10.1 cm (4.0 in)	11.0 cm (4.3 in)

BRASSY MINNOW *Hybognathus hankinsoni*

Hybognathus—*hybos*: hump; *gnathus*: jaw; a slight bump is sometimes seen on the front of the lower jaw.
hankinsoni: named after Thomas Hankinson, a professor of zoology at Michigan State Normal School.

Be careful when identifying this species because not all individuals are brassy, and it is not the only brassy-coloured minnow in Ontario.

DESCRIPTION: The Brassy Minnow is a slightly deep-bodied fish usually golden yellow in colour. The snout usually overhangs the mouth. It has a small mouth that is crescent-shaped when viewed from below (p. 136). There is a deep groove at the end of the upper jaw, sloping diagonally forward. The scales, including those in front of the dorsal fin, are large (36–41 **lateral scales**). The **lateral line** is complete (p. 26). The dorsal fin is not distinctly pointed. The spawning male develops minute **nuptial tubercles** on the pectoral fins.

SIMILAR SPECIES: The Fathead Minnow is often similarly coloured, but differs in having small crowded scales in front of the dorsal fin (p. 136). It has an incomplete **lateral line** with small **pores** that are often difficult to see. Where they are found together in eastern Ontario, the Brassy Minnow and Eastern Silvery Minnow may be very difficult to tell apart. The fins of the Eastern Silvery Minnow are more pointed. Positive identification often requires examination of the scales with a microscope.

FEEDING: The Brassy Minnow feeds in schools, eating aquatic insect **larvae**, tiny crustaceans, and algae from the bottom.

REPRODUCTION: Large schools of spawning Brassy Minnows form in shallow marshy areas in spring. One or more males approach a female and, if she is ready to spawn, the group vibrates, releasing eggs and sperm over vegetation. If the female is not ready to spawn, she leaps out of the water away from the males. The eggs are left to develop unguarded.

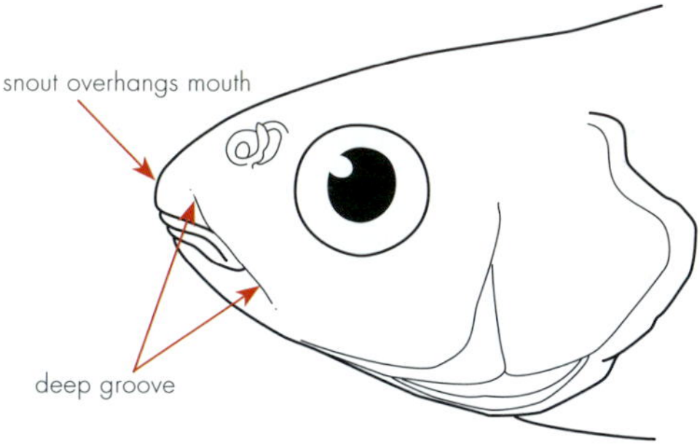

HABITAT: The Brassy Minnow lives in cool, slow-moving streams and lakes, and is found over a wide range of bottom types, but prefers silt, sand, and gravel.

STATUS: G5; N5; S5.

Maximum Age: 3	Ontario Average	Ontario Record	World Record
Length:	6.5 cm (2.6 in)	9.6 cm (3.8 in)	9.7 cm (3.8 in)

BRIDLE SHINER *Notropis bifrenatus*

Notropis—*noto*: back; *tropis*: **keel**. The **genus** was described from a specimen with a keeled back—likely due to the method of preservation.

bifrenatus—*bi*: two; *frena*: bridle; *atus*: provided with; refers to the dark stripes in front of each eye that unite on the snout.

The Bridle Shiner is uncommon and found only in southeastern Ontario in streams and lakes with abundant aquatic plants. Like other **blackline shiners**, it is threatened by the destruction of its clear-water, weedy habitat.

DESCRIPTION: This small elongate shiner has a dark lateral stripe. The snout is short and does not usually overhang the mouth. The upper jaw extends backwards to below the posterior half of the nostril. The scales are large (33–36 **lateral scales**). The dorsal fin starts above or slightly behind the **origin** of the pelvic fin. It has 7, sometimes 8, anal rays. The lower lip and chin are usually pale. There is a black lateral stripe (sometimes inconspicuous on live fishes) extending from the tip of the snout, including the upper lip, and usually ending in a small spot at the base of the tail. The black lateral stripe has crescent-shaped or zig-zag markings and a green-blue iridescence. The back is straw-coloured with large scales that are darkly outlined. There is a pale stripe above the dark lateral stripe. The belly is white or silvery, and yellow in spawning males. Spawning individuals have tails and dorsal and anal fins that are faint yellow. Males develop minute **nuptial tubercles** on the pectoral fins and sometimes on the head and back in front of the dorsal fin.

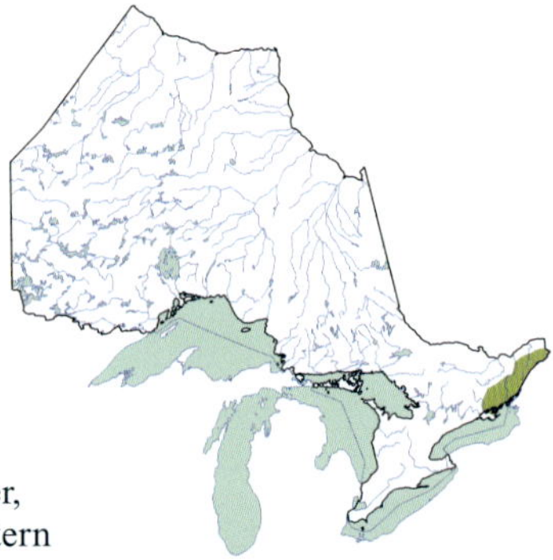

SIMILAR SPECIES: The Bridle Shiner is most easily confused with other **blackline shiners** (Blackchin, Blacknose, and Pugnose). The Blackchin Shiner differs in having a black lower lip. The Pugnose Shiner has a grey or black chin and a much smaller, more upturned mouth extending to only below the front of the nostril. The Weed Shiner, suspected to be present in northwestern

♀

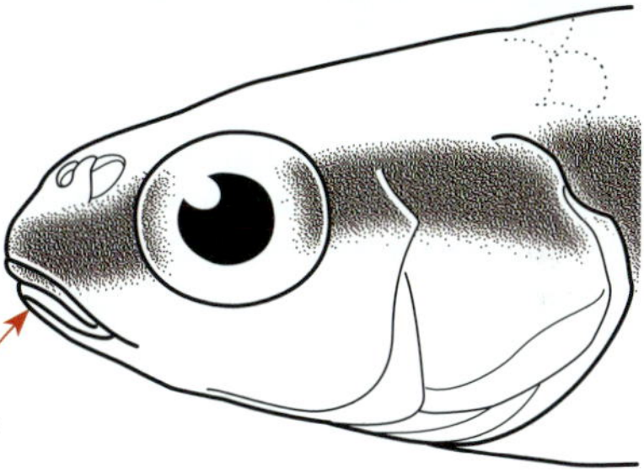

Ontario, has a more prominent spot at the base of the tail, and the dorsal fin usually starts in front of the pelvic fins. The Blacknose Shiner has a longer snout that overhangs the mouth, and usually has 8 anal rays.

FEEDING: The Bridle Shiner feeds during the day on algae, crustaceans, and aquatic insect **larvae**.

REPRODUCTION: Spawning occurs in spring and summer in calm pools with dense vegetation when the water temperature is between 14°C and 26°C. One or two males pursue a female and swim alongside her. The pair or trio quivers, and eggs and sperm are released. Spawning occurs many times per season with different partners. Only a few eggs are released each time. The eggs sink to the bottom and adhere to vegetation. The young hatch in just a few days and remain hidden in the vegetation.

HABITAT: In Ontario, the Bridle Shiner is found only in cool, clear, heavily vegetated areas of the St. Lawrence River and its tributaries.

STATUS: G3; N3; S2; SC.

Maximum Age: 2	Ontario Average	Ontario Record	World Record
Length:	5.0 cm (2.0 in)	5.9 cm (2.3 in)	6.5 cm (2.6 in)

CENTRAL STONEROLLER *Campostoma anomalum*

Campostoma—campo: curved; *stoma*: mouth.
anomalum: abnormal; refers to the unique ridge on the lower jaw.

The range of this species is expanding in Ontario. This expansion is likely the result of climate change and introductions through bait buckets. Releasing baitfishes is not only bad for the environment but also illegal.

DESCRIPTION: The Central Stoneroller is a slightly deep-bodied minnow. The snout overhangs the mouth (p. 26). The groove that separates the upper lip from the snout is continuous (p. 26). The lower lip has a hard cartilaginous ridge that is difficult to see and best detected by touch. The mouth lacks a **barbel** and is crescent-shaped when viewed from below. There are usually 49–55 **lateral scales**. In adults, the dorsal and anal fins have a black crescent-shaped bar through the middle of the fin. A dark lateral stripe is usually evident on juveniles and some adults. The back is brown, olive, or grey, and the belly is white or silvery. The spawning male has orange fins and **nuptial tubercles** over most of the body.

SIMILAR SPECIES: No other Ontario minnow has a cartilaginous ridge on the lower jaw. The Blacknose Dace has a groove between the upper lip and snout that is not continuous, more **lateral scales** (56–68), and a U-shaped mouth when viewed from below. The Brassy Minnow has fewer **lateral scales** (36–41). The Hornyhead and River chubs have a small **barbel** in the corners of the mouth.

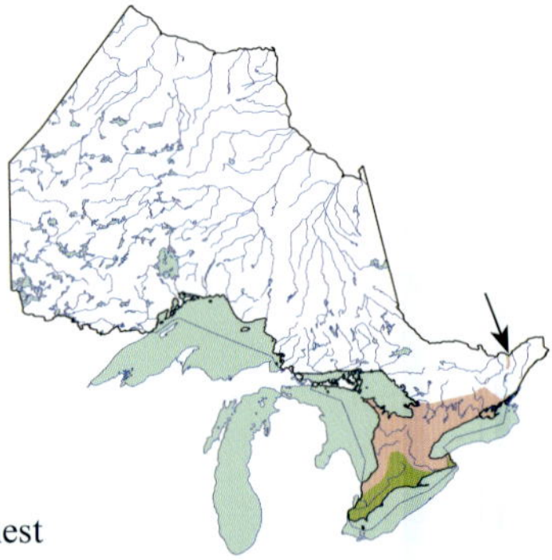

FEEDING: Often feeding in schools, this grazing minnow scrapes **encrusted algae** from rocks with its stiff lower lip. It has an elongate gut, which is necessary to digest algae.

REPRODUCTION: The Central Stoneroller spawns in spring when the water temperature reaches 14°C. The male excavates a shallow nest

Spawning ♂

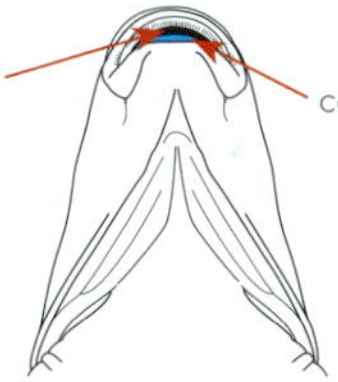

by pushing stones with his head or picking them up in his mouth. The male aggressively defends his nest from other males. A female enters a nest to spawn, and nearby males rush in for a mating frenzy. Fertilized eggs are covered with sand and gravel during the flurry of activity and left to hatch on their own.

HABITAT: The Central Stoneroller lives in the shallows of warmwater streams, over bottoms of exposed bedrock or gravel and stones covered with its preferred food, **encrusted algae**.

STATUS: G5; N4; S4; NAR.

Maximum Age: 6	Ontario Average	Ontario Record	World Record
Length:	10.0 cm (3.9 in)	15.6 cm (6.2 in)	28.7 cm (11.3 in)

COMMON SHINER *Luxilus cornutus*

Luxilus—*lux*: light; *illus*: somewhat; refers to the shiny pigmentation. *cornutus*: horned; refers to the **nuptial tubercles** on spawning males.

Although the male may build and defend its own nest, spawning often takes place in the nests of other species. This sometimes leads to offspring that are **hybrids** of the Common Shiner and the builder of the nest.

DESCRIPTION: The Common Shiner is a large, deep-bodied, silvery minnow. The upper jaw extends backwards to below or behind the front edge of the eye. The chin is usually pigmented only along the outer edge (p. 134). It has large scales (36–42 **lateral scales**). The **lateral scales** at the front of the body are more than twice as high as wide (p. 25). It has small scales on the back in front of the dorsal fin (16–30, usually more than 18, **anterior dorso-lateral** scales) (p. 136). The **origin** of the dorsal fin is usually directly above the **origin** of the pelvic fins (p. 137). There are 9, occasionally 8, anal rays. Adult males grow larger than females and have a pair of golden stripes and a pair of purple or grey-blue parallel stripes on the back (p. 136). Spawning males have rosy fins and small **nuptial tubercles** on the head and on the back in front of the dorsal fin.

SIMILAR SPECIES: The Golden Shiner and Rudd have small upturned mouths, more decurved **lateral lines**, dorsal fins set farther back on the body, and usually more than 9 anal rays. The Fallfish is not as deep-bodied, and has smaller scales (43–50 **lateral scales**) and a longer snout overhanging the mouth. The **origin** of the dorsal fin is behind the **origin** of the pelvic fin in the Fallfish. The Redside Dace has a larger mouth, protruding lower jaw, and smaller scales (63–70 **lateral scales**). The Redfin Shiner has a dark blotch at the base of the dorsal fin. The adult Spotfin Shiner has a dark blotch at the posterior part of the dorsal fin, and the scale outlines form a cross-hatched pattern on the body. The Striped

♂

Shiner has larger scales on the back in front of the dorsal fin (13–19 **anterior dorso-lateral** scales), and the pigment on the chin is evenly distributed. The adult Striped Shiner has faint stripes on the back that converge behind the dorsal fin.

FEEDING: The Common Shiner is **omnivorous**, eating aquatic insects, worms, plants, and algae.

REPRODUCTION: In spring, the male develops **nuptial tubercles** to clear the nest site of stones and to defend his territory from other fishes, including other male Common Shiners. Spawning occurs in water temperatures between 14°C and 28°C. The female moves onto the nest site, the male wraps around her, and eggs and sperm are released into the nest. Spawning is repeated many times with the same, or different, pairings.

HABITAT: The Common Shiner is usually found in the cool, shallow waters of pools and runs in streams. It is occasionally found in lakes.

STATUS: G5; N5; S5.

Maximum Age: 6	Ontario Average	Ontario Record	World Record
Length:	8.3 cm (3.3 in)	18.0 cm (7.1 in)	20.8 cm (8.2 in)

CREEK CHUB *Semotilus atromaculatus*

Semotilus: banner; refers to the dorsal fin.
atromaculatus—ater: black; *macula*: spot; refers to the black spot on the dorsal fin.

The Creek Chub may act as the top predator in a lake or stream when other, more typical predators (e.g., trout, bass) are absent. As a top predator, it often preys on other fishes.

DESCRIPTION: The Creek Chub is a slightly deep-bodied minnow. The upper lip is black. It has a large mouth, the upper jaw extends backwards to below the front part of the eye. A **barbel** is usually present in a groove above the upper lip, near the corners of the mouth, but is small, hidden, and rarely visible to the naked eye. It has small scales (52–62 **lateral scales**). The lobes of the tail are rounded. At the front base of the dorsal fin, there is a dark spot in fishes greater than 5 cm in length. The back is olive-green, and the sides are silvery with a dark lateral stripe that fades or disappears in large individuals. The belly is silvery white. Adult males have a prominent black bar behind the head, and the body is tinted with orange, purple, blue, or yellow. This colouration is particularly intense on the spawning male. The male is larger than the female, and his pectoral fins are longer. The spawning male develops 2 rows of large, sharp **nuptial tubercles** on top of the head and small **nuptial tubercles** on the pectoral fins.

SIMILAR SPECIES: Species that could be confused with the Creek Chub lack a dark spot on the dorsal fin. In addition, the Lake Chub has a **barbel** that is usually visible to the naked eye. The Northern Pearl Dace has smaller scales (usually 65–75 **lateral scales**) and a smaller mouth. The Fallfish has larger scales (43–50 **lateral scales**), and the tail's lobes are pointed.

FEEDING: Creek Chub feed on a wide variety of food items, including aquatic and terrestrial insects, plants, crustaceans, small fishes, and algae.

REPRODUCTION: Spawning occurs in spring when the water temperature is

♂ with nuptial tubercles

Juveniles

between 13°C and 27°C. In streams with gravel bottoms, just above **riffles**, the male makes a pit by removing pebbles with his mouth and vigorously swimming on the bottom to clear debris. He aggressively defends his nest from other male Creek Chub, but allows other minnow species to enter and spawn. When a female Creek Chub enters the nest, the male supports her with his pectoral fin, wraps himself around her, and eggs and sperm are released into the gravel. The male covers the fertilized eggs with gravel and guards them while excavating adjacent pits and spawning with the same, or another, female.

HABITAT: The Creek Chub is found in a wide variety of coolwater habitats in lakes and streams.

STATUS: G5; N5; S5.

Maximum Age: 10+	Ontario Average	Ontario Record	World Record
Length:	10.0 cm (3.9 in)	29.7 cm (11.7 in)	30.3 cm (11.9 in)

CUTLIP MINNOW *Exoglossum maxillingua*

Exoglossum—*exo*: external; *glossa*: tongue; refers to the tongue-like shape of the lower jaw.

maxillingua—*maxilla*: jaw; *lingua*: tongue; refers to the unique jaw shape.

This species is also known as the "eye-picker" because it picks out the eyes of other fishes using its unusual lower jaw.

DESCRIPTION: The Cutlip Minnow is a slightly deep-bodied fish. It has a uniquely shaped **trilobed** lower jaw consisting of a central bony projection with a fleshy lobe on each side. The groove between the upper lip and snout is not continuous (p. 26). There are no **barbels** at the corners of the mouth. It has small scales (50–53 **lateral scales**). The back is olive-grey or olive-green. The sides are grey-silver, sometimes with a greenish purple sheen, and the belly is white. The fins are grey, sometimes with a reddish tinge. The young Cutlip Minnow has a dark lateral stripe extending from the snout to the tail, where it ends in a distinct dark spot. The spawning male has small **nuptial tubercles** on the pectoral and pelvic fins.

SIMILAR SPECIES: No other Ontario fish has a **trilobed** lower jaw. The Blacknose and Longnose daces also have a groove between the upper lip and snout that is not continuous, but differ in having much smaller scales (more than 55 **lateral scales**) and a small **barbel** at the corners of the mouth.

FEEDING: The Cutlip Minnow has a diet of crustaceans, molluscs, and aquatic insect **larvae**, particularly caddisflies.

REPRODUCTION: In spring, spawning males build large circular nests made of stones that are carried by mouth to the nest. The female approaches once the nest is complete, and spawning occurs. A male will mate with the same, or other, females several times during the spawning season. Once hatched, the young remain in the nest unguarded.

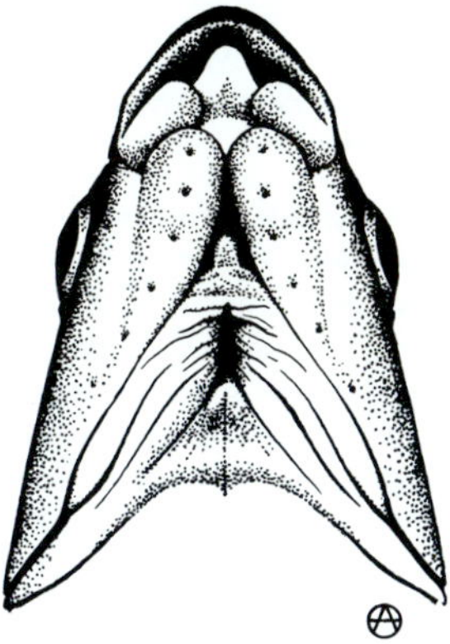

underside of head showing **trilobed** lower jaw

HABITAT: The Cutlip Minnow prefers pools and runs of warmwater streams with bottoms of gravel and **cobble**.

STATUS: G5; N4; S2; SC^F; T^P.

Maximum Age: 4	Ontario Average	Ontario Record	World Record
Length:	10.0 cm (3.9 in)	14.0 cm (5.5 in)	16.0 cm (6.3 in)

EASTERN SILVERY MINNOW *Hybognathus regius*

Hybognathus—hybos: hump; *gnathus*: jaw; refers to a slight bump that is sometimes seen on the front of the lower jaw.
regius: royal, for its beauty.

The Eastern Silvery Minnow survived the last Ice Age east of the Appalachian Mountains. This is why it is found only in the southeastern portion of Ontario.

DESCRIPTION: The Eastern Silvery Minnow is a slightly deep-bodied fish that is, as its name suggests, silvery in colour. The snout usually overhangs the mouth, which is small and crescent-shaped when viewed from below (p. 136). There is a deep groove at the end of the upper jaw, sloping diagonally forward. It has large scales (38–40 **lateral scales**). The dorsal fin is pointed. The spawning male develops small **nuptial tubercles** on the head, body, and pectoral and pelvic fins. The **nuptial tubercles** on females are smaller and fewer.

SIMILAR SPECIES: Where they are found together in eastern Ontario, the Eastern Silvery and Brassy minnows are very difficult to tell apart. The body of the Brassy Minnow is usually golden yellow, and its dorsal fin is more rounded.

FEEDING: The Eastern Silvery Minnow has an elongate gut and specialized **pharyngeal teeth** for eating algae.

REPRODUCTION: In spring, large schools migrate into the shallows of creeks and backwaters. One female is flanked by several males, the group vibrates, and eggs and sperm are released over bottoms with or without vegetation.

HABITAT: The Eastern Silvery Minnow lives in the cool, vegetated, slow-moving waters of lakes and streams. It is found over a range of bottom types, but prefers sand and gravel.

STATUS: G5; N4; S2; NAR.

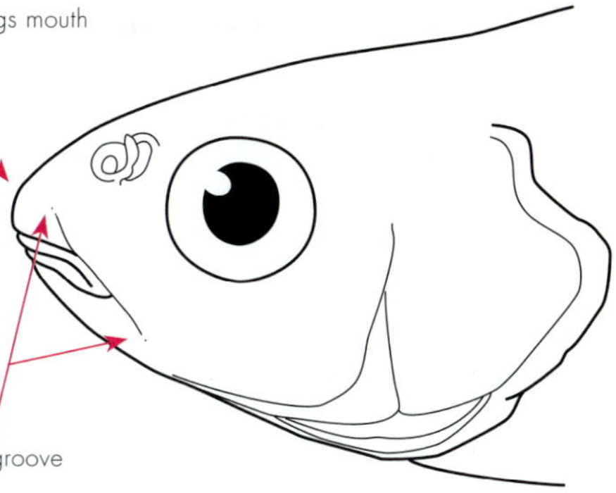

Maximum Age: 3	Ontario Average	Ontario Record	World Record
Length:	7.5 cm (3.0 in)	10.8 cm (4.3 in)	15.0 cm (5.9 in)

EMERALD SHINER *Notropis atherinoides*

Notropis—*noto*: back; *tropis*: **keel**. The **genus** was described from a specimen with a keeled back—likely due to the method of preservation.
atherinoides—*atherin*: smelt; *oides*: like; refers to the similarity it has to a slender, silvery smelt.

The Emerald Shiner is the most important species in the commercial baitfish industry in Ontario. It is harvested in large quantities in Lake Erie, and is in highest demand during ice-fishing season.

DESCRIPTION: The Emerald Shiner has an elongate, silvery body. The snout is bluntly pointed and relatively short (p. 137). Its large scales (38–43 **lateral scales**) come off easily while handling the fish. The dorsal fin is set farther back than in most shiners, beginning well behind the pelvic fin base (p. 137). The anal fin is large (11–13 rays) and has a concave posterior edge. The back is light olive-green or silvery, with a blue-green to yellow-green iridescence. There is a faint stripe along the midline of the back. The belly is silvery white. Juveniles are translucent. Spawning males develop minute **nuptial tubercles** on the top of the pectoral fins.

SIMILAR SPECIES: The Emerald Shiner has more anal rays than most minnow species. Of the minnow species with 9 or more anal rays, the Common, Striped, and Golden shiners and the Rudd have deeper bodies. The Common and Striped shiners have the **origin** of their dorsal fin directly above the **origin** of the pelvic fins. The Golden Shiner and the Rudd have a more decurved **lateral line**. The Redfin Shiner has a dark blotch at the front base of the dorsal fin. The Emerald Shiner is very difficult to distinguish from the Rosyface and Silver shiners. Suspected specimens of these three species longer than 10 cm (4 in.) are most likely to be Silver Shiners, which have a dorsal fin that originates above or slightly behind the pelvic fin base. The Rosyface and Silver shiners have a longer and more pointed snout.

FEEDING: The Emerald Shiner prefers to feed on a variety of **zooplankton** from midwater depths and drifting terrestrial and aquatic insects at the surface.

REPRODUCTION: Spawning occurs throughout the spring and summer in water temperatures between 20°C and 23°C. In lakes, spawning occurs in open water, over gravel shoals where immense schools containing thousands of fish form. A male approaches a female, and the pair swims together and rolls while releasing eggs and sperm. In streams, Emerald Shiners spawn in the shallows over gravel.

HABITAT: The Emerald Shiner prefers the cool, open waters of lakes, but is also found in the lower reaches of streams connected to lakes, particularly during spawning.

STATUS: G5; N5; S5.

Maximum Age: 4	Ontario Average	Ontario Record	World Record
Length:	7.5 cm (3.0 in)	12.4 cm (4.9 in)	13.0 cm (5.1 in)

FALLFISH *Semotilus corporalis*

Semotilus: banner; refers to the dorsal fin.
corporalis: a variation of its original common name, "corporal."

The Fallfish is the largest native minnow in Ontario. Remember: not all minnows are small and not all small fishes are minnows!

DESCRIPTION: The Fallfish is a large, silvery, slightly deep-bodied fish. The snout slightly overhangs the large mouth. There is a small, triangular, flap-like **barbel** in a groove above the upper lip near the corners of the mouth. It has large scales (43–50 **lateral scales**). The lobes of the tail are pointed. The back is dark olive-green, brown, or black, the sides are silvery, and the belly is silvery white. The juvenile has a dark lateral stripe, which fades or disappears in the adult. There is usually a spot at the base of the tail. A dark crescent is present at the front of each scale on the sides of the body (faint or absent in juveniles). The male develops small **nuptial tubercles** on the snout and top of head, and very small ones on the lower gill cover and fins (particularly the pectoral fins), and behind the anal fin.

SIMILAR SPECIES: The Common and Striped shiners have deeper bodies, larger scales (36–42 **lateral scales**), and shorter snouts that do not overhang the mouth, and the **origins** of their dorsal fins are directly over the **origins** of their pelvic fins. The Hornyhead and River chubs have a **barbel** at the corners of the mouth, and the lobes of the tail are rounded. The Creek Chub has smaller scales (52–62 **lateral scales**), rounded tail lobes, and a distinct black spot on the dorsal fin.

FEEDING: The food of the Fallfish includes aquatic insects, terrestrial insects taken at the surface, crustaceans, and small fishes.

REPRODUCTION: The Fallfish spawns in spring when the water temperature is above 16°C. In streams with gravel bottoms, the male moves stones with his mouth to build a mound up to 90 cm high. Males establish a hierarchy by butting and biting other males. The dominant

♂ with nuptial tubercles

male begins spawning and others follow suit. Communal spawning occurs with several males and females congregating over the same mound and releasing eggs and sperm. Other minnow species may share the same mound, and **hybridization** may occur.

HABITAT: The Fallfish prefers the cool, clear waters of streams with gravel bottoms. It is occasionally found in lakes.

STATUS: G5; N5; S4.

Maximum Age: 9	Ontario Average	Ontario Record	World Record
Length:	17.0 cm (6.7 in)	47.0 cm (18.5 in)	51.0 cm (20.1 in)
Weight: Overall	0.1 kg (0.2 lbs)	1.4 kg (3.2 lbs)	1.6 kg (3.5 lbs)
Angling	–	1.4 kg (3.2 lbs)	1.6 kg (3.5 lbs)

FATHEAD MINNOW *Pimephales promelas*

Pimephales—pime: fat; *phales*: head; refers to the swollen heads of spawning males.
promelas—pro: in front; *melas*: black; refers to the black heads of spawning males.

The Fathead Minnow is the "lab rat" of the fish world. It is often used in laboratory experiments to examine the impacts of a wide range of chemicals on aquatic life.

DESCRIPTION: The Fathead Minnow is a small, deep-bodied fish. It has a rounded snout and a small upturned mouth. The scales on the side are moderately large (41–54 **lateral scales**). The **lateral line** is incomplete (p. 26). The scales on the back are small and particularly crowded just behind the head (p. 136). Adults have a rounded dorsal fin with a black blotch at the front, and often at the back, of the fin. The anal fin is small and rounded with 7 rays. There is a dark lateral stripe (faint in silvery fish) running from the head to the base of the tail. There is often a pale bar followed by a dark bar at the base of the tail. The back is dark olive-green or brown, the sides have a silvery or brassy reflection, and the belly is silvery white. The spawning male becomes dark overall. He develops a spongy pad on the back in front of the dorsal fin, and several large **nuptial tubercles** on the snout and lower jaw.

SIMILAR SPECIES: The Bluntnose Minnow has a more slender body, a snout that overhangs the mouth, and a spot at the base of the tail. The Pugnose Minnow is a more elongate and paler fish with 9 dorsal rays. The Brassy Minnow has larger scales on the back in front of the dorsal fin and a complete **lateral line**, and its snout usually overhangs the mouth. An orange-coloured form of the Fathead Minnow, commonly called a Rosy Red, is cultured for use as feeder,

♂

Rosy Red

bait, and as a pond fish. Rosy Reds have been occasionally captured in the wild in Ontario as the result of illegal introduction or escape from garden ponds.

FEEDING: The Fathead Minnow feeds from the bottom on aquatic insect **larvae**, **zooplankton**, and algae.

REPRODUCTION: In spring, the male chooses a spawning site, and spawning occurs from June through to August at water temperatures between 16°C and 29°C. After circling around each other, the male lures the female into position, and she deposits adhesive eggs with her **ovipositor** onto the underside of the rock or wood he has chosen. The male guards the nest and fans the eggs. Eggs hatch in less than one week.

HABITAT: The Fathead Minnow is found in a wide range of shallow habitats in lakes and streams.

STATUS: G5; N5; S5.

Maximum Age: 5	Ontario Average	Ontario Record	World Record
Length:	5.0 cm (2.0 in)	10.1 cm (4.0 in)	10.1 cm (4.0 in)

FINESCALE DACE *Chrosomus neogaeus*

Chrosomus—*chro*: colour; *somus*: body; refers to the bright body colours.

neogaeus—*neo*: new; *gaeus*: world; thought to be related to "the minnow" (*Phoxinus phoxinus*) found only in Eurasia (i.e., the Old World).

Cloning is the production of offspring that have the DNA of only one parent. The Finescale Dace often **hybridizes** with its close relative, the Northern Redbelly Dace. The **hybrid** offspring are all female, which mate with males of either species. However, the sperm does not fertilize the egg but merely triggers it to grow and hatch. Therefore, the offspring of the **hybrids** are clones, having only the DNA of their mother.

DESCRIPTION: The Finescale Dace is a slightly deep-bodied minnow. It has a large mouth, the upper jaw extends backwards to below the front part of the eye. The **lateral line** is incomplete (p. 26), usually ending below the dorsal fin. It has very small scales (63–85 **lateral scales**), which are often difficult to see with the naked eye except in large individuals. There is a single dark lateral stripe, a wide pale stripe just above it, and a distinct straight edge between the pale stripe and the uniformly dark back. The lower sides and belly lack dark markings and can be silvery, white, bright yellow, or bright red. Colours are more intense during spawning. The spawning male has tiny **nuptial tubercles** on the head, throat, breast, pectoral fins, body above the anal fin, and the lower lobe of the tail.

SIMILAR SPECIES: The Northern Pearl Dace is a more elongate, less deep-bodied minnow with a smaller mouth. It has a complete **lateral line**, and it usually has scattered dark scales on the sides and belly. The Northern Redbelly Dace has a smaller mouth and 2 dark lateral stripes. **Hybrids** between Northern Redbelly Dace and Finescale Dace show characteristics intermediate to the two parent species. For example, the **hybrid** frequently has a shorter second lateral stripe (similar to the Northern Redbelly

Upper jaw extends backwards to below the front part of the eye

♂

Dace), but also has a darker back that lacks the 2 rows of spots (more characteristic of the Finescale Dace).

FEEDING: The Finescale Dace feeds on small molluscs, aquatic and terrestrial insects, and algae.

REPRODUCTION: Spawning occurs in late spring when the water temperature is between 13°C and 18°C. Schools of ripe males and females form near submerged logs and brush. The male chases the female and nips her while she swims in circles. He places his enlarged pectoral fin under her and curls his tail over hers. The pair vibrates, and eggs and sperm are released. Both males and females spawn repeatedly over several days. The eggs are left unguarded.

HABITAT: The Finescale Dace prefers the cool, heavily vegetated, slow-moving, shallow waters of lakes and streams with bottoms of silt and **detritus**. In Ontario, it is most often found in clear but "tea-stained" waters of the Canadian Shield and Hudson Bay Lowlands.

STATUS: G5; N5; S5.

Maximum Age: 6	Ontario Average	Ontario Record	World Record
Length:	7.5 cm (3.0 in)	10.6 cm (4.2 in)	11.0 cm (4.3 in)

GHOST SHINER *Paranotropis buchanani*

Paranotropis-para: near; *noto*: back; *tropis*: keel. closely resembles, but is distinct, from members of the genus Notropis.
buchanani: named after Dr. John Lee Buchanan, an American educator and friend of the person who described the species.

Until recently, the Ghost Shiner was not recognized as different from the Mimic Shiner in Ontario. Distinguishing these species is often very difficult and requires a microscope to examine a **sensory canal** under the eye, which is absent in the Ghost Shiner.

DESCRIPTION: The Ghost Shiner is a small, translucent, slightly deep-bodied shiner with very little pigment on its body. The rounded snout slightly overhangs the mouth, and the upper jaw is shorter than the eye diameter. The breast is not scaled. It has large scales (30–35 **lateral scale**s) and 8 anal rays. Tips of pelvic fins usually extend to, or past, the origin of the anal fin and stripe along midside absent or reduced to a few faint speckles. Spawning males develop small **nuptial tubercles** on top of the head, and minute ones on the rest of the head, front of the body, and pectoral fins.

SIMILAR SPECIES: The Ghost Shiner is difficult to distinguish from the River and Sand shiners, both of which have mid-dorsal stripes and usually 7 anal rays. The Mimic Shiner has shorter pelvic fins that do not reach the origin of the anal fin, and the midside stripe is more darkly pigmented on the back half of the body although it may be quite pale in **turbid** water.

FEEDING: There has been nothing reported on the feeding habits of the Ghost Shiner, but it is thought to eat aquatic insect **larvae**, tiny crustaceans, and algae.

REPRODUCTION: Little is known of the spawning habits of the Ghost Shiner except that it spawns in spring over sand and gravel bottoms

HABITAT: The Ghost Shiner is found in slow-moving areas of large warm streams (such as the Detroit River) and Lake St. Clair in southwestern Ontario. It is tolerant of high **turbidity** and is found over silt and clay bottoms.

STATUS: G5; N3; S3; NAR.

Maximum Age: 2	Ontario Average	Ontario Record	World Record
Length:	4.8 cm (1.9 in)	5.8 cm (2.3 in)	6.4 cm (2.5 in)

GOLDEN SHINER *Notemigonus crysoleucas*

Notemigonus—*noto*: back; *gonia*: angle; refers to the body shape. *crysoleucas*—*chryso*: gold; *leuko*: white; refers to the body colour.

Although schooling, such as found in the Golden Shiner, lowers the odds of any given individual being consumed, it is not clear how schooling works. To predators, schools may appear as a single large organism or may simply confuse them.

DESCRIPTION: The Golden Shiner is a large, deep-bodied minnow that is thin from side to side. The mouth is small and upturned. The scales are medium to large (44–54 **lateral scales**), and there are 9–12 rows of scales above the **lateral line**. The **lateral line** is decurved (p. 26). There is a small scaleless **keel** on the abdomen between the pelvic and anal fins. The **origin** of the dorsal fin is behind the **origin** of the pelvic fin base. The anal fin is large (more than 9 rays). The back is olive-green to dark brown, and the sides are brassy or silvery. It has a dark lateral stripe that becomes less distinct in adults. The fins are yellow or colourless. The spawning male develops **nuptial tubercles** on the head, body, and all fins.

SIMILAR SPECIES: The Golden Shiner can be confused with other minnows with deep bodies, such as Common, Redfin, Spotfin, and Striped shiners. The adult Spotfin Shiner has a dark blotch at the posterior part of the dorsal fin, and the scale outlines form a cross-hatched pattern on the body. The Common and Striped shiners have a smaller anal fin (8–9 rays) and a dorsal fin set farther forward, its **origin** usually directly above the **origin** of the pelvic fin. The Redfin Shiner has a black blotch on the dorsal fin. The Golden Shiner can be confused with other minnows with a steeply upturned mouth, such as the Pugnose Shiner and the Pugnose Minnow, which are not deep-bodied and have a smaller anal fin (7–8 rays). The Golden Shiner is most similar to the Rudd, which has orange-red fins, a scaled **keel**, and larger scales (38–42 **lateral scales**).

FEEDING: The Golden Shiner feeds mainly on small crustaceans, aquatic and terrestrial insects, and, to a lesser extent, algae and **larval** fishes.

REPRODUCTION: Spawning occurs over an extended period from May to August in water temperatures between 20°C and 27°C. One or more males chase a female, eggs and sperm are released, and adhesive eggs are deposited on algae and submerged weed beds. The eggs are left unguarded.

HABITAT: The Golden Shiner prefers cool, heavily vegetated waters of lakes and streams.

STATUS: G5; N5; S5.

Maximum Age: 9	Ontario Average	Ontario Record	World Record
Length:	10.0 cm (3.9 in)	20.4 cm (8.0 in)	32.0 cm (12.6 in)

GRAVEL CHUB *Erimystax x-punctatus*

Erimystax—*eri*: very; *mystax*: moustached; refers to the **barbels** around the mouth.
x-punctatus—*punctatus*: spotted; refers to the X-shaped markings on the sides of the body.

The Gravel Chub is the rarest fish in Ontario, having been collected only twice—both times in the lower Thames River. It was last seen in 1958 and is likely **extirpated** from Canada as a result of **siltation**.

DESCRIPTION: The Gravel Chub is a small, elongate, silvery fish. The snout greatly overhangs the mouth (p. 26). A small but distinct **barbel** is present at the corners of the mouth (p. 27). Its large eye has a diameter equal to or longer than the length of the upper jaw. It has large scales (38–45 **lateral scales**). The **origin** of the dorsal fin is ahead of the **origin** of the pelvic fins (p. 137). The back is olive-green or olive-brown with darkly outlined scales. The sides are silvery with a bluish sheen, and the belly is milky white. The body has W-, X-, or Y-shaped dark markings, which may be faint. The spawning male develops a hardened pad on the cheek and minute **nuptial tubercles** on the head, throat, and sometimes the front half of the body.

SIMILAR SPECIES: The Hornyhead and River chubs lack black W-, X-, or Y-shaped markings on the body and have snouts that only slightly overhang the mouth. They both have a dorsal fin **origin** over or slightly behind the pelvic fin **origin**. The Silver Chub lacks black markings and has a lower caudal lobe with a white leading edge.

FEEDING: The Gravel Chub searches the bottom for molluscs, aquatic vegetation, and insects.

REPRODUCTION: The Gravel Chub spawns in spring in swift **riffles.** The female swims close to the bottom, and the male approaches her. With the help of his nuptial cheek pad, the male remains in close contact with the female during spawning. Rapid vibrations occur, and eggs and sperm are released over gravel and stones. The eggs are left to develop on their own.

HABITAT: In Ontario, the Gravel Chub was found only in the cooler waters of the lower Thames River, a large **turbid** river with a moderate flow. As its name suggests, it prefers gravel bottoms.

STATUS: G4; NX; SX; XP.

Maximum Age: ?	Ontario Average	Ontario Record	World Record
Length:	7.5 cm (3.0 in)	9.4 cm (3.7 in)	11.0 cm (4.3 in)

HORNYHEAD CHUB *Nocomis biguttatus*

Nocomis—*Nokomis*: Indigenous word for "daughter of the moon" from Longfellow's *Song of Hiawatha.*

biguttatus—*bi*: two; *guttatus*: spotted; refers to the two spots on the body.

The Hornyhead Chub is named for the **nuptial tubercles** found on the head of males. These small horny bumps are termed "nuptial," as they are most prominent during spawning season. Many minnow species have **nuptial tubercles**.

DESCRIPTION: The Hornyhead Chub is a large, slightly deep-bodied minnow. There is a small **barbel** at the corners of the mouth (p. 27). The snout slightly overhangs the mouth. The eye is close to the mouth (p. 137). The scales are large (40–48 **lateral scales**). The **origin** of the dorsal fin is over or slightly behind the **origin** of the pelvic fins (p. 137). The lobes of the tail are rounded. It has a round black spot at the base of the tail, which is not always evident in large individuals. The back is olive-brown, the sides are silvery, and the belly is creamy white. The spawning male has a red spot behind the eye and develops large **nuptial tubercles** covering the entire head

SIMILAR SPECIES: The Lake Chub has smaller scales (more than 52 **lateral scales**). The Creek Chub, Fallfish, and Northern Pearl Dace have a small **barbel** rarely visible to the naked eye. The Creek Chub has a dark spot at the front of the dorsal fin. The Northern Pearl Dace has smaller scales (65–75 **lateral scales**). The lobes of the tail are pointed in the Fallfish. The Gravel Chub has a snout that greatly overhangs the mouth, a dorsal fin **origin** ahead of the pelvic fin **origin**, and black markings on the body. It is often very difficult to distinguish the Hornyhead Chub from the River Chub, which lacks a spot at the base of the tail, has the eye farther from the mouth, and lacks a red spot and **nuptial tubercles** behind the eyes in large males.

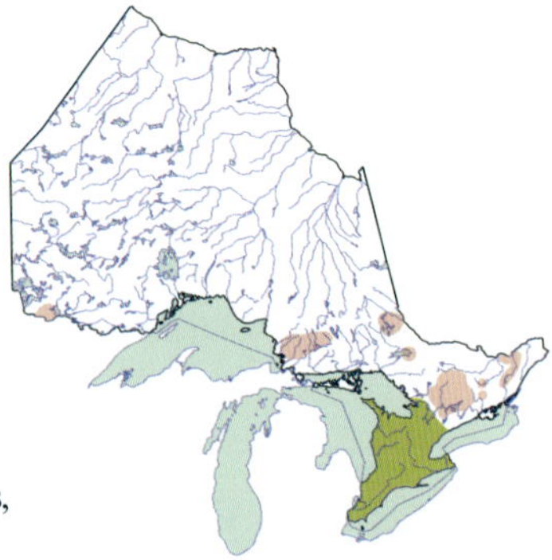

FEEDING: The Hornyhead Chub is **omnivorous**, feeding on aquatic insects, crayfishes, snails, small fishes, algae, and plant material.

Juvenile

♂ with nuptial tubercles

REPRODUCTION: Spawning occurs in spring when the water temperature is between 18°C and 26°C. The male prepares a nest in shallows by moving stones with his mouth and chin. Nests may be as large as 1 m across and 15 cm high. The male entices a female into his nest, presses her against the stones with his caudal peduncle, and eggs and sperm are released. The male covers the eggs with more stones and continues to enlarge the nest in preparation for the next female. Both females and males spawn several times with more than one mate.

HABITAT: The Hornyhead Chub prefers the pools of cool streams with rocky **substrates**.

STATUS: G5; N4; S4; NAR.

Maximum Age: 4	Ontario Average	Ontario Record	World Record
Length:	9.0 cm (3.5 in)	16.0 cm (6.3 in)	26.0 cm (10.2 in)

LAKE CHUB *Couesius plumbeus*

Couesius: named after E. Coues, collector of the **type specimen**.
plumbeus: lead; refers to the body colour.

The Lake Chub is the most widely distributed of all Canadian fishes and is found in every province and territory.

DESCRIPTION: The Lake Chub is an elongate fish that is greyish silver overall. There is a continuous groove that separates the upper lip from the snout (p. 26). The snout usually overhangs the mouth (p. 26). A small **barbel** is usually visible at the corners of the mouth (p. 27). It has small scales (53–79, usually more than 58, **lateral scales**). The edge of the dorsal fin is concave. The pectoral fins are larger in males than in females. The back can vary in colour from pale olive to brown to almost black. Its sides are often sprinkled with small dark spots, and the belly is silvery white. A dark lateral stripe is most prominent in juveniles, but may persist in adults. Spawning males are red or orange around the mouth, at the top of the gill cover, and at the base of the pectoral and pelvic fins. Females may be rosy at the base of the pectoral fins. The spawning male develops tiny **nuptial tubercles** on the head, back, dorsal fin, and pectoral fins. **Nuptial tubercles** on females are smaller and fewer.

SIMILAR SPECIES: The Longnose and Blacknose daces have a groove between the upper lip and snout that is not continuous. The Lake Chub is very difficult to distinguish from the Northern Pearl Dace. The Northern Pearl Dace has a **barbel** that is rarely visible and a rounded dorsal fin; the spawning male has a red stripe on the lower sides of the body.

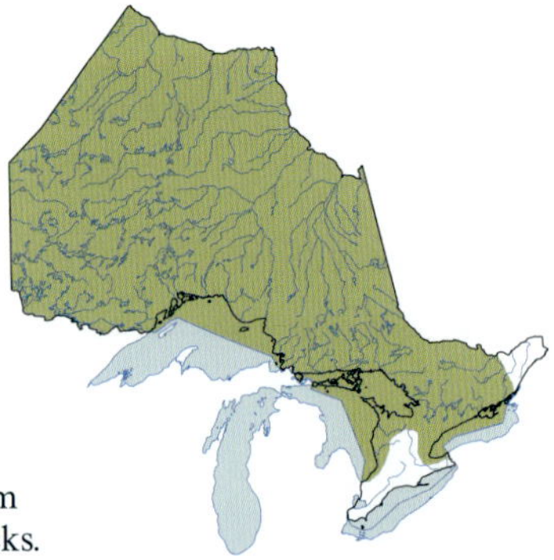

FEEDING: The Lake Chub feeds mainly on aquatic insect **larvae**, although **zooplankton** and algae make up a small part of the diet.

REPRODUCTION: Large schools of Lake Chub migrate from lakes to tributary streams in early spring. Several males approach a female, press against her, and eggs and sperm are released over sand, gravel, or rocks.

♂

♂

Males and females spawn several times with the same or different mates. Fertilized eggs are left unguarded.

HABITAT: The Lake Chub lives in the cold, **pelagic** waters of larger lakes, including the Great Lakes, except during spawning migrations.

STATUS: G5; N5; S5.

Maximum Age: 5	Ontario Average	Ontario Record	World Record
Length:	10.0 cm (3.9 in)	20.7 cm (8.1 in)	23.0 cm (9.1 in)

LONGNOSE DACE *Rhinichthys cataractae*

Rhinichthys—*rhini*: snout; *ichthys*: fish; refers to the prominent snout. *cataractae*: cataract, as in fast-flowing water. The specimen used to describe the species was caught near Niagara Falls.

The streamlined shape and large pectoral fins of the Longnose Dace make it hydrodynamically adapted to maintaining its position in the fast-flowing waters that it prefers.

DESCRIPTION: The Longnose Dace is an elongate fish with a long snout. The snout greatly overhangs the mouth, and the upper jaw is well below the eye level. The groove between the upper lip and snout is not continuous (p. 26). There is a small **barbel** at the corners of the mouth (p. 27). The scales are small (61–72 **lateral scales**). A dark lateral stripe, which extends from the snout to the base of tail, is usually present in the juvenile but fades or disappears in the adult. The back is olive-green, grey, or brown. There are usually 3 pale spots on the back: 1 in front of the dorsal fin, 1 immediately behind the dorsal fin, and 1 in front of the tail. The sides are usually paler than the back and may be speckled. The belly is silvery white. The spawning male has orange or red colouration around the mouth and the base of the fins. This colouration is particularly intense at the base of the pectoral fins. The male develops small tubercles on the head, body, and pectoral fins, and has longer pectoral fins than the female.

SIMILAR SPECIES: Most members of the sucker family have much thicker lips with ridges or **papillae**. The Blacknose Dace has a shorter snout that does not greatly overhang the mouth, which is higher on the head, and a more prominent dark lateral stripe.

FEEDING: The Longnose Dace usually feeds at night on aquatic insects, worms, crustaceans, and molluscs.

REPRODUCTION: Spawning occurs throughout spring and summer when

♂ with nuptial tubercles

Juvenile

the water temperature is between 11°C and 24°C. The male Longnose Dace defends a territory in shallow **riffles**. When a female enters his territory, the two swim together, vibrate, and release eggs and sperm. The fertilized eggs settle into, and adhere to, the **substrate**.

HABITAT: The Longnose Dace prefers the cool, fast-flowing waters of streams with rocky bottoms. It is occasionally found in the shallow waters of lakes.

STATUS: G5; N5; S5.

Maximum Age: 5	Ontario Average	Ontario Record	World Record
Length:	7.5 cm (3.0 in)	15.2 cm (6.0 in)	22.5 cm (8.9 in)

MIMIC SHINER *Paranotropis volucellus*

Paranotropis-para: near; *noto*: back; *tropis*: keel. closely resembles, but is distinct from, members of the genus *Notropis*
volucellus: swift (reason unknown).

This is one of the most common minnows in Ontario but is rarely recognized, as it is generally plain in appearance.

DESCRIPTION: The Mimic Shiner is a small, elongate, silvery minnow. The snout slightly overhangs the mouth, and the upper jaw is shorter than the eye diameter. It has large scales (36–39 **lateral scales**). It has 8 anal rays, rarely 7 or 9. The body is generally silvery, the back may appear cross-hatched, and the belly is silvery white. The mid-dorsal stripe is faint or absent and does not continue along each side of the dorsal fin. The anus is surrounded by black pigment. Tips of pelvic fins do not reach the origin of the anal fin and the stripe along the middle of the side is developed on the back half of the body. The Mimic Shiner is generally moderately pigmented, but pale when found in **turbid** water. Spawning males develop minute **nuptial tubercles** on the head.

SIMILAR SPECIES: The Mimic Shiner is difficult to distinguish from the Sand and River shiners, both of which usually have 7 anal rays. The River Shiner has a scaled breast and a more prominent mid-dorsal stripe that continues along each side of the dorsal fin. The Sand Shiner lacks black pigment around the anus. The Ghost Shiner is much paler in colour and is often translucent in life with a dark bar at the base of the tail. It has longer pelvic fins that extend to, or past, the origin of the anal fin and the dusky stripe along the middle of the sides is absent or reduced to a few speckles.

FEEDING: The Mimic Shiner feeds on crustaceans, insects, and algae.

REPRODUCTION: The Mimic Shiner spawns in June and July. Spawning occurs over vegetation, and the adhesive eggs become attached to aquatic plants.

HABITAT: The Mimic Shiner prefers vegetated areas of lakes and slow-moving streams with bottoms of sand and gravel.

STATUS: G5; N5; S5.

Maximum Age: 2	Ontario Average	Ontario Record	World Record
Length:	6.0 cm (2.4 in)	8.2 cm (3.2 in)	8.2 cm (3.2 in)

NORTHERN PEARL DACE *Margariscus nachtriebi*

Margariscus—margarita: pearl; *iscus*: little; refers to the iridescent colouration.
nachtriebi: named after Professor Henry Nachtrieb of the University of Minnesota, and former director of the Minnesota Zoological Survey.

Once thought to be closely related to the Creek Chub, the Northern Pearl Dace is now thought to be more related to the Lake Chub, which it closely resembles.

DESCRIPTION: The Northern Pearl Dace is an elongate minnow. It has a small mouth, the upper jaw extends backwards to below the nostril. A **barbel** is present in a groove above the upper lip, near the corners of the mouth, but is small, hidden, and rarely visible to the naked eye. The upper lip is grey. It has small scales (usually 65–75 **lateral scales**), and the **lateral line** is complete (p. 26) except in some young. The dorsal fin is rounded. The back is dark or black, the sides are silvery grey with scattered darkened scales, and the belly is white. A dark lateral stripe is distinct in young, faint at the front in adults, and usually ends in a small distinct spot at the base of the tail. The adult male, and occasionally female, has a red stripe on the lower side that extends from the head to the tail and, during the spawning season, develops small **nuptial tubercles** on the front half of the pectoral fins and minute ones on the head.

SIMILAR SPECIES: The Finescale Dace has a larger mouth, the upper jaw extending backwards to below the front of the eye, and the **lateral line** is incomplete. The Creek Chub has larger scales (52–62 **lateral scales**) and a larger mouth, and individuals longer than 50 mm have a brown or black spot at the front base of the dorsal fin. The Lake Chub has a dorsal fin with a concave posterior edge and a larger visible **barbel** at the corners of the mouth; the spawning male lacks a red stripe on the lower side.

FEEDING: The diet consists mainly of small crustaceans, **larval** aquatic insects, molluscs, and terrestrial insects that fall into the water.

♂

♂

Juvenile

REPRODUCTION: Spawning occurs in spring when the water temperature is between 13°C and 18°C. Males and females initiate chases, and then the male places his pectoral fins under the female to keep her in close proximity. The male curls his tail over the female, the pair vibrates, and eggs and sperm are released over sand or gravel. Both males and females spawn with several mates during the spawning season. The eggs are left unguarded.

HABITAT: The Northern Pearl Dace prefers shallow, vegetated areas in cool and cold lakes and streams throughout Ontario.

STATUS: G5; N5; S5.

Maximum Age: 4	Ontario Average	Ontario Record	World Record
Length:	9.0 cm (3.5 in)	16.0 cm (6.3 in)	16.0 cm (6.3 in)

NORTHERN REDBELLY DACE *Chrosomus eos*

Chrosomus—chrom: colour; *somus*: body; refers to the bright body colours.
eos: dawn; alludes to the belly colouration, which is similar to a sunrise.

The Northern Redbelly Dace readily **hybridizes** with the Finescale Dace. **Hybrids** of these two species are common in northern Ontario.

DESCRIPTION: The Northern Redbelly Dace is a slightly deep-bodied fish and one of our most colourful minnows. It has a small mouth, the upper jaw extends backwards to below the nostril. It has very small scales (70–90 **lateral scales**) that are difficult to see with the naked eye. It has 2 dark lateral stripes: 1 along the middle of the sides and 1 above the first lateral stripe. This latter stripe is sometimes faint in adults and usually absent in small young. There is often a row of spots along each side of the back. The lower sides and belly lack dark markings and can be silvery, white, bright yellow, or bright red. Colours are more intense during spawning. The spawning male has tiny **nuptial tubercles** on the head, throat, breast, pectoral fins, and the lower body behind the anal fin.

SIMILAR SPECIES: The Northern Pearl Dace has only 1 lateral stripe and scattered darkened scales on the sides. The Finescale Dace has a larger mouth and only 1 lateral stripe. **Hybrids** between Northern Redbelly Dace and Finescale Dace show characteristics intermediate to the two parent species. For example, the **hybrid** frequently has a shorter second lateral stripe (similar to the Northern Redbelly Dace), as well as a darker back that lacks the 2 rows of spots (more characteristic of the Finescale Dace).

FEEDING: The Northern Redbelly Dace feeds on crustaceans, insects, plants, and algae.

REPRODUCTION: The Northern Redbelly Dace is a **fractional spawner**, releasing small numbers of eggs at a time over several months in the summer at water temperatures between 21°C and 27°C. The female, accompanied by several males, darts into algal

Upper jaw does not extend backwards to below the eye

♂

♂

beds, and eggs and sperm are released. The fertilized eggs are left unattended.

HABITAT: The Northern Redbelly Dace prefers cool, heavily vegetated, shallow waters of lakes and slow-moving streams with bottoms of silt and **detritus**. In Ontario, it is most often found in the clear but "tea-stained" waters of the Canadian Shield.

STATUS: G5; N5; S5.

Maximum Age: 3	Ontario Average	Ontario Record	World Record
Length:	5.5 cm (2.2 in)	8.2 cm (3.2 in)	8.2 cm (3.2 in)

PUGNOSE MINNOW *Opsopoeodus emiliae*

Opsopoeodus—*opso*: food; *odus*: teeth; refers to the **serrated pharyngeal teeth**.
emiliae: Emily. Dr. Oliver Hay, an American palaeontologist, described the species and named it in honour of his wife.

Sometimes, fishes exhibit deformities as a result of mutations caused naturally or induced by chemicals or parasites. Flattened (so-called "pug") snouts are a common deformity. The snout of the Pugnose Minnow is not a deformity—it is natural!

DESCRIPTION: The Pugnose Minnow is a small, slightly deep-bodied, silvery or translucent fish. It has a rounded snout and a very small, steeply upturned mouth, the upper jaw extends backwards to below the front half of the nostril. It has large scales (35–41 **lateral scales**). The dorsal fin usually has 9 rays. The lower lip is usually pale. The back is pale yellow or olive-green, with darkly outlined scales extending down the sides and appearing cross-hatched. The belly is white. A prominent lateral stripe starts on the snout and ends in a spot at the base of the tail. The dorsal fin is dark in spawning males, with middle rays that are clear or white. The lower half of the anal fin is bright white in spawning males. Spawning males have fine stubble-like **nuptial tubercles** on the snout, lips, and chin.

SIMILAR SPECIES: The Pugnose Minnow can be confused with other minnows with a small, steeply upturned mouth, such as the Golden Shiner and Pugnose Shiner. The Golden Shiner has a body that is deeper and thinner from side to side, and a large anal fin with more than 11 rays and a concave posterior edge. The Pugnose Shiner always has a dark lower lip and a dorsal fin with 8 rays, and the scale outlines do not form a cross-hatched pattern.

FEEDING: The Pugnose Minnow feeds on algae, crustaceans, and tiny molluscs.

REPRODUCTION: Little is known of the spawning habits of the Pugnose Minnow except that it spawns in spring.

♂

Steeply upturned mouth

HABITAT: In Ontario, the Pugnose Minnow is found in the warm, vegetated, slow-moving areas of **turbid** streams (including the Detroit River) with bottoms of silt, sand, or gravel.

STATUS: G3; N2; S2; T. E^F, T^P

Maximum Age: 2	Ontario Average	Ontario Record	World Record
Length:	5.0 cm (2.0 in)	5.7 cm (2.2 in)	6.6 cm (2.6 in)

PUGNOSE SHINER *Miniellus anogenus*

Miniellus-mini: small or little; *ellus*: smaller form; refers to the small size among North American minnows
anogenus—an: without; *genys*: chin; refers to the blunt-shaped face.

This small and globally rare species has disappeared from some Lake Erie wetlands. The cause of the disappearance is unknown, but it coincides with an increase in the number and diversity of potential predators and competitors.

DESCRIPTION: The Pugnose Shiner is a small elongate shiner with a dark lateral stripe and a very small upturned mouth, the upper jaw extends backwards to below the front part of the nostril. It has large scales (34–38 **lateral scales**) and usually 8 dorsal and 8 anal rays. The chin is dark. The dark lateral stripe (sometimes inconspicuous on live fishes) extends onto the snout, and there is usually a pale stripe above the dark lateral stripe. The back has yellow tints, and the sides are silvery. There is often a small but distinct spot on the tail. Spawning males develop numerous minute **nuptial tubercles** on the top of the pectoral fins.

SIMILAR SPECIES: The Pugnose Shiner can be confused with other minnows with a steeply upturned mouth, such as the Golden Shiner and Rudd, which are deep-bodied and have a larger anal fin (more than 9 rays). The Pugnose Shiner is often difficult to distinguish from other **blackline shiners** (Blackchin, Blacknose, and Bridle). These species have larger, less upturned mouths. The Blacknose and Bridle shiners have a pale chin and crescent-shaped markings along the lateral stripe. The Blackchin Shiner has a dark lateral stripe, often with a zigzag appearance. The Pugnose Minnow has scale outlines that form a cross-hatched pattern and a dorsal fin with 9 rays.

FEEDING: The Pugnose Shiner prefers to eat small crustaceans, aquatic insects, and algae.

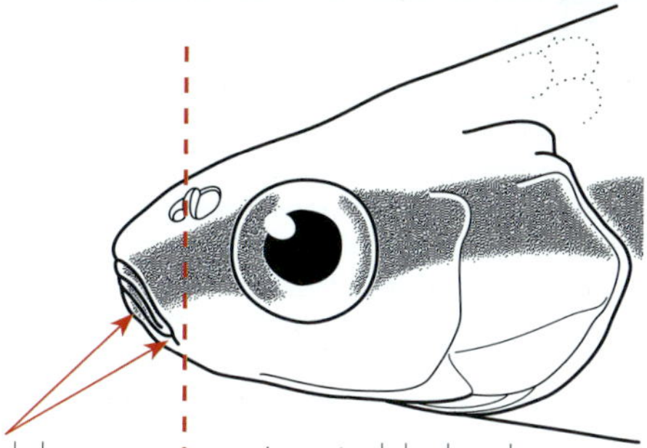

REPRODUCTION: Spawning occurs in spring when the water temperature is between 21°C and 29°C, but little is known of the spawning habits of this species.

HABITAT: The Pugnose Shiner is found only in cool, clear, shallow, heavily vegetated wetlands of the St. Lawrence River, and lakes Erie, Huron, and St. Clair. It is often associated with wild rice.

STATUS: G3; N2; S2; T.

Maximum Age: 3	Ontario Average	Ontario Record	World Record
Length:	5.0 cm (2.0 in)	5.6 cm (2.2 in)	5.8 cm (2.3 in)

REDFIN SHINER *Lythrurus umbratilis*

Lythrurus—lythron: blood; *uro*: tail; refers to the red colouration of the tail.
umbratilis: of the shade; refers to the black blotch in front of the dorsal fin.

The Redfin Shiner often spawns in the nests of sunfishes. Interestingly, they will not use nests if the sunfishes are not actually spawning, suggesting that the sunfishes may release a chemical cue that triggers spawning in the Redfin Shiner.

DESCRIPTION: The Redfin Shiner has a small, slightly deep, silvery body. The lower jaw often projects slightly beyond the upper jaw. It has large scales on the sides (39–46 **lateral scales**), but the scales on the back are small and crowded. The **lateral line** is decurved (p. 26). It has a large anal fin (10–12 rays) with a concave posterior edge. There is a black blotch at the base of the front of the dorsal fin. Spawning males are steel-blue on the sides, with reddish fins. They have small **nuptial tubercles** on the lower jaw and sides and top of the head, which extend back to the dorsal fin, and there are tiny ones on the sides of the body and pectoral fins.

SIMILAR SPECIES: All other shiners in Ontario, including the Golden Shiner, which also has a decurved **lateral line**, lack the black blotch at the front base of the dorsal fin. The Creek Chub, which has a black spot at the front base of the dorsal fin, is not deep-bodied and has more than 52 **lateral scales**.

FEEDING: The Redfin Shiner eats algae, aquatic plants, crustaceans, worms, and insect **larvae** from the bottom.

REPRODUCTION: The Redfin Shiner spawns in summer when the water temperature is above 21°C. The male defends his territory, often including a sunfish nest, by chasing away other males. Once

Juvenile

a female enters the nest, the couple swims together and spawning occurs. The eggs are left to develop in the gravel nests without parental care.

HABITAT: The Redfin Shiner is found only in the shallow, slow-moving, often **turbid** waters of vegetated streams.

STATUS: G5; N4; S4; NAR.

Maximum Age: 3	Ontario Average	Ontario Record	World Record
Length:	6.0 cm (2.4 in)	7.3 cm (2.9 in)	8.8 cm (3.5 in)

REDSIDE DACE *Clinostomus elongatus*

Clinostomus—clino: slanted; *stomus*: mouth.
elongatus: elongate; refers to the shape of the body.

The Redside Dace is particularly sensitive to changes in its habitat associated with urbanization, introduced predators, and intensive agricultural practices. As a result, it is quickly disappearing throughout its range in southwestern Ontario.

DESCRIPTION: The Redside Dace is a slightly deep-bodied minnow. It has a pointed snout, and the lower jaw protrudes beyond the upper jaw. The mouth is large, the upper jaw extends backwards to below the middle of the eye. The scales are small (63–70 **lateral scales**). During the spring, adult Redside Dace have bright red sides (ending below the dorsal fin), but often lose this red colouration later in the summer and fall. The spawning male develops minute **nuptial tubercles** over most of its body, which are larger on the head, back, and pectoral fins. Females also have **nuptial tubercles**, but they are smaller and fewer.

SIMILAR SPECIES: The Common Shiner has a smaller mouth and larger scales (36–42 **lateral scales**), and the lower jaw does not protrude. Other species with red sides, such as the Northern Pearl Dace, Blacknose Dace, Northern Redbelly Dace, and Finescale Dace, have lower jaws equal in length to the upper jaws, and the red stripe, if present, extends past the dorsal fin.

FEEDING: Redside Dace jump out of the water to catch flying insects, such as gnats and midges, that hover above the surface.

REPRODUCTION: Spawning occurs in spring when males congregate in **riffles** and shallow, flowing pools. Females, often accompanied by two or more males, move into nests of other minnow species and spawning occurs. The eggs are left unguarded.

HABITAT: The Redside Dace lives in small coolwater streams. It prefers quiet pools.

STATUS: G3G4; N1; S1; E.

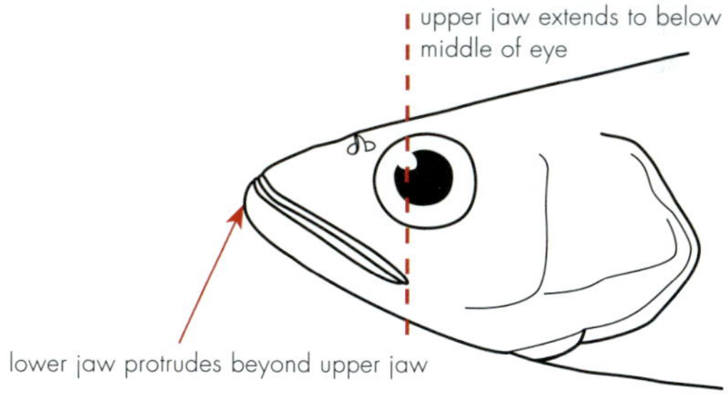

Maximum Age: 4	Ontario Average	Ontario Record	World Record
Length:	7.5 cm (3.0 in)	10.9 cm (4.3 in)	12.0 cm (4.7 in)

RIVER CHUB *Nocomis micropogon*

Nocomis—Nokomis: Indigenous word for "daughter of the moon" from Longfellow's *Song of Hiawatha.*
micropogon—micro: little; *pogon*: beard; refers to the **barbel** at the corners of the mouth.

During the spawning season, two male River Chub will battle over nesting territories by swimming parallel to each other. Each male beats his tail and rams the side of his opponent with the large "horns" on his head.

DESCRIPTION: The River Chub is a large, slightly deep-bodied minnow. It has a small eye. There is a small **barbel** at the corners of the mouth. The eye is far from the mouth (p. 137). The scales are large (39–43 **lateral scales**). The **origin** of the dorsal fin is usually directly above the **origin** of the pelvic fins (p. 137). The lobes of the tail are rounded. It lacks a round spot at the base of the tail, although the lateral stripe may widen in front of the tail and resemble a large oval spot. The back is olive-brown, the sides are silvery with a dark lateral stripe that is faint in adults but prominent in juveniles, and the belly is creamy white. The spawning male has a rosy hue on the lower part of the head and body, and develops a swelling on top of the head. There are large **nuptial tubercles** on the snout in front of the eye and smaller ones on the pectoral fins.

SIMILAR SPECIES: The Lake Chub has smaller scales (more than 52 **lateral scales**). The Creek Chub, Fallfish, and Northern Pearl Dace have a small **barbel** rarely visible to the naked eye. The lobes of the tail are pointed in the Fallfish. The Gravel Chub has a snout that greatly overhangs the mouth, a dorsal fin **origin** ahead of the pelvic fin **origin**, and black markings on the body. It is often very difficult to distinguish the River Chub from the Hornyhead Chub, which has a spot on the base of the tail, eyes closer to the mouth, and a red spot and tubercles behind the eyes in large males.

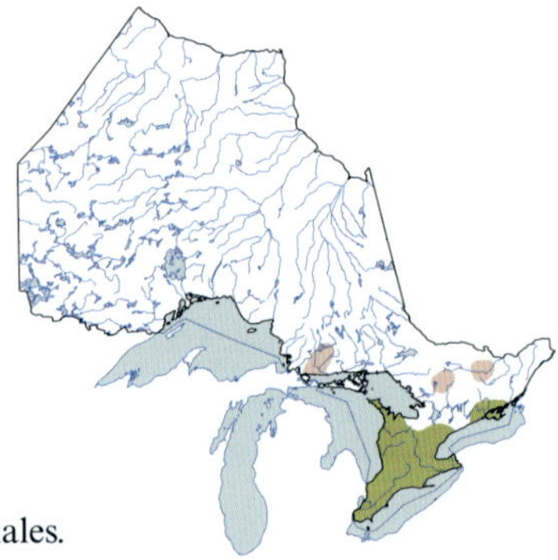

♂ with nuptial tubercles

Nest building

FEEDING: The River Chub is **omnivorous,** feeding on small aquatic insects, crustaceans, algae, and plant material.

REPRODUCTION: In spring, the male builds a nest by moving stones into a mound up to 100 cm in diameter and 33 cm in height. One nest was found to contain 7,050 stones and took 30 hours to complete. Prior to spawning, the male digs a trough in the nest, positions himself over it, and vibrates to attract a female. A female enters and is supported by the male with his pectoral fins. Eggs and sperm are released, and then the male chases her away. He covers the eggs with stones and builds another trough in preparation for the next female to enter the nest. Both females and males spawn several times with more than one mate.

HABITAT: The River Chub is found in the cool waters of pools and runs in streams with rocky **substrates**, including large rivers such as the Detroit River.

STATUS: G5; N4; S4; NAR.

Maximum Age: 5	Ontario Average	Ontario Record	World Record
Length:	10.0 cm (3.9 in)	25.6 cm (10.1 in)	33.0 cm (13.0 in)

RIVER SHINER *Alburnops blennius*

Alburnops-alburn: shining or white; *ops*: resembling or appearance; refers to the resemblance to European members of the genus *Alburnus*

blennius: superficially resembles a blenny fish.

The River Shiner was first recorded in Ontario in 2004, when it was captured in the Rainy River. Rather than being recently introduced, the River Shiner is likely native to Ontario but may be a case of mistaken identity—it had not been previously distinguished from similar species. This view is supported by the capture of the species on the Minnesota side of the Rainy River since the 1940s.

DESCRIPTION: The River Shiner has an elongate, silvery body. The mouth is large; the upper jaw is usually longer than the eye diameter. The snout is even with, or slightly overhangs, the mouth. It has large scales (32–41 **lateral scales**). The breast is scaled. There are 7 anal rays, rarely 8. The body is generally silvery with yellowish tints, the scales are weakly outlined on the back, and the body does not appear cross-hatched. The belly is silvery white. There is no **stitching** along the **lateral line**. There is a distinct dark mid-dorsal stripe in front of the dorsal fin that continues along each side of the fin. The anus is surrounded by little or no pigment. The spawning male develops minute **nuptial tubercles** on the snout, top of the head, pectoral fins, and the leading edges of the dorsal and anal fins.

SIMILAR SPECIES: The River Shiner is difficult to distinguish from the Mimic and Ghost shiners, which usually have 8 anal rays and unscaled breasts. The mid-dorsal stripe is absent or very faint in the Ghost Shiner, and the Mimic Shiner has black pigment around the anus. The River Shiner is very difficult to distinguish from the Sand Shiner, which also has 7 anal rays. The Sand Shiner has an unscaled breast, an upper jaw shorter than the eye diameter, a body more strongly cross-hatched, a **lateral line** usually appearing darkly **stitched**, and a mid-dorsal stripe usually not continuing along each side of the dorsal fin.

FEEDING: The River Shiner feeds on a wide variety of aquatic and terrestrial insect **larvae**, algae, and plants.

REPRODUCTION: The River Shiner spawns several times throughout the summer months until late August. Spawning occurs over sand and gravel bars.

HABITAT: The River Shiner is found in clear waters of large pools and channels of large streams. It may also be found in **turbid** waters over silt, sand, and gravel.

STATUS: G5; N5; S1?

Maximum Age: 4	Ontario Average	Ontario Record	World Record
Length:	7.5 cm (3.0 in)	9.7 cm (3.9 in)	13.0 cm (5.1 in)

ROSYFACE SHINER *Notropis rubellus*

Notropis—*noto*: back; *tropis*: **keel**. The **genus** was described from a specimen with a keeled back—likely due to the method of preservation.
rubellus: reddish; refers to the colouration in spawning males.

In Canada, the Rosyface Shiner was once considered to be present in Manitoba, Ontario, and Quebec. However, a recent study concluded that the Manitoba population is actually a different species, the Carmine Shiner.

DESCRIPTION: The Rosyface Shiner has an elongate, silvery body. It has a long pointed snout. It has large scales (37–41 **lateral scales**). The dorsal fin is set farther back than in most shiners, its **origin** well behind the pelvic fin base (p. 137). It has a large anal fin with 9–11 rays and a straight posterior edge. The body is generally silvery with an olive-green back and silvery white belly. The spawning male has an orange or red head and light-red belly; spawning females are paler red. Spawning males develop minute **nuptial tubercles** on the head, the back in front of the dorsal fin, and the pectoral fins.

SIMILAR SPECIES: The Rosyface Shiner has more anal rays than most minnow species. Of the minnow species with 9 or more anal rays, the Common, Striped, and Golden shiners and the Rudd have deeper bodies. The Common and Striped shiners have the **origin** of their dorsal fin directly above the **origin** of the pelvic fins. The Golden Shiner and the Rudd have a more decurved **lateral line**. The Redfin Shiner has a dark blotch at the front base of the dorsal fin. The Rosyface Shiner is very difficult to distinguish from the Emerald and Silver shiners. The Emerald Shiner has a shorter, more rounded snout, and the edge of its anal fin is concave. Suspected specimens of these three species larger than 10 cm (4 in.) are most likely to be Silver Shiner, which have a dorsal fin that originates above or slightly behind the pelvic fin base.

FEEDING: The Rosyface Shiner feeds near the surface on aquatic and terrestrial insects and plants.

REPRODUCTION: The Rosyface Shiner spawns in late spring when the water temperature is between 20°C and 29°C. Schools are formed in the **riffles** of streams, and much thrashing occurs before spawning. Smaller groups of males and females vibrate together, and eggs and sperm are released. This behaviour is repeated several times. Spawning may occur over nests (depressions in the gravel) made by other minnow species.

HABITAT: The Rosyface Shiner is usually found in cool to warm streams of various depths over bottoms of sand and gravel, and it is occasionally found in lakes.

STATUS: G5; N4; S4; NAR.

Maximum Age: 3	Ontario Average	Ontario Record	World Record
Length:	6.5 cm (2.6 in)	8.7 cm (3.4 in)	9.0 cm (3.5 in)

RUDD *Scardinius erythrophthalmus*

Scardinius: Latin word for "minnow."
erythrophthalmus—erythro: red; *ophthalmus*: eye; refers to the red fleck on the iris.

The Rudd is native to Europe. It was brought to North America early in the 20th century as a food and game fish and, more recently, to be raised for use as bait. As a result, self-reproducing populations have become **established** in southern Ontario and elsewhere. Remember: leftover baitfishes should never be released after fishing!

DESCRIPTION: The Rudd is a large, very deep-bodied minnow, which is thin from side to side. The mouth is small and upturned. There may be a red fleck on the golden-coloured iris. The scales are large (36–45 **lateral scales**), and there are 7–9 rows of scales above the **lateral line**. The **lateral line** is decurved (p. 26). There is a small scaled **keel** on the abdomen between the pelvic and anal fins. The **origin** of the dorsal fin is set far back on the body, beginning behind the pelvic fin base (p. 137). The anal fin is large (10–11 rays). The back is brown-green, the sides are silver or golden with red tints in large fish, and the belly is silvery white. The fins are orange or red. The spawning male develops fine white **nuptial tubercles** on the head and body.

SIMILAR SPECIES: The Golden Shiner has clear or yellow fins, a scaleless **keel**, and smaller scales (44–54 **lateral scales**). **Hybrids** between Golden Shiner and Rudd are possible. They may be recognized by partially scaled **keels** and scale counts that are intermediate to those of the Golden Shiner and Rudd.

FEEDING: The Rudd is **omnivorous**, feeding on aquatic plants, insect **larvae**, crustaceans, molluscs, and, occasionally, fish eggs and **fry**. The young feed on **zooplankton**.

REPRODUCTION: In its native Europe, the Rudd spawns in spring in water temperatures between 18°C and 20°C. A female, often accompanied by two males, deposits eggs over aquatic

Juvenile

vegetation. The eggs are fertilized and adhere to plants. The eggs hatch in three to five days, and the young remain attached to the plants until their yolk supply is depleted. The reproductive habits of the Rudd in Ontario are unknown, although they are assumed to be similar to those in Europe.

HABITAT: In its native range, the Rudd generally prefers the cool, vegetated waters of lakes and streams. This is consistent with the few locations in Ontario where it has been found. However, its preferred habitat in Ontario is unknown due to its limited distribution.

STATUS: G5; NNA; SNA.

Maximum Age: 19	Ontario Average	Ontario Record	World Record
Length:	20.0 cm (7.9 in)	44.1 cm (17.4 in)	61.7 cm (24.3 in)
Weight: Overall	0.2 kg (0.4 lbs)	0.9 kg (2.0 lbs)	2.7 kg (6.0 lbs)
Angling	–	–	2.7 kg (6.0 lbs)

SAND SHINER *Miniellus stramineus*

Miniellus-mini: small; *ellus*: smaller form, refers to their small size among North American minnows
stramineus: of straw; refers to the colouration of its back.

The Sand Shiner is generally widespread in Ontario, but not typically common in biological surveys. Biological surveys use a variety of methods, such as nets and traps, to determine the fish species present in a waterbody. The preferred habitat of the Sand Shiner is not often sampled by biological surveys, thus explaining its rarity in surveys.

DESCRIPTION: The Sand Shiner is a small, elongate, silvery minnow. The upper jaw is shorter than the eye diameter, and the snout is even with, or overhangs, the mouth. It has large scales (31–38 **lateral scales**). The breast is not scaled. There are 7 anal rays, rarely 8. The body is generally silvery with yellowish tints, the back appears cross-hatched, and the **lateral line** usually appears darkly **stitched**. The belly is silvery white. There is a mid-dorsal stripe in front of the dorsal fin of varying intensity that does not continue along each side of the fin. The anus is surrounded by little or no pigment. Spawning males develop minute **nuptial tubercles** on the head.

SIMILAR SPECIES: The Sand Shiner is difficult to distinguish from the Ghost and Mimic shiners, both of which usually have 8 anal rays. The mid-dorsal stripe is absent or very faint in the Ghost Shiner. The Mimic Shiner, and often the Ghost Shiner, have black pigment around the anus. The Sand Shiner is very difficult to distinguish from the River Shiner, which also has 7 anal rays. The River Shiner has a scaled breast and an upper jaw that is longer than the eye diameter, the body is not cross-hatched, the **lateral line** is not darkly **stitched**, and the mid-dorsal stripe continues along each side of the dorsal fin.

FEEDING: The Sand Shiner feeds on a variety of small items, including aquatic insects, crustaceans, and, to a lesser degree, algae and plants.

REPRODUCTION: Spawning takes place from late spring to mid-summer when the water temperature is above 21°C. Eggs and sperm are released over vegetation or sandy **substrates**.

HABITAT: The Sand Shiner is found in the slow-moving, warm areas of streams with bottoms of sand and gravel, and in the shallow, sandy areas of lakes, including the Great Lakes.

STATUS: G5; N5; S4.

Maximum Age: 3	Ontario Average	Ontario Record	World Record
Length:	6.5 cm (2.6 in)	8.5 cm (3.3 in)	8.5 cm (3.3 in)

SILVER CHUB *Macrhybopsis storeriana*

Macrhybopsis—*macros*: long; *hybos*: humped; *opsis*: face; refers to the long humped face.
storeriana: named after David Storer, an American **ichthyologist**.

The Silver Chub was nearly **extirpated** in Lake Erie in the 1950s as a result of the disappearance of mayflies, its preferred prey, due to declining water quality. As water quality improved by the early 2000s, the mayflies returned and so did the Silver Chub. However, water quality is once again declining and so too the Silver Chub.

DESCRIPTION: The Silver Chub is a large silvery minnow that is slightly deep-bodied. The snout is rounded and greatly overhangs the mouth (p. 26). There is a small **barbel** at the corners of the mouth. It has large scales (35–41 **lateral scales**). The **origin** of the dorsal fin is ahead of the **origin** of the pelvic fin. The back is pale grey-green, the sides are silvery, and the belly is silvery white. The tail is grey with a white bottom edge. Males develop very small **nuptial tubercles** on the top of the pectoral fins.

SIMILAR SPECIES: The Spottail Shiner lacks a small **barbel** at the corners of the mouth, and usually has a large spot at the base of the tail.

FEEDING: The Silver Chub eats crustaceans and small molluscs, such as Zebra and Quagga mussels, as well as a variety of insects.

REPRODUCTION: Spawning occurs in late spring and summer when the water temperature is between 19°C and 23°C. The reproductive habits are unknown.

HABITAT: Although it is a river inhabitant throughout most of its range, the Silver Chub is found only in the cool waters of lakes Erie and St. Clair and connecting rivers in Ontario.

STATUS: G5; N2; S2; E[F], T[P] (Great Lakes –Upper St. Lawrence populations).

Maximum Age: 4	Ontario Average	Ontario Record	World Record
Length:	12.0 cm (4.7 in)	22.5 cm (8.9 in)	23.0 cm (9.1 in)

SILVER SHINER *Notropis photogenis*

Notropis—noto: back; *tropis*: **keel**. The **genus** was described from a specimen with a keeled back—likely due to the method of preservation.

photogenis—photino: shiny, bright; *gena*: cheek; refers to the shiny cheek (and body).

In the past, our largest *Notropis* species was not distinguished from Emerald and Rosyface shiners. Although it was first identified in Ontario in 1973, collections are known from as early as 1936, and it was likely always present in southern Ontario.

DESCRIPTION: The Silver Shiner is a large, elongate, silvery minnow. The snout is long and pointed. The eye is large; its diameter is equal to or slightly less than the snout length. It has large silvery scales (36–43 **lateral scales**). The dorsal fin usually originates above or slightly behind the pelvic fin base (p. 137). The anal fin has 9–11 rays. There are often 2 black crescents between the nostrils. A clearly defined dark or orange stripe is often found along the middle of the back. Spawning males are not brightly coloured, and males develop **nuptial tubercles** on the head, front of the body, and pectoral fins.

SIMILAR SPECIES: The Silver Shiner has more anal rays than most minnow species. Of the minnow species with 9 or more anal rays, the Common, Striped, and Golden shiners and the Rudd have deeper bodies. The Common and Striped shiners have the **origin** of the dorsal fin directly above the **origin** of the pelvic fins. The Golden Shiner and the Rudd have a more decurved **lateral line**. The Redfin Shiner has a dark blotch at the front base of the dorsal fin. The Silver Shiner is very difficult to distinguish from the Emerald and Rosyface shiners. Suspected specimens of these three species longer than 10 cm (4 in.) are most likely Silver Shiners. The Emerald and Rosyface shiners have a dorsal fin starting farther back, well behind the pelvic fin base. They also have a faint dark stripe along the middle of the back. The Emerald Shiner has a shorter snout.

FEEDING: The Silver Shiner feeds on a wide variety of terrestrial and aquatic insects, tiny crustaceans, worms, and algae, which are often taken at the surface. It has been reported to leap above the surface to catch flying insects.

REPRODUCTION: Spawning occurs in the spring, but little else is known of their spawning habits.

HABITAT: The Silver Shiner is found in the cool-to-warm, clear waters of streams, over bottoms of **cobble** and boulders.

STATUS: G5; N2N3; S2S3; T.

Maximum Age: 3	Ontario Average	Ontario Record	World Record
Length:	10.0 cm (3.9 in)	14.3 cm (5.6 in)	14.3 cm (5.6 in)

SPOTFIN SHINER *Cyprinella spiloptera*

Cyprinella: small minnow.
spiloptera—spilos: spot; *pteron*: fin; refers to the dark blotch on the dorsal fin.

The Spotfin Shiner is expanding its range in Ontario, likely as a result of bait-bucket transfers, tolerance to degraded waters, and protection of its eggs from predators.

DESCRIPTION: This silvery minnow is slightly deep-bodied with a pointed head. It has large scales (35–41 **lateral scales**), and their outlines form a cross-hatched pattern on the body. The anal fin usually has 8 rays (range: 7–9). There is a black stripe running along the middle of the chin. There is a black blotch on the posterior part of the dorsal fin, which is inconspicuous or absent in smaller individuals. A black lateral stripe, if present, is found only on the posterior half of the body and is most evident on preserved specimens. Adult males are bluish silver with yellow fins, and have white tips on the tail and dorsal and anal fins. The spawning male develops pointed **nuptial tubercles** on the head, lower jaw, back, and pectoral fins, and on and above the anal fin.

SIMILAR SPECIES: It is most often confused with the Common Shiner. The Common and Striped shiners usually have 9 anal rays and lack a black stripe in the middle of the chin and black blotch on the dorsal fin. Their scale outlines do not form a distinct cross-hatched pattern on the body.

FEEDING: The Spotfin Shiner feeds on a variety of terrestrial and aquatic insects, often near the bottom during the day and near the surface at night.

REPRODUCTION: The Spotfin Shiner is a **fractional spawner**, spawning repeatedly throughout the summer. The male chooses a spawning site over rock crevices or fallen trees and stumps. He is highly territorial and defends his spawning site by biting, butting, and chasing away other males. To

Juvenile

attract the female, the male erects his fins and vibrates. The female approaches the male, and spawning occurs. The fertilized eggs fall into crevices where they are protected from **predation**.

HABITAT: The Spotfin Shiner prefers the slow-moving areas of streams with gravel or sand bottoms. It is occasionally found in lakes Erie, Huron, and Ontario, and the St. Lawrence River.

STATUS: G5; N4N5; S4.

Maximum Age: 5	Ontario Average	Ontario Record	World Record
Length:	7.5 cm (3.0 in)	11.5 cm (4.5 in)	12.0 cm (4.7 in)

SPOTTAIL SHINER *Hudsonius hudsonius*

Hudsonius: This species was first described from the Hudson River, a major waterway in the northeastern USA.
hudsonius: the specimen used to describe this species was caught in the Hudson River, USA.

The Spottail Shiner is very abundant in the Great Lakes and, as a result, is an important prey source for larger fishes. It is also an important baitfish, particularly in northern Ontario.

DESCRIPTION: The Spottail Shiner is a relatively large, elongate, silvery minnow with a large black spot at the base of the tail. Its rounded snout overhangs the mouth (p. 26). The scales, including those on the back in front of the dorsal fin, are large (37–39 **lateral scales**). The dorsal and anal fins are long and pointed with a concave posterior edge (p. 25). The body is generally silvery with yellow-golden overtones, with a pale green to olive-green back and a silvery white belly. The spot at the base of the tail is most obvious in young fishes and is sometimes hidden by silvery scales in large adults. Spawning males develop minute **nuptial tubercles** on the head and pectoral fins.

SIMILAR SPECIES: The Bluntnose Minnow and Hornyhead Chub also have prominent spots on the base of the tail. The Bluntnose Minnow has noticeably smaller scales in front of the dorsal fin, rounded dorsal and anal fins, and a dark lateral stripe that extends onto the snout. The Silver Chub is easily confused with large Spottail Shiners that have a hidden spot on the tail. The Silver Chub and Hornyhead Chub both differ in having a small **barbel** at the corners of the mouth, which is obvious only upon close examination.

FEEDING: The Spottail Shiner feeds on a wide variety of crustaceans, aquatic insects, **larval** fishes, and algae.

Juvenile

REPRODUCTION: In late spring and early summer, large schools congregate over sandy shoals or may migrate into lower reaches of tributaries. Spawning occurs in water temperatures between 18°C and 22°C, and there is no parental care of the eggs.

HABITAT: The Spottail Shiner is most often found in the open, clear, cold or cool waters of large lakes and streams. It is also found in tributaries to these waterbodies in moderately flowing waters, over sand or gravel bottoms.

STATUS: G5; N5; S5.

Maximum Age: 5	Ontario Average	Ontario Record	World Record
Length:	9.0 cm (3.5 in)	14.2 cm (5.6 in)	15.0 cm (5.9 in)

STRIPED SHINER *Luxilus chrysocephalus*

Luxilus—*lux*: light; *illus*: somewhat; refers to the shiny pigmentation.
chrysocephalus—*chryso*: gold; *cephalo*: head; refers to the gold iridescence on the head.

The Striped Shiner was not recognized as a separate species from the Common Shiner, with which it frequently **hybridizes**, until 1964.

DESCRIPTION: The Striped Shiner is a silvery, deep-bodied fish and our largest shiner. It has an upper jaw that extends backwards almost to below the eye. The chin is evenly pigmented. It has large scales (36–42 **lateral scales**). The **lateral scales** at the front of the body are more than twice as high as wide (p. 25). The scales on the back in front of the dorsal fin are large (13–19 **anterior dorso-lateral** scales) (p. 136). The **origin** of the dorsal fin is usually directly above the **origin** of the pelvic fins (p. 137). There are 9, occasionally 8, anal rays. Adults have faint stripes on the back that converge behind the dorsal fin. Spawning males develop rosy fins and small **nuptial tubercles** covering the top of the head and back in front of the dorsal fin.

SIMILAR SPECIES: The Golden Shiner and Rudd have small upturned mouths, more decurved **lateral lines**, and usually more than 9 anal rays. The Fallfish is not as deep-bodied. It has smaller scales (43–50 **lateral scales**) and a longer snout overhanging the mouth. The **origin** of its dorsal fin is behind the **origin** of the pelvic fin. The Redside Dace has a larger mouth, a protruding lower jaw, and smaller scales. The Redfin Shiner has a dark blotch at the base of the dorsal fin, and small scales on the back in front of the dorsal fin. The Spotfin Shiner has a dark blotch on the posterior part of the dorsal fin, and the scale outlines form a cross-hatched pattern on the body. The Common Shiner has a smaller dorsal fin (usually more than 18 **anterior dorso-lateral** scales). The adult Common Shiner has stripes on the back that do not converge, and chin pigmentation is usually confined to the outer edge of the chin.

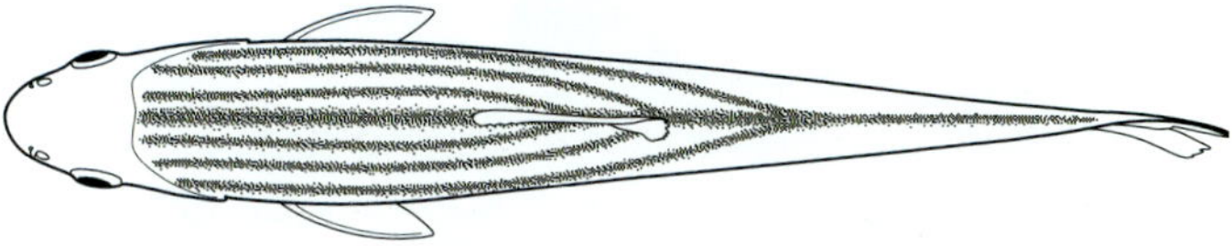

stripes on the back converge behind the dorsal fin

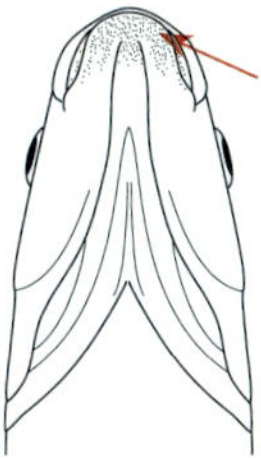

chin pigmented evenly

FEEDING: The Striped Shiner is an **omnivore**, feeding from the surface and the bottom on aquatic insects, algae, and plant material.

REPRODUCTION: In spring, males excavate shallow nests over gravel or use nests of other species. Males use their **nuptial tubercles** to move stones and aggressively defend their nests. Females move into the nest area, and spawning occurs with the male curling around the female. The spawning act is repeated many times with the same, or different, pairings. **Hybrids** frequently occur as several species use the same nest, resulting in a mix of eggs and sperm from different species.

HABITAT: The Striped Shiner is usually found in the cool, shallow waters of pools and runs in streams.

STATUS: G5; N4; S4; NAR.

Maximum Age: 6	Ontario Average	Ontario Record	World Record
Length:	12.9 cm (5.1 in)	23.8 cm (9.4 in)	24.0 cm (9.4 in)

WESTERN BLACKNOSE DACE *Rhinichthys obtusus*

Rhinichthys—*rhini*: snout; *ichthys*: fish; refers to the prominent snout.
obtusus: blunt, refers to the shape of the snout.

♀

♂

The Blacknose Dace has been recently separated into two species, the Eastern Blacknose Dace (*Rhinichthys atratulus*) and Western Blacknose Dace (*Rhinichthys obtusus*), based on a genetics study. It appears that only the Western Blacknose Dace is present in Ontario.

DESCRIPTION: The Western Blacknose Dace is a slightly deep-bodied minnow. The snout overhangs the mouth (p. 26), and the groove between the upper lip and snout is not continuous (p. 26). The upper lip is about level with the lower edge of the eye. There is a small **barbel** at the corners of the mouth (p. 27). The mouth is U-shaped when viewed from below (p. 136). The scales are small (56–68 **lateral scales**). It has a black stripe extending from the snout to the base of the tail, and the back and sides are usually heavily spotted in most individuals from Ontario. Spawning males develop an orange lateral stripe and small **nuptial tubercles** on the head, body, and pectoral fins. Males can be recognized by their longer pelvic fins, which reach the anal fin, and the posterior edge of the anal fin is nearly at a right angle to the body.

SIMILAR SPECIES: The Longnose Dace differs in having a longer snout that greatly overhangs the mouth, and its upper lip is much lower than the eye. The dark lateral stripe and spotting are usually not as prominent. The Central Stoneroller lacks **barbels** and has larger scales (49–55

Spawning ♂

lateral scales), a continuous groove that separates the upper lip from the snout, and a mouth that is crescent-shaped when viewed from below. The Eastern Blacknose Dace is very difficult to distinguish from the Western Blacknose Dace. The eastern species tends to be less heavily spotted, and the mature males have bright red pectoral fins.

FEEDING: The Western Blacknose Dace feeds primarily on aquatic insect **larvae** and, to a lesser extent, worms and algae.

REPRODUCTION: Spawning occurs in spring when water temperatures are between 12°C and 27°C. The male Western Blacknose Dace clears and defends a territory in shallow **riffles**. As a female approaches from deeper pools, the male swims beside her, maintains contact with the help of his **nuptial tubercles**, and curls his tail around her. The female uses her **ovipositor** to push eggs into the **substrate**, where they are fertilized. The male vigorously guards the eggs from other species that try to eat them.

HABITAT: The Western Blacknose Dace prefers small, shallow, cool streams with instream and **riparian** cover.

STATUS: G5; N5; S5.

Maximum Age: 3	Ontario Average	Ontario Record	World Record
Length:	6.4 cm (2.5 in)	10.0 cm (3.9 in)	12.4 cm (4.9 in)

TINCIDAE
Tenches

The Tench is native to Europe and Asia. It was introduced to North America in the late 1800s for sport fishing. Until recently, the Tench was considered to belong in the family Cyprinidae, sharing characteristics such as no teeth in the mouth and no spines in the fins. Genetic studies indicate that this family is unique from carps and minnows. Other characters of the Tench include short anal and dorsal fins, a deep caudal peduncle (p. 23), and **barbels** at the corners of the mouth.

In its native Europe, the Tench is commercially fished and angled because of its fighting abilities. However, when introduced outside of its native range, the Tench outcompetes native species and impacts the food web. An increase in the Tench population causes a decline in molluscs, their preferred prey. Fewer molluscs cause an explosion in **periphyton**, the food that molluscs eat. In turn, excessive **periphyton** causes a decrease in aquatic plants. This cascading effect in the food web underscores the vulnerability of Ontario's freshwater ecosystems.

The Tench was imported into Quebec from Europe in the 1980s to develop pond aquaculture for human food. However, a market never developed, and Tench escaped from farm ponds into the nearby Richelieu River. From there, it spread northward to the St. Lawrence River and now extends from Quebec City in the east to Lake St. Francis in Ontario in the west. The capture of a juvenile Tench on the Quebec side of Lake Saint Francis in fall 2019 indicates it is likely to soon become **established** in Ontario.

There is only one species in the family.

< Tench feeding

TENCH *Tinca tinca*

Tinca: Latin name for Tench.

The Tench was first found in the Great Lakes, in the eastern basin of Lake Ontario, soon after a scientific paper published in 2018 identified it as the next Great Lakes invader.

DESCRIPTION: The Tench is a medium-sized, deep-bodied fish with a deep caudal peduncle (p. 23). It has a a single prominent **barbel** on each side of the mouth. It has very small embedded scales (95–105 **lateral scales**) and a short dorsal fin with 8–9 rays. It is overall olive to dark green to almost black with a golden sheen. The belly is golden. Fins are dark. The tail is slightly forked with rounded lobes. Some mature males have a large tubercle on the side of the body.

SIMILAR SPECIES: No other fish in Ontario has a combination of a deep body, very small scales, a pair of **barbels** at the corner of the mouth, and a slightly forked tail with rounded lobes.

FEEDING: The Tench is **omnivorous**, eating a wide variety of aquatic insects, algae, crustaceans, molluscs, and plants. Usually feeding at night, the Tench depends on its **barbels** for taste and touch perception and its sense of smell to detect food.

REPRODUCTION: The Tench spawns in warm, vegetated shallows in late spring and summer when water temperatures reach 20°C. The female releases sticky eggs over submerged plants, and one or two males follow behind releasing sperm. Females and males release eggs and sperm several times during the spawning season.

HABITAT: The Tench prefers the slow-moving shallows of streams, ponds, wetlands, and lakes with dense vegetation and muddy or sandy bottoms.

Juvenile

STATUS: G5; NNA; SNA.

Maximum Age: 20–30	Ontario Average	Ontario Record	World Record
Length:	-	46.5 cm (18.5 in)	84.0 cm (33.1 in)
Weight: Overall	-	1.4 kg (3.1 lbs)	6.9 kg (15.2 lbs)
Angling	-	-	6.9 kg (15.2 lbs)

XENOCYPRIDIDAE
Xenocarps

Until recently, species in this new fish family were in the family Cyprinidae. Recent studies split the family into multiple families (see p. 129). The family Xenocyprididae is native to eastern Asia, ranging from Thailand to Siberia.

Starting in the 1960s, four xenocarp species were introduced to aquaculture ponds in the southcentral USA to control water quality. The Black Carp (see p. 467) was introduced to control snails, the Bighead Carp (see p. 457) to control **zooplankton**, the Grass Carp (see p. 220) to control aquatic vegetation, and the Silver Carp (see p. 467) to control **phytoplankton**. During floods, these species escaped into, and have since spread throughout, the Mississippi basin. As the species increased in abundance, so did the concern about their impacts on the ecosystems they invaded. These large fishes, growing greater than 1 m in length and 50 kg in weight, appeared to be outcompeting native fishes. As a result, Canada and the USA conducted risk assessments that concluded the species could survive and reproduce in much of North America and have significant ecological and economic impacts.

To prevent these species from invading the Great Lakes, an electrical barrier was built in a canal between the Mississippi basin and Lake Michigan. Although the barrier appears to be effective, a few Bighead Carp and a lot of Grass Carp have been captured in the Great Lakes, including Canadian waters. Although the Bighead Carp is likely not **established**, the Grass Carp is reproducing on the American side of Lake Erie.

There are 161 species worldwide, at least one of which, Grass Carp, is likely to soon become **established** in Ontario.

< Bighead Carp

GRASS CARP *Ctenopharyngodon idella*

Ctenopharyngodon—cteno: comb; *pharyng*: throat; *odon*: tooth; refers to the distinct grooves on the comb-like **pharyngeal teeth**.
idella—idios: distinct, perhaps referring to the distinctive **pharyngeal teeth**.

The Grass Carp has been reproducing in American tributaries to Lake Erie since 2012 or earlier. Given the substantial impacts predicted by risk assessments, it is disappointing that attempts to eradicate the species were not undertaken early enough. It is likely too late for such attempts to be successful now; therefore, we are including this species account with the expectation that the Grass Carp will soon be reproducing in Ontario waters.

DESCRIPTION: The Grass Carp is a large, slightly deep-bodied fish. The eyes are low on the head, and the lower edge of the eye is below the gape of the mouth. The snout does not overhang the mouth, and there are no **barbels**. The **pharyngeal teeth** are slender with distinct grooves (requires dissection to see). It has large scales (34–45 **lateral scales**) that are darkly outlined. The dorsal fin is short with 7–8 rays and lacks a **serrated** spine at the leading edge. The upper lip is much thicker at the front than on the sides. The belly is rounded, without a **keel**. Colour is variable, with the back usually olive or grey, sides silvery or yellow, and belly white. Fins are clear to grey-brown. Spawning males develop **nuptial tubercles** on the head, pectoral fins, front of the dorsal fin, and top of the caudal peduncle.

SIMILAR SPECIES: The Common Carp and Goldfish have a long dorsal fin of 15–23 dorsal rays and a strong, **serrated** spine at the front of the dorsal and anal fins. The Bighead and Silver carps have very small scales (more than 84 **lateral scales** vs. 34–45). The Black Carp is golden grey to dark brown and has **pharyngeal teeth** that are club-like and without grooves. The Fallfish has an eye that is higher on the head, the lower edge of the eye is above the upper lip, which is about as thin at the front as it is on the side.

FEEDING: The Grass Carp is **omnivorous**, feeding primarily on aquatic

Juvenile

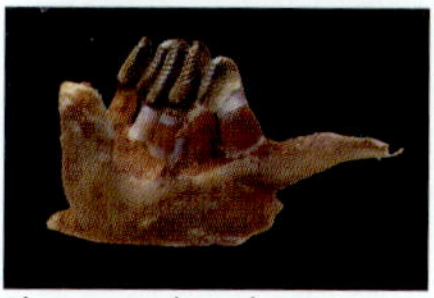

Pharyngeal teeth

plants. It consumes up to 40% of its body weight per day, which causes a drastic reduction in aquatic plants and, in turn, negatively impacts native fishes and **invertebrates**.

REPRODUCTION: The Grass Carp spawns in large **turbid** rivers when the water temperature reaches 18°C. Spawning occurs near the surface during high-flow events in turbulent water. A female is followed by two or more males. Males push their heads against the female and roll to one side. Eggs and sperm are released. The fertilized, semi-buoyant eggs must remain in the flowing water column for them to hatch, usually in one to three days.

HABITAT: The Grass Carp lives in warm, vegetated waters of slow-moving streams and lakes, including nearshore areas of the Great Lakes.

STATUS: G5; NNA; SNA.

Maximum Age: 21	Ontario Average	Ontario Record	World Record
Length:	76.0 cm (29.9 in)	125.7 cm (49.5 in)	150.0 cm (59.1 in)
Weight: Overall	3.8 kg (8.4 lbs)	11.8 kg (26.0 lbs)	45.0 kg (99.2 lbs)
Angling	-	-	39.8 kg (87.6 lbs)

CATOSTOMIDAE
Suckers

Suckers are adapted for feeding on the bottom, with thick, fleshy lips usually located on the underside of the head. This family is largely limited to North America and occurs from the Arctic south into Guatemala. There are two suckers that occur outside North America: the Longnose Sucker, with a range that extends from North America into eastern Siberia, and the Chinese Sucker, which occurs only in the Yangtze River drainage. Suckers are recognized by their lips, which are both touch and taste sensitive, and covered in folds or ridges (known as **plicae**) and bumps (known as **papillae**). They lack teeth in the mouth, but have ten or more long, comb-like **pharyngeal teeth** on each side of the throat. The head lacks scales and **barbels**, and the body has **cycloid scales**. There is a single dorsal fin and no adipose fin.

Known as the harbingers of spring to the angler, the Longnose and White suckers can be observed swimming up streams during their spawning runs just as the ice is melting from the lakes. Often referred to as a coarse fish, the White Sucker can be caught using a dip net, bow and arrow, and spear in certain parts of Ontario in the spring. The flesh of suckers can be firm and tasty, and is often marketed as "mullet."

There are 87 species worldwide, 14 of which occur in Ontario.

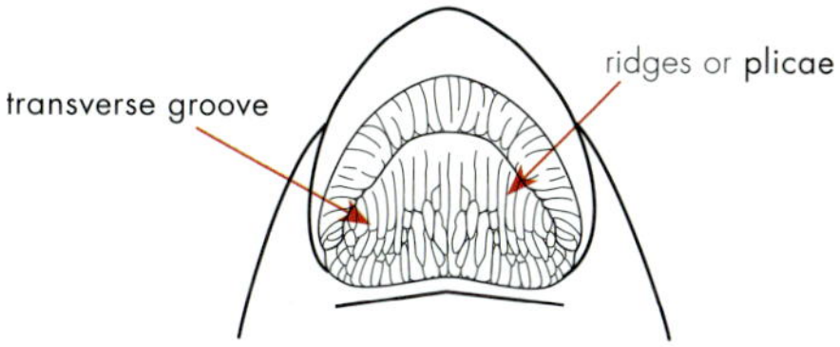

< Longnose Sucker

Sucker lips

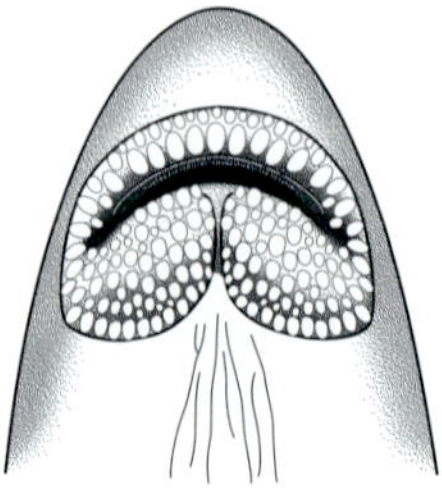

Longnose Sucker

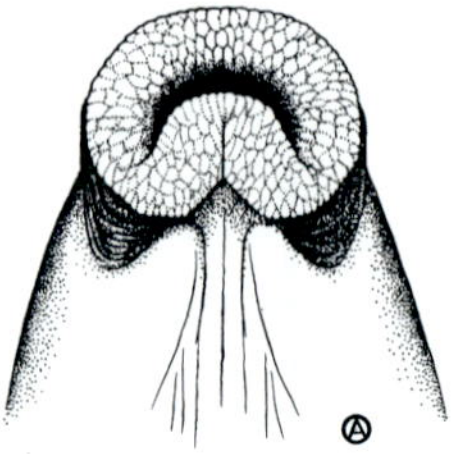

Northern Hog Sucker

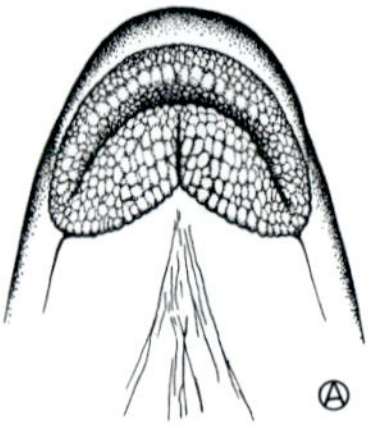

White Sucker

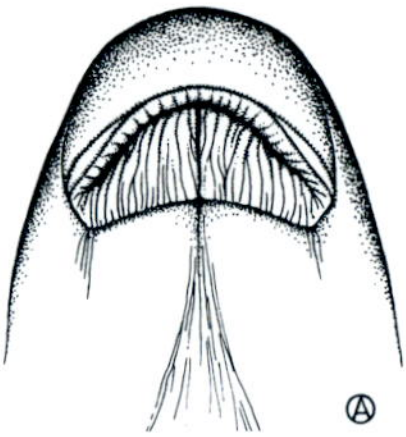

Black Redhorse

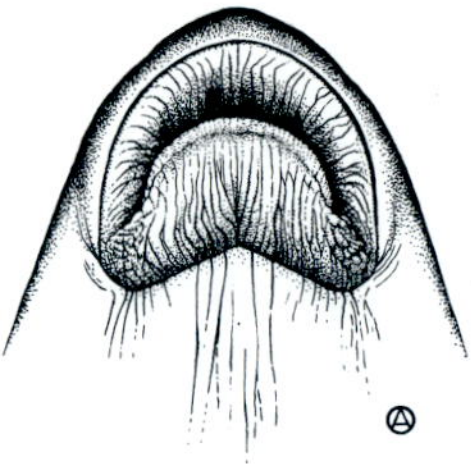

Golden Redhorse

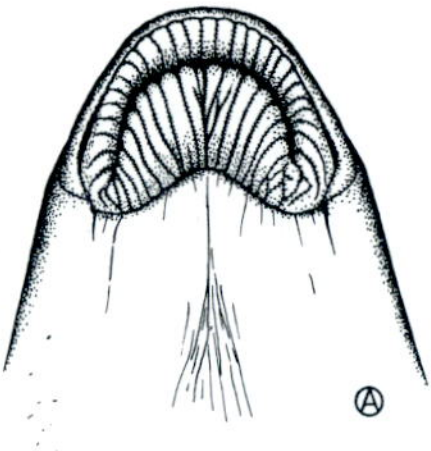

Greater Redhorse

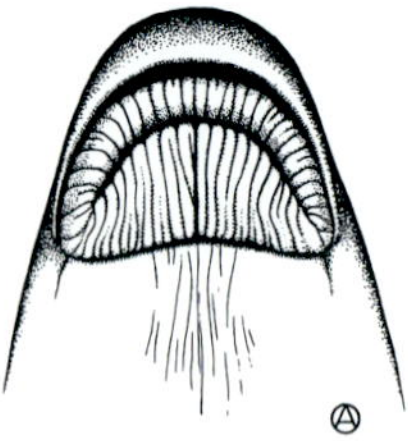

River Redhorse

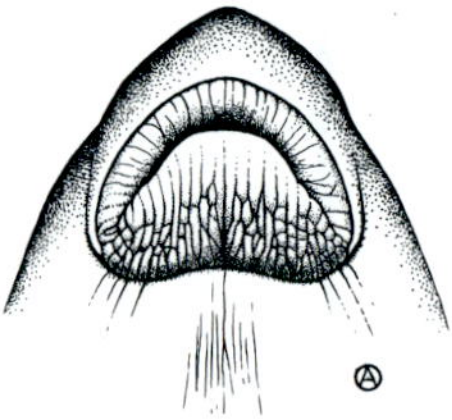

Shorthead Redhorse

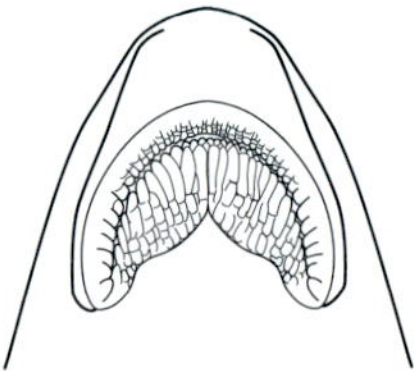

Silver Redhorse

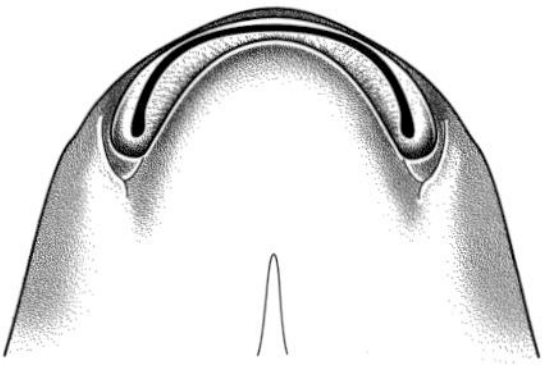

Bigmouth Buffalo

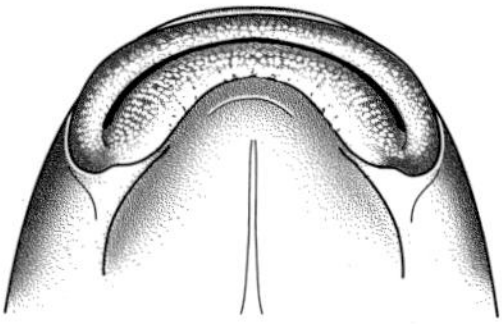

Black/Smallmouth buffaloes or **hybrid**

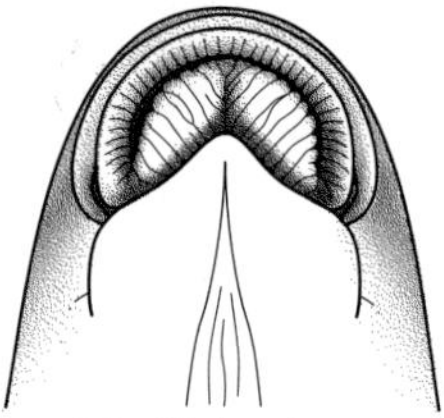

Lake Chubsucker

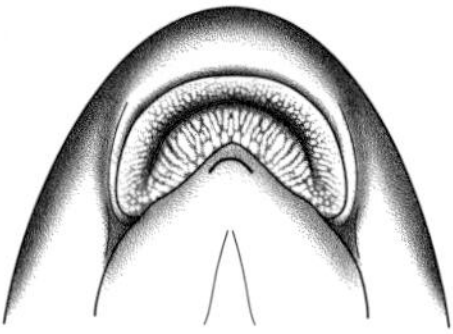

Quillback

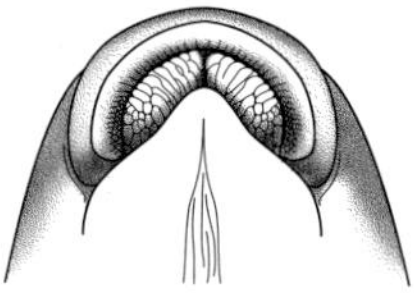

Spotted Sucker

Posterior edge of lower lip in redhorses

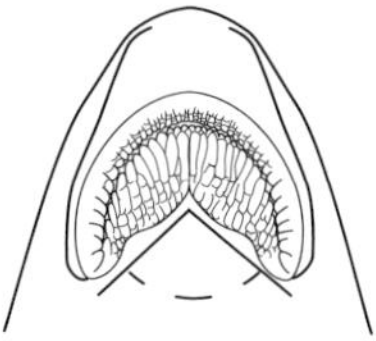

slightly greater than 90°

considerably greater than 90°

Vertical mouth positions in buffaloes

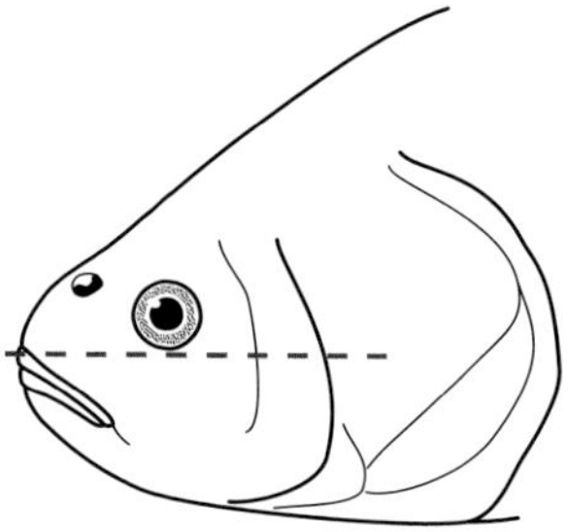

upper lip level with lower edge of eye (Bigmouth Buffalo)

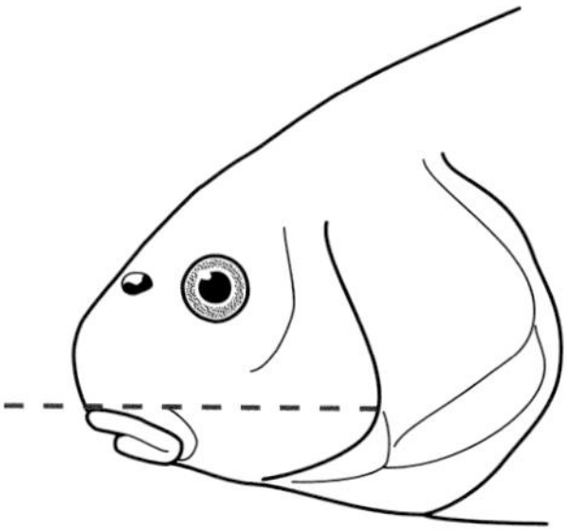

upper lip well below eye (e.g., Black Buffalo)

BIGMOUTH BUFFALO *Ictiobus cyprinellus*

Ictiobus—ictio: fish; *bus*: bull.
cyprinellus: little carp.

Although first discovered in Ontario in 1957, it has likely been here much longer. Since its first discovery in Lake Erie, it has also been found in lakes Huron, Ontario, and St. Clair, and their tributaries.

DESCRIPTION: The Bigmouth Buffalo is a large, very deep-bodied sucker. The lips are thin for a sucker and have faint ridges (p. 225). It has a large upturned mouth, with the upper lip level with the lower edge of the eye (p. 225). The scales are very large (35–41 **lateral scales**). The dorsal fin is long (23–30 rays), and the front part of it is bluntly pointed and much higher than the rest of the fin. The back varies from brown to olive, and the sides are lighter, fading to a white belly. The iris is usually dark. The scales are often darkly outlined, and the body may have an overall greenish cast. The fins are generally darker than the body. Colouration in spawning individuals becomes more intense. Minute **nuptial tubercles** may occur on the body, fins, and head during spawning.

SIMILAR SPECIES: The Common Carp and Goldfish have a **serrated** spine at the front of the dorsal and anal fins. In addition, the Common Carp has 2 **barbels** on each side of the mouth, and the Goldfish has larger scales (fewer than 32 **lateral scales**). The Quillback has a snout that greatly overhangs the small mouth, a more silvery body, paler pectoral and pelvic fins, and a higher dorsal fin. The other buffaloes and **hybrids** have a mouth that is not upturned, and the upper lip is below eye level.

FEEDING: Like other suckers, the Bigmouth Buffalo feeds on the bottom on aquatic insects, molluscs, and crustaceans. Unlike other suckers, it also feeds in the water column on **plankton**.

Juvenile

REPRODUCTION: In spring, adults move into shallow streams, wetlands, and flooded areas. Spawning occurs when the water temperature reaches 15°C. Several males thrash with a female, pushing her to the surface. The spawning commotion is very intense, causing foaming of the water and a great deal of noise. Fertilized adhesive eggs fall to the bottom and are left unattended.

HABITAT: The Bigmouth Buffalo is found in warm, **turbid** lakes and large streams.

STATUS: G5; N5; S2?; NAR (Great Lakes–Upper St. Lawrence populations).

Maximum Age: 26	Ontario Average	Ontario Record	World Record
Length:	45.0 cm (17.7 in)	91.4 cm (36.0 in)	123.0 cm (48.4 in)
Weight: Overall	–	11.1 kg (24.5 lbs)	31.9 kg (70.3 lbs)
Angling	–	–	31.9 kg (70.3 lbs)

BLACK BUFFALO *Ictiobus niger*
SMALLMOUTH BUFFALO *Ictiobus bubalus*

Ictiobus—*ictio*: fish; *bus*: bull.
niger: black.
bubalus: buffalo.

The Black and Smallmouth buffaloes were introduced into the Great Lakes in the 1920s. Genetic studies have shown that these species extensively **hybridize** with each other and with the Bigmouth Buffalo in the Great Lakes. As a result, many buffaloes are virtually impossible to identify to species in Ontario.

DESCRIPTION: The Black and Smallmouth buffaloes are large, very deep-bodied suckers. The lips of these species are thick and deeply grooved (p. 225). They have a small horizontal mouth, with the upper lip well below eye level (p. 225). The scales are large (36–39 **lateral scales**). The dorsal fin is long (26–31 rays), and the front part of it is higher than the rest of the fin. The dorsal fin is higher in females than in males. The back is black to copper, the sides are lighter, and the belly is yellow or white. The iris is usually dark. The scales are often darkly outlined, and the body may have an overall greenish cast. The pectoral, pelvic, and anal fins are dark. Minute **nuptial tubercles** may occur on the body, fins, and head during spawning.

SIMILAR SPECIES: The Common Carp and Goldfish have a **serrated** spine at the front of the dorsal and anal fins. In addition, the Common Carp has 2 **barbels** on each side of the mouth, and the Goldfish has larger scales (fewer than 32 lateral scales). The Bigmouth Buffalo has an upturned mouth with an upper lip that is level with the lower edge of the eye. The Quillback has a more silvery body, a higher dorsal ray, and paler irises and pectoral and pelvic fins.

Black Buffalo

FEEDING: These buffaloes feed on the bottom on molluscs, aquatic insects, and crustaceans. They also use their thick lips to remove algae from rocks.

REPRODUCTION: Although little is known of the spawning habits of these species in Ontario, there is movement into shallow water in spring. The eggs are scattered over the **substrate** and left unguarded.

HABITAT: These species are found in warm, **turbid** lakes and large streams.

STATUS: Black Buffalo: G5; NNA; SNA; DD.
Smallmouth Buffalo: G5; NNA; SNA.

Maximum Age: 24	Ontario Average	Ontario Record	World Record
Length:	40.0 cm (15.7 in)	67.0 cm (26.4 in)	123.0 cm (48.4 in)
Weight: Overall	–	–	37.3 kg (82.2 lbs)
Angling	–	–	37.3 kg (82.2 lbs)

BLACK REDHORSE *Moxostoma duquesnei*

Moxostoma—moxo: misspelling of *myzo*, to suck; *stoma:* mouth. *duquesnei*: named after Fort Duquesne, an old name for Pittsburgh, PA, where the **type specimen** was caught.

The Black Redhorse is one of the rarest redhorses in the Great Lakes basin, and is the rarest one in Ontario. This is likely the result of more specialized habitat requirements and greater sensitivity to environmental changes than the other redhorses.

DESCRIPTION: The Black Redhorse is a slightly deep-bodied sucker. The snout overhangs the mouth. The ridges of the lips are not broken by **transverse grooves** (p. 224). The angle of the posterior edge of the lower lip is considerably greater than 90° (120°–170°) when the mouth is closed (p. 225). Scales are large (43–51, usually 44–47, **lateral scales**), and there are 12–13 scales around the narrowest part of the caudal peduncle. The edge of the dorsal fin is usually concave, rarely straight (p. 25). The back is olive, gold, or brassy, the sides are paler, and the belly is silver or white. The scales often have a greenish or bluish cast. Young are silvery and often darkly mottled on the back and sides. The lower fins are often pale red or orange, and the tail and dorsal fins are grey, but may appear red from bleeding caused by damage when captured. During the spawning season, the male develops large **nuptial tubercles** on the anal fin and lower lobe of the tail, and minute tubercles on other fins. Females may have minute **nuptial tubercles** on the head and body.

SIMILAR SPECIES: The Northern Hog Sucker has dark markings on the fins, and forward-diagonal bars on the back and sides. The Spotted Sucker has rows of distinct dark spots on the back and sides. The Lake Chubsucker is very deep-bodied and has a smaller mouth that is upturned. The Greater, River, and Shorthead redhorses usually have a red tail. The ridges of the

Juvenille

lower lip of the Shorthead Redhorse are broken by **transverse grooves**. The Silver Redhorse is more deep-bodied, and the ridges of both lips are broken by **transverse grooves**. The Golden Redhorse is most similar, but differs in having slightly larger scales (37–45, usually 40–42, **lateral scales**).

FEEDING: The Black Redhorse sucks up bottom matter, extracting food such as aquatic plants and insects.

REPRODUCTION: In spring, males and females move into **riffles** when the water temperature reaches 13°C. Males defend a territory by chasing off other males. A female approaches a male, and a second male moves in to flank her on the opposite side. The three vibrate vigorously, and eggs and sperm are released. The fertilized eggs are left unguarded.

HABITAT: The Black Redhorse prefers the cool bottom waters of large streams with moderate flows.

STATUS: G5; N2; S2; T.

Maximum Age: 17	Ontario Average	Ontario Record	World Record
Length:	28.5 cm (11.2 in)	53.7 cm (21.1 in)	56.9 cm (22.4 in)
Weight: Overall	0.2–0.7 kg (0.4–1.5 lbs)	1.5 kg (3.4 lbs)	2.0 kg (4.4 lbs)
Angling	–	–	1.0 kg (2.2 lbs)

GOLDEN REDHORSE *Moxostoma erythrurum*

Moxostoma—moxo: misspelling of *myzo*, to suck; *stoma*: mouth.
erythrurum—erythros: red; *urus*: tail; refers to the red colour of the tail, a misnomer as the tail is actually grey.

The origin of the common name "redhorse" is unknown, but is likely derived from the horse-like head and red fins of these species.

DESCRIPTION: The Golden Redhorse is a slightly deep-bodied sucker. The ridges of the lips are not usually broken by **transverse grooves** (p. 224). The angle of the posterior edge of the lower lip is considerably greater than 90° (120°–170°) when the mouth is closed (p. 225).The scales are large (37–45, usually 40–42, **lateral scales**), and there are 12–13 scales around the narrowest part of the caudal peduncle. The edge of the dorsal fin is concave (p. 25). The back is olive to gold, the sides are bronze to yellow, and the belly is silver or white. Young are silvery and often darkly mottled on the back and sides. The lower fins are often pale red or orange, and the tail and dorsal fin are grey or olive, but may appear red from bleeding caused by damage when captured. During the spawning season, the male develops **nuptial tubercles** on the head, fins, and body. The largest tubercles are found on the head, anal fin, and lower lobe of the tail. Females may have minute **nuptial tubercles**.

SIMILAR SPECIES: The Northern Hog Sucker has dark markings on the fins, and forward-diagonal bars on the back and sides. The Spotted Sucker has rows of distinct dark spots on the back and sides. The Lake Chubsucker is very deep-bodied and has a smaller mouth that is upturned. The Greater, River, and Shorthead redhorses usually have a red tail. The lower lip of the Shorthead Redhorse has fine **transverse grooves**. The Silver Redhorse is more deep-bodied and has **transverse grooves** on both lips. The

♂ with nuptial tubercles

Juvenile

Black Redhorse is most similar, but differs in having slightly smaller scales (43–51, usually 44–47, **lateral scales**).

FEEDING: Food is sucked from the bottom and consists of aquatic insects, molluscs, and aquatic plants.

REPRODUCTION: Spawning occurs when the water temperature reaches 15°C, later in spring than for other redhorse suckers. Males are aggressive and defend sites over gravel beds in shallow streams by butting other males with their **nuptial tubercles**. A typical sucker spawning act occurs with two males flanking a single female. The threesome vibrates, and eggs and sperm are released.

HABITAT: The Golden Redhorse prefers the bottom waters of warm streams with moderate flows.

STATUS: G5; N4; S4; NAR.

Maximum Age: 11	Ontario Average	Ontario Record	World Record
Length:	33.0 cm (13.0 in)	49.5 cm (19.5 in)	78.0 cm (30.7 in)
Weight: Overall	–	–	1.9 kg (4.1 lbs)
Angling	–	–	1.9 kg (4.1 lbs)

GREATER REDHORSE *Moxostoma valenciennesi*

Moxostoma—moxo: misspelling of *myzo*, to suck; *stoma*: mouth.
valenciennesi: named after Achille Valenciennes, a French naturalist who first described this species from a Lake Ontario specimen.

The Greater Redhorse was originally thought to be rare in North America. Although still relatively rare, it has been found in many more locations as a result of using new fisheries methods to sample large, fast-flowing, deep streams.

DESCRIPTION: The Greater Redhorse is a slightly deep-bodied sucker. Most of the ridges of the lips are not broken by **transverse grooves** (p. 224). The angle of the posterior edge of the lower lip is considerably greater than 90° (110°–170°) when the mouth is closed (p. 225). The head is large (23–26% of **standard length**). The scales are large (41–45 **lateral scales**), and there are 15–16 scales around the narrowest part of the caudal peduncle**.** The edge of the dorsal fin is usually straight or rounded (p. 25). The back is bronze to olive-green, the sides are silver or golden, and the belly is silver or white. All fins are red or orange in life. The juvenile is silvery and often darkly mottled on the back and sides. Spawning males develop large **nuptial tubercles** on the anal fin and lower lobe of the tail.

SIMILAR SPECIES: The Northern Hog Sucker has dark markings on the fins, and forward-diagonal bars on the back and sides. The Spotted Sucker has rows of dark spots on the back and sides. The Lake Chubsucker has a very deep body and a smaller mouth that is upturned. All other redhorses in Ontario have 12–14 scales around the narrowest part of the caudal peduncle. In addition, the Black, Golden, and Silver redhorses have grey tails. The Shorthead Redhorse has a smaller head and smaller lips, and the ridges of the lower lip are broken by **transverse grooves**. In the River Redhorse, the edge of the dorsal fin is often concave.

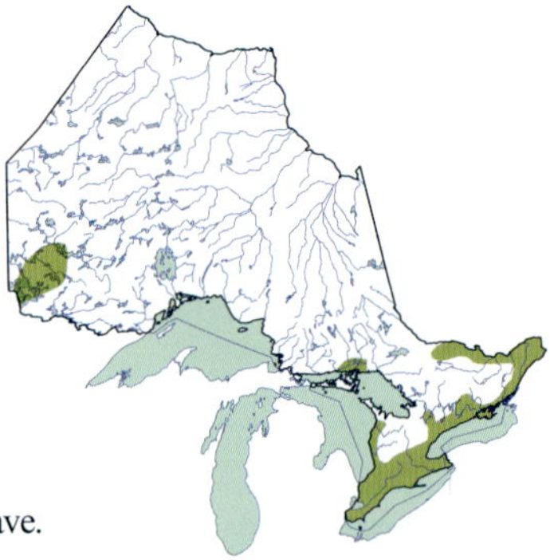

Juvenile

FEEDING: Food is taken from the bottom and consists of aquatic insects, molluscs, crustaceans, and aquatic plants.

REPRODUCTION: Spawning occurs in late spring to early summer when the water temperature reaches 13°C. An upstream migration occurs into suitable habitats of rocky **substrates**, often in **riffles**. The female enters the spawning site and is flanked by two or more males. The males may break the surface of the water and roll over each other vying for position. The males press against the female, they vibrate, and eggs and sperm are released into the **substrate**. The fertilized eggs are left unguarded.

HABITAT: The Greater Redhorse prefers the cool bottom waters of large streams with substantial flows.

STATUS: G4; N4; S3.

Maximum Age: 28	Ontario Average	Ontario Record	World Record
Length:	41.0 cm (16.1 in)	68.8 cm (27.1 in)	80.0 cm (31.5 in)
Weight: Overall	1.0 kg (2.2 lbs)	7.2 kg (16.0 lbs)	7.2 kg (16.0 lbs)
Angling	–	–	4.2 kg (9.2 lbs)

LAKE CHUBSUCKER *Erimyzon sucetta*

Erimyzon—*eri*: very; *myzo*: to suck; refers to the sucking lips. *sucetta:* from the French *sucet*, to suck.

Wetlands, the preferred habitat of Lake Chubsucker, are among the most degraded aquatic habitats in the Great Lakes basin. As a result, the Lake Chubsucker is one of the rarest fishes in Ontario.

DESCRIPTION: The Lake Chubsucker is a small, very deep-bodied sucker that is thin from side to side. The mouth is small and slightly upturned. The scales are large (33–45 **lateral scales**, usually 35–41), and there is no **lateral line**. It has a large, rounded dorsal fin (p. 25). The back and upper sides are bronze to deep olive-green and have a vague cross-hatched pattern in adults. The lower sides are gold to silver, and the belly is green-yellow to yellow. The juvenile has a black stripe along the front edge of the dorsal fin and a wide, prominent black lateral stripe that terminates in a dark spot at the base of the tail. During spawning season, the male becomes dark overall and develops large **nuptial tubercles** on the snout and anal fin.

SIMILAR SPECIES: Minnows with distinct lateral stripes have thin lips without ridges or **papillae**. The Quillback and buffaloes have deeper bodies and a longer dorsal fin with more than 20 rays. The Northern Hog Sucker, redhorse suckers, and Spotted Sucker are less deep-bodied and have a large mouth that is not upturned. In addition, redhorse suckers have a **lateral line**, and the Spotted Sucker has rows of distinct dark spots along the sides of the body.

FEEDING: The Lake Chubsucker is **omnivorous**, feeding on the bottom on small crustaceans, molluscs, aquatic insects, **filamentous algae**, and plant matter.

REPRODUCTION: The Lake Chubsucker spawns in spring. Eggs are broadcast over vegetation and left unguarded.

Juvenile

HABITAT: The Lake Chubsucker requires the warm, clear, heavily vegetated wetlands in the Great Lakes and their tributaries.

STATUS: G5; N2; S2; E.

Maximum Age: 8	Ontario Average	Ontario Record	World Record
Length:	20.0 cm (7.9 in)	28.0 cm (11.0 in)	41.0 cm (16.1 in)
Weight: Overall	–	–	0.9 kg (2.0 lbs)

LONGNOSE SUCKER *Catostomus catostomus*

Catostomus—cato: beneath; *stomus*: mouth. The position of the mouth is low on the head.

The Longnose Sucker and White Sucker often spawn in the same streams at the same time of year. **Hybridization** is minimized, as the Longnose Sucker generally spawns several days before the White Sucker.

DESCRIPTION: The Longnose Sucker is a slightly deep-bodied fish. The long snout greatly overhangs the mouth. Scales are very small (91–120 **lateral scales**). The back and sides are dark olive, grey, or black, with brassy reflections, and the belly is cream-coloured to white. The juvenile is mottled on the back and sides. During the spawning season, the back is green-gold to coppery brown in the female and almost black in the male. A red or pink stripe, which is more intense in the male, extends along the side from the snout to the tail. The lower body and fins may be pink, orange, and yellow. The male develops **nuptial tubercles** on the head, anal fin, and lower lobe of the tail.

SIMILAR SPECIES: In Ontario, the Longnose Sucker is most similar to the White Sucker, but it can be readily distinguished from this, and all other Ontario suckers, by its long snout and very small scales.

FEEDING: Food taken from the bottom sediments includes aquatic insects, worms, other **invertebrates**, and plants.

REPRODUCTION: The Longnose Sucker spawns for about a week in spring as soon as the water temperature exceeds 5°C. Several males crowd around a female, clasping and pressing her with their fins. The group vibrates vigorously, and eggs and sperm are released. Each spawning act lasts 3–5 seconds and may occur up to 60 times in an hour for both females and males. The adhesive eggs are left unguarded and hatch in a few weeks.

Juvenile

Spawning

HABITAT: The Longnose Sucker prefers the cold bottom waters of lakes and streams. In southern Ontario, it is largely limited to lakes except during spring spawning runs into tributaries.

STATUS: G5; N5; S5.

Maximum Age: 20	Ontario Average	Ontario Record	World Record
Length:	33.5 cm (13.2 in)	50.5 cm (19.9 in)	64.0 cm (25.2 in)
Weight: Overall	0.3 kg (0.7 lbs)	–	3.3 kg (7.3 lbs)
Angling	–	–	3.0 kg (6.5 lbs)

NORTHERN HOG SUCKER *Hypentelium nigricans*

Hypentelium—*hypo*: under; *pent*: five; *elium*: lobes; inaccurately refers to the shape of the lower lip.
nigricans: blackish.

Suckers are the preferred live bait of anglers fishing for Northern Pike. The Northern Hog Sucker is often found in bait shops in southern Ontario.

DESCRIPTION: The Northern Hog Sucker is a slightly deep-bodied fish with a long tubular snout. The lips are large and fleshy with **papillae** (p. 224). The eyes are high on the head and, in individuals longer than 5 cm, the head is flat or concave between the eyes when viewed from the front. The scales are medium-sized (44–54 **lateral scales**). The back is olive, grey, or brown, the sides are lighter brown to yellow, with a brassy sheen, and the belly is white or silvery. Two to five forward-diagonal bars are present on the back and sides except in individuals longer than 30 cm. The tail and dorsal, pectoral, and pelvic fins have dark markings. During the spawning season, the male develops large **nuptial tubercles** on the anal fin and tail and smaller ones on the body, other fins, and head. Females develop small tubercles on the lower fins.

SIMILAR SPECIES: All other suckers have lower fins without distinct dark markings, and lack forward-diagonal bars on the back and sides. The White and Longnose suckers have smaller scales, and the redhorse suckers usually have lips with ridges instead of **papillae**.

FEEDING: The Northern Hog Sucker feeds on algae, aquatic insects, and crustaceans that are suctioned up as it roots through rubble.

REPRODUCTION: Spawning occurs in spring when the water temperature reaches 16°C. Females move into **riffles** of shallow streams over fine gravel.

Juvenile

Juvenile top view

Several males crowd around a female, often head-down with their tails thrashing out of the water. Eggs and sperm are released, and the non-adhesive fertilized eggs are abandoned.

HABITAT: The Northern Hog Sucker is found on the bottom of warm, shallow streams and, rarely, lakes.

STATUS: G5; N4; S4.

Maximum Age: 11	Ontario Average	Ontario Record	World Record
Length:	19.0 cm (7.5 in)	38.0 cm (15.0 in)	61.0 cm (24.0 in)
Weight: Overall	–	0.7 kg (1.5 lbs)	0.8 kg (1.8 lbs)
Angling	–	–	0.8 kg (1.8 lbs)

QUILLBACK *Carpiodes cyprinus*

Carpiodes: carp-like.
cyprinus: **genus** name of the carp, as it has a similar appearance to this species.

There are three carpsucker species in North America. These species get this name from their sucker-like mouths and carp-like dorsal fins. The Quillback is the only carpsucker species found in Canada.

DESCRIPTION: The Quillback is a silvery and very deep-bodied sucker, which is thin from side to side. The rounded snout greatly overhangs the small mouth. The scales are large (35–41 **lateral scales**). The dorsal fin is long (25–30 rays), and the front part of it is pointed and much higher than the rest of the fin. The back is olive, grey, beige, or light brown, the sides are silvery, and the belly is cream-coloured to white. The iris is usually silvery or white. The pectoral and pelvic fins are colourless, orange, or grey. The male develops **nuptial tubercles** on the lower half of the head, throat, and dorsal, pectoral, and pelvic fins.

SIMILAR SPECIES: The Common Carp and Goldfish have a **serrated** spine at the front of the dorsal and anal fins, and the snout does not overhang the mouth. In addition, the Common Carp also has 2 **barbels** on each side of the mouth, and the Goldfish has larger scales (25–32 **lateral scales**). The buffaloes and their **hybrids** have dark irises, a lower dorsal fin, and darker, less silvery bodies with darker pectoral, pelvic, and anal fins. The Bigmouth Buffalo has a larger upturned mouth.

FEEDING: Food is taken from the bottom sediments and includes plant material, aquatic insects, and other **invertebrates**.

REPRODUCTION: Quillback migrate upstream in spring to flooded areas

Juvenile

Fry

in streams or lakes. Spawning occurs when water temperatures are above 18°C. Eggs are randomly deposited over sand and mud bottoms and left unguarded.

HABITAT: The Quillback is found in the cool bottom waters of lakes and large slow-moving streams.

STATUS: G5; N5; S4.

Maximum Age: 11	Ontario Average	Ontario Record	World Record
Length:	31.5 cm (12.4 in)	62.0 cm (24.4 in)	66.0 cm (26.0 in)
Weight: Overall	1.8–2.3 kg (4–6 lbs)	2.7 kg (6.0 lbs)	3.7 kg (8.1 lbs)
Angling	–	–	3.7 kg (8.1 lbs)

RIVER REDHORSE *Moxostoma carinatum*

Moxostoma—moxo: misspelling of *myzo*, to suck; *stoma*: mouth. *carinatum—carina*; refers to the ridges on the skull.

The River Redhorse has a very unusual, fragmented distribution in Ontario. The reasons for this enigmatic distribution are unknown, but may be related to its specialized habitat or climate changes since the last Ice Age.

DESCRIPTION: The River Redhorse is a slightly deep-bodied, silvery sucker. The snout greatly overhangs the upper lip. The ridges of both lips are rarely broken by **transverse grooves** (p. 224). The angle of the posterior edge of the lower lip is considerably greater than 90° (100°–170°) when the mouth is closed (p. 225). The head is large (21–27%, usually 23–26%, of **standard length**). Scales are large (41–46, usually 42–44, **lateral scales**), and there are 12–13 scales around the narrowest part of the caudal peduncle. The edge of the dorsal fin is usually concave or straight (p. 25). The back is bronze to olive-green, the sides are silver or gold, and the belly is silver or white. The lower fins are usually pale red or orange, and the tail and dorsal fins are red. The juvenile is silvery or brassy, and often darkly mottled on the back and sides. During the spawning season, the male develops large **nuptial tubercles** on the snout, anal fin, and lower lobe of the tail, and minute tubercles on its other fins. Females may have inconspicuous **nuptial tubercles** on the anal fin.

SIMILAR SPECIES: The Northern Hog Sucker has dark markings on the fins, and forward-diagonal bars on the back and sides. The Spotted Sucker has rows of distinct dark spots on the back and sides. The Lake Chubsucker has a very deep body and a smaller mouth that is upturned. The Black, Golden, and Silver redhorses have a grey tail. The Shorthead Redhorse has a smaller head and lips, and the ridges of the lower lip are broken

Spawning ♂ with nuptial tubercles

by **transverse grooves**. The Greater Redhorse has 15–16 scales around the narrowest part of the caudal peduncle, and the edge of the dorsal fin is usually straight or rounded.

FEEDING: The molar-like **pharyngeal teeth** of the River Redhorse crush large molluscs that are taken from the bottom. Aquatic insects and crustaceans are also consumed.

REPRODUCTION: Spring spawning migration occurs when the water temperature reaches 18°C. The male arrives first over gravel-bottomed **riffles**. When a female approaches the male, he swims rapidly back and forth and is joined by a second male who synchronizes his movements. The female then assumes a position between the males. The three vibrate vigorously, and eggs and sperm are released.

HABITAT: The River Redhorse prefers the cool bottom waters of very large streams with substantial flows.

STATUS: G4; N2N3; S2; SC.

Maximum Age: 28	Ontario Average	Ontario Record	World Record
Length:	58.0 cm (22.8 in)	81.3 cm (32.0 in)	81.3 cm (32.0 in)
Weight: Overall	–	5.5 kg (12.1 lbs)	7.7 kg (17.1 lbs)
Angling	–	5.5 kg (12.1 lbs)	7.7 kg (17.1 lbs)

SHORTHEAD REDHORSE *Moxostoma macrolepidotum*

Moxostoma—moxo: misspelling of *myzo*, to suck; *stoma*: mouth.
macrolepidotum—macro: long (often mistakenly used to mean large); *lepido*: scale; refers to the large scales.

In the past, large numbers of redhorses were commercially harvested in the Great Lakes (termed "mullet" in the trade) for fertilizers, pet food, and even human consumption. Shorthead and Silver redhorses were the main species harvested.

DESCRIPTION: The Shorthead Redhorse is a slightly deep-bodied sucker with a small head. The ridges of the lower lip are broken by **transverse grooves** (p. 224). The angle of the posterior edge of the lower lip is nearly straight (140°–180°) when the mouth is closed (p. 225). The head is small (18–25%, usually 19.5–22.5%, of **standard length**). The scales are large (39–46, usually 42–44, **lateral scales**), and there are 12–14 scales around the narrowest part of the caudal peduncle. The edge of the dorsal fin is concave (p. 25). The back is dark olive to tan, the sides are yellow or silvery, often with a copper or greenish cast, and the belly is silver or white. All fins, including the dorsal fin and tail, are orange or red, although the colour may quickly disappear after death. The juvenile is silvery and often darkly mottled on the back and sides. During the spawning season, the male develops large **nuptial tubercles** on the anal fin and lower lobe of the tail, and minute tubercles on the head, body, and other fins.

SIMILAR SPECIES: The Northern Hog Sucker has dark markings on the fins, and forward-diagonal bars on the back and sides. The Spotted Sucker has rows of distinct dark spots on the back and sides. The Lake Chubsucker has a very deep body and a smaller mouth that is upturned. The Black, Golden, and Silver redhorses have grey tails. The lower lips of all other redhorses, except the Silver Redhorse, are not broken by **transverse grooves**. The

Juvenile

Silver Redhorse is more deep-bodied, the posterior edge of the lower lip is slightly greater than 90°, and the ridges of the upper lip are broken by **transverse grooves**. The Greater and River redhorses have larger heads. The Greater Redhorse has more scales (15–16) around the narrowest part of the caudal peduncle.

FEEDING: Food consists of aquatic insects, molluscs, and crustaceans sucked up from the bottom.

REPRODUCTION: Spawning migration occurs in spring from larger bodies of water into streams. Males arrive first and defend territories in **riffles** over gravel. The female is flanked by two males as she enters the spawning grounds. The males press against her, they vibrate, and eggs and sperm are released. The fertilized eggs are left in the gravel unguarded.

HABITAT: The Shorthead Redhorse prefers the cool bottom waters of large lakes and streams.

STATUS: G5; N5; S5.

Maximum Age: 20	Ontario Average	Ontario Record	World Record
Length:	41.0 cm (16.1 in)	61.5 cm (24.2 in)	75.0 cm (29.5 in)
Weight: Overall	–	2.5 kg (5.6 lbs)	2.7 kg (6.0 lbs)
Angling	–	2.5 kg (5.6 lbs)	2.5 kg (5.6 lbs)

SILVER REDHORSE *Moxostoma anisurum*

Moxostoma—moxo: misspelling of *myzo*, to suck; *stoma*: mouth. *anisurum—aniso*: unequal; *uro*: tail. The upper and lower tail lobes are not equal in length.

All six redhorse species in Ontario have similar habitats and diets. In some rivers, as many as six redhorse species are known to occur in the same stretch of stream. In many cases, only very small differences in their habitat and food preferences allow them to co-exist.

DESCRIPTION: The Silver Redhorse is a deep-bodied, silvery sucker. The snout does not overhang, or only slightly overhangs, the mouth. Both upper and lower lips have ridges that are broken with numerous fine **transverse grooves** (p. 224). The angle of the posterior edge of the lower lip is only slightly greater than 90° when the mouth is closed (p. 225). The scales are large (38–48, usually 40–42, **lateral scales**), and there are 12–13 scales around the narrowest part of the caudal peduncle. The edge of the dorsal fin is straight or rounded (p. 25). The back is bronze to olive-green, the sides are silver or gold, and the belly is silver or white. The lower fins are often pale red or orange, and the tail and dorsal fin are grey, but may appear red from bleeding caused by damage when captured. The juvenile is silvery and often darkly mottled on the back and sides. During the spawning season, the male develops **nuptial tubercles** on the anal fin and lower lobe of the tail, and many tubercles on the body and other fins. Females may have inconspicuous **nuptial tubercles** on the anal fin.

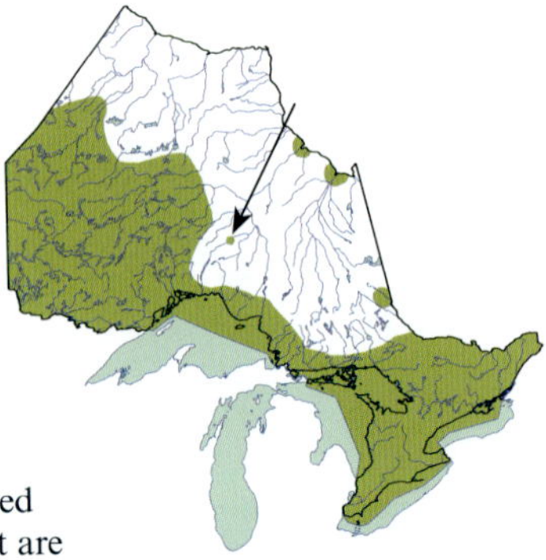

SIMILAR SPECIES: The Northern Hog Sucker has dark markings on the fins, and forward-diagonal bars on the back and sides. The Spotted Sucker has rows of distinct dark spots on the back and sides. The Lake Chubsucker has a very deep body and a smaller mouth that is upturned. The Greater, River, and Shorthead redhorses usually have a red tail, and an upper lip with ridges that are

Juvenile

not broken by **transverse grooves**. The Black and Golden redhorses are more slender, and the ridges of both lips are not broken by **transverse grooves**. The Black, Golden, and Shorthead redhorses usually have a concave dorsal fin edge.

FEEDING: The Silver Redhorse sucks aquatic insects, molluscs, and crustaceans from the bottom.

REPRODUCTION: Spawning occurs in spring when the water temperature reaches 13°C. Males and females move into the main channel of swift-flowing streams. After spawning occurs, the fertilized eggs are abandoned.

HABITAT: The Silver Redhorse prefers the cool bottom waters of large streams and lakes.

STATUS: G5; N5; S4.

Maximum Age: 25	Ontario Average	Ontario Record	World Record
Length:	40.0 cm (15.7 in)	71.1 cm (28.0 in)	74.0 cm (29.1 in)
Weight: Overall	0.7 kg (1.5 lbs)	4.3 kg (9.5 lbs)	10.8 kg (23.8 lbs)
Angling	–	4.3 kg (9.5 lbs)	5.2 kg (11.4 lbs)

SPOTTED SUCKER *Minytrema melanops*

Minytrema—miny: small; *trema*: hole; refers to the reduced **lateral line**.
melanops—melan: black; *ops*: eyes or spots; refers to the rows of dark spots on the body.

The Spotted Sucker was first discovered in Canada in 1962. Since that first discovery in Lake Erie, it has also been found in Lake St. Clair and its tributaries.

DESCRIPTION: The Spotted Sucker is a slightly deep-bodied fish. The snout only slightly overhangs the mouth. The lips have both **plicae** and **papillae** (p. 225). The scales are large (42–47 **lateral scales**), and there are 16 scales around the narrowest part of the caudal peduncle. The back varies in colour from olive to brown, the sides are silver, bronze-green, or copper-coloured, and the belly is grey, white, or silver. There are 8–12 rows of distinct dark spots on the back and sides. These are faint in small juveniles. The fins are usually dark, although the pectoral and pelvic fins may also be white. Spawning males have 2 dark lateral stripes separated by a pinkish grey stripe. Females may also have this pinkish stripe. **Nuptial tubercles** are most prominent on the anal fin and head of the male.

SIMILAR SPECIES: The White and Longnose suckers have smaller scales. The Lake Chubsucker has a very deep body and a more upturned mouth. The Northern Hog Sucker and redhorses lack regular rows of distinct dark spots.

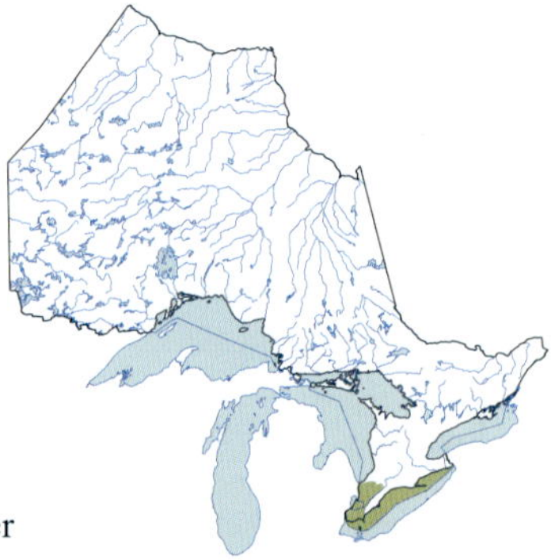

FEEDING: The Spotted Sucker feeds on aquatic insects, molluscs, crustaceans, and algae that are sucked from the bottom.

REPRODUCTION: Spawning occurs in spring when the water temperature reaches 12°C. Males and females congregate in shallow **riffles** of streams where males defend a territory from other males. A female settles on the bottom with one or two males by her

Large juvenile

side. Nudging and pressing against her body, the males propel the spawning group to the surface, releasing eggs and sperm. Eggs are adhesive and left unguarded.

HABITAT: The Spotted Sucker prefers the warm bottom waters of lakes and large streams.

STATUS: G5; N2; S2; SC.

Maximum Age: 6	Ontario Average	Ontario Record	World Record
Length:	31.0 cm (12.2 in)	51.0 cm (20.1 in)	51.0 cm (20.1 in)
Weight: Overall	0.2–0.7 kg (0.4–1.5 lbs)	–	2.4 kg (5.2 lbs)
Angling	–	–	2.4 kg (5.2 lbs)

WHITE SUCKER *Catostomus commersonii*

Catostomus—*cato*: beneath; *stomus*: mouth. The position of the mouth is low on the head.
commersonii: named after Philibert Commerson, a French naturalist.

The White Sucker is one of the most common and widespread fishes in Ontario. It is probably best known for its large spawning migrations into even the smallest streams in spring.

DESCRIPTION: The White Sucker is a slightly deep-bodied fish. The snout overhangs the mouth. The scales are small (53–85 **lateral scales**). The back and upper sides are grey, brown, or black. The lower sides and belly are cream-coloured to white. The pectoral, pelvic, and anal fins are often orange. The juvenile is usually mottled on the back and sides, which often have 3 prominent black spots. During the spawning season, the male has a prominent, wide pale stripe on each side of the back and a dark lateral stripe. It develops prominent **nuptial tubercles** on the anal fin, lower lobe of the tail, and some scales behind the anal fin. There are minute **nuptial tubercles** on the lower head and throat. Females may have poorly developed **nuptial tubercles**.

SIMILAR SPECIES: All other suckers, except the Longnose Sucker and some Northern Hog Suckers, have larger scales than White Suckers. In Ontario, the White Sucker is most similar to the Longnose Sucker, which differs in having smaller scales (more than 90 **lateral scales**) and a snout that greatly overhangs the mouth.

FEEDING: The White Sucker feeds from the bottom on aquatic insects, small crustaceans, molluscs, other **invertebrates**, and plants. Although it also feeds on fish eggs, they likely represent a very small proportion of its diet.

REPRODUCTION: In early spring, when the water temperature reaches

Juveniles

Juvenile

Spawning ♂ with minnows

10°C, White Suckers typically migrate upstream in schools to suitable spawning grounds. Several males crowd around a female, pressing and holding her, with the aid of **nuptial tubercles,** on the anal fins and tails. An individual may spawn up to 40 times in an hour, and the spawning season may last up to a month. Fertilized eggs adhere to the gravel and hatch within two weeks.

HABITAT: Although it prefers cool water, the White Sucker is found in a wide range of habitats in Ontario, and is never far from the bottom.

STATUS: G5; N5; S5.

Maximum Age: 17	Ontario Average	Ontario Record	World Record
Length:	41.0 cm (16.1 in)	61.0 cm (24.0 in)	64.0 cm (25.2 in)
Weight: Overall	0.5 kg (1.1 lbs)	2.6 kg (5.1 lbs)	2.9 kg (6.5 lbs)
Angling	–	2.6 kg (5.8 lbs)	2.9 kg (6.5 lbs)

ICTALURIDAE
North American Catfishes

As their name suggests, catfishes have the appearance of a whiskered cat, as their mouths are surrounded by eight **barbels**. This is a North American family, occurring from southern Canada to Guatemala. Catfishes have an adipose fin, spines on the leading edges of the dorsal and pectoral fins, and no scales. Several species not found in Canada live in caves and lack eyes.

Catfishes are known to have very keen senses, particularly taste and smell. Known as "swimming tongues," Channel Catfish have large numbers of taste buds covering their entire body, with the greatest number, 25 buds per square millimetre, occurring on the **barbels**. Their taste buds can detect a substance in the water at concentrations of one part per billion parts of water, giving them the keenest sense of taste of any vertebrate, including sharks. Their exceptional senses enable catfishes to find food in dark or muddy waters, even at great distances. Anglers often take advantage of their keen senses by presenting stinkbaits or other bait with a strong odour.

The Flathead Catfish is one of the newest additions to the fauna of Ontario. Although several adults have been caught in the Canadian waters of Lake Erie since the 1980s, the capture of two juveniles in the lower Thames River since 2016 strongly indicates that reproduction has occurred in Ontario.

There are 52 species of North American Catfishes, 10 of which are found in Ontario.

< Brown Bullhead

Adipose fins and tails

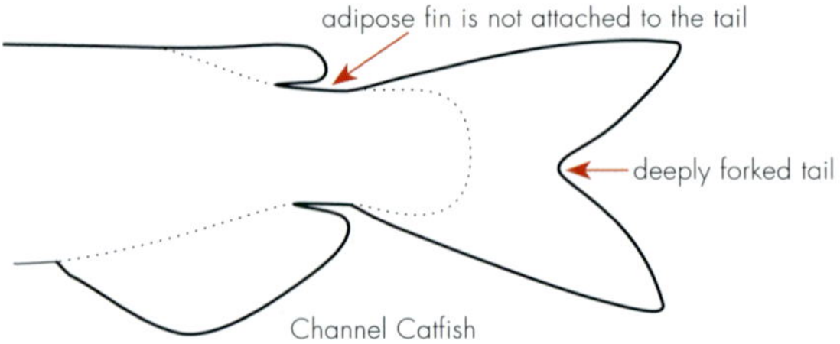

Channel Catfish

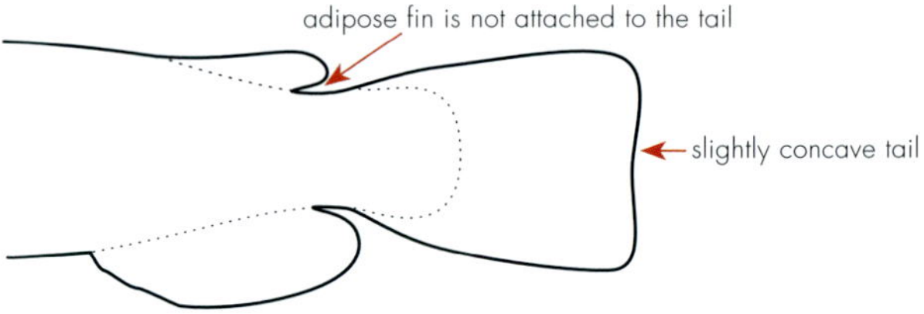

e.g., Brown Bullhead

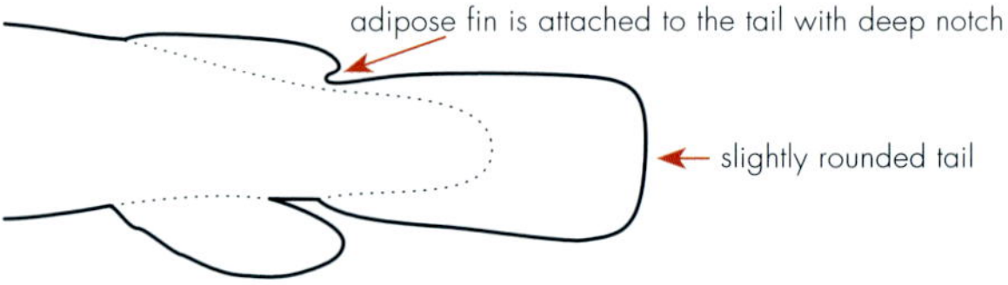

Northern Madtom

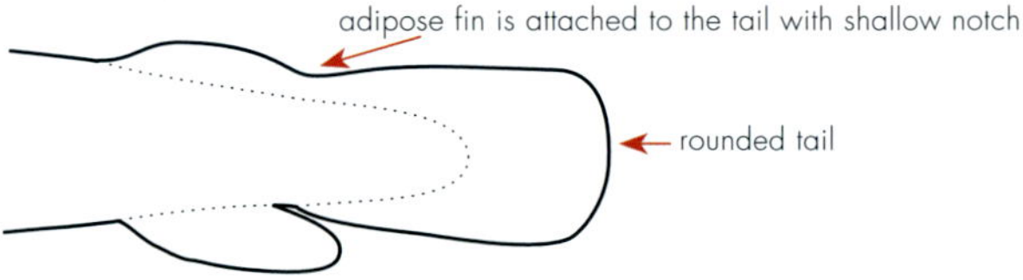

e.g., Tadpole Madtom

Pectoral fins

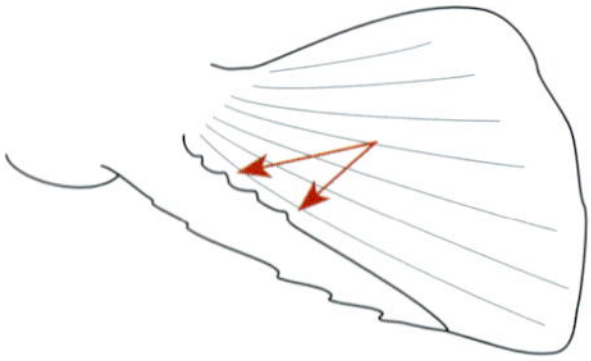

weakly **serrated** pectoral spine

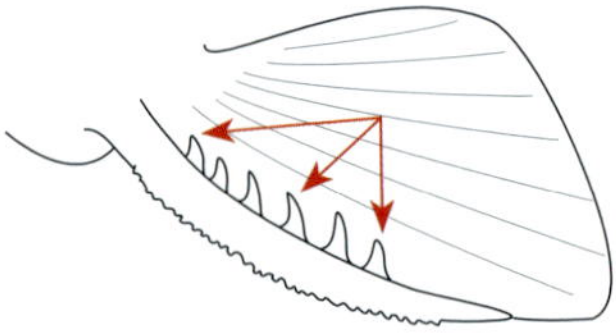

strongly **serrated** pectoral spine

Pectoral spines

Channel Catfish

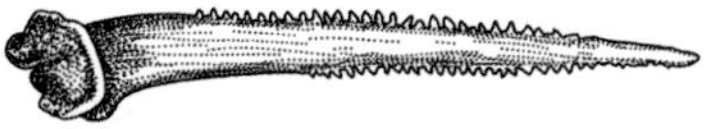

Flathead Catfish

Black Bullhead

Brown Bullhead

Yellow Bullhead

Brindled Madtom

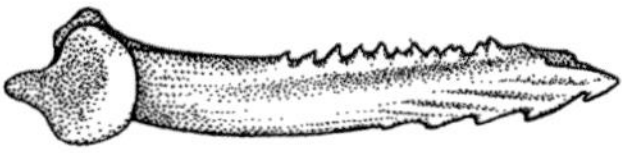

Margined Madtom

Northern Madtom

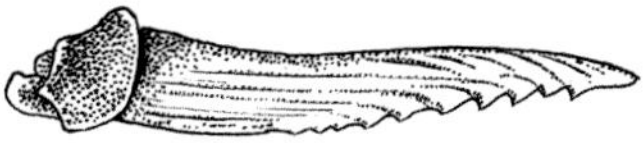

Stonecat

Tadpole Madtom

BLACK BULLHEAD *Ameiurus melas*

Ameiurus—*a*: without; *meiurus*: curtailed; refers to the slightly rounded edge of the tail.
melas: black.

The bullheads likely derive their common name from their large head relative to their body. Bullheads are the catfishes most commonly caught by anglers in Ontario.

DESCRIPTION: The Black Bullhead is a robust, dark catfish. The lower jaw does not protrude. It has 4 pairs of dark **barbels**. The top of the head is rounded. The body lacks scales. The back is olive to black, the sides are lighter, and the belly is white or yellow. There is usually a pale bar at the base of the tail. The adipose fin is not attached to the tail, which is square or slightly concave (p. 256). The **fin membranes** are usually intense black and are darker than the fin rays. The leading edges of the dorsal and pectoral fins each have a spine (p. 256). The pectoral spines are smooth or weakly **serrated** on the posterior edges (p. 257). The anal fin is short, never reaching the tail when depressed. Spawning males become black with a bright yellow or white belly.

SIMILAR SPECIES: Madtoms have adipose fins that are attached to the tail. The Channel Catfish has a deeply forked tail. The Flathead Catfish has a flattened head, protruding lower jaw, and in young, a white patch on the upper lobe of the tail. The Yellow Bullhead has pale **barbels** on the chin, and the anal fin reaches the tail when depressed. The Brown and Yellow bullheads lack the pale bar at the base of the tail, usually have grey **fin membranes**, and have stronger **serrations** on the posterior edges of their pectoral spines.

FEEDING: The Black Bullhead is secretive during the day and feeds almost exclusively at night. It is **omnivorous**, feeding on almost anything it can find on the bottom, including crustaceans, worms, molluscs, **larval** insects, aquatic plants, small fishes, and fish eggs.

On nest

REPRODUCTION: The Black Bullhead spawns in late spring when the water temperature reaches 21°C. The female prepares a saucer-shaped nest in mud, sand, or gravel by pushing pebbles away with her mouth and fanning smaller objects away with her tail. The male enters the nest, the two nudge each other, and the male wraps his tail over her head. Eggs and sperm are released during several spawning acts, and the pair guards the eggs and fans them to clear debris. They hatch in about a week, with the parents continuing to guard the young **fry** that remain together in tight balls or schools. After a few weeks, the young leave the nest area to fend for themselves.

HABITAT: The Black Bullhead lives on the bottom in warm, shallow lakes and slow-moving streams. It prefers some form of cover, such as aquatic plants or fallen trees.

STATUS: G5; N5; S4.

Maximum Age: 10	Ontario Average	Ontario Record	World Record
Length:	15.5 cm (6.1 in)	26.0 cm (10.2 in)	66.0 cm (26.0 in)
Weight: Overall	0.2 kg (0.4 lbs)	–	3.7 kg (8.1 lbs)
Angling	–	–	3.7 kg (8.1 lbs)

BRINDLED MADTOM *Noturus miurus*

Noturus—*noto*: back; *uro*: tail. The adipose fin and tail fin are attached as one.
miurus—*miuros*: curtailed; refers to the short body.

The Brindled Madtom was once considered very rare in Canada, largely as a result of its cryptic behaviour of hiding in crevices of various structures. Recent sampling using collecting gear better suited to its behaviour has indicated that it is not as rare as once thought.

DESCRIPTION: The Brindled Madtom is a small, slightly deep-bodied catfish. The snout overhangs the mouth. The body lacks scales. The adipose fin is attached to the tail, and there is a shallow notch where they join (p. 256). The posterior edge of the tail is rounded (p. 256). The leading edge of the dorsal and pectoral fins each have a spine. The pectoral spines have large **serrations** on their posterior edges (p. 257). The back is pale with 2–3 large dark saddles, the sides are pale with small irregular dark spots, and the belly is white or pale yellow. Dorsal and adipose fins with black blotches that extend to fin margins.

SIMILAR SPECIES: The Channel Catfish, Flathead Catfish, and bullheads have adipose fins that are not attached to the tail. The Stonecat, Tadpole Madtom, and Margined Madtom are uniform brown or grey without obvious saddles. The Northern Madtom has a deep notch where the adipose fin joins the tail, small light spots in front of the dorsal fin, and dorsal and adipose fins with black blotches that do not extend to fin margins.

FEEDING: The Brindled Madtom is nocturnal, hiding on the bottom during the day and feeding on aquatic insects and crustaceans at night. Prey is frequently scavenged from the bottom with the aid of its sensitive **barbels**.

REPRODUCTION: Spawning occurs throughout the summer when the water temperature reaches 24°C. Nests are prepared in cavities under stones or debris. The male guards the eggs and young for several weeks once they hatch.

HABITAT: The Brindled Madtom lives on bottoms of sand, gravel, and woody debris in the warm shallows of slow-moving streams.

STATUS: G5; N2; S2; NAR.

Maximum Age: 3	Ontario Average	Ontario Record	World Record
Length:	7.0 cm (2.8 in)	12.2 cm (4.8 in)	13.0 cm (5.1 in)

BROWN BULLHEAD *Ameiurus nebulosus*

Ameiurus—*a*: without; *meiurus*: curtailed; refers to the slightly rounded edge of the tail.
nebulosus: cloudy; refers to the mottled colour pattern.

To protect themselves from predators, young bullheads are often found in large schools that superficially resemble large masses of tadpoles. Such schools are best viewed nearshore at night by flashlight. Watch out for water snakes—a common nocturnal predator of the bullhead.

DESCRIPTION: The Brown Bullhead is a robust, dark catfish. The snout overhangs the mouth. It has 4 pairs of dark **barbels**; however, the base of the **barbels** on the chin may be pale. The top of the head is rounded. The body lacks scales. The back is yellowish brown, olive, or grey, to almost blue-black, the sides are often mottled with faint brown blotches, and the belly is pale yellow or white. The adipose fin is not attached to the tail (p. 256), and the end of the tail is square or slightly concave (p. 256). The **fin membranes** are not obviously darker than the fin rays. The leading edges of the dorsal and pectoral fins each have a spine. The pectoral spines have large **serrations** on their posterior edges (p. 257). The anal fin is short, never reaching the tail when depressed.

SIMILAR SPECIES: Madtoms have an adipose fin that is attached to the tail. The Flathead Catfish has a flattened head, protruding lower jaw, and in young, a white patch on the upper lobe of the tail. The Channel Catfish has a deeply forked tail. The Yellow Bullhead has chin **barbels** that are pale along their entire length and an anal fin that reaches the tail when depressed. The Black Bullhead usually has a pale bar at the base of the tail, **fin membranes** obviously darker than fin rays, and weak **serrations** on the posterior edge of the pectoral spine.

Juvenile

FEEDING: The Brown Bullhead is an **opportunist**, feeding on crustaceans, worms, insect **larvae**, crayfishes, small fishes, fish eggs, and plant material. Prey is frequently scavenged from the bottom at night with the aid of sensitive **barbels**.

REPRODUCTION: The Brown Bullhead spawns in late spring and early summer when the water temperature reaches 21°C. Males and/or females clear stones to prepare saucer-shaped nests in the shallows of lakes or in stream banks. Nests have even been found in rubber tire bumpers along docks. The male and female caress each other with their **barbels**, hover side by side over the nest, facing opposite directions, and release eggs and sperm. Both parents care for the eggs by fanning them with their pelvic fins. Once the eggs hatch, the parents keep the young in tight balls by swimming around them. Young are guarded by the parents until they reach about 50 mm in length, and strays may be picked up in the parents' mouths and returned to the school.

HABITAT: The Brown Bullhead lives on the bottom of warm, shallow lakes and slow-moving streams. It prefers some form of cover, such as aquatic plants or fallen trees.

STATUS: G5; N5; S5.

Maximum Age: 11	Ontario Average	Ontario Record	World Record
Length:	28.0 cm (11.0 in)	44.6 cm (17.6 in)	55.0 cm (21.7 in)
Weight: Overall	0.3–0.5 kg (0.7–1.1)	1.5 kg (3.4 lbs)	3.4 kg (7.4 lbs)
Angling	–	1.5 kg (3.4 lbs)	3.4 kg (7.4 lbs)

CHANNEL CATFISH *Ictalurus punctatus*

Ictalurus—ich: fish; *ailouros*: cat; hence catfish.
punctatus—punctum: spot; refers to the spotted colour pattern.

This is the largest catfish native to Canada. It has a small but dedicated following of anglers who fish for it. Every year, "mudcat" fishing derbies are held for this species in Ontario.

DESCRIPTION: The Channel Catfish is an elongate fish with a forked tail. The snout overhangs the mouth. There are 4 pairs of dark **barbels** around the mouth. The top of the head is rounded. The body lacks scales. The adipose fin is not attached to the tail (p. 256). The forked tail has pointed lobes (p. 256). The back is pale blue, pale olive, or grey. The sides are lighter, often with black spots, and the belly is greyish to yellow to silver white. Spawning males may be brighter blue. Albinos are sometimes encountered.

SIMILAR SPECIES: All other Ontario catfishes have tails that are rounded, slightly concave, or square.

FEEDING: The Channel Catfish, an **opportunist**, feeds during night or day by sight, as well as by touch and taste, by using its sensitive **barbels**. Its diet consists of a wide variety of **invertebrates**, fishes, and plant material. Larger Channel Catfish feed almost exclusively on fishes.

REPRODUCTION: Spawning occurs in late spring and summer when the water temperature reaches 21°C. Nests are constructed by males and females in secluded areas, such as undercut banks and hollow logs. An active and prolonged courtship occurs with the male and female swimming close together but facing opposite directions. Each fish wraps its tail around the other's head, the male quivers, and then eggs and sperm are released into the nest. The male chases the female out of the nest and then tends to the eggs and young for several weeks once they hatch.

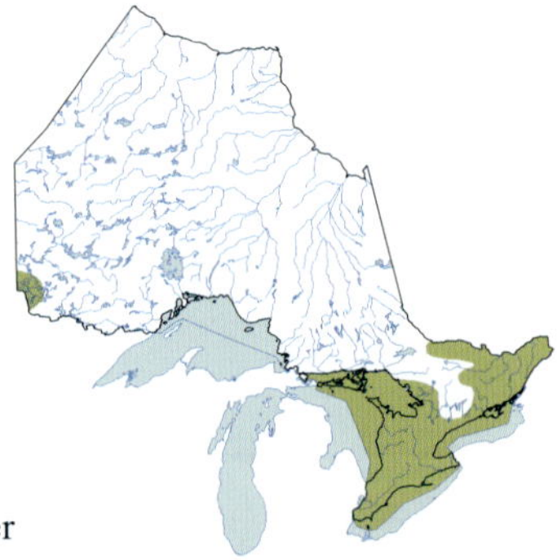

HABITAT: The Channel Catfish is found in a wide variety of warmwater

habitats in both lakes and streams and is not as closely associated with the bottom as bullheads and madtoms.

STATUS: G5; N5; S4.

Maximum Age: 24	Ontario Average	Ontario Record	World Record
Length:	44.5 cm (17.5 in)	99.8 cm (39.2 in)	132.0 cm (52.0 in)
Weight: Overall	0.9–1.8 kg (2.0–4.0 lbs)	15.1 kg (33.4 lbs)	26.3 kg (58.0 lbs)
Angling	–	15.1 kg (33.4 lbs)	26.3 kg (58.0 lbs)

FLATHEAD CATFISH *Pylodictis olivaris*

Pylodictis—mud fish.
olivaris—olive coloured, referring to the colour of the body.

Prior to 2016, only seven large adult Flathead Catfish had been caught in Canadian waters, four in Lake Erie and three in Lake St. Clair. Between 2016 and 2018, 11 additional individuals were caught in the lower Thames River, including several juveniles representing the first evidence of reproduction in Canada. Although the origin of the species in the Great Lakes is debated and it was first reported in Lake Erie in 1890, the Flathead Catfish has since spread to the American waters of lakes St. Clair, Huron, and Michigan.

DESCRIPTION: The Flathead Catfish is a mottled catfish with a robust, flattened head and elongate body. The mouth is wide, and the lower jaw protrudes in front of the upper jaw, except in juveniles. It has 4 pairs of dark **barbels**. The top of the head is flat. The body lacks scales. Colour is variable. The back and sides are yellow, olive, or brown, mottled with darker brown or black. The belly is pale yellow to creamy white. Juveniles and young adults have a white patch on the upper lobe of the tail and may be nearly black. The large adipose fin is not attached to the tail (p. 256), and the end of the tail is square or slightly concave (p. 256). The **fin membranes** are dark. The leading edges of the dorsal and pectoral fins each have a spine. The pectoral spines have **serrations** on both the anterior and posterior edges (p. 257). The anal fin is short, with 13–17 total rays.

SIMILAR SPECIES: No other catfish in Ontario has a protruding lower jaw and a flattened head. Madtoms have adipose fins attached to the tail. The Channel Catfish has a forked tail and a longer anal fin. It is most like the Brown and Black bullheads but differs in having **serrations** on the anterior edge of the pectoral spines and a shorter anal fin (13–17 total rays, vs. 17–26 in the Brown and Black bullheads).

FEEDING: The Flathead Catfish is typically an **ambush predator**, waiting

Juvenile

motionless on the bottom with its mouth open to strike at prey. It may also pursue prey. It feeds almost exclusively on live fishes and, occasionally, crayfishes. Young Flathead Catfish feed on aquatic insect **larvae** and **zooplankton**. Flathead Catfish do not feed in the winter, and they congregate in deep pools.

REPRODUCTION: Spawning occurs in late spring and summer when the water temperature reaches 21°C. Nests are constructed by one or both parents, near submerged logs or natural hollows. A lengthy courtship occurs sporadically over several hours. The pair swims close together, while the male rubs against the female with his **barbels** and belly. The male then encircles the female's head with his caudal fin and, with bellies touching, eggs and sperm are released into the nest. The male then chases the female out of the nest and tends to the eggs and young after they hatch.

HABITAT: The Flathead Catfish is found in large tributaries of the Great Lakes. It prefers the hard bottom of deep, slow pools with submerged logs or rocks for cover. Studies in the United States have shown that Flathead Catfish rarely travel far from their preferred location.

STATUS: G5; NNA; SNA; DD.

Maximum Age: 25	Ontario Average	Ontario Record	World Record
Length:	66.7 cm (26.3 in)	112 cm (44.1 in)	155.0 cm (61.0 in)
Weight: Overall	8.2 kg (18.1 lbs)	17.2 kg (37.9 lbs)	56.7 kg (126.0 lbs)
Angling	–	–	55.8 kg (123.0 lbs)

MARGINED MADTOM *Noturus insignis*

Noturus – noto: back; *uro*: tail. The adipose fin and tail fin are attached as one.
insignis: marked. The margins of the fins are marked or outlined.

The limited and disjunct distribution of this species has led to an ongoing debate regarding its origin in Ontario. Its current distribution may be the result of the fragmentation of a formerly wider range or the result of release from bait buckets.

DESCRIPTION: The Margined Madtom is a small elongate catfish. The snout overhangs the mouth. The body lacks scales. The adipose fin is attached to the tail, and there is a very shallow notch where they join (p. 256). The posterior edge of the tail is straight or slightly rounded (p. 256). The leading edges of the dorsal and pectoral fins each have a spine. The pectoral spines have small **serrations** on their posterior edges (p. 257). The back is dark brown and lacks a light spot behind the dorsal fin. The sides are a lighter brown, and the belly is white. The back, sides, and fins are tinted with olive or yellow. The edges of the tail and dorsal and anal fins are black. The muscle segments are not usually obvious on the posterior half of the body.

SIMILAR SPECIES: The Channel Catfish, Flathead Catfish, and bullheads have adipose fins that are not attached to the tail. No other madtom in Ontario has dark-edged fins. In addition, the Brindled and Northern madtoms have a paler body with dark saddles. The Tadpole Madtom has a narrow black lateral stripe, obvious muscle segments on the posterior half of the body, and a snout that does not overhang the mouth. The Stonecat has a light spot just behind the dorsal fin.

FEEDING: The Margined Madtom is nocturnal, hiding on the bottom during the day and feeding on aquatic insects, crustaceans, and, occasionally, small fishes at night. Prey is frequently scavenged from the bottom with the aid of sensitive **barbels**.

REPRODUCTION: Nothing is known of the spawning habits of this species in

Ontario. In the United States, spawning occurs in summer at night. Nests are constructed under rocks in quiet areas near **riffles**. Eggs and sperm are released, and the fertilized eggs cling together in a ball. The male guards the eggs and young for several weeks once they hatch.

HABITAT: The Margined Madtom lives on bottoms of sand, gravel, and rubble in the warm shallows of streams and lakes.

STATUS: G5; N1?; SU; DD.

Maximum Age: 4	Ontario Average	Ontario Record	World Record
Length:	8.0 cm (3.1 in)	15.9 cm (6.3 in)	17.9 cm (7.0 in)

NORTHERN MADTOM *Noturus stigmosus*

Noturus—noto: back; *uro*: tail. The adipose fin and tail fin are attached as one.
stigmosus: full of marks.

This endangered species is one of the rarest freshwater fish in Ontario. Fewer than 300 specimens have ever been collected in Canada, all in southwestern Ontario.

DESCRIPTION: The Northern Madtom is a small, slightly deep-bodied catfish. The snout overhangs the mouth. The body lacks scales. The adipose fin is attached to the tail, and there is a deep notch where they join (p. 256). The tail is slightly rounded (p. 256). The leading edges of the dorsal and pectoral fins each have a spine. The pectoral spines have large **serrations** on their posterior edges (p. 257). The back is pale with 2–3 large dark saddles, the sides are pale with small irregular dark spots, and the belly is white or pale yellow. There are 2 light spots slightly smaller than the eye, just in front of the dorsal fin. The dorsal and adipose fins have wide pale edges.

SIMILAR SPECIES: The Channel Catfish, Flathead Catfish, and bullheads have adipose fins that are not attached to the tail. The Stonecat, Tadpole Madtom, and Margined Madtom are brown or grey, without obvious dark saddles. The Brindled Madtom has a shallower notch where the adipose fin joins the tail and a black tip on the dorsal fin, and lacks pale edges on the dorsal and adipose fins.

FEEDING: The Northern Madtom is nocturnal, hiding on the bottom during the day and feeding on aquatic insects and crustaceans at night. Prey is frequently scavenged from the bottom with the aid of sensitive **barbels**.

REPRODUCTION: Spawning occurs during summer nights, over a one month period. Nests are constructed in cavities beneath flat rocks and logs, or in crayfish burrows. The male guards the eggs and newly hatched young for several weeks.

HABITAT: In Canada, the Northern Madtom is found on the rocky bottoms in the warm shallows of large lakes and streams.

STATUS: G3; N1; S1; E.

Maximum Age: 5	Ontario Average	Ontario Record	World Record
Length:	10.0 cm (3.9 in)	13.2 cm (5.2 in)	17.8 cm (7.0 in)

STONECAT *Noturus flavus*

Noturus—noto: back; *uro*: tail; refers to the connection of the adipose fin to the tail.
flavus: yellow; refers to the colour of parts of the body and fins.

The Stonecat is the largest of the madtoms in Canada. Its streamlined shape makes it highly adapted to maintaining its position in fast-flowing waters.

DESCRIPTION: The Stonecat is an elongate catfish. The snout overhangs the mouth. The body lacks scales. The adipose fin is attached to the tail, and there is a shallow notch where they join (p. 256). The posterior edge of the tail is straight or slightly rounded (p. 256). The leading edges of the dorsal and pectoral fins each have a spine. The pectoral spines lack **serrations** on the posterior edge (p. 257). The back is usually brown or grey with a light spot just behind the dorsal fin, the sides are paler, and the belly is grey to white. The tail is usually bordered on the top and bottom by white or yellow.

SIMILAR SPECIES: The Channel Catfish, Flathead Catfish, and bullheads have adipose fins that are not attached to the tail. The Brindled and Northern madtoms have a paler body with dark saddles across the back. The Tadpole Madtom has a deeper body, a black lateral stripe, and a snout that does not overhang the mouth. The Margined Madtom has dark-edged fins.

FEEDING: The Stonecat is **omnivorous**, feeding primarily on aquatic insects, crustaceans, molluscs, and, less frequently, small fishes and algae. Prey is frequently scavenged from the bottom at night with the aid of sensitive **barbels**.

REPRODUCTION: Spawning occurs during the warm summer months when the water temperature exceeds 23°C. The male prepares a nest under flat stones. Eggs and sperm are released nto the nest, and the eggs and young are guarded by the male.

HABITAT: The Stonecat is found in shallow, fast-flowing, warm waters of *riffles* with gravel bottoms.

STATUS: G5; N5; S4.

Maximum Age: 7	Ontario Average	Ontario Record	World Record
Length:	17.5 cm (6.9 in)	26.7 cm (10.5 in)	31.0 cm (12.2 in)

TADPOLE MADTOM *Noturus gyrinus*

Noturus—*noto*: back; *uro*: tail. The adipose fin and tail fin are attached as one.
gyrinus: tadpole; refers to its resemblance to a tadpole.

As its common name suggests, smaller individuals of this species bear a remarkable resemblance to frog tadpoles. Be careful when handling this madtom—its pectoral spines carry a mild venom and cause a sting similar to that of a bee.

DESCRIPTION: The Tadpole Madtom is a small, deep-bodied catfish. The snout does not overhang the mouth, and the lower jaw does not protrude. The top of the head is rounded. The body lacks scales. The adipose fin is attached to the tail, and there is a very shallow notch where they join (p. 256). The posterior edge of the tail is rounded (p. 256). The leading edges of the dorsal and pectoral fins each have a spine. The pectoral spines lack **serrations** on their posterior edges (p. 257). The back is dark brown, the sides are lighter brown, and the belly is tan to yellowish brown. There is a narrow black lateral stripe beginning under the dorsal fin, and there may be fainter dark stripes running above and below it. The muscle segments are often distinct on the posterior half of the body.

SIMILAR SPECIES: The Channel Catfish, Flathead Catfish, and bullheads have adipose fins that are not attached to the tail. The Brindled and Northern madtoms have a paler body with dark saddles. The Stonecat and the Margined Madtom are more slender, have snouts overhanging their mouths, and lack a black lateral stripe and distinct muscle segments. The Stonecat has a light spot just behind the dorsal fin. The Margined Madtom has dark-edged fins.

FEEDING: The Tadpole Madtom is nocturnal, hiding on the bottom during the day and feeding on aquatic insects and crustaceans at

night. Prey is frequently scavenged from the bottom with the aid of sensitive **barbels**.

REPRODUCTION: Spawning occurs in summer, with nests being built in cavities under stones. Eggs and sperm are released, and the fertilized eggs adhere to one another and to the nest. Both the male and female, or sometimes only the male, guard the eggs and young.

HABITAT: The Tadpole Madtom lives over bottoms of sand, gravel, and woody debris in the warm shallows of slow-moving or still waters.

STATUS: G5; N5; S4.

Maximum Age: 3	Ontario Average	Ontario Record	World Record
Length:	7.0 cm (2.8 in)	11.7 cm (4.6 in)	13.0 cm (5.1 in)

YELLOW BULLHEAD *Ameiurus natalis*

Ameiurus—*a*: without; *meiurus*: curtailed; refers to the slightly rounded edge of the tail.
natalis—*natis*: rump; perhaps refers to the swollen, furrowed posterior part of the head in spawning males.

Bullheads can often survive long periods of time out of water because they can obtain some oxygen through their scaleless skin. Many anglers have been surprised when their catch, thought to be long dead, comes back to life in the kitchen sink while being cleaned.

DESCRIPTION: The Yellow Bullhead is a robust, slightly deep-bodied catfish. The snout overhangs the mouth. It has 4 pairs of **barbels**; the 2 pairs on the chin are pale. The top of the head is rounded. The body lacks scales. The back is olive to black, the sides are yellowish brown, and the belly is white. The adipose fin is not attached to the tail, and the end of the tail is slightly rounded (p. 256). The **fin membranes** are usually grey. The leading edges of the dorsal and pectoral fins each have a spine (p. 256). The pectoral spines are strongly **serrated** on the posterior edges (p. 257). The anal fin is long, usually reaching the tail when depressed.

SIMILAR SPECIES: Madtoms have adipose fins that are attached to the tail. The Flathead Catfish has a flattened head, protruding lower jaw, and in young, a white patch on the upper lobe of the tail. The Channel Catfish has a deeply forked tail. The Black Bullhead usually has a pale bar at the base of the tail, black **fin membranes**, and weak **serrations** on the posterior edge of the pectoral spines. The Black and Brown bullheads have dark chin **barbels**, and their anal fins do not reach the tail when depressed.

FEEDING: The Yellow Bullhead is most active at night, feeding on crustaceans, worms, molluscs, **larval**

insects, aquatic plants, small fishes, and fish eggs. Its **barbels** have well-developed sensory organs used for touch and taste, as it commonly scavenges in muddy, dark waters.

REPRODUCTION: Spawning occurs in spring when the water temperature reaches 21°C. Both males and females excavate a nest that is often a depression in the bottom sediment, but may be a burrow dug into the stream bank or under a log. Eggs and sperm are released over the nest. The adhesive fertilized eggs are guarded by the male and fanned to keep them from being buried in sediment. Once the eggs hatch, the male continues to guard the brood until the young reach about 50 mm in length.

HABITAT: The Yellow Bullhead lives on the bottom in warm, shallow lakes and slow-moving streams. It prefers some form of cover, such as aquatic plants or fallen trees.

STATUS: G5; N4; S4.

Maximum Age: 7	Ontario Average	Ontario Record	World Record
Length:	25.5 cm (10.0 in)	36.8 cm (14.5 in)	47.0 cm (18.5 in)
Weight: Overall	0.2–0.5 kg (0.4–1.1 lbs)	–	2.9 kg (6.4 lbs)
Angling	–	–	2.9 kg (6.4 lbs)

ESOCIDAE
Pikes and Mudminnows

The familiar Northern Pike and Muskellunge belong to this family as do the lesser known pickerels and mudminnows. The Northern Pike has the widest distribution, being found in the cool waters of the northern hemisphere throughout Eurasia and North America. Seven other species are native to North America, and two occur in Siberia. The Muskellunge, Northern Pike, and pickerels are easily distinguished by their large heads with a flattened, elongate snout, which resembles a duck's bill. There are large canine teeth in the jaws, as well as smaller teeth on the roof of the mouth and tongue. Mudminnows are small, reaching a length of 15 cm (6 in.). Like all esocids, they have **cycloid scales**, and a single dorsal fin and anal fin placed well back on the body.

Several species of this family lived in North America during the late Cretaceous Period, 83–70 million years ago, but are now extinct. Fossils of *Oldmanesox canadensis* were discovered in the Oldman Formation in Dinosaur Provincial Park, Alberta, and show a strong resemblance to Northern Pike and Muskellunge of today. Fossils of the extinct mudminnow *Novumbra oregonensis* were also discovered on the western side of North America, dating back 40 million years ago. Both of these indicate that members of the pike family dispersed into North America from Eurasia when these two continents were still joined.

Researchers no longer recognize Umbridae, used in our previous edition, as a separate family and classify the mudminnows with Esocidae.

There are 14 species worldwide, five of which are found in Ontario.

< Juvenile Northern Pike

Scales on cheeks and gill cover

Chain and Grass pickerels

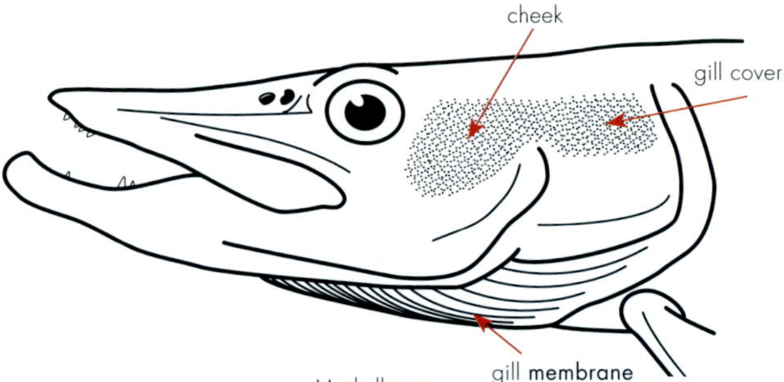

Muskellunge

Northern Pike

Pores on lower jaw, and rays in gill membranes

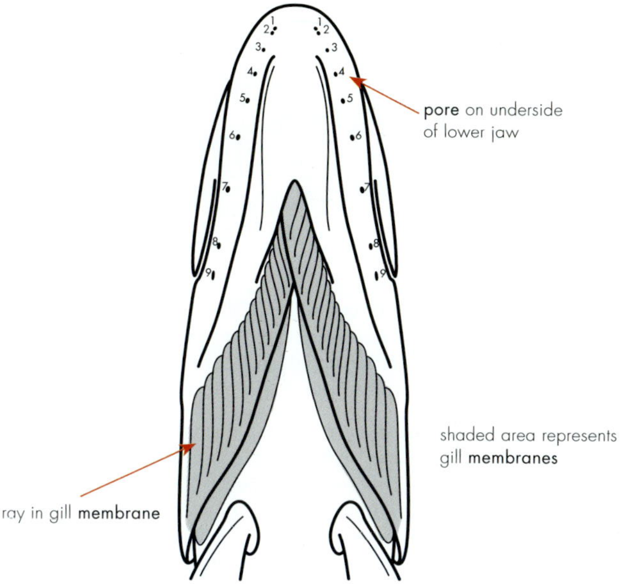

Heads of Chain and Grass pickerels

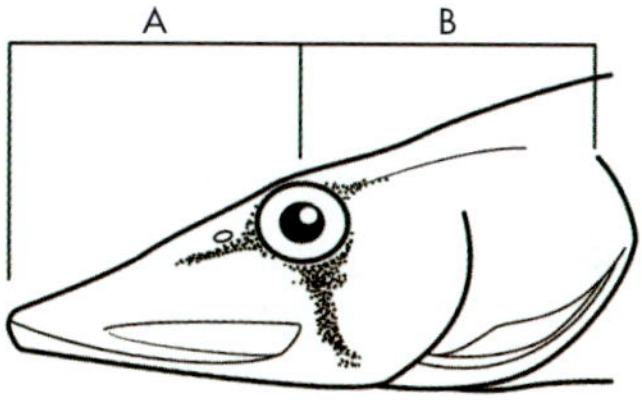

Distance **A** is equal to distance **B** (Grass Pickerel)

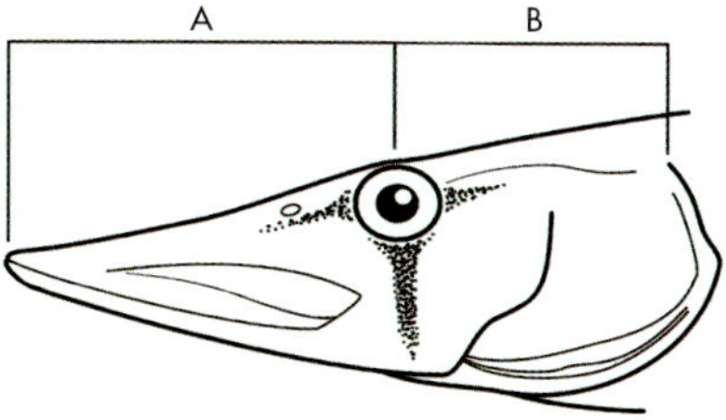

Distance **A** is greater than distance **B** (Chain Pickerel)

CENTRAL MUDMINNOW *Umbra limi*

Umbra: shade, as these fish prefer cover.
limi—limus: mud; often found in muddy habitats.

Superficially, the Central Mudminnow looks like a minnow or a killifish. However, despite its small size, it is related to pikes, not minnows or killifishes. Mudminnows are capable of breathing air using their **swim bladders** and can readily survive in water with little oxygen.

DESCRIPTION: The Central Mudminnow is a small, dark, and slightly deep-bodied fish. It has large scales (34–37 **lateral scales**). The upper jaw extends backwards to below the front of the eye. The tail is rounded. The back and sides are usually dark olive-green to brownish black, the sides have irregular darker brown markings often formed into bars, and the belly is yellow to white. There is a dark bar at the base of the tail. The fins are grey to brown. During spawning, females are more brightly coloured than the males, and both have a green iridescence, particularly on the anal fin.

SIMILAR SPECIES: Members of the minnow family have forked tails. The Blackstripe Topminnow has a prominent black lateral stripe on a pale body. The Banded Killifish has pale sides with more distinct bars, and its upper jaw does not extend backwards to below the eye.

FEEDING: The Central Mudminnow hides by day and feeds by night, quickly darting after small crustaceans, insect **larvae**, and molluscs. Occasionally, small fishes are eaten by adult females.

REPRODUCTION: In spring, the Central Mudminnow moves into shallow, weedy areas and spawns when the water temperature reaches 13°C. Eggs and sperm are released, and the fertilized eggs stick to submerged vegetation There is no parental care given to the eggs or young.

HABITAT: The Central Mudminnow prefers the quiet, vegetated waters of cool lakes and streams.

STATUS: G5; N5; S5.

Maximum Age: 4	Ontario Average	Ontario Record	World Record
Length:	7.5 cm (3.0 in)	16.1 cm (6.3 in)	16.1 cm (6.3 in)

CHAIN PICKEREL *Esox niger*

Esox—an old European name for pike.
niger—black, referring to the colouration of the juvenile.

Native to eastern Canada, the Chain Pickerel has been moving into Ontario likely from the American side of Lake Ontario. The capture of a juvenile Chain Pickerel in a Lake Ontario wetland suggests that it is now reproducing in Ontario. This should be of concern as it has had negative ecological impacts where it has been introduced elsewhere in Canada.

DESCRIPTION: The Chain Pickerel is a medium-sized, elongate fish. It has a fully scaled cheek and a fully scaled gill cover (p. 280). The snout is long; the distance from its tip to the middle of the eye is distinctly greater than the distance from the middle of the eye to the rear edge of the gill cover (p. 281). The underside of the lower jaw has 8–9 **pores** (usually 4 on each side), and each gill **membrane** has 14–17 rays (p. 281). The scales are very small (117–135 **lateral scales**). The back is green to nearly brown with a golden stripe in front of the dorsal fin, the sides are yellow to yellow-green with dark markings resembling chains, and the belly is creamy white. The anal and pelvic fins have little pigment. There is a prominent dark bar below the eye, which is vertical or, occasionally, slopes forward. The juvenile is darker, with a golden stripe on the back in front of the dorsal fin. Its sides have irregular bars or are occasionally mottled, and there may, occasionally, be a faint pale stripe.

SIMILAR SPECIES: The Muskellunge has a partially scaled cheek and gill cover, a total of 12–18 **pores** on the underside of the lower jaw, and a pale body often with dark bars or spots. The Northern Pike has a partially scaled gill cover, a total of 10 **pores** on the underside of the lower jaw, and a dark body with light bars or spots. Juveniles of Northern Pike, and some Muskellunge, have a dark bar below the eye, which is not as prominent and disappears with growth. The Grass Pickerel has a shorter snout, the distance from its tip to the middle of the eye is equal to, or less than, the distance from the middle

Juvenile

of the eye to the rear edge of the gill cover, the bar below its eye slopes backwards, and it has larger scales (97–118 **lateral scales**).

FEEDING: The Chain Pickerel is a sight predator, overtaking prey smaller than itself. Its diet consists of fishes and frogs, but also includes small turtles, mice, and ducklings. Young feed on aquatic insect **larvae** and worms.

REPRODUCTION: Spawning begins in early spring when water temperatures reach 9°C. A female, accompanied by one or two smaller males, moves in over flooded vegetation along shorelines of lakes, streams, and ponds. A pair swims side by side then rolls, putting ventral surfaces together, and eggs and sperm are released. Fertilized eggs adhere to vegetation. No parental care is given to the eggs or young. Eggs hatch in about two weeks. **Larvae** have adhesive glands on their snouts, allowing them to attach to vegetation. Feeding begins about two weeks after hatch.

HABITAT: The Chain Pickerel prefers warm marshes and bays of lakes and large streams with aquatic vegetation. It often occurs in dark, acidic waters.

STATUS: G5; N3; SNA; NAR[F].

Maximum Age: 9	Ontario Average	Ontario Record	World Record
Length:	42.0 cm (16.5 in)	59.4 cm (23.4 in)	99.0 cm (39.0 in)
Weight: Overall	0.4–0.7 kg (0.9–1.5 lbs)	1.5 kg (3.3 lbs)	5.6 kg (12.2 lbs)
Angling	–	–	4.2 kg (9.4 lbs)

GRASS PICKEREL *Esox americanus vermiculatus*

Esox: an old European name for pike.
americanus: for its homeland, North America.
vermiculatus: worm-like; refers to the wavy, dark lines on the body.

The common name "pickerel" means small pike and should be used for only certain members of the pike family and not for the Walleye. The Grass Pickerel is currently considered a subspecies of the Redfin Pickerel (*Esox americanus*), but research indicates that it may be a separate species (*Esox vermiculatus*).

DESCRIPTION: The Grass Pickerel is a small elongate fish. It has a fully scaled cheek and a fully scaled gill cover (p. 280). The snout is short; the distance from its tip to the middle of the eye is equal to, or less than, the distance from the middle of the eye to the rear edge of the gill cover (p. 281). The underside of the lower jaw has 8 **pores** (usually 4 on each side), and each gill **membrane** has 11–13 rays (p. 281). The scales are very small (97–118 **lateral scales**). The back is green with a golden stripe in front of the dorsal fin, the sides have 15–23 olive to black irregular, wavy bars, and the belly is beige to white. The anal and pelvic fins are grey to yellow. There is a prominent dark bar below the eye, which slopes backward. The juvenile has a golden green stripe on the sides, which breaks up and gradually disappears with growth.

SIMILAR SPECIES: The Grass Pickerel is frequently confused with juvenile Northern Pike or Muskellunge. It differs from these two species in having a fully scaled gill cover, only 8 **pores** on the underside of the lower jaw, and 13–15 rays in the gill **membrane**. Juveniles of the Northern Pike, and some Muskellunge, have a dark bar below the eye that is not as prominent and disappears with growth. The Chain Pickerel has a longer snout, the bar below its eye is usually vertical, each gill **membrane** has 14–17 rays, and it has smaller scales (117–135 **lateral scales**).

FEEDING: The Grass Pickerel is a sight predator, feeding on fishes and crayfishes, and, less frequently,

Juveniles

on aquatic insects. Frogs and tadpoles may also occasionally be eaten. Young individuals prefer **larval** aquatic **invertebrates**.

REPRODUCTION: Spawning occurs in spring when the water temperature reaches 8°C. Males move onto flooded stream margins or marshy areas with abundant vegetation and are later joined by females. Eggs and sperm are released, and the fertilized eggs adhere to the vegetation. Parental care is not provided to the eggs or young. The eggs hatch in about two weeks, and the young begin to feed two weeks after they hatch.

HABITAT: The Grass Pickerel is found in the heavily vegetated, warm waters of streams and wetlands in southern Ontario.

STATUS: G5T5; N3; S3; SC.

Maximum Age: 7	Ontario Average	Ontario Record	World Record
Length:	17.5 cm (6.9 in)	32.8 cm (12.9 in)	39.4 cm (15.5 in)
Weight: Overall	–	0.2 kg (0.4 lbs)	1.0 kg (2.2 lb)
Angling	–	–	0.5 kg (1.1 lb)

MUSKELLUNGE *Esox masquinongy*

Esox: an old European name for pike.
masquinongy: from the Indigenous words *mashk*: deformed; *kinonga*: pike.

In 1988, the largest Muskellunge angled in Canada (weighing 29.5 kg) was captured in Georgian Bay and, at that time, was considered to be the fourth-largest Muskellunge ever caught. Since then, two Muskellunge, believed to be larger and caught in the 1950s, have been deemed hoaxes based on forensic examination of their photographs. The only Muskellunge now considered larger is also suspect. It's quite possible that the Georgian Bay fish may one day become the undisputed world-record Muskellunge.

DESCRIPTION: The Muskellunge is a very large, elongate fish. It has a partially scaled cheek and a partially scaled gill cover (p. 280). There are 12–18 **pores** on the underside of the lower jaw (6–9 on each side), and each gill **membrane** has 16–19 rays (p. 281). It has very small scales (132–167 **lateral scales**). The colour pattern is variable, but can generally be described as dark markings on a light background. The back may be green-gold, brown, grey, or silver. The sides are lighter, and the belly is creamy to milky white. The head and body may be covered with dark blotches, wavy bars, or both, or may lack them altogether. Fins are green to reddish brown with dark blotches. Juveniles up to about 15 cm in length are pale with a dark back and have black blotches or bars on the side. There is a small dark vertical bar below the eye in the juvenile, which disappears as the fish grows.

SIMILAR SPECIES: The Northern Pike has a fully scaled cheek, a total of 10 **pores** on the underside of the lower jaw, 14–15 rays in each gill **membrane**, and a colour pattern of light bars or spots on a dark background. The Grass Pickerel and Chain Pickerel have fully scaled gill covers, and, usually, a total of 8 **pores** on the underside of the lower jaw. The juvenile Grass Pickerel has a pale lateral stripe, and the juvenile Chain Pickerel has sides that have irregular bars or are mottled. The adult Grass Pickerel has

Barred

Silver

Spotted

15–23 irregular dark bars and a prominent dark vertical bar below the eye. The adult Chain Pickerel has sides with chain-like markings. The **hybrid** between Muskellunge and Northern Pike is known as the Tiger Muskellunge. The Tiger Muskellunge often has a fully scaled cheek, a total of 10–16 **pores** on the underside of the lower jaw, and typically a colour pattern of irregular dark bars and spots on a light background.

FEEDING: The Muskellunge is an **ambush predator**, waiting motionless in weed beds to strike at prey. Adults feed almost exclusively on fishes with other vertebrates, such as frogs, mice, muskrats, and ducklings, making up a small percentage of their diet. There is a relationship

Juvenile

Tiger Muskellunge

between size and prey size, with larger adults seizing only larger prey species. Young Muskellunge feed on large **zooplankton** and aquatic insects for the first few weeks of their life.

REPRODUCTION: Spawning begins in spring when the water temperature reaches 10°C. Muskellunge home to their birthplace spawning grounds over shallow, heavily vegetated floodplains of streams or lakes. A larger female is approached by one or two smaller males. They swim together then roll, putting their ventral surfaces close together. Eggs and sperm are released. This is repeated many times over the week-long spawning period. A nest is not built, nor is parental care provided to the eggs or young. The fertilized eggs are scattered over the vegetation and hatch in about two weeks.

HABITAT: The Muskellunge is found in the cool waters of lakes and larger streams, usually near aquatic plants, particularly wild rice.

STATUS: G5; N4; S4.

Maximum Age: 30	Ontario Average	Ontario Record	World Record
Length:	96.5 cm (38.0 in)	147.3 cm (58.0 in)	183.0 cm (72.0 in)
Weight: Overall	7.2 kg (16.0 lbs)	29.5 kg (65.0 lbs)	31.8 kg (70.1 lbs)
Angling	–	29.5 kg (65.0 lbs)	30.6 kg (67.5 lbs)

NORTHERN PIKE *Esox lucius*

Esox: an old European name for pike.
lucius: pike.

The Northern Pike is one of the most common fishes in Ontario, except in the Kawarthas and Algonquin Park. These areas of Ontario were isolated soon after the last Ice Age, which prevented Northern Pike from colonizing their lakes and streams.

DESCRIPTION: The Northern Pike is a large elongate fish. It has a fully scaled cheek and a partially scaled gill cover (p. 280). There is a total of 10 **pores** on the underside of the lower jaw (5 on each side), and each gill **membrane** usually has 14–15 rays (p. 281). It has very small scales (105–148 **lateral scales**). The colour pattern is variable, but can generally be described as light markings on a dark background. Background colour varies from green to brown and is dark on the back fading to creamy white on the belly. In juveniles up to about 38 cm long, the light markings are shaped into 8–12 pale bars, which gradually break up into small bean-shaped spots as the fish grows. The tail and the dorsal and anal fins are yellow, green, orange, or pale red, and blotched with irregular black marks. There is a small dark vertical bar below the eye in the juvenile, which disappears as the fish grows.

SIMILAR SPECIES: The Muskellunge has a partially scaled cheek, a total of 12–18 **pores** on the underside of the lower jaw, 16–19 rays in each gill **membrane**, and a colour pattern of dark bars or spots on a light background. The Grass Pickerel and Chain Pickerel have fully scaled gill covers and, usually, a total of 8 **pores** on the underside of the lower jaw. The juvenile Grass Pickerel has a pale lateral stripe. The adult Grass Pickerel has 15–23 irregular dark bars and a prominent dark bar below the eye. Although the juvenile Chain Pickerel has markings similar to the juvenile Northern Pike, the adult Chain Pickerel has chain-like markings on the sides (vs. bean-shaped pale spots). The **hybrid** between Muskellunge and Northern Pike is known as the Tiger Muskellunge. The Tiger Muskellunge has characteristics

Northern Pike (continued)

Juvenile

intermediate to the two parent species, and typically a colour pattern of irregular dark bars and spots on a light background.

FEEDING: The Northern Pike is an **ambush predator**, waiting motionless in weed beds for prey to swim by. It is an **opportunist**, feeding on whatever is readily available, with fishes making up 90% of the adult diet. Frogs, crayfishes, mice, muskrats, and ducklings may also supplement its diet. Young pike feed on large **zooplankton** and aquatic insects for the first few weeks of their life.

REPRODUCTION: Spawning begins in early spring when the water temperature reaches 5°C. A spawning migration occurs into shallow, heavily vegetated floodplains of streams or lakes. A larger female is approached by one or two smaller males. They swim together then roll, putting their ventral surfaces close together. Eggs and sperm are released. This is repeated many times during daytime over several days. A nest is not built, nor is parental care provided to the eggs or young. The fertilized eggs adhere to the vegetation and hatch in about two weeks.

HABITAT: Northern Pike are found in a wide variety of coolwater habitats, from the smallest headwater streams to the nearshore waters of the Great Lakes. They are almost always found near aquatic plants that provide camouflage for concealment and hunting.

STATUS: G5; N5; S5.

Maximum Age: 30	Ontario Average	Ontario Record	World Record
Length:	61.0 cm (24.0 in)	134.6 cm (53.0 in)	150.0 cm (59.1 in)
Weight: Overall	1.6 kg (3.5 lbs)	19.1 kg (42.1 lbs)	28.4 kg (62.6 lbs)
Angling	–	19.1 kg (42.1 lbs)	25.0 kg (55.1 lbs)

OSMERIDAE
Smelts

This family includes small, silvery fishes that are found in marine and freshwater habitats in the northern hemisphere. They are often **anadromous**, living their adult lives in the Arctic, Atlantic, and Pacific oceans, and then migrating into streams during spring spawning runs. Smelts have a large mouth with teeth on the jaws, tongue, and roof of the mouth. Similar to salmons and trouts, smelts have small **cycloid scales** and a single dorsal fin in the middle of the back followed by a small adipose fin. Unlike salmons and trouts, there is no pelvic axillary process (see top fig. page 23).

The name "smelt" likely has its origin from the old English word *smoelt,* meaning silvery and shiny, although this origin is disputed by some. Other possible roots include the smell they exude, which is somewhat like cucumber, or the German word *schmelzen,* meaning to melt, as the flesh melts in your mouth.

There are 15 species worldwide, one of which is found in Ontario.

< Rainbow Smelt

RAINBOW SMELT *Osmerus mordax*

Osmerus: odorous; refers to the cucumber-like scent that the Rainbow Smelt exudes.
mordax: biting, as this species has many teeth on the jaws, tongue, and roof of the mouth.

In Ontario, the Rainbow Smelt is native only to a few lakes in the Ottawa Valley. However, it has been spread throughout Ontario and beyond largely through bait buckets and subsequent dispersal.

DESCRIPTION: The Rainbow Smelt is a small, elongate, silvery fish. The snout does not overhang the large mouth. There are large canine teeth on the tongue and roof of the mouth. It has small scales (62–72 **lateral scales**) that come off easily. On the back, there is a single dorsal fin with 8–11 rays and a small adipose fin without rays (p. 23). The anal fin is medium-sized with 12–16 rays. There is no pelvic axillary process (p. 23). The back is green, and the silvery sides have iridescent purple, blue, and pink reflections. The belly is white. Individuals from some lakes may be darker in colour. Spawning males have small **nuptial tubercles** on the head, body, and fins. **Nuptial tubercles** are seldom present on females.

SIMILAR SPECIES: Minnows lack an adipose fin and teeth in their mouths (their teeth are in their throat!). The whitefishes and ciscoes have a deeper body and a pelvic axillary process. They lack large teeth on the tongue and roof of the mouth. The Brook Silverside has 2 dorsal fins with rays and a longer anal fin.

FEEDING: The Rainbow Smelt is a schooling fish, feeding on small fishes, crustaceans, insect **larvae**, and worms.

REPRODUCTION: The marine Rainbow Smelt is **anadromous,** migrating into fresh water to spawn. In Ontario, it is **landlocked**, and large schools of smelt move in early spring from lakes to streams and shorelines to spawn. Spawning runs begin once the water temperature reaches 5°C and often occur under ice.

Spawning run

Males are usually first on the spawning grounds, and both males and females stay for about three weeks. Two males flank a female, and eggs and sperm are released. The fertilized eggs are attached by a thread to vegetation and sway in the current in a balloon-like manner. After a few weeks, the eggs hatch and the young drift back downstream to the lake.

HABITAT: When not spawning, the Rainbow Smelt spends most of its life in the cold, deep waters of lakes.

STATUS: G5; N5; S5.

Maximum Age: 7	Ontario Average	Ontario Record	World Record
Length:	19.0 cm (7.5 in)	29.8 cm (11.8 in)	35.6 cm (14.0 in)
Weight: Overall	<0.1 kg (0.1 lbs)	0.2 kg (0.4 lbs)	0.2 kg (0.4 lbs)
Angling	–	0.2 kg (0.4 lbs)	0.2 kg (0.4 lbs)

SALMONIDAE
Trouts and Salmons

This family includes some of the most familiar sport and commercial fishes in Ontario. The family includes not only the trouts and salmons, but also whitefishes and graylings. Occurring naturally throughout the Northern Hemisphere, family members have been successfully introduced in many coldwater localities throughout the world for sport and aquaculture. Their streamlined body has small **cycloid scales** and a single dorsal fin in the middle of the back followed by an adipose fin. There is a small pelvic axillary process (see top fig. page 23).

Salmon have the amazing ability to home to their birthplace streams to spawn. Some Pacific salmon travel as far as 7,400 km round trip from their spawning grounds, downstream to the ocean, and then back several years later. Many hypotheses have been tested to find the cue that guides salmon, including the sun, ocean currents, temperature, odour, and magnetic stimuli. Although all of these cues may be used to some extent, odour is considered to be the strongest. Young salmon become imprinted to the distinctive smell of their home stream, and this is later used as the adults migrate back to their birthplace stream to spawn.

There are 261 species recognized worldwide, 18 of which are found in Ontario.

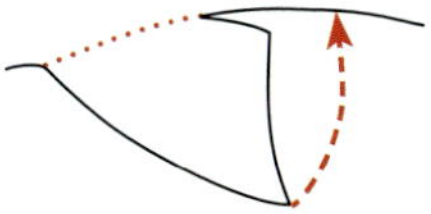

tip of anal fin extends well past anal fin base when depressed against the body (e.g., Rainbow Trout)

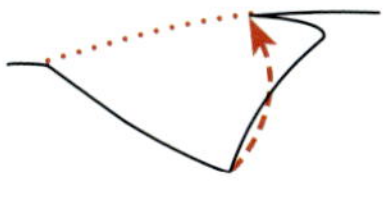

tip of anal fin extends to end of anal fin base when depressed against the body (e.g., Coho Salmon)

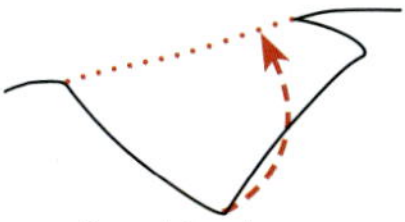

tip of anal fin does not extend to anal fin base when depressed against the body (e.g., Chinook Salmon)

< Brook Trout spawning

ATLANTIC SALMON *Salmo salar*

Salmo: name for salmon of the Atlantic.
salar: from *salio*, to leap.

In Ontario, the Atlantic Salmon was native only to Lake Ontario and its tributaries. It was **extirpated** from the lake in the late 1800s, largely as a result of dams that blocked its migration and pollution that destroyed its spawning grounds. Attempts to reintroduce Atlantic Salmon in Lake Ontario have had limited success, likely due to habitat degradation and **competition** for spawning grounds from introduced Pacific salmons, although reintroduction efforts are ongoing.

DESCRIPTION: The Atlantic Salmon is an elongate, moderately deep-bodied fish. The upper jaw extends backwards to below the posterior edge of the eye, and farther backwards in large males. It has very small scales (109–121 **lateral scales**). There are fewer than 12 anal rays, and when the anal fin is depressed against the body, its tip extends well behind the anal fin base (p. 299). The gums and inside of the mouth are pale. In the Great Lakes, the back is brown, blue, or green, the sides are silvery, and the belly is white. There are small dark spots, or X-shaped markings, on the back and sides, and few or no spots on the tail. The dark spots may be faint or absent in silvery individuals. When entering streams, these individuals lose their silver colour and become darker. The dark spots become prominent on the head, back, sides, and on the dorsal and adipose fins. There are often red spots on the sides. The dark and red spots may have pale edges. The adipose fin is rarely orange or red. Spawning males develop a hooked lower jaw.

SIMILAR SPECIES: Chinook, Coho, and Pink salmons have black tongues and more than 12 anal rays, and when their anal fins are depressed against the body, the tips do not extend far behind the base, if at all. The Rainbow Trout has a reddish lateral stripe, numerous small dark spots on the tail, and spots without pale edges on the body. Brook Trout and Lake Trout have pale spots on a dark body and white leading edges on the lower fins. The Brown Trout's body has a larger mouth, the upper jaw extends backwards beyond the

Juvenile

Eggs

eye in adults, and the juvenile has an orange or red adipose fin. The Atlantic Salmon occasionally **hybridizes** with Brown Trout. These **hybrids** are difficult to distinguish from the parent species.

FEEDING: Young Atlantic Salmon feed on aquatic insect **larvae** before migrating downstream. Once in Lake Ontario, their diet becomes mostly **piscivorous**. During the spawning run, adults do not feed, although they readily strike at artificial flies.

REPRODUCTION: Atlantic Salmon typically spawn in the fall, although spawning migrations up tributary streams may occur anytime from spring to fall. In **riffle** areas, the female hollows out a nest (known as a **redd**) in the gravel by lying on her side and beating vigorously with her tail. The male enters the **redd**, and eggs and sperm are released. The female covers the fertilized eggs with gravel. Both males and females spawn more than once, and then rest in the river for a short period before returning to the lake. Some males may remain in the river all winter. Atlantic Salmon often spawn for several successive years before dying.

HABITAT: In Ontario, the Atlantic Salmon spends most of its life in the cold waters of the Great Lakes and Trout Lake near North Bay.

STATUS: G5TXQ; NX; SX; X (Lake Ontario population).

Maximum Age: 13	Ontario Average	Ontario Record	World Record
Length:	46.0 cm (18.1 in)	89.2 cm (35.1 in)	150.0 cm (59.1 in)
Weight: Overall	1.2 kg (2.6 lbs)	11.0 kg (24.3 lbs)	46.8 kg (103.1 lbs)
Angling	–	11.0 kg (24.3 lbs)	35.9 kg (79.1 lbs)

Smolt

♂

Jumping the falls

DEEPWATER CISCOES *Coregonus* spp.

These deepwater fishes were originally described as species in the Great Lakes and Lake Nipigon based on their distinct body shapes and number of gill rakers. Recent genetic analyses suggest that these fishes evolved from a common ancestor, probably Cisco (*C. artedi*), independently in each Great Lake, and several other lakes, since the end of the last Ice Age. For now, we continue to include their scientific names here until scientists formally rename the species.

DESCRIPTION: These are elongate, silvery fishes. The snout does not overhang the mouth and the head is somewhat pointed. There are 2 flaps of skin between the nostrils. The scales are small (63–95 **lateral scales**). There is a single dorsal fin with 8–11 rays and a small adipose fin without rays. A pelvic axillary process is present. The pectoral and pelvic fins are noticeably long in Kiyi. The back ranges from black to blue to light tan, the sides are silver with pink to purple iridescence, and the belly is white. The Shortnose Cisco has a black snout. In most species, the pelvic and anal fins may be milky or opaque, with a sprinkling of black. The other fins are generally colourless, but may have varying amounts of black, particularly along the outer edges. The fins of the Blackfin Cisco are generally very black. **Nuptial tubercles** are present in spawning males and, in some species, spawning females.

SIMILAR SPECIES: Minnows, Goldeye, and Mooneye lack an adipose fin. The Rainbow Smelt is more elongate, has large canine teeth, and lacks a pelvic axillary process. The snouts in the Round, Pygmy, and Lake whitefishes overhang the mouths. To the untrained eye, it is virtually impossible to tell all ciscoes apart.

FEEDING: These species feed on a wide variety of small prey, including **zooplankton**, insects, molluscs, algae, and, occasionally, small fishes. The Bloater feeds in the water column, while other species feed on the bottom (Blackfin Cisco, Deepwater Cisco, Shortjaw Cisco) or in both locations (Kiyi, Shortnose Cisco).

REPRODUCTION: Little is known about the spawning habits of these fishes. They generally spawn over 2–3 month periods between August and May, depending on the species and lake. It is believed that the males congregate first and migrate to greater depths up to 175 m. When later joined by females, eggs and sperm are released, and the fertilized eggs are left unattended.

HABITAT: These species are, or in some cases were, found in the cold, deep waters of the Great Lakes and preferred different depths; the Bloater prefers the shallowest depths (10–121 m), while the Deepwater Cisco preferred and the Kiyi prefers the deepest depths (30–200 m).

BLOATER *Coregonus hoyi*
Coregonus—kore: eye; *gonia*: angle.
hoyi: named after Dr. Philo Hoy, a Wisconsin naturalist.

STATUS: G4; N4; S4; NAR.

BLACKFIN CISCO *Coregonus nigripinnis*
Coregonus—kore: eye; *gonia*: angle.
nigripinnis—niger: black; *pinnis*: fin.

STATUS: G1Q; NU; SU; DD.

DEEPWATER CISCO *Coregonus johannae*
Coregonus—kore: eye; *gonia*: angle.
johannae: life companion of George Wagoner, who described the species.

STATUS: GX; NX; SX; X.

KIYI *Coregonus kiyi*

Coregonus—kore: eye; *gonia*: angle.
kiyi: name used for this species by Lake Michigan fishermen.

STATUS: G3G4TNR; N3; S3; SC (Upper Great Lakes). G3G4TX; NX; SX; E (Lake Ontario).

LONGJAW CISCO *Coregonus alpenae*

Coregonus—kore: eye; *gonia*: angle.
alpenae: named after the fishing town of Alpena, Michigan

STATUS: GNR; NNR; SNR.

NIPIGON CISCO *Coregonus nipigon*

Coregonus—kore; eye; *gonia*: eye; *gonia*: angle.
nipigon: named after Lake Nipigon.

STATUS: G3G5; NU; SU.

SHORTJAW CISCO *Coregonus zenithicus*
Coregonus—*kore*: eye; *gonia*: angle.
zenithicus: named after Duluth, Minnesota (the Zenith City).

STATUS: G3; N2; S2; T.

SHORTNOSE CISCO *Coregonus reighardi*
Coregonus—*kore*: eye; *gonia*: angle.
reighardi: in honour of Jacob Reighard, an American **ichthyologist** from the University of Michigan.

STATUS: GH; NH; SH; E.

Cisco

BROOK TROUT *Salvelinus fontinalis*

Salvelinus—salvelin: an old name for **char**, meaning blood-coloured; alludes to their red belly.
fontinalis: living in springs.

The Brook Trout (or Speckled Trout) is one of Ontario's most colourful and highly prized sport fishes. Several forms of Brook Trout are recognized in Ontario. The Aurora Trout, which lacks the distinctive markings of a Brook Trout, is native to two lakes in northeastern Ontario. The coaster Brook Trout lives a large part of its life in the nearshore waters of Lake Superior.

DESCRIPTION: The Brook Trout is a deep-bodied fish. It has minute scales (210–244 **lateral scales**). The upper jaw extends backwards to well beyond the eye. When the anal fin is depressed against the body, its tip extends well behind the anal fin base (p. 299). The tail is square or slightly forked. The gums and inside of the mouth are usually pale. The back is olive-green, brown, or black, with pale wavy lines that extend onto the dorsal fin. The sides are lighter with white, yellow, and red spots, some of which have blue edges. The belly is silvery or white. The lower fins have white leading edges followed by a black stripe. The spawning male develops a hook on the lower jaw and an orange-red belly with black pigmentation.

SIMILAR SPECIES: All other trouts and salmons, except the Lake Trout, have dark spots on the body that may be faint in silvery individuals. The Chinook, Coho, and Pink salmons have black tongues and more than 12 anal rays. When their anal fins are depressed against the body, the tips do not extend far behind the base. The Rainbow Trout often has a reddish stripe along the side. The Lake Trout has a deeply forked tail and lacks wavy lines on the back and a black stripe behind the white leading edge of the lower fins. The Atlantic Salmon has an upper jaw that does not extend behind the eye and a more deeply forked tail. The Brown Trout has dark spots on the body, often with pale edges. The Brook Trout occasionally **hybridizes**

Spawning

Juvenile

♂ Aurora Trout

♀ Aurora Trout

Tiger Trout

♂ and ♀ circle around nest

♂ chases away rivals

♂ chases away rivals

♀ covers fertilized eggs with gravel

with the Brown Trout, producing the Tiger Trout, with striking zebra-like markings.

FEEDING: Brook Trout feed on aquatic and terrestrial insects, crustaceans, and, occasionally, fishes, amphibians, and small mammals.

REPRODUCTION: Spawning occurs in the fall when the water temperature drops below 10°C. The male moves into **riffle** areas of streams, or lake shorelines with **groundwater upwellings**, and defends a territory. The female enters and hollows out a nest (known as a **redd**) and may help the male to chase off rival males. The male presses against the female, the pair vibrates, and eggs and sperm are released. This may occur several times, and then the female covers the fertilized eggs with gravel. The eggs develop unattended for two to three months before hatching.

HABITAT: In southern Ontario, the Brook Trout is largely limited to the upper reaches of coldwater tributaries to the Great Lakes. In the rest of Ontario, Algonquin Park northward, it is found in the cold waters of lakes, streams, and James Bay.

STATUS: Brook Trout: G5T5; N5; S5.
Aurora Trout: G5TNRQ; NNR; S1.

Maximum Age: 24	Ontario Average	Ontario Record	World Record
Length:	28.0 cm (11.0 in)	81.6 cm (32.1 in)	86.0 cm (33.9 in)
Weight: Overall	0.2 kg (0.4 lbs)	6.6 kg (14.5 lbs)	8.0 kg (17.6 lbs)
Angling	–	6.6 kg (14.5 lbs)	8.0 kg (17.6 lbs)

BROWN TROUT *Salmo trutta*

Salmo: name for salmon of the Atlantic.
trutta: name for trout.

The Brown Trout is native to Europe and was one of the first species introduced into Ontario in the 1800s. Most populations in Ontario are self-reproducing, and widespread stocking no longer occurs.

DESCRIPTION: The Brown Trout is a slightly deep-bodied fish. The upper jaw extends backwards well beyond the eye in adults. It has very small scales (120–130 **lateral scales**). There are 10–12 anal rays, and when the anal fin is depressed against the body, its tip extends well behind the anal fin base (p. 299). The gums and inside of the mouth are pale. In individuals from streams, the back is brown, the sides are pale brown or silvery, and the belly is white. There are usually prominent dark spots on the head, back, sides, and dorsal and adipose fins. Many spots have pale edges. There are often red spots with blue edges on the sides. The adipose fin is usually orange or red. The lower fins have white leading edges followed by a black stripe. The tail has no dark spots except in large individuals, which often have dark spots along the upper and lower margins. In Great Lakes individuals, the back is brown, blue, or green, the sides are silvery, and the belly is white. The spots may be faint or absent. When entering streams, these individuals lose their silver colour and become darker. Spawning males develop a hooked lower jaw.

SIMILAR SPECIES: The Chinook, Coho, and Pink salmons have black tongues and more than 12 anal rays. When their anal fins are depressed against the body, the tips do not extend far behind the base, if at all. The Rainbow Trout has a reddish lateral stripe, numerous small dark spots on the tail, and spots without pale edges on the body. The Brook Trout and Lake Trout have pale spots on a dark body. The Atlantic Salmon has a smaller mouth and X-shaped black markings on the sides, and the juvenile lacks an orange or red adipose fin. The Brown Trout occasionally **hybridizes** with the Brook Trout, producing the Tiger Trout, with striking zebra-like markings.

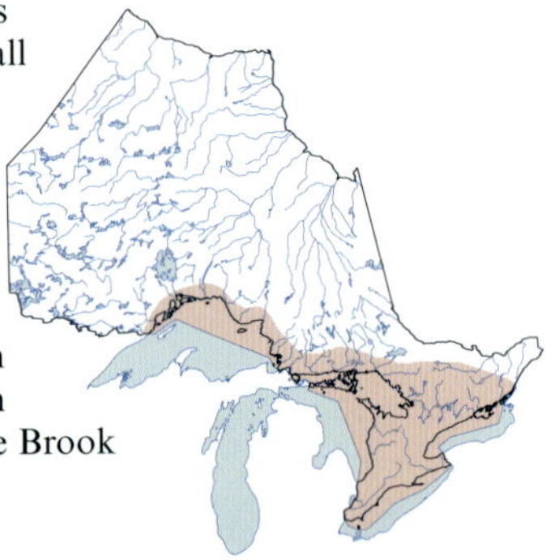

Juvenile

The Brown Trout also occasionally **hybridizes** with the Atlantic Salmon. These **hybrids** are difficult to distinguish from the parent species.

FEEDING: The Brown Trout feeds on a variety of items, including aquatic and terrestrial insects, crustaceans, molluscs, fishes, amphibians, and small mammals.

REPRODUCTION: In the fall, spawning occurs in shallow streams or rocky shorelines of lakes when the water temperature drops below 9°C. The female hollows out a nest (known as a **redd**), the male enters, and eggs and sperm are released. Spawning may occur several times for both males and females. The female then covers the fertilized eggs with gravel. Young may spend their first years in the stream before migrating downstream.

HABITAT: The Brown Trout is found in the cool waters of the Great Lakes and their tributaries. It is rarely found in small lakes.

STATUS: G5; NNA; SNA.

Maximum Age: 38	Ontario Average	Ontario Record	World Record
Length:	41.0 cm (16.1 in)	96.5 cm (38.0 in)	140.0 cm (55.1 in)
Weight: Overall	0.8 kg (1.8 lbs)	15.6 kg (34.4 lbs)	50.0 kg (110.2 lbs)
Angling	–	15.6 kg (34.4 lbs)	19.6 kg (42.1 lbs)

CHINOOK SALMON *Oncorhynchus tshawytscha*

Oncorhynchus—onco: hook; *rhyncho*: snout; refers to the hooked snout in spawning males.
tshawytscha: common name for this fish in Kamchatka, Russia, where it was first discovered.

The Chinook are Indigenous Peoples who inhabit parts of western North America and once depended on salmon as a dietary staple. The Chinook Salmon was first introduced into the Great Lakes around a hundred years ago, but it didn't establish reproducing populations until it was more intensively stocked in the late 1960s.

DESCRIPTION: The Chinook Salmon is an elongate, moderately deep-bodied fish. It has very small scales (130–165 **lateral scales**). There are 15–17 anal rays. When the anal fin is depressed against the body, its tip usually does not extend to the end of the anal fin base (p. 299). The inside of the mouth and gums are black. In the Great Lakes, the back is blue or green, the sides are silvery, and the belly is white. There are numerous small dark spots without pale edges on the back and both lobes of the tail. The dark spots may be faint on silvery individuals. Individuals in streams lose their silver colour, become darker, and the back and sides become olive-brown to purple, with the colour darker in males. The spawning male develops a hooked snout and large teeth.

SIMILAR SPECIES: The Brook Trout and Lake Trout have pale spots on a dark body. The Atlantic Salmon and Brown Trout have black and red spots with pale edges on the body and few or no spots on the tail. In these four species and Rainbow Trout, when the anal fin is depressed against the body, its tip extends well behind the anal fin base. The Rainbow Trout has a pale mouth and gums, and usually a reddish stripe. The Coho Salmon has pale gums and dark spots usually only on the upper lobe of the tail.

FEEDING: Young Chinook Salmon feed on aquatic insect **larvae**. After migrating

Juveniles

into the Great Lakes, the young's diet becomes mostly **piscivorous**. Adult Chinook Salmon feed on Alewife, Rainbow Smelt, and other forage fishes in the shallows in spring and in deeper waters in summer.

REPRODUCTION: In fall, Chinook Salmon congregate in river mouths, waiting for the fall rains to begin before migrating upstream. Once on the spawning grounds, the female hollows out a nest (known as a **redd**) near **riffles** by lying on her side and beating vigorously with her tail. She then pairs up with a large male, and several smaller males may join in. Eggs and sperm are released, and the female covers the eggs with gravel. Both males and females spawn several times and die shortly thereafter. The eggs hatch in the spring, and juveniles may migrate downstream to the lake during summer or remain in the stream for one to two years before migrating.

HABITAT: In Ontario, the Chinook Salmon spends most of its life in the cold waters of the Great Lakes until it returns to tributaries to spawn.

STATUS: G5; N4; SNA.

Maximum Age: 9	Ontario Average	Ontario Record	World Record
Length:	88.0 cm (34.6 in)	119.4 cm (47.0 in)	150.0 cm (59.1 in)
Weight: Overall	7.6 kg (16.7 lbs)	21.0 kg (46.4 lbs)	61.4 kg (135.4 lbs)
Angling	–	21.0 kg (46.4 lbs)	44.1 kg (97.2 lbs)

CISCO *Coregonus artedi*

Coregonus—kore: eye; *gonia*: angle.
artedi: named after the Swedish naturalist Peter Artedi.

Several forms of ciscoes were once very abundant in the Great Lakes. However, overfishing in the 19th and early 20th centuries led to dramatic decline and, in two cases (Deepwater Cisco and Shortnose Cisco), extinction. Before the **collapse** of this "chub" fishery, annual landings in the Great Lakes averaged 10 million kg. These fishes were sold fresh, frozen, or smoked—the last still available through a much smaller fishery.

DESCRIPTION: The Cisco is a slightly deep-bodied, silvery fish. The head is pointed and the snout does not overhang the mouth. There are 2 flaps of skin between the nostrils. It has small scales (63–94 **lateral scales**). There is a single dorsal fin with 10–15 rays and a small adipose fin without rays (p. 23). It has a pelvic axillary process (p. 23). The back is green, blue, grey, light brown, or black. The sides are silvery with a pink to purple iridescence, and the belly is white. The pelvic and anal fins may be milky or opaque, with a sprinkling of black. The other fins are generally colourless, but may have varying amounts of black, particularly along the outer edges. Spawning individuals develop **nuptial tubercles** on the sides. These are larger and more numerous in males.

SIMILAR SPECIES: Minnows, Goldeye, and Mooneye lack an adipose fin. The Rainbow Smelt is more elongate, has large canine teeth, and lacks a pelvic axillary process. The snouts in the Round, Pygmy, and Lake whitefishes overhang the mouths. To the untrained eye, it is virtually impossible to tell ciscoes apart.

FEEDING: The Cisco feeds in the water column on a wide variety of small prey, including **zooplankton**, crustaceans, **larval** insects, algae, and, occasionally, small fishes.

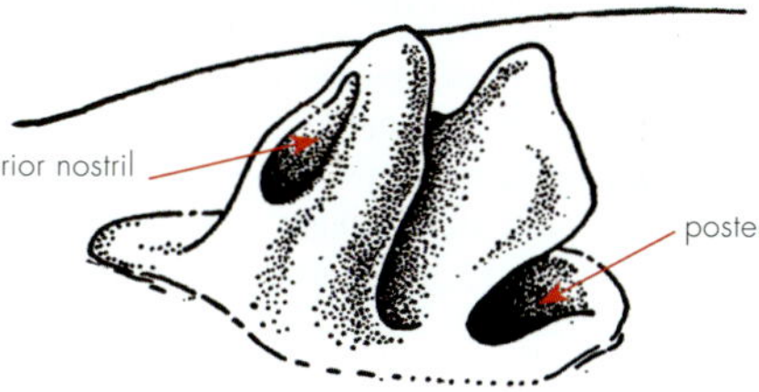

2 flaps of skin between nostrils

REPRODUCTION: The Cisco typically spawns over gravel or rocky bottoms in late fall when the water temperature drops below 5°C. Males congregate first and migrate in large numbers to shallow depths in smaller lakes, but may spawn at any depth to 64 m in the Great Lakes. Upon arrival of the females, eggs and sperm are released, and the fertilized eggs are left unattended.

HABITAT: This species is generally found in the cold, deeper waters of lakes and, occasionally, large streams. In winter and spring, it may be found in cold, shallow waters.

STATUS: G5; N5; S5.

Maximum Age: 11	Ontario Average	Ontario Record	World Record
Length:	25.0 cm (9.8 in)	59.7 cm (23.5 in)	59.7 cm (23.5 in)
Weight: Overall	0.1 kg (0.2 lbs)	2.0 kg (4.3 lbs)	3.4 kg (7.4 lbs)
Angling	–	2.0 kg (4.3 lbs)	3.4 kg (7.4 lbs)

COHO SALMON *Oncorhynchus kisutch*

Oncorhynchus—onco: hook; *rhyncho*: snout; refers to the hooked snout in spawning males.
kisutch: common name for this fish in Kamchatka, Russia, where it was first discovered.

The Coho and Chinook salmons, native to western North America, were first introduced into the Great Lakes in the late 1800s. However, reproducing populations of these species did not become established until the 1960s when they were stocked in large numbers.

DESCRIPTION: The Coho Salmon is a deep-bodied fish that is thin from side to side. It has very small scales (121–148 **lateral scales**). There are 13–15 anal rays, and when the anal fin is depressed against the body, its tip reaches the end of or extends slightly behind the anal fin base (p. 299) except in juveniles, where the tip extends well past the base. The inside of the mouth is black and the gums are pale. In the Great Lakes, the back is blue or green, the sides are silvery, and the belly is white. There are small dark spots on the back and usually only on the upper half of the tail. None of the spots has a pale edge. The dark spots may be faint on silvery individuals. In streams, the back and head become darker, and the sides dull. The spawning male develops a hooked snout, large teeth, and brilliant red sides.

SIMILAR SPECIES: Brook Trout and Lake Trout have pale spots on a dark body. Atlantic Salmon and Brown Trout have black and red spots with pale edges on the body and few or no spots on the tail. When the anal fin in these four species and in the Rainbow Trout is depressed against the body, its tip extends well behind the anal fin base. The Rainbow Trout has a pale mouth and gums, usually a reddish lateral stripe, and numerous rows of spots on both the upper and lower tail. The Chinook Salmon has black gums and dark spots on the upper and lower tail, and when the anal fin is depressed against the body, its tip usually does not extend to the end of the anal fin base.

FEEDING: Young Coho Salmon feed on aquatic insect **larvae**. After migrating into the Great Lakes, their diet becomes mostly **piscivorous**. Adult Coho Salmon feed on Alewife, Rainbow

♂ spawner

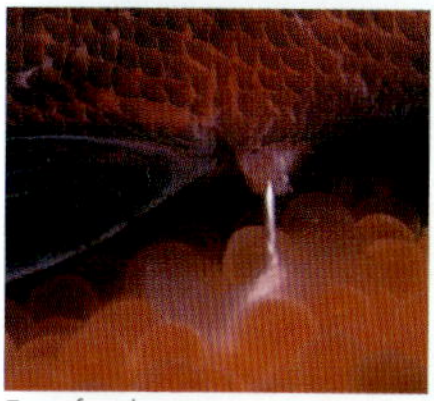

Egg fertilization

Eggs

Newly hatched yolk-sac **larvae**

Juvenile

Smelt, and other forage fishes in the shallows in spring and in deeper waters in summer.

REPRODUCTION: Spawning runs occur in the fall from the Great Lakes into tributaries. In **riffle** areas, the female hollows out a nest (known as a **redd**) in the gravel by lying on her side and beating vigorously with her tail. The male enters the **redd**, and eggs and sperm are released. The female covers the fertilized eggs with gravel and guards the nest as long as she can. Both adults die soon after spawning. The eggs hatch the following spring. Some young migrate immediately to the Great Lakes, while others remain in the stream for up to two years. Although Coho Salmon spawn in Great Lakes tributaries, this species is largely maintained through stocking by Ontario and several American states.

HABITAT: The Coho Salmon spends most of its life in the cold, deep waters of the Great Lakes until it returns to streams to spawn.

STATUS: G5; N5; SNA.

Maximum Age: 5	Ontario Average	Ontario Record	World Record
Length:	63.5 cm (25.0 in)	106.7 cm (42.0 in)	108.0 cm (42.5 in)
Weight: Overall	2.3 kg (5.0 lbs)	13.3 kg (29.2 lbs)	15.2 kg (33.5 lbs)
Angling	–	13.3 kg (29.2 lbs)	15.1 kg (33.2 lbs)

LAKE TROUT *Salvelinus namaycush*

Salvelinus—salvelin: an old name for **char**, meaning blood-coloured; alludes to their red belly.
namaycush: Indigenous name meaning tyrant of the lakes.

By the 1950s, the Lake Trout was decimated in the Great Lakes by overfishing and **predation** by the newly arrived Sea Lamprey. In the 1950s, the Province of Ontario developed and began stocking a **hybrid** of Lake Trout and Brook Trout (Speckled Trout) named Splake. Splake are intermediate in appearance to the parent species, and grow faster than either parent.

DESCRIPTION: The Lake Trout is a slightly deep-bodied fish. It has minute scales (175–228 **lateral scales**). There are 8–10 anal rays, and when the anal fin is depressed against the body, its tip extends well behind the anal fin base (p. 299). The tail is deeply forked. The gums and inside of the mouth are pale. The back is green, grey, brown, or almost black, the sides are lighter, and the belly is white. The head, body, and fins are covered with numerous pale spots, which are sometimes indistinct in silvery individuals from large lakes. There are no red spots. The lower fins have narrow, white leading edges that are not followed by a black stripe. Spawning individuals develop minute **nuptial tubercles** around the anus.

SIMILAR SPECIES: All other trouts and salmons, except the Brook Trout, have dark spots on the body, although these may be faint in silvery individuals. The Chinook, Coho, and Pink salmons have black tongues and anal fins with more than 12 rays, and when their anal fins are depressed against the body, the tips do not extend far behind the anal fin base, if at all. The Rainbow Trout often has a reddish stripe along the side. The Brook Trout has a square or slightly forked tail, wavy lines on the back and dorsal fin, red spots on the sides, and a black stripe behind the white leading edge of the lower fins.

FEEDING: The Lake Trout feeds on a variety of aquatic and terrestrial insects, crustaceans, fishes, amphibians, and small mammals.

REPRODUCTION: Spawning occurs in the fall in rocky areas of lakes, often with **groundwater upwellings**, when

Splake (**hybrid** Brook Trout and Lake Trout)

Juvenile

the water temperature falls below 11°C. A nest is not constructed, but Lake Trout clean the area by brushing rocks with their bodies and tails. Spawning occurs at night, often at depths of 10 m or more. The male presses against the female, and eggs and sperm are released. A female may spawn with one or two males at a time, or a group may spawn together. Fertilized eggs fall between rock crevices and remain there for several months before hatching.

HABITAT: In Ontario, the Lake Trout is found in the Great Lakes and coldwater lakes on the Canadian Shield. It is rarely found in streams, although it is known to migrate into some Great Lakes tributaries in the fall.

STATUS: G5; N5; S5.

Maximum Age: 50	Ontario Average	Ontario Record	World Record
Length:	50.0 cm (19.7 in)	130.8 cm (51.5 in)	150.0 cm (59.1 in)
Weight: Overall	1.2 kg (2.6 lbs)	28.6 kg (63.1 lbs)	46.3 kg (102.0 lbs)
Angling	–	28.6 kg (63.1 lbs)	32.7 kg (72.0 lbs)

LAKE WHITEFISH *Coregonus clupeaformis*

Coregonus—*kore*: eye; *gonia*: angle.
clupeaformis—*clupea*: herring; *formis*: shape; refers to its herring-like shape.

An important food item of the Lake Whitefish is the scud, a small bottom-dwelling crustacean. In the Great Lakes, scud populations have declined dramatically due to **competition** from the invasive Zebra and Quagga Mussels. As a result, Lake Whitefish have become thinner, have declined in abundance, and feed at greater depths where the scud are able to persist because there are no invasive Mussels.

DESCRIPTION: The Lake Whitefish is a deep-bodied, silvery fish. Its snout overhangs the small mouth. There are small weak teeth in the juvenile that disappear in the adult. There are 2 flaps of skin between the nostrils. There is no notch in the lower posterior section of the **eyelid**. The scales are small (70–97 **lateral scales**). There is a single dorsal fin with 11–13 rays and a small adipose fin without rays (p. 23). It has a pelvic axillary process (p. 23). The back is greenish brown, the sides are silvery, and the belly is silvery white. **Nuptial tubercles** develop on the sides of spawning individuals and are larger and more numerous in males.

SIMILAR SPECIES: Minnows, Goldeye, and Mooneye lack an adipose fin. The Rainbow Smelt is more elongate, has large canine teeth in the mouth, and lacks a pelvic axillary process. The snout in ciscoes does not overhang the mouth. The Round and Pygmy whitefishes have only a single flap of skin between the nostrils. The Round Whitefish has a notch in the lower posterior section of the **eyelid**.

FEEDING: The Lake Whitefish feeds from the bottom on **invertebrates**, including scuds, molluscs, aquatic insect **larvae**, and, occasionally, small fishes.

REPRODUCTION: Spawning occurs in fall when the water temperature drops below 8°C, typically in depths less than

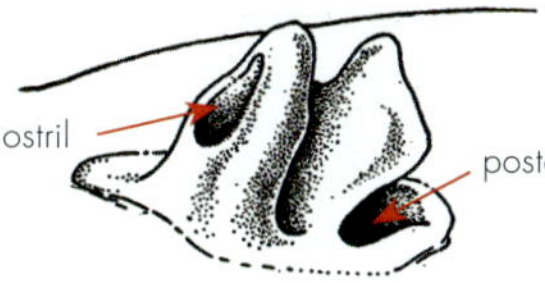

2 flaps of skin between nostrils

8 m. Eggs and sperm are deposited randomly over the stony bottom, and fertilized eggs are left unattended.

HABITAT: This species is generally found in the cold, deeper waters of lakes and, occasionally, large streams. In winter and spring, it may be found in cold, shallow waters.

STATUS: G5; N5; S5.
GNR, NNR, SNR, X^F (Como Lake populations).
G5TNRQ; NU; SU; T (Opeongo Lake populations).

Maximum Age: 50	Ontario Average	Ontario Record	World Record
Length:	38.0 cm (15.0 in)	74.9 cm (29.5 in)	100.0 cm (39.4 in)
Weight: Overall	0.5 kg (1.1 lbs)	6.7 kg (14.8 lbs)	19.0 kg (41.8 lbs)
Angling	–	6.7 kg (14.8 lbs)	6.5 kg (14.4 lbs)

PINK SALMON *Oncorhynchus gorbuscha*

Oncorhynchus—onco: hook; *rhyncho*: snout; refers to the hooked snout in spawning males.
gorbuscha: an old Russian name for this species.

The Pink Salmon, native to western North America, was accidentally released into Lake Superior when a hatchery flooded in the 1950s. It subsequently spread and **established** reproducing populations in a few tributaries across the Great Lakes basin.

DESCRIPTION: The Pink Salmon is a slightly deep-bodied fish that is thin from side to side. It has tiny scales (147–205, usually more than 170, **lateral scales**). There are 13–19 anal rays. When the anal fin is depressed against the body, its tip may vary from not reaching, to extending slightly beyond, the anal fin base (p. 299). In the Great Lakes, the back is blue or green, the sides are silvery, and the belly is white. In streams, the back and head become darker, and the sides lose their silver colour and become pale red with brown to olive-green blotches. There are large dark spots on the body, which may be faint on silvery individuals. On the tail, these spots are often longer than the eye diameter. The spawning male develops a hooked snout and a hump behind the head.The juvenile lacks **parr marks** and has no spots on the dorsal fin and tail.

SIMILAR SPECIES: No other trout or salmon has dark markings on the tail that are as long as the eye diameter. The Pink Salmon occasionally **hybridizes** with the Chinook Salmon.

FEEDING: In the Great Lakes, Pink Salmon primarily eat small fishes.

REPRODUCTION: After spending two years in the Great Lakes, the Pink Salmon begins its spawning run into streams in late summer when the water temperature is about 10°C. Once arriving at its spawning grounds, the female hollows out a nest (known as a **redd**) in the gravel by lying on her side and beating vigorously with her tail to remove silt and gravel. The male

Juvenile

Migration

arrives on the **redd** and may aggressively defend it from other males. Eggs and sperm are released, and the fertilized eggs are covered by the female. Exhausted from the migration and spawning, the female guards the nest as long as she can, but both females and males die within a few days of spawning.

HABITAT: The Pink Salmon spends most of its life in the cold, deep, open waters of the Great Lakes until it returns to tributaries to spawn.

STATUS: G5; N5; SNA.

Maximum Age: 3	Ontario Average	Ontario Record	World Record
Length:	61.0 cm (24.0 in)	83.0 cm (32.7 in)	83.0 cm (32.7 in)
Weight: Overall	1.8 kg (4.0 lbs)	5.9 kg (13.1 lbs)	6.8 kg (15.0 lbs)
Angling	–	5.9 kg (13.1 lbs)	6.7 kg (14.9 lbs)

PYGMY WHITEFISH *Prosopium coulterii*

Prosopium: a mask; refers to the large bones in front of the eyes. *coulterii*: named for Dr. John Coulter, an American botanist.

The Pygmy Whitefish population in Lake Superior was the only one known east of the foothills of the Rockies until recently, when it was found in several lakes northwest of Lake Superior. This very unusual and highly disjunct distribution is puzzling to biologists.

DESCRIPTION: The Pygmy Whitefish is a small, elongate, and silvery fish. Its snout overhangs the small mouth. Small weak teeth are present only on the tongue. There is only a single flap of skin between the nostrils. It has small scales (50–70 **lateral scales**). There is a single dorsal fin with 11–12 rays and a small adipose fin without rays (p. 23). It has a pelvic axillary process (p. 23). The back is brown, the sides are silvery, and the belly is white. Spawning individuals develop **nuptial tubercles** on the back, sides, and fins, which are larger and more numerous in males.

SIMILAR SPECIES: Minnows lack an adipose fin. The Rainbow Smelt has large canine teeth in the mouth and lacks a pelvic axillary process. The snout in ciscoes does not overhang the mouth. The Lake Whitefish has 2 flaps of skin between the nostrils. The Round Whitefish has smaller scales and, usually, dark spots on the top of the head and adipose fin. Its adult length exceeds 142 mm in Ontario.

FEEDING: The Pygmy Whitefish feeds on a variety of crustaceans, aquatic insects, molluscs, and, occasionally, fish eggs.

REPRODUCTION: Little is known of the spawning habits of the Pygmy Whitefish. It spawns in the fall, likely over gravel bottoms. The fertilized eggs hatch in spring.

HABITAT: In Ontario, the Pygmy Whitefish is found in the cold, deep waters of Lake Superior and in at least one inland lake in northwestern Ontario.

STATUS: G4TNRQ; N2; SU; T[F] (Great Lakes–Upper

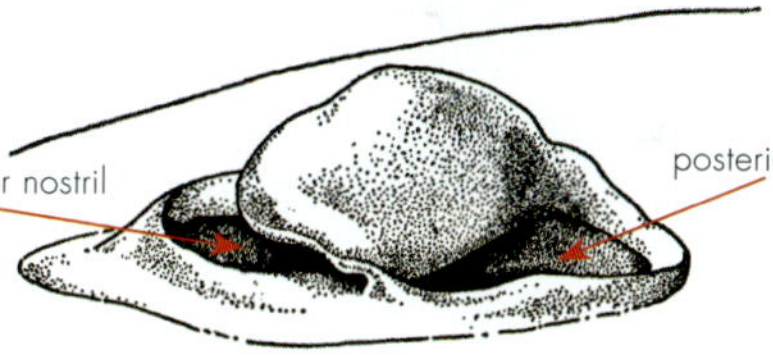

single flap of skin between the nostrils

St. Lawrence populations).
G4TNRQ; N1N2; SU; DD[F] (Saskatchewan–Nelson River populations.

Maximum Age: 9	Ontario Average	Ontario Record	World Record
Length:	11.5 cm (4.5 in)	14.2 cm (5.6 in)	28.0 cm (11.0 in)

RAINBOW TROUT *Oncorhynchus mykiss*

Oncorhynchus—onco: hook; *rhyncho*: snout; refers to the hooked snout in spawning males.
mykiss: common name for this fish in Kamchatka, Russia, where it was described.

The Rainbow Trout, native to western North America, is one of the most widely introduced species in Ontario. Individuals that undergo spawning migrations in the Great Lakes and its tributaries are termed "steelhead."

DESCRIPTION: The Rainbow Trout is an elongate, moderately deep-bodied fish. It has very small scales (100–150 **lateral scales**). There are fewer than 13 anal rays, and when the anal fin is depressed against the body, its tip extends well behind the anal fin base (p. 299). The gums and inside of the mouth are usually pale. The back is olive-brown to purple, and the sides are paler with a prominent reddish lateral stripe. There are numerous small dark spots on the back and tail, none of which has a pale edge. In Great Lakes individuals, the back is blue or green, the sides are silvery, and the belly is white. The reddish lateral stripe and dark spots may be faint or absent on the body. When entering streams, these individuals lose their silver colour and become darker.

SIMILAR SPECIES: The Brook Trout and Lake Trout have pale spots on a dark body. The Atlantic Salmon and Brown Trout have black and red spots with pale edges on the body and few or no spots on the tail. The Chinook, Coho, and Pink salmons have black mouths. When the anal fin is depressed against the body, its tip does not extend behind the anal fin base in the Chinook and Pink salmons, and only slightly behind the anal fin base in the Coho Salmon.

FEEDING: In streams, Rainbow Trout mostly eat aquatic insects. They usually feed on the bottom, but may rise to the surface in search of emerging or egg-laying insects. Small fishes, snails, leeches, and fish eggs may also supplement their diet. In the Great Lakes, they are mostly **piscivorous**, feeding on Alewife,

Steelhead

Juvenile

Rainbow Smelt, and other forage fishes in the shallows in spring and in deeper waters in summer.

REPRODUCTION: Rainbow Trout usually spawn in the spring when the water temperature reaches 5°C. The female hollows out a nest (known as a **redd**) in the gravel with her tail, and is joined by one or two males. Eggs and sperm are released, and the female covers the eggs with gravel. There is no parental care given to the eggs or young. Spawning runs occur from the Great Lakes into tributary streams in fall and spring. Unlike the Chinook, Coho, and Pink salmons, Rainbow Trout return to the lake and may migrate and spawn for up to five successive years before dying.

HABITAT: The Rainbow Trout is found in cold streams and lakes. The steelhead spends most of its life in the cold waters of the Great Lakes until it returns to tributaries to spawn.

STATUS: G5; N5; SNA.

Maximum Age: 11	Ontario Average	Ontario Record	World Record
Length:	53.0 cm (20.9 in)	99.3 cm (39.1 in)	122.0 cm (48.0 in)
Weight: Overall	1.5 kg (3.3 lbs)	18.5 kg (40.7 lbs)	25.4 kg (56.0 lbs)
Angling	–	18.5 kg (40.7 lbs)	21.8 kg (48.0 lbs)

ROUND WHITEFISH *Prosopium cylindraceum*

Prosopium: a mask; refers to the large bones in front of the eyes. *cylindraceum*: shaped like a cylinder.

The Round Whitefish is much more common in northwestern Canada than in Ontario, where it is rarely encountered as a result of its small size, low abundance, and preference for deep waters.

DESCRIPTION: The Round Whitefish is a very elongate, silvery fish. Its snout overhangs the small mouth. Small weak teeth are present only on the tongue. There is only a single flap of skin between the nostrils. There is a notch in the lower posterior section of the **eyelid**. It has very small scales (74–108 **lateral scales**). There is a single dorsal fin with 11–15 rays and a small adipose fin without rays (p. 23). It has a pelvic axillary process (p. 23). The back is light greenish brown to almost black, the sides are silvery, and the belly is silvery white. Spawning individuals develop **nuptial tubercles** on the sides and on the back behind the head, which are larger and more numerous in males.

SIMILAR SPECIES: Minnows lack an adipose fin. The Rainbow Smelt, ciscoes, and Lake Whitefish lack a notch in the lower posterior section of the **eyelid**. The Rainbow Smelt has large canine teeth in the mouth and lacks a pelvic axillary process. The snout in ciscoes does not overhang the mouth. The Lake Whitefish has 2 flaps of skin between the nostrils. The Pygmy Whitefish has larger scales and lacks dark spots on the top of the head and adipose fin, and its length rarely exceeds 142 mm in Ontario.

FEEDING: The Round Whitefish feeds from the bottom on aquatic insect **larvae**, crustaceans, molluscs, and, occasionally, fish eggs and small fishes.

REPRODUCTION: Spawning occurs in the fall when the water temperature drops below 5°C. Males migrate to the shallow waters of lakes and streams, followed by females. Eggs and sperm are released over gravel bottoms. No parental care is given to the fertilized eggs or young.

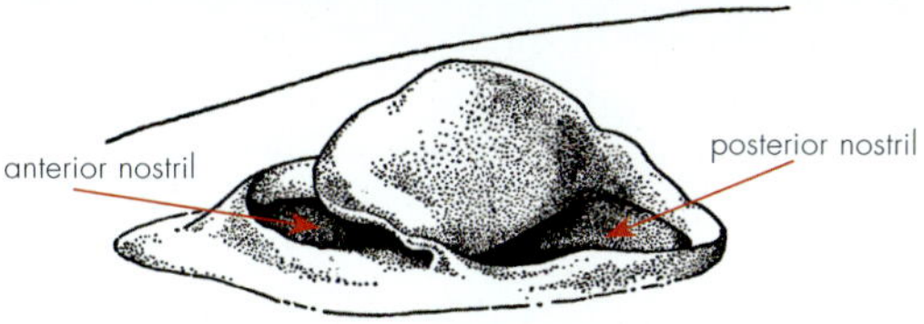

single flap of skin between the nostrils

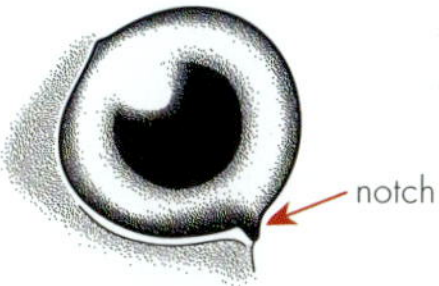

eye showing notch on the lower posterior section of the **eyelid**

HABITAT: The Round Whitefish is found in the cold waters of the Great Lakes and inland lakes on the Canadian Shield. It is rarely found in streams.

STATUS: G5; N5; S4.

Maximum Age: 16	Ontario Average	Ontario Record	World Record
Length:	25.0 cm (9.8 in)	54.2 cm (21.3 in)	59.0 cm (23.2 in)
Weight: Overall	–	–	2.7 kg (6.0 lbs)
Angling	–	–	2.7 kg (6.0 lbs)

PERCOPSIDAE
Trout-perches

The Trout-perches are so named for their resemblance to both trouts and perches. There are two species in this family, both of which are found only in the fresh waters of North America. Trout-perches are small, silvery fishes with dark spots and a large head. The dorsal fin has one or two soft spines and is followed by an adipose fin. The anal fin also has one or two soft spines at its leading edge. The pelvic fins are located far forward, below the pectoral fins.

The Trout-perches are surviving members of a much larger family that dates back to the Eocene Epoch, 55 to 34 million years ago. The members of this family are considered to link the more ancient soft-rayed families, such as salmons and trouts, with the more recently appearing spiny-rayed families, such as perches and darters, as they have characteristics common to both groups. These characteristics include the adipose fin and scaleless head found in trouts, and **ctenoid scales** and fin spines found in perches.

There are two living species, only one of which is found in Ontario.

< Trout-perch

TROUT-PERCH *Percopsis omiscomaycus*

Percopsis—perke: perch; *ops*: like; similar characteristics to a perch. *omiscomaycus*: Indigenous word for this fish.

Trout-perch move inshore in the evening to feed and offshore in the morning to seek shelter. They provide a vital link between these habitats by transporting nutrients from shallow to deep waters, where Trout-perch are preyed upon by coldwater species such as Lake Trout.

DESCRIPTION: The Trout-perch is a small, elongate fish. It has small **ctenoid scales** (43–60 **lateral scales**). On the back, there is a single dorsal fin with 2 spines, followed by 9–11 soft rays and a small adipose fin without rays (p. 23). The pelvic fins originate below the middle of the pectoral fin. The back and sides are yellow-olive, silvery, or translucent, with 5 rows of black spots or markings. The belly is silvery white or translucent.

SIMILAR SPECIES: The darters, Freshwater Drum, minnows, Ruffe, and suckers do not have an adipose fin. The ciscoes, Rainbow Smelt, and whitefishes have **cycloid scales**, and their pelvic fin **origins** are behind the pectoral fins.

FEEDING: The Trout-perch moves into shallow water at night to feed on aquatic insects and small crustaceans. Large adults may also feed on small fishes and fish eggs.

REPRODUCTION: Spring spawning runs occur when the water temperature reaches 10°C, although some Ontario populations spawn well into the summer. Males and females congregate in shallow, rocky streams or the nearshore waters of lakes. Two or more males press against the female, and the spawning group often breaks the surface of the water as they release eggs and sperm. The fertilized eggs ink and adhere to the bottom. The Trout-perch is a **fractional spawner**, producing and releasing small batches of eggs several times during the spawning season.

HABITAT: The Trout-perch prefers the cool waters of lakes, but may occasionally be found in streams.

STATUS: G5; N5; S5.

Maximum Age: 4	Ontario Average	Ontario Record	World Record
Length:	9.0 cm (3.5 in)	15.0 cm (5.9 in)	20.0 cm (7.9 in)

GADIDAE
Cods

Members of this family are usually found in large schools throughout the Northern Hemisphere. Most species occur in the deep, open oceans, except for the Burbot, which occurs only in fresh waters. The cods usually have one **barbel** under the chin, two or three dorsal fins, one long or two shorter anal fins, and pelvic fins positioned underneath the gill opening and in front of the pectoral fins. They have small **cycloid scales**.

This family includes many highly prized species, such as the Atlantic Cod, Haddock, and Pollock, and is second by volume only to the herring family in global commercial fish landings. The Atlantic Cod had been fished off Newfoundland's coast for more than 500 years; however, a moratorium was placed on cod fishing in 1992 due to the **collapse** of the species. Cod stocks have still not rebounded, and this may be partially due to irreversible changes in the marine ecosystem.

There are 26 species worldwide, one of which is found in Ontario.

< Burbot

BURBOT *Lota lota*

Lota—lotte: a French word for codfish.

The Burbot is rarely encountered in the summer, but is frequently caught by anglers ice-fishing for Lake Trout. This species is generally referred to by anglers as "ling" or "ling cod."

DESCRIPTION: The Burbot is a large elongate fish. It has minute embedded scales that are not visible to the naked eye except in large fish. It has a single **barbel** on the chin. There are 2 dorsal fins, a short one followed by a long one, a rounded tail, and a long anal fin. The pelvic fins are located below the gill opening and in front of the pectoral fins. The back and sides are yellow, brown, or black, and are often mottled. The belly is white.

SIMILAR SPECIES: The Emerald Bowfin has large scales. Ontario catfishes have more than 1 **barbel**. The tail and dorsal and anal fins are continuous in the American Eel. None of these fishes has a single **barbel** on the chin, or pelvic fins in front of the pectoral fins.

FEEDING: The Burbot is considered to have a voracious appetite, and forages at night on the bottom for crustaceans and a wide variety of fishes.

REPRODUCTION: The Burbot is the only species in Ontario that spawns in winter under the ice when the water temperature is 1°C. Spawning occurs in shallow bays over sand or on gravel shoals. Males arrive first, followed by the females three to four days later. Spawning takes place at night with 10–12 males and females forming a writhing ball that rolls across the bottom. Eggs and sperm are scattered, and the fertilized eggs are given no parental care.

HABITAT: The Burbot prefers the cold bottom waters of lakes, but may occasionally be found in cold streams.

STATUS: G5; N5; S5.

Spawning Burbot

Maximum Age: 20	Ontario Average	Ontario Record	World Record
Length:	38.0 cm (15.0 in)	104.1 cm (41.0 in)	152.0 cm (59.8 in)
Weight: Overall	0.4 kg (0.9 lbs)	8.1 kg (18.0 lbs)	34.0 kg (75.0 lbs)
Angling	–	8.1 kg (18.0 lbs)	11.4 kg (25.1 lbs)

ATHERINOPSIDAE
New World Silversides

Members of this family are distributed in the fresh and salt waters of North, Central, and South America. They are usually small and elongate and have a wide silvery stripe. They have two widely separated dorsal fins; the first is short with weak spines, and the second is longer with a single spine followed by soft rays. The pectoral fins are placed high on the body, and the pelvic and anal fins each have a small spine. **Cycloid scales** are found on the head and body.

The marine Atlantic Silverside occurs in a broad latitudinal range, from Canada's Gulf of St. Lawrence to Florida. This species is very short lived, usually maturing at age one, spawning several times in the spring, and then dying. To adapt to the short growing season in Canadian waters, eggs that hatch early in the spring are mostly females. This allows the females the longest time possible to grow to a larger size and produce more eggs, which will be laid the next year. In southern waters where the growing season is longer, females and males hatch at the same rate throughout the spawning season. This strategy is called "temperature-dependent sex determination."

There are 108 species in this family, one of which occurs in Ontario.

< Brook Silverside

BROOK SILVERSIDE *Labidesthes sicculus*

Labidesthes—labidos: pair of forceps; refers to the jaw shape. *sicculus—siccus*: dried; it is sometimes found in drying pools of streams.

On a moonlit night, schools of Brook Silverside can be seen "flying" out of the water in a low arc, and individuals may travel up to 10 times their body length before re-entry. This unusual behaviour is made possible by their pectoral fins, which are set high on the body, similar to those in flying fishes.

DESCRIPTION: The Brook Silverside is an elongate, silvery fish. There are minute teeth on the jaws, but none on the tongue or roof of the mouth. It has very small scales (75–95 **lateral scales**). There are 2 dorsal fins—a short one with 4 spines followed by a long one with 11–12 rays. It has a long anal fin with 24–28 rays. The body is pale green or olive, and the sides have a silvery stripe. The tip of the first dorsal fin is black in spawning males. The male has a short, conical **genital papilla**, whereas the female has a wide, round, fleshy one.

SIMILAR SPECIES: Minnows have only a single dorsal fin and lack teeth in their mouth. The Rainbow Smelt has a single dorsal fin, a fleshy adipose fin, and a shorter anal fin.

FEEDING: This species schools near the surface and leaps out of the water to feed on flying insects. Aquatic insects and crustaceans may also be eaten.

REPRODUCTION: Spawning occurs in shallow, well-vegetated areas in spring and summer when the water temperature reaches 17°C. Males defend a territory and chase females, who often dart out of the water. Eventually, a pair releases eggs and sperm as they glide to the bottom. Males and females possess **genital papillae,** through which eggs and sperm are released. Eggs have adhesive filaments and microscopic hairs that aid in attachment to vegetation. The Brook Silverside is a **fractional spawner**, releasing eggs and sperm in intervals throughout the spring and summer. Adults usually die shortly after the spawning season.

HABITAT: The Brook Silverside prefers the warm surface waters of clear streams and the nearshores of lakes.

STATUS: G5; N4; S4; NAR.

Maximum Age: 2	Ontario Average	Ontario Record	World Record
Length:	7.5 cm (3.0 in)	10.8 cm (4.2 in)	13.0 cm (5.1 in)

FUNDULIDAE
Topminnows

This family is closely related to the live bearers (Poeciliidae), which includes guppies. The topminnows are found in marine and fresh waters from eastern Canada to Manitoba and south to Bermuda, Cuba, and Yucatan. Topminnows are highly adapted for surface feeding with heads that are flattened on top and mouths that are small, **protrusible**, and upturned. They have one dorsal fin behind the middle of the back and a rounded or squared tail. **Cycloid scales** are found on the head and body.

Some fishes lay their eggs out of water and then rely on seasonal rainfall or high tides for egg hatching. This occurs on Canada's east coast, where a topminnow, the Mummichog, consistently spawns at night during the highest spring tides with a new or full moon. The fertilized eggs attach to vegetation that is left high and dry until the next high tide several weeks later—at which time the eggs rapidly rehydrate and hatch, and the young are washed into tide pools. This remarkable stranding behaviour is thought to allow the eggs to incubate in safety, away from wave disturbance and **predation**.

There are 45 species worldwide, two of which are found in Ontario.

< Blackstripe Topminnow (♀ top, ♂ bottom)

BANDED KILLIFISH *Fundulus diaphanus*

Fundulus—*fundus*: bottom; *ulus*: little; a small bottom-dwelling fish. *diaphanus*: transparent; the body has a transparent look.

This species is related to the Mosquitofish and looks quite similar with its small size and upturned mouth. The Mosquitofish, aptly named for its propensity to feed on mosquito **larvae**, is native to the southern United States and Mexico but has been introduced throughout the world to control mosquitoes. The Banded Killifish also feeds on mosquitoes, but never gets abundant enough in Ontario to control mosquito populations.

DESCRIPTION: The Banded Killifish is a small elongate fish. The upper jaw does not extend to the eye. It has large scales (40–51 **lateral scales**). The tail is square. The back is olive-green to dark brown, the sides are silver to pale yellow with 12–20 vertical dark bars, and the belly is yellow to white. The dorsal and anal fins often have black markings, whereas the tail and pectoral and pelvic fins are clear. The female has fewer and more widely spaced vertical bars. The male is more brightly coloured than the female at spawning time.

SIMILAR SPECIES: No minnows in Ontario have vertical bars or square tails. The Blackstripe Topminnow has sides with a distinct dark lateral stripe crossed by short bars in the male. The Central Mudminnow has a larger mouth, an upper jaw that extends backwards to below the front of the eye, darker sides with more irregular-shaped bars, and a black bar at the base of the tail.

FEEDING: The Banded Killifish feeds on aquatic insect **larvae**, crustaceans, molluscs, and plants.

REPRODUCTION: Spawning occurs in quiet, heavily vegetated waters in spring and summer when the water temperature reaches 20°C. The male defends a territory by chasing away other males and pursuing a female until she extrudes a single egg, which hangs from her body by a thin thread. The male then presses against her, holds her with his dorsal and anal fins, quivers, and releases sperm. The

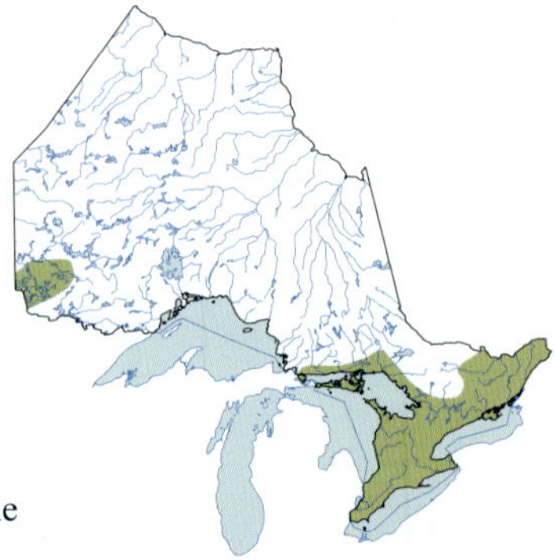

♂

♀

female then extrudes eggs in small batches of 5–10. The fertilized eggs have long adhesive threads that attach to vegetation. The eggs are abandoned and hatch in about two weeks.

HABITAT: The Banded Killifish prefers the warm surface waters of clear streams and the nearshores of lakes.

STATUS: G5; N5; S5; NAR.

Maximum Age: 3	Ontario Average	Ontario Record	World Record
Length:	7.0 cm (2.8 in)	9.8 cm (3.9 in)	13.0 cm (5.1 in)

BLACKSTRIPE TOPMINNOW *Fundulus notatus*

Fundulus—*fundus*: bottom; *ulus*: little; a small bottom-dwelling fish. *notatus*: spotted.

The Blackstripe Topminnow has one of the most restricted distributions of any freshwater fish in Canada. It is found only in small sections of several streams in southwestern Ontario.

DESCRIPTION: The Blackstripe Topminnow is a small elongate fish. It has very large scales (29–36 **lateral scales**). The tail is rounded. The back is olive-green to dark brown, the sides have a prominent dark lateral stripe, and the belly is yellow to white. The top of the head often has a white spot. The tail and dorsal and anal fins frequently have small dark spots. In males, the chin is blue, the gill **membranes** are yellow, and there are short dark bars along the lateral stripe. In females, the gill **membranes** are white. The male has larger dorsal and anal fins than the female.

SIMILAR SPECIES: No minnows in Ontario have rounded tails. The Central Mudminnow and the Banded Killifish have vertical bars and lack a dark lateral stripe.

FEEDING: The Blackstripe Topminnow feeds on terrestrial insects taken from the surface, as well as molluscs and crustaceans.

REPRODUCTION: Spawning occurs throughout the spring and summer when the water temperature reaches 21°C. A male and female form a pair and defend a territory in shallow areas with heavy vegetation, chasing out other topminnows. The male follows the female below and behind her. When ready to spawn, he presses against her and holds her with his dorsal and anal fins, and they both quiver. The female releases a cluster of 5–10 eggs that hang from her by an adhesive thread. The male fertilizes and then places the cluster onto vegetation, where they adhere. A total of 20–30 eggs are deposited in this way over several days, and then the process is repeated later in the season when the female is ready to release another batch of eggs.

♂

♀ top, ♂ bottom

Blackstripe Topminnow and its reflection off the surface of the water

HABITAT: The Blackstripe Topminnow prefers the warm surface waters of small streams.

STATUS: G5; N2; S2; SC.

Maximum Age: 2	Ontario Average	Ontario Record	World Record
Length:	5.5 cm (2.2 in)	6.7 cm (2.6 in)	8.0 cm (3.1 in)

GASTEROSTEIDAE
Sticklebacks

This is one of the most studied fish families because of the unique reproductive behaviour of its members. Sticklebacks are found in the fresh and salt waters of Eurasia and North America. They are small and easily recognized, as they have 3–16 isolated dorsal spines followed by a soft-rayed dorsal fin. The spines may stick straight up (e.g., Brook Stickleback) or may lean to one side or the other (e.g., Ninespine Stickleback). The pectoral fins are fan-like, and the pelvic fins, found below the pectoral fins, have one spine with one or two soft rays. The body is scaleless and may be covered with bony plates.

Sticklebacks on the west coast of Canada are of great interest to evolutionary biologists, as they have evolved at an extremely rapid rate since the end of the last Ice Age 10,000 years ago. In several isolated lakes, **species pairs** have evolved independently from their ancestor, the marine Threespine Stickleback. In each lake, the two members of the **species pair** differ in size and behaviour and occupy a different **niche**, with one being benthic (inhabiting the bottom of the lake) and the other limnetic (living in open waters). These **species pairs** are at risk of extinction due to **hybridization** and the introduction of **invasive species**.

There are 21 species worldwide, four of which occur in Ontario.

< Ninespine Stickleback nesting (♂ top, ♀ bottom)

BROOK STICKLEBACK *Culaea inconstans*

Culaea: derived from the original name *eucalia*—*eu*: true; *calathus*: basket; refers to the nest shape.
inconstans: variable; refers to variation in colour pattern or number of spines.

The sticklebacks typically have several spines on their back and bony plates on their sides. These small fishes are protected from **predation** by these spines and plates, which often vary in number depending on the presence of predators.

DESCRIPTION: The Brook Stickleback is a small, slightly deep-bodied fish. It has no scales. There are 4–7, usually 5, short, isolated dorsal spines that are about equal in length and stick straight up. The back and sides are olive-green with numerous pale spots or wavy lines, and the belly is silvery white to light green. The spawning male is dark green to black, sometimes with a copper tint, and may have red pelvic fins. Spawning females become darker.

SIMILAR SPECIES: The Ninespine Stickleback has 7–12, usually 9, short dorsal spines that often lean to the left or the right. The Threespine Stickleback has 2–4, usually 3, dorsal spines. The Fourspine Stickleback has 3–4, usually 4, dorsal spines that vary in length and often lean to the left or the right.

FEEDING: The Brook Stickleback consumes aquatic insect **larvae**, crustaceans, and, occasionally, fish eggs.

REPRODUCTION: Stickleback spawning behaviour is renowned for its complexity. In summer, the male arrives on the spawning grounds first and constructs a round nest from leaves and twigs held together by a thread that he secretes. The male courts a female and lures her into the nest with nips, butts, and nudges. The male prods her belly and eggs are released. She is then chased out of the nest, and the male fertilizes the eggs. Several females may spawn in his nest over the season. He guards the eggs and young by attacking intruders or by performing an aggressive display with erected spines and a quivering body.

Spawning ♂ (black) and ♀ inside nest

♂ displaying spawning colour

Skeleton stained with red and blue dye

HABITAT: The Brook Stickleback is found not only in brooks, but also in the cool, shallow waters of larger streams, lakes, and wetlands and in the deep waters of the Great Lakes.

STATUS: G5; N5; S5.

Maximum Age: 3	Ontario Average	Ontario Record	World Record
Length:	5.0 cm (2.0 in)	7.6 cm (3.0 in)	8.7 cm (3.4 in)

FOURSPINE STICKLEBACK *Apeltes quadracus*

Apeltes—a: without; *peltes*: shield; refers to the lack of protective plates.
quadracus—quad: four; *acus*: spines; refers to the four spines on the back.

The Fourspine Stickleback is found only in the Thunder Bay area of Ontario. It is native to eastern Canada, and its occurrence in Thunder Bay is clearly the result of transfer in the ballast water of ships travelling through the St. Lawrence Seaway.

DESCRIPTION: The Fourspine Stickleback is a small, slightly deep-bodied fish. It has no scales. There are 3–4, usually 4, isolated dorsal spines that often lean to the left or right. The back is olive-green to brown, the sides are darkly mottled, and the belly is silver or white. The spawning male may be almost black with red pelvic fins.

SIMILAR SPECIES: The Ninespine Stickleback has 7–12, usually 9, short dorsal spines that are about equal in length. The Brook Stickleback has 4–7, usually 5, short dorsal spines that are about equal in length and stick straight up. The Threespine Stickleback has 2–4, usually 3, dorsal spines that stick straight up.

FEEDING: The Fourspine Stickleback consumes tiny **invertebrates** and algae.

REPRODUCTION: Stickleback spawning behaviour is renowned for its complexity. In spring and summer, the male constructs a cup-shaped basket out of leaves and twigs held together and attached to vegetation by a thread he secretes. The male then performs a dance for the female by rapidly swimming around her and displaying his red pelvic fins. The female enters the nest and, in a head-up position, releases between 15 and 50 eggs. The male picks up stray eggs in his mouth and places them in the nest before fertilizing them. The female is chased out of the nest, and the male aerates the fertilized eggs by sucking water through the nest. Up to four nests may

Dorsal spines

be built, one on top of the other, and guarded by a single male. The male may chase, ram, and bite intruders.

HABITAT: In Ontario, the Fourspine Stickleback is known only from the shallow, cool waters of Thunder Bay harbour.

STATUS: G5; N5; SNA.

Maximum Age: 3	Ontario Average	Ontario Record	World Record
Length:	4.5 cm (1.8 in)	5.3 cm (2.1 in)	6.4 cm (2.5 in)

NINESPINE STICKLEBACK *Pungitius pungitius*

Pungitius: pricking; refers to the isolated spines on the back.

Some populations of the Ninespine Stickleback from western Canada have lost their pelvic fins and underlying supporting bones, particularly on the right side, during the course of evolution. The Florida Manatee, a large marine mammal, has also lost its hindlimbs and supporting bones, typically on the right side. The independent evolution of unique characteristics in different species is known as parallel evolution.

DESCRIPTION: The Ninespine Stickleback is a small elongate fish. It has no scales. There are 7–12, usually 9, short, isolated dorsal spines that often lean to the left or right and are about equal in length. The back is light grey to olive, the sides are pale with irregular dark bars or blotches, and the belly is silver. Spawning individuals have a reddish tint, and spawning males become black with white pelvic fins.

SIMILAR SPECIES: The Threespine Stickleback has 2–4, usually 3, dorsal spines that stick straight up. The Fourspine Stickleback has 3–4, usually 4, dorsal spines that vary in length. The Brook Stickleback has 4–7, usually 5, short dorsal spines that stick straight up.

FEEDING: The Ninespine Stickleback consumes aquatic insects, crustaceans, molluscs, worms, and, occasionally, fish eggs.

REPRODUCTION: Stickleback spawning behaviour is renowned for its complexity. In summer, the male constructs a tunnel-shaped nest from leaves and twigs held together with a thread he secretes. The male lures the female into the nest by performing an intricate dance of zigzag swimming patterns in front of the nest opening with his head down and spines erect. The male vibrates against the female, and eggs are released. She is then chased out of the opposite end of the nest, and the male fertilizes the

Nesting ♂ top, ♀ bottom

eggs. Several females may spawn in his nest over the season. The male fans the fertilized eggs with his pectoral fins and guards the eggs and young from intruders.

HABITAT: The Ninespine Stickleback is found in the cool, shallow waters of streams, lakes, and wetlands, and also in the deep waters of the Great Lakes.

STATUS: G5; N5; S5.

Maximum Age: 5	Ontario Average	Ontario Record	World Record
Length:	6.5 cm (2.6 in)	8.9 cm (3.5 in)	9.0 cm (3.5 in)

THREESPINE STICKLEBACK *Gasterosteus aculeatus*

Gasterosteus—*gastro*: belly; *osteus*: bony; refers to the bony ventral plates.
aculeatus: with spines; refers to the spines on the back.

In Ontario, the Threespine Stickleback is native only to southeastern Ontario, downstream of Niagara Falls, and the James Bay Lowlands. Its recent sporadic occurrence in the upper Great Lakes is undoubtedly the result of transfer in the ballast water of ships travelling through the St. Lawrence Seaway.

DESCRIPTION: The Threespine Stickleback is a small, slightly deep-bodied fish. It has no scales, but it usually has large plates on the sides. There are 2–4, usually 3, isolated dorsal spines that stick straight up, with the first 2 spines being the longest. The back is silvery green to olive-brown, sometimes darkly mottled. The sides are pale with silvery reflections, and the belly is silver. In the spawning male, the eyes are blue, the dorsal surface has a bluish sheen, and the sides and belly are red. Spawning females are golden with dark grey vertical stripes along their sides.

SIMILAR SPECIES: The Ninespine Stickleback has 7–12, usually 9, short dorsal spines that are about equal in length. The Brook Stickleback has 4–7, usually 5, short dorsal spines that are about equal in length. The Fourspine Stickleback has 3–4, usually 4, dorsal spines that often lean to the left or right.

FEEDING: The Threespine Stickleback consumes small crustaceans, aquatic and terrestrial insects, molluscs, worms, and, occasionally, fish eggs.

REPRODUCTION: Stickleback spawning behaviour is renowned for its complexity. In summer, the male constructs a tunnel-shaped nest from leaves and twigs, which he assembles with a thread he secretes. The male lures the female into the nest by performing an intricate zigzag dance in front of the nest opening. The male prods her belly and eggs are released. She is then chased out of the nest, and the male fertilizes the eggs.

♀

♂

Several females may spawn in his nest over the season. The male fans the fertilized eggs and guards them from intruders. Schools of egg-eating females may raid the nest, and the defending male tries to draw them away. To distract the females, he swims away from the nest and then rolls to expose his shiny, silvery belly.

HABITAT: The Threespine Stickleback prefers the cool waters (both shallow and deep) of the Great Lakes and lower portions of their tributaries. It is also found in the brackish waters of the James Bay Lowlands.

STATUS: G5; N5; S4S5.

Maximum Age: 8	Ontario Average	Ontario Record	World Record
Length:	5.0 cm (2.0 in)	7.5 cm (3.0 in)	11.0 cm (4.3 in)

COTTIDAE
Sculpins

Most members of this family are small, bottom-dwelling freshwater fishes in lakes and rivers in the Northern Hemisphere. A few move into salt water either to feed or reproduce.

Sculpins in this family have a large, flattened head with large eyes placed high on the head and spines at the front of the gill cover. The body usually lacks scales although **prickles** or plates are often present. There are two dorsal fins – the first one is small with spines, and the second is larger with soft rays. In some species, these two fins are joined by a very small **membrane**.

The colour pattern helps them blend into their surroundings. They are often difficult to identify and additional studies are required to resolve their relationships

There are 118 species worldwide, three of which are found in Ontario.

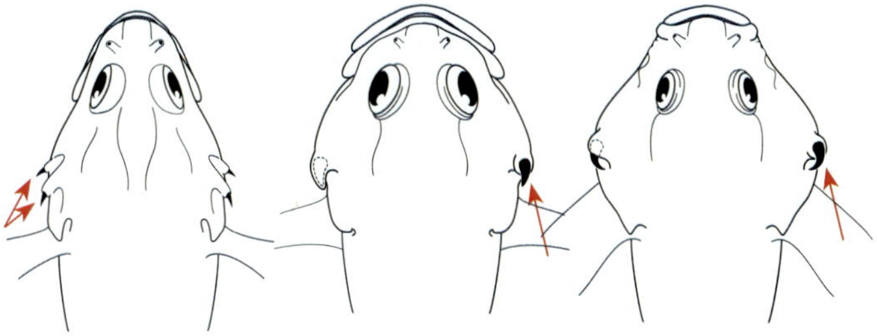

2 prominent spines at the front of the gill cover (Deepwater Sculpin)

prominent spine at the front of the gill cover, straight or slightly curved, its length usually less than 2/3 eye diameter (e.g., Slimy Sculpin)

prominent spine at the front of the gill cover. Strongly curved, its length usually more than 2/3 eye diameter (Spoonhead Sculpin)

< Mottled Sculpin

MOTTLED SCULPIN *Cottus bairdii*

Cottus—kottos: head; refers to the large head.
bairdii: named after Spencer Baird, first US Fish Commissioner.

The popular trout fly known as the "muddler minnow" is meant to mimic a sculpin. The Mottled and Slimy sculpins are common inhabitants of trout streams in Ontario.

DESCRIPTION: The Mottled Sculpin is a small slightly deep-bodied fish with a large, slightly flattened head. The body is scaleless except for patches of fine **prickles** that may be present on the sides just behind the head. A prominent spine about ½ the eye diameter in length is present at the front of the gill cover (p. 361). The gill **membranes** are attached to the body (p. 27). There are 4 pelvic rays. The back is brown with dark saddles, the sides are darkly mottled, and the belly is white. The chin and pelvic fins are darkly mottled. In spawning males, the spiny dorsal fin is black with an orange edge.

SIMILAR SPECIES: Gobies have pelvic fins that are joined together to form a disc. The Deepwater Sculpin has 2 prominent spines at the front of the gill cover, and the gill **membranes** are not attached to the body. The Spoonhead Sculpin has a more flattened head with a larger, sickle-shaped spine at the front of the gill cover. The Slimy Sculpin is very difficult to distinguish from the Mottled Sculpin. It tends to have only 3 pelvic rays in Ontario, and the chin and pelvic fins are usually not mottled. Slimy and Mottled sculpins occasionally **hybridize**, and their **hybrids** are virtually impossible to distinguish from the parent species.

FEEDING: The Mottled Sculpin feeds on aquatic insect **larvae** and, occasionally, worms and small crustaceans. Its lower jaw has tiny nerve endings that are able to detect vibrations from prey that are buried in the bottom. Once prey is detected, the Mottled Sculpin bites into the bottom to capture its prey.

REPRODUCTION: Spawning occurs in spring when the water temperature

Juvenile

reaches 5°C. The male chooses a nesting site and lures the female to spawn with a courtship display that includes head shaking, swelling his gill covers, and making drumming sounds by slapping the **substrate**. Females usually choose to spawn with large males. However, if the male is much larger than the female, the male may eat her. Large males spawn with up to 13 different females in a spawning season. Eggs are deposited on the underside of a rock or ledge, after which the male chases the female away. He then fertilizes the eggs, guards them, and fans them with his pectoral fins.

HABITAT: The Mottled Sculpin is found in the cold waters of streams and lakes.

STATUS: G5; N5; S5.

Maximum Age: 4	Ontario Average	Ontario Record	World Record
Length:	7.5 cm (3.0 in)	13.3 cm (5.2 in)	15.0 cm (5.9 in)

SLIMY SCULPIN *Cottus cognatus*

Cottus—kottos: head; refers to the large head.
cognatus: kindred, because of its similarity to a European sculpin.

The Slimy Sculpin is one of the few species found with Brook Trout in the cold headwaters of streams. As a result, it is important prey for large Brook Trout.

DESCRIPTION: The Slimy Sculpin is a small elongate fish with a large, slightly flattened head. The body is scaleless except for patches of fine **prickles** that may be present on the sides just behind the head. A prominent spine, about ½ the eye diameter in length, is present at the front of the gill cover (p. 361). The gill **membranes** are attached to the body (p. 27). There are 2 dorsal fins that are rarely joined. In Ontario, there are 3–4 pelvic fin rays; if present, the fourth is greatly reduced in length. The back is brown, green, or grey, with dark saddles, the sides are darkly mottled, and the belly is white. The chin and pelvic fins are uniform in colour. Spawning males are darker, and their first dorsal fin is black with an orange edge.

SIMILAR SPECIES: Gobies have pelvic fins that are joined together to form a disc. The Deepwater Sculpin has 2 prominent spines at the front of the gill cover, and the gill **membranes** are not attached to the body. The Spoonhead Sculpin has a more flattened head with a larger, sickle-shaped spine at the front of the gill cover. The Mottled Sculpin is very difficult to distinguish from the Slimy Sculpin. It has 4 pelvic rays, and the chin and pelvic fins are usually mottled. Mottled and Slimy sculpins occasionally **hybridize**, and their **hybrids** are virtually impossible to distinguish from the parent species.

FEEDING: The Slimy Sculpin feeds at the bottom on aquatic insect **larvae** and, occasionally, worms and small crustaceans.

REPRODUCTION: Spawning occurs in spring when the water temperature reaches 4°C. The male

chooses a nesting site and lures the female to spawn with a courtship display that includes head shaking and swelling the gill covers. Eggs are deposited on the underside of a rock or ledge, after which the male chases the female away. He then fertilizes the eggs and guards and fans them with his pectoral fins. Large males often have eggs from more than one female in their nesting sites.

HABITAT: The Slimy Sculpin is found in the cold waters of streams and lakes.

STATUS: G5; N5; S5.

Maximum Age: 7	Ontario Average	Ontario Record	World Record
Length:	7.5 cm (3.0 in)	11.5 cm (4.5 in)	12.1 cm (4.8 in)

SPOONHEAD SCULPIN *Cottus ricei*

Cottus—kottos: head; refers to the large head.
ricei: named after Marcus Rice, an American zoology student who first discovered the species.

As a result of its deepwater habitat, the Spoonhead Sculpin is rarely encountered by anglers or biologists. It is most likely to be seen in the stomach contents of a deepwater predator, such as Lake Trout or Burbot.

DESCRIPTION: The Spoonhead Sculpin is a small elongate fish with a large flat head. The body is scaleless and covered in **prickles**, sometimes restricted to the head in large females. A single, large, sickle-shaped spine more than ½ the eye diameter in length is present at the front of the gill cover (p. 361). The gill **membranes** are attached to the body (p. 27). There are 2 dorsal fins that are narrowly joined or widely separated. The back is brown with dark saddles or spots, the sides are spotted or mottled, and the belly is white.

SIMILAR SPECIES: Gobies have pelvic fins that are joined together to form a disc. The Deepwater Sculpin has 2 prominent spines at the front of the gill cover, and the gill **membranes** are not attached to the body. In the Mottled and Slimy sculpins, the head is less flattened and the spine at the front of the gill cover is smaller and less curved.

FEEDING: The Spoonhead Sculpin feeds from the bottom on aquatic insect **larvae** and small crustaceans.

REPRODUCTION: Information on the spawning habits of this deepwater species is limited. Several specimens caught in August from Ontario and Quebec contained eggs and sperm that were advanced in development; hence, they would likely have spawned in the fall.

HABITAT: In Ontario, the Spoonhead Sculpin prefers the cold waters of very deep lakes, including the Great Lakes. In northern Canada, it prefers streams.

STATUS: G5; N5; S4; NAR.

Maximum Age: 6	Ontario Average	Ontario Record	World Record
Length:	5.5 cm (2.2 in)	12.0 cm (4.7 in)	13.4 cm (5.3 in)

PSYCHROLUTIDAE
Fathead Sculpins

Most members of this family are cold-water, bottom-dwelling marine fishes, found to depths of 2800 meters, in the Northern Hemisphere. The name comes from the Greek psychrolouteo meaning "to have a cold bath". Once restricted to just a small number of species, recent research has shown that most sculpins are more closely related to the bizarre marine Blobfish than they are to sculpins that live in fresh waters. Ontario's Deepwater Sculpin, although living in fresh waters, is also more closely related to marine sculpins and has been reclassified into Psychrolutidae. Sculpins in this family usually lack scales and have plates on the body with prickles. They are often called tadpole sculpins because of their large heads that taper to small, flat tails.

In the Great Lakes, the Deepwater Sculpin is a species at risk and was once thought to be extirpated from Lake Ontario. It has seen a comeback since 2016, where it has been discovered in several locations in lakes Superior, Huron, and Ontario. Century-old records of this species from the Royal Ontario Museum's fish collection aided in this search for current Deepwater Sculpin habitats.

There are 216 species worldwide, one of which occurs in Ontario.

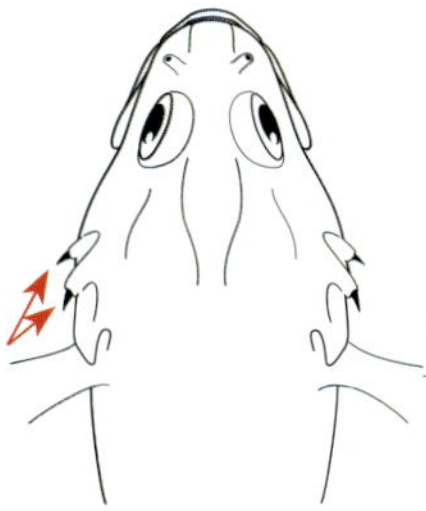

2 prominent spines at the front of the gill cover (Deepwater Sculpin)

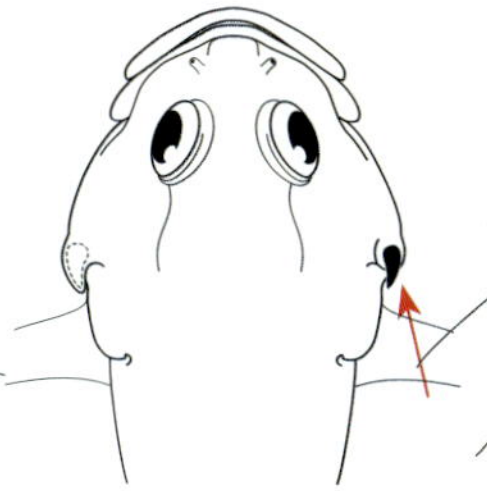

prominent spine at the front of the gill cover, straight or slightly curved, its length usually less than $2/3$ eye diameter (e.g., Slimy Sculpin)

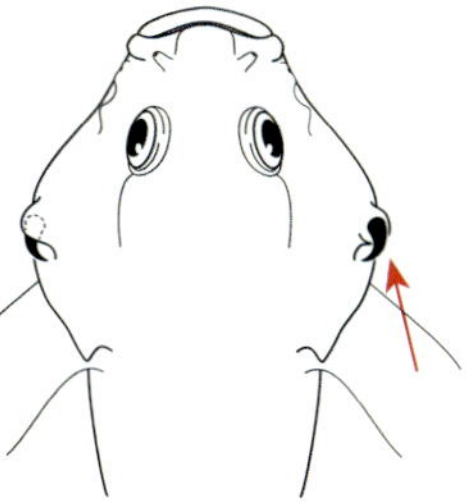

prominent spine at the front of the gill cover. Strongly curved, its length usually more than $2/3$ eye diameter (Spoonhead Sculpin)

< Deepwater Sculpin on nest

DEEPWATER SCULPIN *Myoxocephalus thompsonii*

Myoxocephalus—myoxo: kind of mouse; *cephalus*: head.
thompsonii: named after Reverend Zadock Thompson, who wrote the *History of the State of Vermont (1833).*

The Deepwater Sculpin, our only Psychrolutidae, plays an important role in the deepwater ecosystems of deep lakes. It feeds on **invertebrates** and, in turn, is fed upon by Lake Trout and Burbot. The dramatic decline in Lake Ontario was followed by a resurgence despite the presence of three invasive fishes, the Alewife, Smelt, and Round Goby as well as Quagga mussels.

DESCRIPTION: The Deepwater Sculpin is a small, elongate fish with a large, slightly flattened head. The body is scaleless except for patches of fine **prickles** on the upper sides. It has 2 prominent spines at the front of the gill cover (p. 361). The gill **membranes** are not attached to the body but broadly joined to each other (p. 27). The back is grey-brown with thin dark saddles or dark spots, the sides are lighter with dark spots or blotches, and the belly is pale.

SIMILAR SPECIES: Gobies have pelvic fins that are joined together to form a disc. The Mottled, Slimy, and Spoonhead sculpins have a single prominent spine at the front of the gill cover, and their gill **membranes** are attached to the body.

FEEDING: The Deepwater Sculpin feeds on crustaceans and fish eggs.

REPRODUCTION: Little is known of the spawning habits of this deepwater species. Spawning occurs in summer and fall. One study on the development of eggs indicated that the Deepwater Sculpin spawns once annually but has a protracted spawning season. Spawning occurs in the fall, winter, or spring. Eggs laid in a nest guarded by a presumed male was observed by an underwater drone in Grand Traverse Bay, Lake Michigan on 16 March 2021

Deepwater Sculpin on nest with eggs

Deepwater Sculpin on nest with Round Goby nearby

at 190m. Are there others at different times? May also be useful to mention that newly hatched larvae are not benthic but ascend into the water column becoming part of the plankton until they reach a length of about 2 cm when they descend to the benthos.

HABITAT: The Deepwater Sculpin is found only in the cold waters of very deep lakes, including the Great Lakes.

STATUS: G5TNRQ; NNR; S3?; SC[F] (Great Lakes–Upper St. Lawrence populations);
G5TNRQ; N4; S4; NAR[F] (Saskatchewan–Nelson River populations).

Maximum Age: 17	Ontario Average	Ontario Record	World Record
Length:	11.4 cm (4.5 in)	18.9 cm (7.4 in)	23.0 cm (9.1 in)

MORONIDAE
Temperate Basses

Often known as "striped basses," North American members of this family are silvery and often have rows of dark stripes along their sides. They are native to the coastal waters of the Atlantic Ocean and Gulf of Mexico and their drainages, although they have been widely introduced in the United States. Two species also occur in Europe and North Africa. Temperate basses have two spines on the posterior edge of the gill cover. They have two dorsal fins—the first one with spines and the second with one spine followed by soft rays. The dorsal fins are joined by a small **membrane** in the White Perch. The pelvic fins are placed far forward, below the pectoral fins. The anal fin has three spines followed by soft rays. The head and body have **ctenoid scales**.

The large Striped Bass, or "striper," is a highly sought sport fish, although it has been in decline for many years. Conservation measures, including closing spawning grounds to recreational fishing in the spring, have had a positive impact on this species in Canadian and US waters. However, population and body sizes remain below historical values. In the past, specimens larger than 26 kg (58 lbs) were regularly caught along the coastal waters of New England. The Canadian angling record Striped Bass weighed 25 kg (55 lbs) and was caught in Nova Scotia in 2008.

There are six species worldwide, two of which are found in Ontario.

< White Perch

WHITE BASS *Morone chrysops*

Morone: of unknown origin.
chrysops—*chryso*: gold; *ops*: eye; refers to the yellow eye.

Hybrids between White Bass and Striped Bass, known as "wipers," are raised in American fish farms. They are often found in live fish markets in Ontario. Several individuals have been caught in the wild in Ontario, including a 9.5 kg (21.0 lbs) individual captured in Lake Ontario in 2012.

DESCRIPTION: The White Bass is a silvery, medium-sized, very deep-bodied fish, which is thin from side to side. It has small scales (52–60 **lateral scales**). There is a spiny and a soft dorsal fin. The anal fin has 3 spines of different lengths. The third spine is the longest and is usually less than ¾ the length of the longest soft anal ray. There are 11–13 soft anal rays. The back is blue-grey to dark green, the sides are silvery with several dark, broken stripes, and the belly is white. The eye is yellow.

SIMILAR SPECIES: The Yellow Perch has 6–8 prominent dark bars on the body. The sunfishes, including Largemouth and Smallmouth basses, have a single, sometimes notched, dorsal fin. In the White Perch, the spiny and soft dorsal fins are joined by a small **membrane**, and the second and third anal spines are about equal in length, the third usually more than ¾ the length of the longest soft anal ray, and there are 8–10 soft anal rays. Wipers can be recognized by their distinctive stripes, which are prominently offset. The White Bass may **hybridize** with White Perch. The **hybrids** are difficult to distinguish from the parent species.

FEEDING: The White Bass is mainly a **piscivore**, feeding on small fishes. It is **crepuscular**, forming large schools at dawn and dusk to feed.

REPRODUCTION: Spawning occurs in the spring when the water temperature

Juvenile

Wiper

reaches 14°C. White Bass move onto shoals, the males preceding the females. Spawning occurs at the surface, with a female swimming in circles around several males. Eggs and sperm are released, and the eggs sink to the bottom, becoming fertilized on the way down. The fertilized eggs are adhesive and attach to the bottom. There is no parental care given to the fertilized eggs or young.

HABITAT: The White Bass prefers cool, clear waters of the Great Lakes and the lower portions of their tributaries, and Lake Nipissing.

STATUS: G5; N4; S4.

Maximum Age: 9	Ontario Average	Ontario Record	World Record
Length:	28.0 cm (11.0 in)	48.5 cm (19.1 in)	48.5 cm (19.1 in)
Weight: Overall	0.2 kg (0.4 lbs)	1.6 kg (3.4 lbs)	3.1 kg (6.8 lbs)
Angling	–	1.6 kg (3.4 lbs)	3.1 kg (6.8 lbs)

WHITE PERCH *Morone americana*

Morone: of unknown origin.
americana: for its homeland, North America.

Native to the Atlantic Coast, the White Perch invaded Lake Ontario through the Erie Canal in the 1950s. It subsequently dispersed through the Welland Canal into Lake Erie and then into the remaining Great Lakes.

DESCRIPTION: The White Perch is a silvery, medium-sized, very deep-bodied fish, which is thin from side to side. It has small scales (46–51 **lateral scales**). The spiny and soft dorsal fins are joined by a small **membrane**. The anal fin has 3 spines, the last 2 about equal in length. The third spine is usually more than ¾ the length of the longest soft anal ray. There are 8–10 soft anal rays. The back is green to almost black, the sides are silvery to brassy with a greenish tint, and the belly is silvery white. In juveniles, the sides may have faint blotches or broken stripes that disappear in the adult. There is a blue tint on the head of spawning adults.

SIMILAR SPECIES: The Yellow Perch has 6–8 prominent dark bars on the body. The sunfishes, including Largemouth and Smallmouth basses, are usually not silvery, and there is a single, sometimes notched, dorsal fin. In the White Bass, the spiny and soft dorsal fins are not joined, the anal spines are different lengths, the longest spine is usually less than ¾ the length of the longest soft anal ray, and there are 11–13 soft anal rays. The White Perch may **hybridize** with the White Bass. The **hybrids** are difficult to distinguish from the parent species.

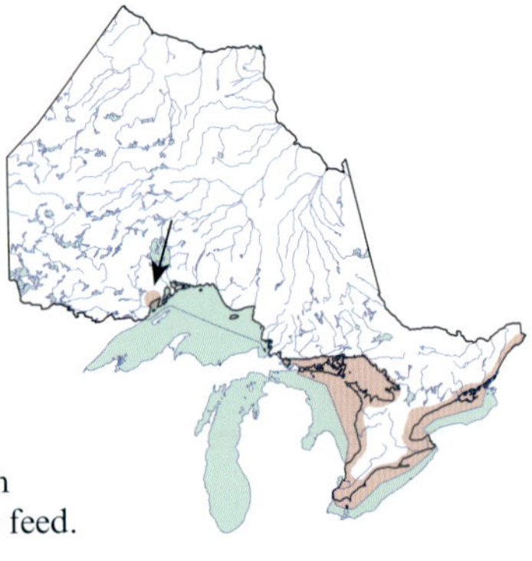

FEEDING: The diet of the White Perch consists mainly of aquatic insect **larvae** and small fishes. Crustaceans, molluscs, worms, and fish eggs may also occasionally be eaten. In addition to feeding during the day in deeper waters, White Perch move to the surface in the evening to feed.

REPRODUCTION: Spawning occurs in spring when the water temperature reaches 11°C. A large school of White Perch forms in shallow water, and eggs and sperm are randomly released over a 1–2 week period. The fertilized eggs are adhesive and become attached to the rocky bottom or to vegetation. No parental care is given to the fertilized eggs or young.

HABITAT: The White Perch prefers the cool waters of the Great Lakes and the lower portions of their tributaries.

STATUS: G5; N5; SNA.

Maximum Age: 17	Ontario Average	Ontario Record	World Record
Length:	15.5 cm (6.1 in)	29.0 cm (11.4 in)	58.0 cm (22.8 in)
Weight: Overall	<0.1 kg (0.1 lbs)	0.7 kg (1.5 lbs)	2.7 kg (6.0 lbs)
Angling	–	0.7 kg (1.5 lbs)	1.6 kg (3.5 lbs)

CENTRARCHIDAE
Sunfishes and Basses

This family is native to the eastern half of North America. However, some members of the family are highly prized for sport and have been introduced worldwide. Sunfishes are thin from side to side and very deep-bodied, whereas basses are oval in cross-section and less deep-bodied. Both have teeth in the mouth and throat. The long dorsal fin has sharp spines followed by soft rays that are generally longer than the spines. The pelvic fins are below the pectoral fins. The anal fin has three or more spines followed by soft rays. The head and body have **ctenoid scales**.

Centrarchids are a model group for studying locomotion and feeding because of their diversity in body shape and ecology. The sunfishes rely primarily on their pectoral fins to manoeuvre their thin, deep bodies. They are adapted to a sedentary life in slow-moving waters, where they feed on small, often motionless, prey. Sunfishes are typical suction feeders, rapidly opening their small mouths to suck in water containing prey. Conversely, the Largemouth and Smallmouth basses use their more muscular, streamlined bodies and tails to swim. They are adapted to the active pursuit of large, fast prey. These basses are ram feeders, having larger mouths and often swimming at high speed to overtake and engulf prey.

There are 43 species worldwide, 11 of which are found in Ontario.

< Bluegill ♂ guarding fry

BLACK CRAPPIE *Pomoxis nigromaculatus*

Pomoxis—poma: gill cover; *oxys*: sharp; refers to the bony, pointed edge of the gill cover.
nigromaculatus—nigro: black; *macula*: spot; refers to the colour pattern.

The Black Crappie is a popular sport fish in the United States and is prized for its sweet-tasting flesh. Angling for crappies is becoming increasingly popular in Ontario, particularly in spring when crappies form large schools.

DESCRIPTION: The Black Crappie is a small, very deep-bodied fish, which is very thin from side to side. The mouth is large, the upper jaw usually extends backwards to below the middle of the eye. It has large **ctenoid scales** (36–41 **lateral scales**). The dorsal fin has 7–8 spines. There is no notch between the spiny and soft portions of the dorsal fin (p. 23). The base of the dorsal fin is about equal in length to the base of the anal fin, which has 6–7 spines. The back is green to golden brown, often with a blue to silver overcast. The sides are lighter green or silver, with dark mottling, and the belly is white. The soft dorsal and anal fins and the tail have dark wavy lines and oblong pale spots. The tips of the pelvic fins are black. Spawning males are darker.

SIMILAR SPECIES: The Largemouth and Smallmouth basses, sunfishes, and the Rock Bass have more than 9 dorsal spines, and the base of the dorsal fin is much longer than the base of the anal fin. The White Crappie has only 6 dorsal spines, sides with faint bars, and an anal fin base longer than the dorsal fin base.

FEEDING: The Black Crappie is usually **crepuscular**, feeding at dawn and dusk on small fishes, crustaceans, and aquatic insects. As this

Juvenile

species feeds throughout the winter, ice fishing for Black Crappie is not uncommon.

REPRODUCTION: Spawning occurs in spring when the water temperature reaches 13°C. Males form colonies in shallow, vegetated areas, and each male prepares a nest by clearing a small depression about 20 cm in diameter. A female approaches and circles the nest site. The male and female swim beside each other, and eggs and sperm are released. The female spawns several times with one male and then moves to another nest to spawn again. The male fans the fertilized eggs with his fins and guards the eggs and young after they hatch.

HABITAT: The Black Crappie prefers the warm waters of lakes and slow-moving streams, usually with abundant vegetation.

STATUS: G5; N5; S4.

Maximum Age: 15	Ontario Average	Ontario Record	World Record
Length:	21.5 cm (8.5 in)	43.2 cm (17.0 in)	49.0 cm (19.3 in)
Weight: Overall	0.2 kg (0.4 lbs)	1.7 kg (3.8 lbs)	2.7 kg (6.0 lbs)
Angling	–	1.7 kg (3.8 lbs)	2.5 kg (5.4 lbs)

BLUEGILL *Lepomis macrochirus*

Lepomis—epis: scale; *poma*: cover; refers to the scales on the gill cover.
macrochirus—macro: large; *chirus*: hand; probably refers to the body shape.

The Bluegill sometimes exhibits an unusual spawning behaviour. Small males, called "sneakers," may enter a nest and release sperm during the spawning act of a larger male and female. This saves the small male the energy of building a nest, defending territory, and competing for a female.

DESCRIPTION: The Bluegill is a small, very deep-bodied fish, which is very thin from side to side. The mouth is small, the upper jaw does not extend to below the middle of the eye. It has large **ctenoid scales** (39–45 **lateral scales**). The dorsal fin has 10–11, usually 10, spines. There is no notch between the spiny and soft portions of the dorsal fin (p. 23). The base of the dorsal fin is about twice the length of the base of the anal fin, which has 3 spines. The pectoral fins are long and pointed and, when folded forward, extend well past the front of the eye. The back and sides are green to brown with faint dark bars. The belly is silver to yellow. The **ear flap** is entirely black without a pale edge. There is a prominent black blotch near the posterior base of the dorsal fin. The spawning male becomes more brightly coloured with an orange belly.

SIMILAR SPECIES: The crappies have 6–8 dorsal spines, and the anal fin base is as long as or longer than the base of the dorsal fin. The Largemouth and Smallmouth basses have a notched dorsal fin, are not as deep-bodied, and have smaller scales (more than 59 **lateral scales**). The Rock Bass has 5–7 anal spines and numerous dark spots arranged in rows on the sides. Other

Bluegill (continued)

Juvenile

Spawning pair

♂ on nest

Green Frog eating Bluegill

sunfishes have pale edges on their **ear flaps**. The Warmouth, Green, and Northern sunfishes have larger mouths and shorter, rounded pectoral fins. The Pumpkinseed and Orangespotted Sunfish have distinct orange or brown spots on the body.

FEEDING: The Bluegill eats aquatic plants and small aquatic and terrestrial insects. It may also nip parasites from turtles.

REPRODUCTION: Spawning occurs in spring and summer when the water temperature reaches 19°C. Males form colonies in shallow water, and the male prepares a nest up to 30 cm in diameter by sweeping with his fins to remove sand and gravel. Larger males compete for central locations in the colony where there is less **predation**. The male makes grunting noises during courtship, likely to attract a female. When a female approaches a male, the two swim in circles over the nest. Then, with the female lying on her side next to the male, eggs and sperm are released. The male defends the eggs and young until they leave the nest, by butting and charging intruders. Males and females spawn more than once with the same, or different, mates.

HABITAT: The Bluegill prefers the warm waters of lakes and slow-moving streams with abundant aquatic vegetation.

STATUS: G5; N5; S5.

Maximum Age: 10	Ontario Average	Ontario Record	World Record
Length:	19.0 cm (7.5 in)	28.2 cm (11.1 in)	41.0 cm (16.1 in)
Weight: Overall	0.1 kg (0.2 lbs)	0.8 kg (1.8 lbs)	2.2 kg (4.7 lbs)
Angling	–	0.8 kg (1.8 lbs)	2.2 kg (4.7 lbs)

GREEN SUNFISH *Lepomis cyanellus*

Lepomis—*lepis*: scale; *poma*: cover; refers to the scales on the gill cover.
cyanellus—*cyano*: dark blue; *ellus*: little; perhaps refers to the blue spots on the body.

Many of the sunfishes **hybridize** with one another, producing offspring that may exhibit a mixture of characters of the two parent species and are often difficult to identify. These **hybrid** offspring may be fertile. The exact reason for **hybridization** is unknown but thought to be related to some form of stress, such as habitat degradation. **Hybrids** involving a Green Sunfish parent are relatively common in southwestern Ontario.

DESCRIPTION: The Green Sunfish is a small deep-bodied fish, which is thin from side to side. The mouth is large, the upper jaw extends backwards to below the middle of the eye. It has large **ctenoid scales** (40–50 **lateral scales**). The dorsal fin has 9–11, usually 10, spines. There is no notch between the spiny and soft portions of the dorsal fin (p. 23). The base of the dorsal fin is more than twice the length of the base of the anal fin, which has 3 spines. In adults, the pectoral fins are short and rounded and, when folded forward, they seldom reach the eye. The back is brown to olive, with an emerald green tint. The sides are yellow-green with blue spots or wavy lines and, sometimes, faint dark bars. The belly is yellow to white. The **ear flap** has a large black spot surrounded by a wide pale red to yellow edge. There is a prominent black blotch near the posterior base of the dorsal fin. The tail and soft dorsal and anal fin have a white to orange edge. Sometimes, the anal fin also has a black blotch near its posterior base. The spawning male has vertical bars on the sides, and prominent pale edges on the tail and dorsal and anal fins.

Juvenile

Hybrid of Green Sunfish and Bluegill

SIMILAR SPECIES: The crappies have 6–8 dorsal spines, and the anal fin base is as long as or longer than the base of the dorsal fin. The Largemouth and Smallmouth basses have a notched dorsal fin, are not as deep-bodied, and have smaller scales (more than 59 **lateral scales**). The Rock Bass has 5–7 anal spines and numerous dark spots arranged in rows on the sides. The Northern Sunfish has larger scales (33–38 **lateral scales**), and lacks a black blotch on the dorsal fin and a pale margin on the anal fin. The Pumpkinseed and Bluegill have smaller mouths, their upper jaws do not extend backwards to below the middle of the eye, and longer, pointed pectoral fins, which extend past the eye when folded forward. The Pumpkinseed lacks a black blotch on the dorsal fin, and the **ear flap** of the Bluegill lacks a pale edge.

FEEDING: The Green Sunfish feeds on aquatic insect **larvae**, crustaceans, molluscs, and small fishes.

REPRODUCTION: Spawning occurs in the spring and summer when the water temperature reaches 15°C. In very shallow water, many males form a colony, and each male hollows out a nest up to 38 cm in diameter by sweeping the bottom with his tail and removing stones with his mouth. Once the nest is complete, the male performs a courtship ritual to attract the female. He first rushes towards her, then slowly swims back to his nest while making a grunting sound. The female enters the nest and, with the male upright and the female

slightly on her side, they vibrate, releasing eggs and sperm. Both males and females spawn with more than one mate. The male cares for the fertilized eggs and young until they leave the nest.

HABITAT: The Green Sunfish prefers the warm waters of streams and wetlands.

STATUS: G5; N4; S4; NAR.

Maximum Age: 9	Ontario Average	Ontario Record	World Record
Length:	9.0 cm (3.5 in)	18.6 cm (7.3 in)	31.0 cm (12.2 in)
Weight: Overall	–	–	1.0 kg (2.1 lbs)
Angling	–	–	1.0 kg (2.1 lbs)

LARGEMOUTH BASS *Micropterus nigricans*

Micropterus—micro: small; *pterus*: fin. Bernard-Germain-Étienne de Lacépède, who described the species, mistook the torn dorsal fin for two fins, one of which was very small.
nigricans-black: refers to the common name "black bass"

The Largemouth Bass is a game fish much sought after by professional and amateur anglers alike. Although they often exceed 2 kg in Ontario, Largemouth Bass fail to reach the large sizes seen in the southern United States. This is the result of longer northern winters during which bass neither feed nor grow significantly.

DESCRIPTION: The Largemouth Bass is a medium-sized, deep-bodied fish. The mouth is very large, the upper jaw extends backwards past the eye (except in individuals less than 20 cm). It has small **ctenoid scales** (60–68 **lateral scales**). The dorsal fin has 9–11, usually 10, spines. The dorsal fin has a distinct notch between the spiny and soft portions (p. 24), which sometimes are separated. The length of the shortest dorsal spine is less than ½ the length of the longest spine. The base of the dorsal fin is more than twice the length of the base of the anal fin, which has 3 spines. The back and sides are green to olive, and the belly is yellow to white. The sides have a dark stripe, which is sometimes faint or broken. Juveniles have a more prominent dark lateral stripe.

SIMILAR SPECIES: The crappies have 6–8 dorsal spines, and the anal fin base is as long as or longer than the base of the dorsal fin. Sunfishes are deeper bodied and have larger scales (fewer than 51 **lateral scales**). The Rock Bass has 5–7 anal spines, and sides with numerous dark spots arranged in rows. The Smallmouth Bass has a smaller mouth, sides with bars, and a less distinct notch between the spiny and soft portions of the dorsal fin.

FEEDING: Adult Largemouth Bass eat mainly fishes, frogs, and crustaceans, while juveniles eat aquatic insects, crustaceans, small fishes, and frogs. It is a sight feeder and often takes its prey spectacularly from the surface.

Largemouth Bass (continued)

Feeding on crayfish

Juvenile

Eggs

Fry in nest

REPRODUCTION: Spawning occurs in spring and summer when the water temperature reaches 16°C. The male prepares a nest up to 90 cm in diameter on a sand or soft mud bottom surrounded by vegetation in 1–4 m of water. The female is attracted to the nest with a courtship display that includes nipping and rubbing. The pair circles the nest and, with the female lying slightly on her side next to the male, eggs and sperm are released. The female may spawn several times with one male, or she may move to another nest to spawn again. Eggs adhere to vegetation. The male fans the fertilized eggs with his fins and guards the eggs and young after they hatch.

HABITAT: The Largemouth Bass prefers the warm waters of lakes and slow-moving streams with extensive aquatic vegetation and other cover such as docks and sunken logs. The habitats of the Largemouth and Smallmouth basses seldom overlap, although they are frequently found in the same lake.

STATUS: G5; NNR; S5.

Maximum Age: 23	Ontario Average	Ontario Record	World Record
Length:	30.0 cm (11.8 in)	55.9 cm (22.0 in)	97.0 cm (38.2 in)
Weight: Overall	0.4 kg (0.9 lbs)	4.7 kg (10.4 lbs)	10.1 kg (22.2 lbs)
Angling	–	4.7 kg (10.4 lbs)	10.1 kg (22.2 lbs)

NORTHERN SUNFISH *Lepomis peltastes*

Lepomis—lepis: scale; *poma*: cover; refers to the scales on the gill cover.
peltastes—pelta: shield; alluding to its large and armored **ear flap**.

The Northern Sunfish has a long upturned **ear flap** or, more correctly, a long opercular flap. Unlike humans, fishes do not have external ears. However, like humans, they have an **inner ear**. Fish ears, along with the **lateral line** and the **sensory canals** on the head, detect vibrations in the water that are then interpreted as sounds.

DESCRIPTION: The Northern Sunfish is a small, very deep-bodied fish, which is thin from side to side. The mouth is medium-sized, the upper jaw extends backwards to below the front half of the eye. It has large **ctenoid scales** (33–38 **lateral scales**). The dorsal fin has 10–11 spines. There is no notch between the spiny and soft portions of the dorsal fin (p. 23). The base of the dorsal fin is more than twice the length of the base of the anal fin, which has 3 spines. The pectoral fins are rounded and short; when folded forward, the pectoral fins extend to, but usually not beyond, the middle of the eye. The back is olive to brown. The sides are paler and spotted or mottled with orange and blue, and sometimes have bars. The belly is red to yellow. The **ear flap** is often elongated and upturned and has a narrow white or red edge. The dorsal and anal fins lack dark spots, but often have pale orange ones. Spawning males are brilliantly coloured with a bright blue or green back, bright orange belly, rusty orange spots on the dorsal and anal fins, and blue-black pelvic fins.

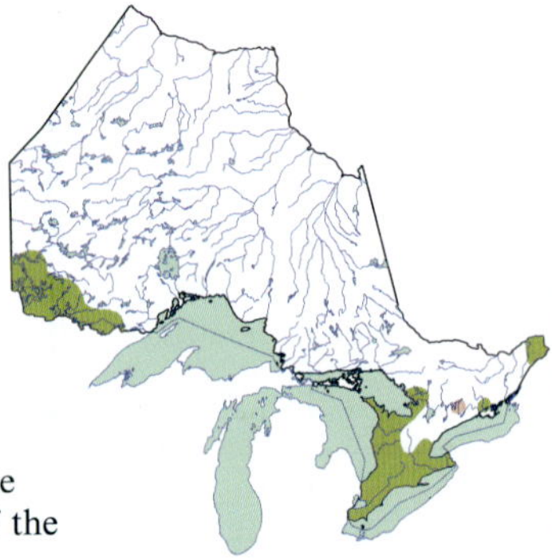

SIMILAR SPECIES: The crappies have 6–8 dorsal spines, and the anal fin base is as long as or longer than the base of the

♂

Juvenile

dorsal fin. The Largemouth and Smallmouth basses have a notched dorsal fin, are not as deep-bodied, and have smaller scales (more than 59 **lateral scales**). The Rock Bass has 5–7 anal spines, and sides with numerous dark spots arranged in rows. The Warmouth has a patch of fine teeth on the tongue and brown bars radiating from the eye. The Bluegill and Green Sunfish have a large black blotch on the dorsal fin. The Pumpkinseed has a prominent red spot on its **ear flap** and dark spots on its dorsal and anal fins. The Orangespotted Sunfish has dark spots on the dorsal fin and distinct orange or brown spots on the body.

FEEDING: The Northern Sunfish feeds on small aquatic and terrestrial insects, crustaceans, molluscs, and small fishes.

REPRODUCTION: Spawning occurs in spring and summer when the water temperature reaches 22°C. Males form colonies in shallow water, and each prepares a nest up to 45 cm in diameter by sweeping with his tail to remove sand and gravel. The male makes grunting noises during courtship, likely to attract a female. Once a female approaches a male, the two swim in circles over the nest. Then, with the female lying on her side next to the male, eggs and sperm are released. The male fans the fertilized eggs with his fins. Other females may invade nests after spawning to eat the eggs.

Northern Sunfish (continued)

HABITAT: The Northern Sunfish prefers the warm waters of slow-moving streams and lakes with aquatic vegetation.

STATUS: G5TNRQ; N3; S3; SC (Great Lakes–Upper St. Lawrence populations).
G5TNRQ; N3?; S3; NAR (Saskatchewan–Nelson River populations).

Maximum Age: 7	Ontario Average	Ontario Record	World Record
Length:	8.0 cm (3.1 in)	11.5 cm (4.5 in)	14.8 cm (5.8 in)

ORANGESPOTTED SUNFISH *Lepomis humilis*

Lepomis—*lepis*: scale; *poma*: cover; refers to the scales on the gill cover.
humilis: small.

The Orangespotted Sunfish is not native to Canada or the Great Lakes. It was introduced into the Lake Erie basin in the early 1900s and has since spread into southwestern Ontario.

DESCRIPTION: The Orangespotted Sunfish is a small, very deep-bodied fish, which is thin from side to side. The mouth is medium-sized, the upper jaw extends backwards to below the front half of the eye. It has large **ctenoid scales** (34–41 **lateral scales**). The dorsal fin has 10–11 spines. There is no notch between the spiny and soft portions of the dorsal fin (p. 23). The base of the dorsal fin is about twice the length of the base of the anal fin, which has 3 spines. The pectoral fins are rounded or bluntly pointed and moderately long. When folded forward, the pectoral fins extend to, but not beyond, the eye. The back is olive with green and blue tints. The sides are paler, often silvery, with several distinct orange spots in the male or distinct brown spots in the female and juvenile. The belly is yellow to white. The back and sides often have wide bars. The **ear flap** has a large dark spot with a wide pale edge. The soft dorsal fin usually has dark spots. Females are smaller and less brightly coloured. Spawning males are brilliantly coloured with reddish orange spots and fins and black edges on the pelvic and anal fins.

SIMILAR SPECIES: The crappies have 6–8 dorsal spines and an anal fin base that is as long as or longer than the base of the dorsal fin. The Largemouth and Smallmouth basses are not as deep-bodied and have smaller scales

Juvenile

♀

♂

(more than 59 **lateral scales**). The Rock Bass has 5–7 anal spines, and sides with numerous dark spots arranged in rows. The Warmouth has a larger mouth and wide brown bars radiating from the eye. The Bluegill and Green Sunfish have a large black blotch on the soft dorsal fin. The Pumpkinseed has a red spot on its **ear flap**. The Northern Sunfish lacks dark spots on the dorsal fin.

FEEDING: The Orangespotted Sunfish feeds on aquatic insects, crustaceans, algae, and small fishes.

REPRODUCTION: Spawning occurs in spring and summer when the water temperature reaches 18°C. The male constructs a bowl-shaped nest up to 18 cm across in the shallows by sweeping the bottom with his tail. He makes grunting noises during courtship, likely to attract a female. Once a female approaches a male, the two swim in circles over the nest. Then, with the female lying on her side next to the male, eggs and sperm are released. The fertilized eggs are adhesive and stick to the bottom. The male defends the eggs until they hatch.

HABITAT: The Orangespotted Sunfish prefers the warm waters of streams and wetlands with abundant aquatic vegetation.

STATUS: G5; NNA; SNA.

Maximum Age: 4	Ontario Average	Ontario Record	World Record
Length:	6.9 cm (2.7 in)	9.7 cm (3.8 in)	15.0 cm (5.9 in)

PUMPKINSEED *Lepomis gibbosus*

Lepomis—*epis*: scale; *poma*: cover; refers to the scales on the gill cover.
gibbosus—*gibbus*: hunched, humped; refers to the back of the adult male.

The Pumpkinseed is one of the most colourful, widespread, and abundant fishes in Ontario. It is often the first species encountered by young anglers dangling a worm in the water.

DESCRIPTION: The Pumpkinseed is a small, very deep-bodied fish, which is thin from side to side. The mouth is small, the upper jaw does not extend backwards to below the middle of the eye. It has large **ctenoid scales** (35–47 **lateral scales**). The dorsal fin has 10–11, usually 10, spines. There is no notch between the spiny and soft portions of the dorsal fin (p. 23). The base of the dorsal fin is about twice the length of the base of the anal fin, which has 3 spines. The pectoral fins are long and pointed and, when folded forward, extend past the front of the eye. The back is golden brown to olive, with dark spots. The sides are golden to silvery with a green or blue tint, numerous brown or orange spots, and faint to prominent dark bars. The belly is bronze to orange. The **ear flap** has a large black spot with a bright red spot on the edge. The soft portions of the dorsal and anal fins have numerous small dark spots or broken dark wavy lines, but there is no large black blotch. The female is paler with more prominent vertical bars. Spawning males become more brightly coloured.

SIMILAR SPECIES: The crappies have 6–8 dorsal spines and an anal fin base that is as long as or longer than the base of the dorsal fin. The Largemouth

♀

♂

Juvenile

Circling over nest

and Smallmouth basses have a notched dorsal fin, are not as deep-bodied, and have smaller scales (more than 59 **lateral scales**). The Rock Bass has 5–7 anal spines, and sides with numerous dark spots arranged in rows. Other sunfishes lack the distinct red spot on the **ear flap**, although the edge may be red. The Green Sunfish and the Warmouth have larger mouths and shorter, rounded pectoral fins. The Bluegill has a black blotch on the dorsal fin. The Northern Sunfish lacks dark spots on the dorsal and anal fins and often has an upturned **ear flap** with a white or red edge.

FEEDING: The Pumpkinseed feeds on aquatic and terrestrial insect **larvae**, crustaceans, molluscs, small fishes, and, occasionally, plants.

REPRODUCTION: Spawning occurs in the spring and summer when the water temperature reaches 13°C. In very shallow water with abundant aquatic vegetation, males form a colony, and each male hollows out a nest up to 40 cm in diameter by sweeping the bottom with his tail and removing stones with his mouth. Once the nest is complete, the male performs a courtship ritual to attract the female, bunting and nipping her. They swim in circles over the nest and then, with the male upright and the female on her side, they vibrate, and eggs and sperm are released. Both males and females spawn with more than one mate. The male cares for the fertilized eggs and young until they leave the nest.

HABITAT: The Pumpkinseed prefers the cool to warm waters of lakes and slow-moving streams with aquatic vegetation. Pumpkinseed are often seen in large numbers near the surface.

STATUS: G5; N5; S5.

Maximum Age: 12	Ontario Average	Ontario Record	World Record
Length:	20.3 cm (8.0 in)	27.4 cm (10.8 in)	40.0 cm (15.7 in)
Weight: Overall	0.2 kg (0.4 lbs)	0.6 kg (1.4 lbs)	0.7 kg (1.5 lbs)
Angling	–	0.6 kg (1.4 lbs)	0.7 kg (1.5 lbs)

ROCK BASS *Ambloplites rupestris*

Ambloplites—*amblys*: blunt; *opilioz*: guard; refers to the flat spine on the gill cover.
rupestris: of rocks; refers to the preferred habitat of this species.

The Rock Bass has been widely introduced within its native range in central Ontario. Where native, the Rock Bass is a healthy member of the ecosystem. Where introduced, it often becomes very abundant while other native species, such as Smallmouth Bass, decline as a result of **competition** for food. Fishes, including Rock Bass, should never be transported between lakes.

DESCRIPTION: The Rock Bass is a small, very deep-bodied fish, which is thin from side to side. The mouth is large, and the upper jaw extends backwards to below the middle of the eye. It has large **ctenoid scales** (37–51 **lateral scales**). The dorsal fin has 10–13 spines. There is no notch between the spiny and soft portions of the dorsal fin (p. 23). The base of the dorsal fin is about twice the length of the base of the anal fin, which has 5–7, usually 6, spines. The back and upper sides are brown to olive, with golden tints, and there are often dark saddles. These saddles are very obvious at night. The sides usually have numerous dark spots arranged in rows (8–10 rows below the **lateral line**), which may be obscured by blotches that can rapidly intensify with stress. The belly is white. The eye is usually red. Spawning males become darker.

SIMILAR SPECIES: The crappies have 6–8 dorsal spines, and the anal fin base is as long as or longer than the base of the dorsal fin. The sunfishes and Largemouth and Smallmouth basses lack 8–10 rows of spots below the **lateral line** and have 3 anal spines.

FEEDING: The Rock Bass eats a wide variety of items, including aquatic insects, crustaceans, and small fishes.

Juvenile

Defence posture

REPRODUCTION: Spawning occurs in spring when the water temperature reaches 15°C. Males often form colonies in shallow water. Each male hollows out a nest up to 60 cm in diameter on the bottom using his pectoral and anal fins. Once the nest is complete, a female approaches, and the male swims beside her over the nest. The pair vibrates, and eggs and sperm are released. Both males and females spawn with more than one mate. The male cares for the fertilized eggs by fanning them with his pectoral fins, and defends the nest by erecting his fins and opening his mouth to scare away intruders. Once the young hatch, the male continues to guard them for up to ten days.

HABITAT: The Rock Bass prefers the cool waters of lakes and slow-moving streams, and is often found over rocky bottoms. Rock Bass are often found in groups with other sunfishes and basses, including Smallmouth Bass and Pumpkinseed.

STATUS: G5; N5; S5.

Feeding on crayfish

Maximum Age: 18	Ontario Average	Ontario Record	World Record
Length:	20.0 cm (7.9 in)	29.2 cm (11.5 in)	43.0 cm (16.9 in)
Weight: Overall	0.2 kg (0.4 lbs)	1.4 kg (3.0 lbs)	1.4 kg (3.0 lbs)
Angling	–	1.4 kg (3.0 lbs)	1.4 kg (3.0 lbs)

SMALLMOUTH BASS *Micropterus dolomieu*

Micropterus—micro: small; *pterus*: fin. Bernard-Germain-Étienne de Lacépède, who described the species, mistook the torn dorsal fin for two fins, one of which was very small.
dolomieu: named after Déodat Gratet de Dolomieu, a French geologist and friend of Lacépède.

The Smallmouth Bass has been widely introduced throughout Ontario, and it is often difficult to distinguish between native and introduced populations. When introduced, the Smallmouth Bass often has a negative impact on other native fishes, such as minnows and Lake Trout, as a result of **predation** or **competition** for food. Fishes, including Smallmouth Bass, should never be transported between lakes.

DESCRIPTION: The Smallmouth Bass is a medium-sized, deep-bodied fish. The mouth is large, and the upper jaw extends backwards to below the posterior half of the eye. It has small **ctenoid scales** (68–78 **lateral scales**). The dorsal fin has 9–11, usually 10, spines. There is a notch between the spiny and soft portions of the dorsal fin (p. 24). The length of the shortest dorsal spine is more than ½ the length of the longest spine. The base of the dorsal fin is more than twice the length of the base of the anal fin, which has 3 spines. The back is brown to green, the sides are lighter with golden tints, and the belly is cream to white. The sides have darker bars, sometimes faint, and the head has dark bars radiating backward from the eye. Juveniles have more prominent bars on the body and a tri-coloured tail with an orange base, a vertical black bar, and white to yellow tips.

SIMILAR SPECIES: The crappies have 6–8 dorsal spines, and the anal fin base is as long as or longer than the base of the dorsal fin. Sunfishes are deeper-bodied and have larger scales (fewer than 51 **lateral scales**) and a dorsal fin without a

Approaching a crayfish

Juvenile

♂ with **fry**

Eggs

Fry

Fry leaving the nest

notch. The Rock Bass has 5–7 anal spines, and sides with numerous dark spots arranged in rows. The Largemouth Bass has a larger mouth, an upper jaw that extends backwards to past the eye in individuals greater than 20 cm, a dark lateral stripe on the side, and a more distinct notch between the spiny and soft portions of the dorsal fin.

FEEDING: In many Ontario habitats, crayfishes make up the largest part of the diet. Other items include aquatic insects, fishes, tadpoles, frogs, and plant material.

REPRODUCTION: Spawning occurs in spring and summer when the water temperature reaches 16°C. The male prepares a nest 0.3–2 m in diameter on a sand, gravel, or rock bottom near logs or dense vegetation in 1–6 m of water. The male often uses the same nest in successive years. The female is attracted to the nest with a courtship display that includes nipping and rubbing. The pair circles the nest and, with the female lying on her side next to the male, eggs and sperm are released. The female may spawn several times with one male or may move to the nest of a different male to spawn again. The male fans the fertilized eggs with his fins and guards the eggs and young after they hatch.

HABITAT: The Smallmouth Bass prefers the cool waters of lakes and streams. It is often found over rocky bottoms, and is associated with various types of cover, such as docks and sunken logs. In the heat of summer, it often retreats to cooler, deeper waters.

STATUS: G5; N5; S5.

Maximum Age: 18	Ontario Average	Ontario Record	World Record
Length:	30.0 cm (11.8 in)	61.0 cm (24.0 in)	69.0 cm (27.2 in)
Weight: Overall	0.4 kg (0.9 lbs)	4.6 kg (10.2 lbs)	5.4 kg (11.9 lbs)
Angling	–	4.6 kg (10.2 lbs)	5.4 kg (11.9 lbs)

WARMOUTH *Lepomis gulosus*

Lepomis—*lepis*: scale; *poma*: cover; refers to the scales on the gill cover.
gulosus: gluttonous, as it is considered to have a voracious appetite.

The Warmouth is Ontario's rarest sunfish. It is found only in several Lake Erie wetlands and is common only at Point Pelee.

DESCRIPTION: The Warmouth is a small, very deep-bodied fish, which is thin from side to side. The mouth is large, the upper jaw extends backwards to below or past the middle of the eye. The tongue has a patch of small fine teeth. It has large **ctenoid scales** (36–42 **lateral scales**). The dorsal fin has 10 spines. There is no notch between the spiny and soft portions of the dorsal fin (p. 23). The base of the dorsal fin is more than twice the length of the base of the anal fin, which has 3 spines. The pectoral fins are rounded and moderately long and, when folded forward, extend to the posterior half of the eye. The back and sides are yellow to olive, with irregular dark brown or olive bars, spots, or mottling. The belly is white, yellow, or grey, and often mottled. There are wide brown bars radiating from the eye. The **ear flap** has a dark spot with a pale to dusky edge. The soft dorsal fin, tail, and anal fin are spotted. The spawning male is more brilliantly coloured and has grey pelvic fins and an orange spot at the base of the soft dorsal fin.

SIMILAR SPECIES: The crappies have 6–8 dorsal spines, and the anal fin base is as long as or longer than the base of the dorsal fin. The Largemouth and Smallmouth basses have a notched dorsal fin, are not as deep-bodied, and have smaller scales (more than 59 **lateral scales**). The Rock Bass has 5–7 anal spines, and sides with numerous dark spots arranged in rows. All other sunfishes lack teeth on

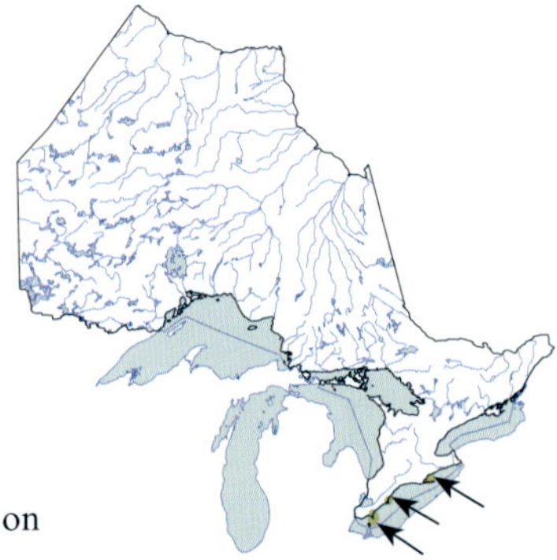

Juvenile

the tongue and wide brown bars radiating from the eye and, except for the Green Sunfish, have smaller mouths. The Bluegill and Green Sunfish have a black blotch on the dorsal fin. The Pumpkinseed has a red spot on its **ear flap**. The Northern Sunfish has an upturned **ear flap** and lacks dark spots on the dorsal and anal fins.

FEEDING: The Warmouth feeds on aquatic insects, crustaceans, and small fishes.

REPRODUCTION: Spawning occurs in late spring when the water temperature reaches 21°C. The male constructs a bowl-shaped nest, up to 15 cm in diameter, in the shallows by sweeping the bottom with his tail. He defends it by charging intruders with his mouth open and gill covers spread. A female is enticed to the nest with similar displays and then the pair swims in circles over the nest. With the female lying on her side next to the male, eggs and sperm are released. The male guards the fertilized eggs and young until they leave the nest.

HABITAT: The Warmouth prefers the warm waters of wetlands with abundant aquatic vegetation.

STATUS: G5; N1; S1; E.

Maximum Age: 8	Ontario Average	Ontario Record	World Record
Length:	12.4 cm (4.9 in)	17.2 cm (6.8 in)	31.0 cm (12.2 in)
Weight: Overall	0.1 kg (0.2 lbs)	–	1.1 kg (2.4 lbs)
Angling	–	–	1.1 kg (2.4 lbs)

WHITE CRAPPIE *Pomoxis annularis*

Pomoxis—*poma*: gill cover; *oxys*: sharp; refers to the bony, pointed edge of the gill cover.
annularis—*annulus*: ring; refers to the dark bars on the body.

The origin of the common name "crappie" is unknown, but may be derived from the French words *crapet* for sunfish or *crapaud* for toad. Canadians typically use the pronunciation "crapee," whereas Americans use "crawpee."

DESCRIPTION: The White Crappie is a small, very deep-bodied fish, which is very thin from side to side. The mouth is large, the upper jaw extends backwards to below the middle of the eye. It has large **ctenoid scales** (34–44 **lateral scales**). The dorsal fin has 6, rarely 7, spines. The base of the dorsal fin is less than the length of the base of the anal fin, which has 6–7 spines. The back is green to brown, often with a silver overcast, the sides are lighter green or silver with faint dark bars, and the belly is silver or white. The soft portions of the dorsal and anal fins and the tail have dark wavy lines or rows of spots. The pelvic fins are white. Spawning males are darker.

SIMILAR SPECIES: The Largemouth and Smallmouth basses, sunfishes, and Rock Bass have more than 8 dorsal spines, and the base of the dorsal fin is 2 or more times longer than the base of the anal fin. The Black Crappie has 7–8 dorsal spines, darkly mottled sides, and an anal fin base equal in length to the base of the dorsal fin.

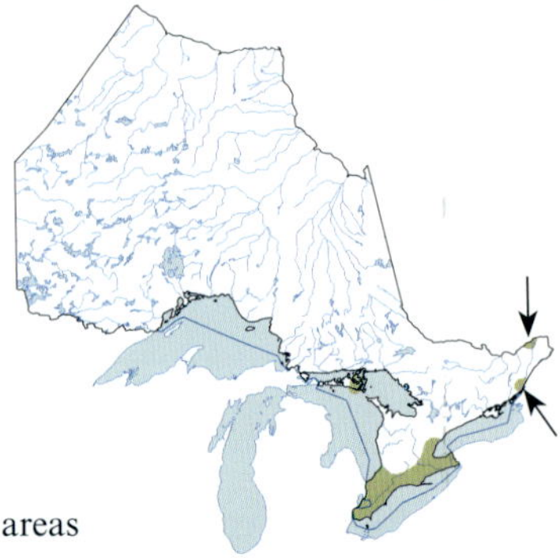

FEEDING: The White Crappie is usually **crepuscular**, feeding at dawn and dusk on small fishes, aquatic insects, and crustaceans.

REPRODUCTION: Spawning occurs in spring when the water temperature reaches 14°C. Males form colonies in shallow, vegetated areas

Juvenile

and, occasionally aided by females, each male prepares a nest about 30 cm across. The female circles the nest and then swims beside the male. The male arches his body and, with the female below him, the pair quivers, and eggs and sperm are released. The female spawns several times with one male and then moves to another nest to spawn again. The male fans the fertilized eggs with his fins and guards the eggs and young after they hatch.

HABITAT: The White Crappie prefers the warm waters of lakes and slow-moving streams.

STATUS: G5; N4; S4.

Maximum Age: 10	Ontario Average	Ontario Record	World Record
Length:	22.0 cm (8.7 in)	40.6 cm (16.0 in)	53.0 cm (20.9 in)
Weight: Overall	0.1 kg (0.2 lbs)	1.3 kg (2.8 lbs)	2.4 kg (5.2 lbs)
Angling	–	1.3 kg (2.8 lbs)	2.4 kg (5.2 lbs)

PERCIDAE
Perches and Darters

This family includes one of the most well-known Ontario fishes, the Yellow Perch. It also includes the Walleye and Sauger, the less well-known darters, and the introduced Ruffe. Members of the family are spread throughout the fresh waters of the northern hemisphere. Perches and darters have teeth in the mouth and throat. They have two dorsal fins (except for the Ruffe, which has one)—the first with sharp spines and the second with one or two spines followed by soft rays. The pelvic fins are below the pectoral fins. The anal fin has one or two spines followed by soft rays. The head and body have **ctenoid scales**.

There are more darters (222 species) in North America than any other group of freshwater fishes, except minnows (444 species). However, there are only 12 darter species in Ontario, likely as a result of a relatively cool climate and young waterbodies (ca. 10,000 years old). Most North American darters prefer warmer waters and evolved in very old waterbodies (more than one million years old). Darters often go unnoticed because they are small bottom dwellers; however, some of them rival coral reef fishes in their beauty. During spawning, darters exhibit strong **sexual dimorphism** in size and colouration. Spawning males are often very brightly coloured.

There are 247 species worldwide, 16 of which occur in Ontario.

< Yellow Perch

BLACKSIDE DARTER *Percina maculata*

Percina: little perch.
maculata—macula: spotted.

The Blackside Darter is native to southwestern Ontario. However, it has been found sporadically throughout southern Ontario. This sporadic occurrence is likely the result of transfer through bait buckets. It is ecologically unsound and illegal to release unused bait into the wild.

DESCRIPTION: The Blackside Darter is a small elongate fish. It has small **ctenoid scales** (56–81 **lateral scales**). The snout is bluntly pointed, and the upper jaw extends in front of the lower jaw. The groove between the upper lip and snout is not continuous (p. 26). The gill **membranes** are not attached to the body but narrowly attached to each other (p. 27). The spiny and soft dorsal fins are separated. The back is yellow to brown with 8–9 vague dark saddles and wavy lines. The sides are yellow and have a row of 6–9 large oval blotches, often connected by a dark stripe that starts on the snout. The belly is white to cream. There is a distinct small spot at the base of the tail. Spawning males become darker.

SIMILAR SPECIES: All other Ontario darters lack, or have smaller, dark blotches along the sides. The Blackside Darter is known to **hybridize** with other species of darters. These **hybrids** are difficult to distinguish from the parent species.

FEEDING: The Blackside Darter eats aquatic insect **larvae** and small crustaceans, usually from the bottom.

REPRODUCTION: Spawning occurs in spring when the water temperatures reach 16°C. Males move into pools, followed shortly after by the females. A female is pursued by several males while she chooses a spawning site. She then wriggles her body into the sand or gravel, and a male lies on top of her, holding her in position between his pelvic fins. The pair vibrates, and eggs are released one at a time and then fertilized by the

Juvenile

male. Both females and males spawn numerous times over several weeks with different partners, with the female laying more than 10 eggs each time. The eggs and young are left unguarded.

HABITAT: The Blackside Darter prefers the slow-moving areas of streams with gravel bottoms.

STATUS: G5; N5; S4.

Maximum Age: 4	Ontario Average	Ontario Record	World Record
Length:	6.0 cm (2.4 in)	9.9 cm (3.9 in)	11.0 cm (4.3 in)

CHANNEL DARTER *Percina copelandi*

Percina: little perch.
copelandi: named after Herbert Copeland, an American biologist who discovered the species.

Populations of Channel Darter in southwestern Ontario have declined, very likely as a result of **invasive species** such as the Zebra Mussel and Round Goby. It is thought to compete with, and be predated by, the Round Goby, but is currently protected in eastern Ontario by its occurrence above dams that act as barriers to gobies.

DESCRIPTION: The Channel Darter is a small elongate fish. It has large **ctenoid scales** (43–61 **lateral scales**). The snout is rounded, and the upper jaw extends in front of the lower jaw. The groove between the upper lip and snout is continuous (p. 26). The gill **membranes** are not attached to the body but narrowly attached to each other (p. 27). There are 2 separate dorsal fins. The first, or (spiny) dorsal fin, has a black edge in males. The back and upper sides are yellow to olive-green, with small black M-, V-, W-, or X-shaped dark markings, and there is a row of small spots along the sides. The belly is pale. Spawning males are darker on the body and head.

SIMILAR SPECIES: All Ontario darters, except the Johnny and Tessellated darters, lack small M-, V-, W-, or X-shaped marks and the continuous groove separating the upper lip from the snout. The River Darter has 2 dark spots on the spiny dorsal fin. Johnny and Tessellated darters have dorsal fins that lack a distinct dark edge, and usually lack a row of small spots along the sides. The Channel Darter is known to **hybridize** with the Logperch, but **hybrids** are very difficult to distinguish from the parent species.

FEEDING: The Channel Darter eats aquatic insect **larvae** and small crustaceans from the bottom.

REPRODUCTION: The Channel Darter spawns in spring when the water temperature reaches 20°C. In nearshore areas of lakes or in fast-flowing streams, the male guards a territory behind a large rock or between several small rocks. The female is

lured into the spawning site with a courtship display by the male. The male lies on top of her, holding her in position between his pelvic fins. Eggs and sperm are released, and the fertilized eggs are buried in the bottom. Parental care is not provided to the eggs or young.

HABITAT: The Channel Darter prefers the sandy nearshores of lakes Erie and St. Clair, and streams with sand and gravel bottoms.

STATUS: G4TNRQ; N1; S1; E^F; SC^P (Lake Erie populations). G4TNRQ; N2; S2; E^F; SC^P (Lake Ontario populations)

Maximum Age: 5	Ontario Average	Ontario Record	World Record
Length:	4.3 cm (1.7 in)	6.1 cm (2.4 in)	6.2 cm (2.4 in)

EASTERN SAND DARTER *Ammocrypta pellucida*

Ammocrypta—ammos: sand; *krypto*: hide; refers to its habit of burying in the sand.
pellucida: transparent, as this fish is almost see-through.

As its common name suggests, the Eastern Sand Darter has a strong preference for sandy habitats. In fact, it often buries itself in sand, usually leaving only its eyes exposed. This behaviour is likely undertaken to conserve energy in fast-flowing streams.

DESCRIPTION: The Eastern Sand Darter is a small, translucent, and very elongate fish. It has small **ctenoid scales** (62–84 **lateral scales**). The spiny dorsal fin is distinctly separated from the soft dorsal fin. The back is pale yellow to iridescent green, usually with a row of spots along the midline and on both sides of the dorsal fins. The sides are pale yellow to silvery, with a golden lateral stripe, and usually have a row of 10–14 small round or oval dark spots. The belly is silvery or white. The pelvic fins of the spawning male are black.

SIMILAR SPECIES: Other darters are less elongate, have spiny and soft dorsal fins close together, lack translucent flesh, and, except for the Channel Darter, have no small round or oval dark spots along the sides.

FEEDING: The Eastern Sand Darter feeds on small aquatic insect **larvae** from the bottom.

REPRODUCTION: Spawning occurs in late spring and early summer when the water temperature reaches 14°C. The male chases a female and rests on her back, using his pelvic fins to hold her. The pair vibrates, burying their tails in the sand, and eggs and sperm are released. Fertilized eggs become buried in the sand, and no parental care is given the eggs or young.

HABITAT: The Eastern Sand Darter is one of the most habitat-specific fishes in Ontario, being almost exclusively found on sandy bottoms of large streams and nearshore areas of the Great Lakes in southern Ontario.

STATUS: G4TNRQ; N2; S2; T (Southwestern Ontario population).
G4TNRQ; N1; S1; T^F; E^P (West Lake population).

Maximum Age: 3	Ontario Average	Ontario Record	World Record
Length:	6.6 cm (2.6 in)	8.4 cm (3.3 in)	8.4 cm (3.3 in)

FANTAIL DARTER *Etheostoma flabellare*

Etheostoma—etheo: to strain; *stoma*: mouth. The biologist who first used this name likely intended it to be *Heterostoma*, meaning different.

flabellare—flabellum: fan; refers to the shape of the tail.

The Fantail Darter develops exaggerated fin ornamentation consisting of yellow-orange fleshy knobs on the dorsal fin rays, which are thought to mimic eggs. As females prefer to spawn with males that are already guarding eggs in the nest, the egg-shaped knobs may trick females into entering the nest even though eggs may not be present.

DESCRIPTION: The Fantail Darter is a small elongate fish. It has small to medium **ctenoid scales** (41–60 **lateral scales**). The snout is pointed, and the lower jaw is even with or extends in front of the upper jaw. The groove between the upper lip and snout is not continuous (p. 26). The gill **membranes** are not attached to the body but broadly attached to each other (p. 27). The dorsal spines are short (shorter in the male), and the spiny and soft dorsal fins are close together. The back is olive to brown. The sides are lighter with 9–13 dark bars that do not reach the belly, and there are often numerous horizontal rows of tiny spots. The belly is white to grey. Spawning males are darker with a black head, and the dorsal spines are tipped with yellow to orange fleshy knobs.

SIMILAR SPECIES: All other Ontario darters have an upper jaw that extends in front of the lower jaw, and males have longer dorsal spines without fleshy knobs. In addition, the Channel, Iowa, Least, Rainbow, and River darters have gill **membranes** that are narrowly attached to each other, and the Greenside Darter has large V-shaped markings on the sides.

FEEDING: The Fantail Darter is able to eat food items almost as long as itself, including aquatic insect **larvae** and crustaceans from the bottom.

REPRODUCTION: In spring, when the water temperature reaches 17°C, the male establishes a territory under a rock in the shallows, and uses the fleshy knobs of his dorsal spines to clean the underside

of the rock. A female enters his territory when he performs a series of circles and figure-eights to encourage her to join him under the rock. Once under the rock, the female turns upside down and is head to tail with the male. They then vibrate and a single egg is released, which sticks to the rock. The male then turns upside down, fertilizes the egg, and then flips right side up again in preparation for another egg to be released. The female may remain on her back for up to two hours, laying 30–40 eggs while the male continues his acrobatic behaviour. Once the female has completed her egg-laying, she leaves the rock and may be replaced by another female. The male guards the eggs and brushes them with his fleshy knobs, which is thought to keep them free of fungi and bacteria.

HABITAT: The Fantail Darter prefers shallow streams with gravel bottoms, slow to moderate flow, and little vegetation.

STATUS: G5; N5; S4.

Maximum Age: 4	Ontario Average	Ontario Record	World Record
Length:	5.0 cm (2.0 in)	8.2 cm (3.2 in)	8.4 cm (3.3 in)

GREENSIDE DARTER *Etheostoma blennioides*

Etheostoma—*etheo*: to strain; *stoma*: mouth. The biologist who first used this name likely intended it to be *Heterostoma*, meaning different mouths.

blennioides—*oides*: like, as this fish resembles a blenny fish.

Historically, the distribution of the Greenside Darter was limited to a few watersheds in southwestern Ontario. Recently, its range has expanded dramatically as a result of accidental release and the increase in its preferred habitat of large **filamentous algae** mats. These algae are becoming increasingly abundant in Ontario in response to agricultural and urban runoffs of organic pollution such as fertilizers.

DESCRIPTION: The Greenside Darter is a small elongate fish. It has small **ctenoid scales** (54–65 **lateral scales**). The snout is rounded, and the upper jaw extends in front of the lower jaw. The groove between the upper lip and snout is continuous at the front but not at the side. The spiny and soft dorsal fins are close together. The gill **membranes** are not attached to the body but broadly attached to each other (p. 27). There are 2 dark bars extending down from the eye. The back is green to brown with 6–7 dark saddles that become faint in adults. The sides are pale green with small brown to dark red spots on the upper sides. There are 6–7 large V-shaped markings in a row, which may become bars in large individuals. The belly is white or cream-coloured. The spawning male develops bright green fins and bright green bars on the sides.

SIMILAR SPECIES: No other Ontario darter has large V-shaped markings on the sides. The Eastern Sand Darter has spiny and soft dorsal fins that are well separated. The Channel, Iowa, Least, Rainbow, and River darters have gill **membranes** that are narrowly attached to each other, and the Fantail Darter has a lower jaw that is even with or extends in front of the upper jaw.

FEEDING: The Greenside Darter feeds on small aquatic insect **larvae** from the bottom.

REPRODUCTION: Spawning occurs in **riffles** in spring when the water temperature reaches 11°C. The male

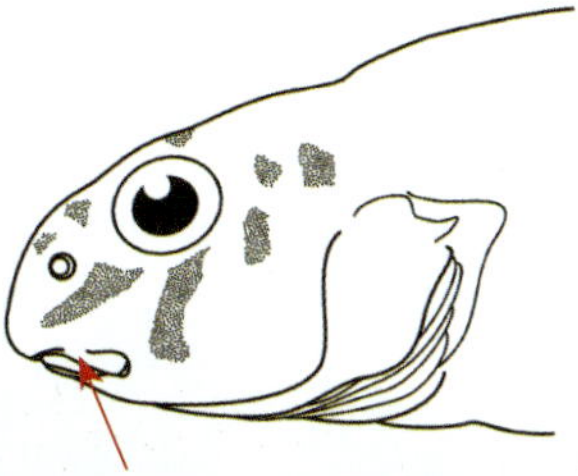

♂

guards a territory, and the female picks a spawning site above an algae-covered rock within the territory. The male lies on top of the female, the pair vibrates, and eggs and sperm are released. Spawning occurs over several weeks, and both males and females spawn with several partners. Fertilized eggs become buried in the gravel bottom, and no parental care is given to the eggs or young.

HABITAT: The Greenside Darter prefers heavily vegetated waters of streams and, rarely, lakes.

STATUS: G5; N4; S4; NAR.

Maximum Age: 5	Ontario Average	Ontario Record	World Record
Length:	7.5 cm (3.0 in)	10.0 cm (3.9 in)	17.0 cm (6.7 in)

IOWA DARTER *Etheostoma exile*

Etheostoma—*etheo*: to strain; *stoma*: mouth. The biologist who first used this name likely intended it to be *Heterostoma*, meaning different mouths.

exile—*exilis*: slender; refers to the body shape.

The Iowa Darter is one of the most widespread darters in Canada. This is the result of its ability to survive in a wide range of water temperatures and habitats.

DESCRIPTION: The Iowa Darter is a small elongate fish. It has small **ctenoid scales** (45–69 **lateral scales**). The snout is rounded, and the upper jaw extends in front of the lower jaw. The groove between the upper lip and snout is not continuous (p. 26). The gill **membranes** are not attached to the body but narrowly attached to each other (p. 27). The spiny and soft dorsal fins are slightly separated. The back is olive to brown, usually with 8 dark saddles. The sides are olive to brown, with 9–14 dark blotches or mottling that does not reach the ventral surface of the body. The belly is yellow or white. Spawning males are very colourful with blue to green and yellow to red tints on the body and fins.

SIMILAR SPECIES: In the Eastern Sand Darter, the spiny and soft dorsal fins are well separated. The Blackside Darter has a dark stripe and large blotches on the sides. The Fantail and Greenside darters have gill **membranes** that are broadly attached to each other. In addition, the Fantail Darter has a lower jaw equal to or extending in front of the upper jaw, and the Greenside Darter has large V-shaped markings on the sides. The Channel, Johnny, and Tessellated darters have small black V-, W-, or X-shaped dark markings on the back and upper sides, and the upper lip is separated from the snout by a continuous groove. The River Darter has 2 dark blotches on the spiny dorsal fin. The Rainbow Darter is deeper-bodied and has vertical bars that encircle the body. The Least Darter has pelvic fins that extend to the anus.

FEEDING: The Iowa Darter feeds from the bottom on aquatic insect **larvae**, small crustaceans, and molluscs.

♂

♂

Juvenile

REPRODUCTION: In spring, when the water temperature exceeds 12°C, adults move into shallow water nearshore, and males establish territories over wood debris or roots, often below undercut banks. Once a female enters the male's territory, he lies on top of her, the pair vibrates, and eggs and sperm are released. The females spawn with several males before moving back into deeper water. The fertilized eggs adhere to the bottom and are left unguarded.

HABITAT: The Iowa Darter can be found in a wide variety of bottom habitats in the clear waters of lakes and streams.

STATUS: G5; N5; S5.

Maximum Age: 3	Ontario Average	Ontario Record	World Record
Length:	5.0 cm (2.0 in)	7.2 cm (2.8 in)	7.2 cm (2.8 in)

JOHNNY DARTER *Etheostoma nigrum*

Etheostoma—etheo: to strain; *stoma*: mouth. The biologist who first used this name likely intended it to be *Heterostoma*, meaning different mouths.
nigrum—niger: black; refers to the colouration of the spawning male.

The Johnny Darter is probably the most common darter in Ontario. This is likely the result of its ability to survive in a wide range of water temperatures and habitats.

DESCRIPTION: The Johnny Darter is a small elongate fish. It has medium-sized **ctenoid scales** (37–52 **lateral scales**). The snout is rounded, and the upper jaw extends in front of the lower jaw. The groove between the upper lip and snout is continuous (p. 26). The gill **membranes** are not attached to the body but narrowly attached to each other (p. 27). The spiny and soft dorsal fins are slightly separated. The soft dorsal fin usually has 12 or fewer rays. The back is yellow to brown, with about 6 dark saddles. The sides are paler with numerous small brown M-, V-, W-, or X-shaped markings or broken wavy lines. The belly is white to yellow. The spawning male becomes grey to black, and the marks on the sides become less distinctive. Its pelvic and pectoral fins develop knob-like white tips, and the spiny dorsal fin may develop a black spot.

SIMILAR SPECIES: All other Ontario darters, except the Channel and Tessellated darters, lack small dark M-, V-, W-, or X-shaped markings. The Channel Darter has a distinct dark edge on the spiny dorsal fin and a row of small spots along the sides. The Johnny Darter is very difficult to distinguish from the Tessellated Darter, which usually has more than 12 rays in the soft dorsal fin and **hybridizes** with the Johnny Darter. **Hybrids** are very difficult to distinguish from the parent species.

FEEDING: The Johnny Darter feeds on aquatic insect **larvae**, and small crustaceans and molluscs off the bottom.

REPRODUCTION: In spring, males enter shallow water to spawn when the water temperature reaches 10°C. The male selects a territory and then cleans a nesting site under a rock while swimming upside down. The female then moves into shallow water and is courted by males until she swims under a rock with one of them. With both the male and female upside down, the female deposits one egg at a time onto the cleaned rock surface, and the male immediately fertilizes it. After depositing 30–200 eggs in succession, the female leaves the site and the male guards and fans the fertilized eggs with his pectoral fins. The male may guard more than 1,000 eggs laid by different females at his nesting site. Females are **fractional spawners**, releasing several small clutches of eggs over a few days or weeks.

HABITAT: The Johnny Darter can be found in a wide variety of bottom habitats in lakes and streams.

STATUS: G5; N5; S5.

Maximum Age: 4	Ontario Average	Ontario Record	World Record
Length:	5.0 cm (2.0 in)	7.6 cm (3.0 in)	7.6 cm (3.0 in)

LEAST DARTER *Etheostoma microperca*

Etheostoma—*etheo*: to strain; *stoma*: mouth. The biologist who first used this name likely intended it to be *Heterostoma*, meaning different mouths.

microperca—*micro*: small; *perca*: perch; refers to the small size of this fish.

The Least Darter is the smallest vertebrate in Canada. Adults of this species are often mistaken for the young of other darter species.

DESCRIPTION: The Least Darter is a very small, slightly deep-bodied fish. It has very large **ctenoid scales** (24–36 **lateral scales**). The snout is rounded and the upper jaw extends in front of the lower jaw. The groove between the upper lip and snout is not continuous (p. 26). The gill **membranes** are not attached to the body but narrowly attached to each other (p. 27). The spiny and soft dorsal fins are slightly separated. The pelvic fins usually extend to or in front of the anus. The back is olive-brown with dark green saddles and a dark, mid-back stripe in front of the dorsal fin. The sides are paler with 7–12 dark blotches, and the belly is whitish with scattered dark spots. Spawning males have orange and black dorsal fins, and orange anal and pelvic fins.

SIMILAR SPECIES: All other darters have smaller pectoral fins and scales (more than 35 **lateral scales**).

FEEDING: The Least Darter feeds on small crustaceans and aquatic insects that are on aquatic plants.

REPRODUCTION: In spring, when the water temperature reaches 12°C, males enter shallow, heavily vegetated inshore areas, and each may defend a territory about 30 cm in diameter. The female then moves into shallow water and, while several males court her, she chooses the largest and most colourful male and a spawning site in his territory. The male chases away his competitors and then lies on top of the female using his enlarged pelvic fins to clasp her. The pair vibrates, and a single adhesive egg is released and

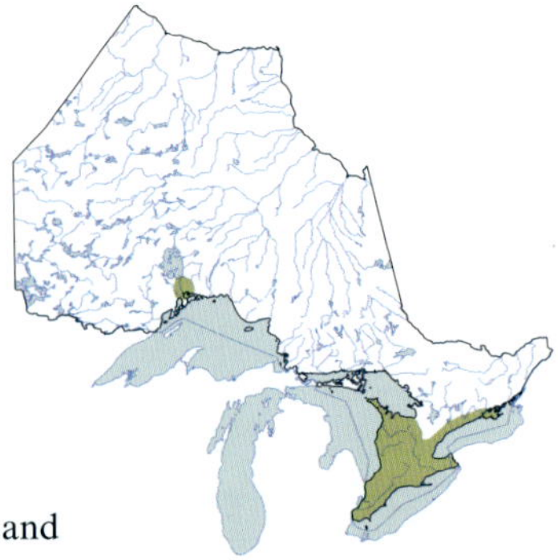

attaches to an aquatic plant. The male then fertilizes the egg. Three or four eggs are laid at a single site, and then the female finds a new site where the pair spawns again. About 30 eggs are released in one day by the female. There is no parental care given to the eggs or young.

HABITAT: The Least Darter prefers the quiet, weedy areas of lakes and streams.

STATUS: G5; N4; S4; NAR.

Maximum Age: 2	Ontario Average	Ontario Record	World Record
Length:	2.5 cm (1.0 in)	4.2 cm (1.7 in)	4.4 cm (1.7 in)

LOGPERCH *Percina caprodes*

Percina: little perch.
caprodes—kapros: pig; refers to the blunt, upturned snout.

Freshwater mussel **larvae**, known as "glochidia," are parasitic usually on fishes. The Logperch, which has the habit of rolling stones in search of prey, occasionally rolls a female snuffbox mussel full of glochidia. The snuffbox rapidly closes its shell onto the snout of the Logperch and expels the glochidia into the gills of the fish. There the **larvae** feed, develop, and eventually fall off to grow as free-living mussels.

DESCRIPTION: The Logperch is a small elongate fish. It has small **ctenoid scales** (67–103 **lateral scales**). The snout is long, pointed, and greatly overhangs the mouth. The groove between the upper lip and snout is not continuous. The gill **membranes** are not attached to the body but narrowly attached to each other (p. 27). The spiny and soft dorsal fins are slightly separated. The back and sides are yellow to dark olive, with 15–25 narrow dark bars that alternate in length. The belly is white. There is a distinct dark spot at the base of the tail. Spawning males are more brightly coloured.

SIMILAR SPECIES: All other Ontario darters have snouts that do not greatly overhang the mouths and fewer or no dark bars on the sides.

FEEDING: The Logperch feeds from the bottom on aquatic insect **larvae** and often rolls stones and debris with its snout to pursue prey.

REPRODUCTION: Spawning occurs when the water temperature reaches 15°C. Males congregate in the shallow waters of lakes or streams with sand and gravel bottoms and current. During spawning, a female swims into a school of males and rests on the bottom. Several males may vie to position themselves on top of the female. The successful male lies on top of her and holds her with his pelvic fins. The pair quivers, causing a cloud of sand to surround them. Eggs and sperm are released, and the fertilized eggs become buried in the cloud of sand as it settles to the bottom. Both females and males spawn numerous

Round Goby competes with Logperch

Snuffbox mussel traps Logperch

times over several weeks, with the female laying 10–20 eggs each time. The eggs and young are left unguarded.

HABITAT: The Logperch is found over rocky and sandy bottoms in lakes and slow- to fast-flowing streams. Although it prefers moderately shallow waters, it has been found at depths of 40 m in Lake Erie.

STATUS: G5; N5; S5.

Maximum Age: 3	Ontario Average	Ontario Record	World Record
Length:	9.0 cm (3.5 in)	18.0 cm (7.1 in)	18.0 cm (7.1 in)

RAINBOW DARTER *Etheostoma caeruleum*

Etheostoma—*etheo*: to strain; *stoma*: mouth. The biologist who first used this name likely intended it to be *Heterostoma*, meaning different mouths.

caeruleum—*caeruleus*: blue; refers to the vivid blue colouring of the spawning male.

As its name implies, the Rainbow Darter is one of the most colourful fishes in Ontario. In fact, darters are often thought to be the most colourful of all freshwater fishes in North America. The colours are likely used for species recognition and mate attraction during spawning.

DESCRIPTION: The Rainbow Darter is a small, slightly deep-bodied fish. The snout is pointed, and the upper jaw extends in front of the lower jaw. It has large **ctenoid scales** (36–57 **lateral scales**). The groove between the upper lip and snout is not continuous (p. 26). The gill **membranes** are not attached to the body but narrowly attached to each other (p. 27). The spiny and soft dorsal fins are close together but not joined. The back is olive-brown with 3–11 dark saddles, of which 2–3 are prominent. The sides have many bars and are most prominent behind the anus, where they encircle the body. The bars are blue and red in the male; brown and yellow, but often vague, in the female. The belly is white or yellow. Spawning males are brilliant blue and green with yellow or orange colouration on the head, body, and fins.

SIMILAR SPECIES: In the Eastern Sand Darter, the spiny and soft dorsal fins are well separated. The Greenside Darter has large V-shaped markings on the sides, and its gill **membranes** are broadly attached to each other. The Least Darter has pelvic fins that usually extend to the anus and very large scales (fewer than 37 **lateral scales**). The Channel, Fantail, Iowa, and River darters are less deep-bodied, and their vertical bars do not encircle the body. In addition, the Channel Darter has an upper lip

♂ (left), ♀ (right)

Juvenile

♀

separated from the snout by a continuous groove, the Fantail Darter has gill **membranes** that are broadly attached to each other, and the River Darter has 2 dark blotches on the spiny dorsal fin.

FEEDING: The Rainbow Darter feeds from the bottom on aquatic insect **larvae**, small crustaceans, and molluscs.

REPRODUCTION: The Rainbow Darter spawns in **riffles** in spring when the water temperature reaches 15°C. The male guards a territory by displaying his brightly coloured fins and chasing away competing males. The female is courted and, when ready to spawn, partially buries herself in the bottom. The male lies on top of the female, the pair vibrates, and eggs and sperm are released. Spawning occurs over several weeks, and both males and females spawn with several partners. Fertilized eggs become buried in the gravel, and no parental care is given to the eggs or young.

HABITAT: The Rainbow Darter prefers shallow streams with gravel bottoms, moderate flow, and little vegetation.

STATUS: G5; N4; S4.

Maximum Age: 3	Ontario Average	Ontario Record	World Record
Length:	5.0 cm (2.0 in)	8.1 cm (3.2 in)	8.1 cm (3.2 in)

RIVER DARTER *Percina shumardi*

Percina: little perch.
shumardi: named after its discoverer, Dr. George Shumard, who was a surgeon for the Pacific Railroad in Missouri.

The River Darter is one of few fishes in Ontario that is more widespread in the north than in the south. This is probably because its preferred habitat is much more common in northern than southern Ontario.

DESCRIPTION: The River Darter is a small elongate fish. It has small **ctenoid scales** (46–62 **lateral scales**). The upper jaw usually extends in front of the lower jaw. The groove between the upper lip and snout is usually not continuous (p. 26), but occasionally there is a very shallow continuous groove. The gill **membranes** are not attached to the body but narrowly attached to each other (p. 27). The spiny and soft dorsal fins are separated. The back is dark olive-green to light brown, with 7–8 faint saddles. The sides are paler with a row of 8–15 dark blotches or short vertical bars. The belly is white. There are 2 dark blotches on the spiny dorsal fin. The spot at the base of the tail may be faint. Spawning males are darker and more colourful.

SIMILAR SPECIES: No other Ontario darter has 2 dark spots on the spiny dorsal fin. The Channel Darter is most similar in colour pattern. It has a deep continuous groove separating the upper lip from the snout, and small, black, M-, V-, W-, or X-shaped markings on the back and upper sides.

FEEDING: The River Darter eats aquatic insect **larvae** and small crustaceans from the bottom.

REPRODUCTION: The River Darter spawns in spring in the shallows of large streams. The males move into the spawning sites first, followed by the females. The female partially buries her body into the sand or gravel, and the male rests on top of her, holding her in position between his pelvic fins. The pair vibrates, eggs are deposited one

at a time, and then are fertilized by the male. Both females and males spawn numerous times over several weeks with different partners. The fertilized eggs and young are left unguarded.

HABITAT: The River Darter prefers clear, large streams with moderate flows and gravel bottoms strewn with rubble and boulders.

STATUS: G5TNRQ; N1; S1; E (Great Lakes–Upper St. Lawrence populations).
G5TNRQ; N4; S4; NAR (Saskatchewan–Nelson River populations and Southern Hudson Bay–James Bay populations).

Maximum Age: 4	Ontario Average	Ontario Record	World Record
Length:	5.6 cm (2.2 in)	7.2 cm (2.8 in)	7.8 cm (3.1 in)

RUFFE *Gymnocephalus cernua*

Gymnocephalus—gymnos: naked; *kephale*: head; refers to the scaleless head.

cernua: turned toward the earth; refers to the position of the mouth.

The Ruffe is native to Europe and was introduced into Lake Superior through the ballast water of ocean-going ships. It was first discovered in Duluth Harbour, Minnesota, and was later transferred, probably by ballast water, to Thunder Bay, where it was discovered in 1991.

DESCRIPTION: The Ruffe is a medium-sized, deep-bodied fish. It has large **ctenoid scales** (34–40 **lateral scales**). The snout overhangs the small mouth, and the upper jaw extends to below the front edge of the eye. The teeth of the lower jaw are small, and there are no enlarged canines. There is 1 long dorsal fin that is distinctly notched between the spiny- and soft-rayed sections. The back is green to brown, the sides are lighter green to brown, with numerous dark spots or blotches, and the belly is light brown to yellow. The dorsal fin and tail are spotted.

SIMILAR SPECIES: The Sauger, Walleye, and Yellow Perch have 2 dorsal fins that are separated. The Yellow Perch has 6–8 wide dark bars on the body, and the Sauger and Walleye have large canine teeth in the lower jaw. The Trout-perch has an adipose fin.

FEEDING: The Ruffe moves into shallow water at night to feed on aquatic insect **larvae** and small crustaceans from the bottom. In northern Europe, it is known to eat the eggs of whitefishes. The Ruffe has well-developed **sensory canals** on its head, likely to aid in detecting and locating moving prey.

REPRODUCTION: The Ruffe spawns in spring and summer when the water temperature reaches 6°C. Spawning occurs on a wide variety of bottom types, from sand and rock to heavily vegetated areas in waters up to 3 m deep. Males and

females enter the spawning grounds, and large numbers of eggs are released and fertilized over an extended period. The fertilized eggs are adhesive, sticking to vegetation or the bottom. Females can produce up to 200,000 eggs per season, allowing for explosive population increases in favourable conditions.

HABITAT: The Ruffe is found in cool, nearshore waters of lakes and stream mouths with aquatic vegetation.

STATUS: G5; NNA; SNA.

Maximum Age: 10	Ontario Average	Ontario Record	World Record
Length:	11.0 cm (4.3 in)	18.0 cm (7.1 in)	25.0 cm (9.8 in)
Weight: Overall	–	–	0.4 kg (0.9 lbs)

SAUGER *Sander canadensis*

Sander: named after its European relative, the Zander.
canadensis: of Canada, as this species was originally described from a Canadian location.

Both the Sauger and Walleye have a structure in their eyes that give them a shiny or "wall-eyed" appearance. This structure, known as a ***tapetum lucidum***, reflects light into the fish's eye, allowing it to see better at night, when these species do most of their feeding.

DESCRIPTION: The Sauger is a large elongate fish. It has small **ctenoid scales** (82–100 **lateral scales**). The mouth is large, and the upper jaw extends to below the posterior edge of the pupil. The lower jaw has enlarged canine teeth. The spiny and soft dorsal fins are separated. The eyes are silver and opaque. The back is grey to brown, with 3–4 darker brown saddles, the sides are paler, often with darker brown blotches or round spots, and the belly is white. The spiny dorsal fin is clear with distinct rows of spots. The pelvic fins are white with dark speckles.

SIMILAR SPECIES: The Ruffe has spots on the body and fins, and a single dorsal fin that is distinctly notched. The Yellow Perch has 6–8 prominent bars on the body. The Walleye has a white tip on the lower lobe of the tail. The dark, spiny dorsal fin has a black blotch and lacks distinct rows of spots. The Saugeye, a hatchery-produced **hybrid** of the Walleye and Sauger, shows characteristics of both parents, such as a barred spiny dorsal fin, blotches on the sides, and a white tip on the lower lobe of the tail.

FEEDING: The Sauger has specialized eyes that allow it to feed in **turbid** or dark waters. It feeds on a variety of fishes, insects, leeches, and crustaceans.

REPRODUCTION: The Sauger spawns in spring when the water temperature reaches 4°C. Spawning occurs at night on gravel shoals that were often previously used by Walleye. Males arrive on the shoals first.

When females arrive, they are usually pursued by, and spawn with, several smaller males. Eggs and sperm are released, and the fertilized eggs drop between the gravel. Females leave after spawning, while the males stay longer and continue to spawn with other females. The eggs and young are left unguarded.

HABITAT: The Sauger is found in a wide variety of coolwater habitats in lakes and streams. As its eyes are light-sensitive, it is typically found in deeper waters during the day or in very **turbid**, shallower waters.

STATUS: G5; N5; S4.

Maximum Age: 18	Ontario Average	Ontario Record	World Record
Length:	33.0 cm (13.0 in)	56.4 cm (22.2 in)	76.0 cm (29.9 in)
Weight: Overall	0.3 kg (0.7 lbs)	2.0 kg (4.4 lbs)	4.0 kg (8.7 lbs)
Angling	–	2.0 kg (4.4 lbs)	4.0 kg (8.7 lbs)

TESSELLATED DARTER *Etheostoma olmstedi*

Etheostoma—etheo: to strain; *stoma*: mouth. The biologist who first used this name likely intended it to be *Heterostoma*, meaning different mouths.
olmstedi: named after Charles Olmstead, an American naturalist who discovered this species.

Until recently, the Johnny and Tessellated darters were considered the same species. They are now considered separate species based on slight anatomical differences. In Ontario, the Tessellated Darter is generally found to the east of the Lake Ontario drainage and the Johnny Darter to the west and north, and both species are found in the Lake Ontario drainage, where they may **hybridize**.

DESCRIPTION: The Tessellated Darter is a small elongate fish. It has medium-sized **ctenoid scales** (36–57 **lateral scales**). The snout is rounded, and the upper jaw extends in front of the lower jaw. The groove between the upper lip and snout is continuous (p. 26). The gill **membranes** are not attached to the body but narrowly attached to each other (p. 27). The spiny and soft dorsal fins are slightly separated. The soft dorsal fin usually has more than 12 rays. The back is yellow to brown, with about 6 dark green saddles. The sides have small, brown, M-, V-, W-, or X-shaped markings. The belly is white to yellow. The spawning male becomes very dark, the markings on the sides become less distinctive, and a black spot may develop on the spiny dorsal fin.

SIMILAR SPECIES: All Ontario darters, except the Channel and Johnny darters, lack small, dark, M-, V-, W-, or X-shaped markings. The Channel Darter has a row of small spots along the sides. The Tessellated Darter is very difficult to distinguish from the Johnny Darter, which usually has 12 or fewer rays in the soft dorsal fin.

FEEDING: The Tessellated Darter feeds during the day on aquatic insects, small crustaceans, and molluscs.

REPRODUCTION: The Tessellated Darter spawns in spring when the water temperature reaches 12°C. The male selects a territory in shallow water and then cleans a nesting site under a rock by fanning it with his pectoral fins. The female then moves into shallow water and is courted by a male until she swims under the rock with him. With both the male and female upside down, the female deposits one egg at a time onto the cleaned rock surface, and the male immediately fertilizes it. After depositing 20 or more eggs in succession, the female leaves the nest and will spawn up to seven more times with the same, or a different, male over several weeks. Larger, dominant males often move to new nesting sites to spawn with other females. Smaller, subordinate males take over the abandoned nests, clean them in preparation for spawning, and, at the same time, clean and care for the fertilized eggs deposited by the previous pair.

HABITAT: The Tessellated Darter is primarily found in slow-moving streams, over gravelly and sandy bottoms.

STATUS: G5; N4N5; S4; NAR.

Maximum Age: 4	Ontario Average	Ontario Record	World Record
Length:	6.2 cm (2.4 in)	8.0 cm (3.1 in)	11.0 cm (4.3 in)

WALLEYE *Sander vitreus*

Sander: named after its European relative, the Zander.
vitreus: glassy; refers to the large, silvery eyes.

In Ontario, the Walleye is widely known as "pickerel." However, the name "pickerel" should be used only for small species of the pike family, such as the Chain Pickerel (*Esox niger*), also found in Ontario. "Walleye," the accepted common name, should always be used.

DESCRIPTION: The Walleye is a large elongate fish. It has small **ctenoid scales** (83–104 **lateral scales**). The mouth is large, and the upper jaw extends to below the posterior edge of the eye. The eyes are silver and opaque. The lower jaw has enlarged canine teeth. The spiny and soft dorsal fins are separated. The back is olive-green to brown with 5–12 dark saddles. The sides are paler with yellow flecks and may have inconspicuous blotches. The belly is yellow to white. The spiny dorsal fin is speckled and has a black blotch. The pelvic fins are yellow to orange. The lower lobe of the tail has a white tip. A grey-blue colour variant of the Walleye occurs occasionally in most populations, but these are not the same as the extinct subspecies, "Blue Pike" (*Sander vitreus glaucus*). Blue Pike was once present in lakes Erie and Ontario and recently found to be genetically the same as Walleye. Blue Pike is the historical name used by commercial fishermen and is the accepted common name.

SIMILAR SPECIES: The Ruffe has dark spots on the body and fins, and a single dorsal fin that is distinctly notched. The Yellow Perch has 6–8 prominent bars on the body. The Sauger lacks a white tip on the lower lobe of the tail and has a clear spiny dorsal fin covered with rows of black spots. The Saugeye, a hatchery-produced **hybrid** of the Walleye and Sauger, shows characteristics of both parents, such as a barred dorsal fin, blotches on the sides, and a white tip on the lower lobe of the tail. The Blue Pike had larger eyes that were closer together. It was dark blue on the back, blue to silvery on the sides, and silvery to white on the belly. The pelvic fins were white.

Blue Pike

FEEDING: The Walleye has large, sensitive eyes that are capable of finding prey in the dark. It generally moves into shallows in the evening, feeding at or near the bottom on fishes, leeches, crustaceans, molluscs, and frogs. The young are thought to have voracious appetites—in one instance, seven juveniles were found attached in a row, each having swallowed the back half of the fish in front!

REPRODUCTION: The Walleye spawns in early spring when water temperatures are above 2°C. Males move onto spawning grounds first, over shallow gravel or rocky shoals of lakes or streams. Once the females arrive, they congregate with the males in small groups, and spawning occurs in the evening with eggs and sperm being released. The fertilized eggs drop into the gravel and are left unguarded.

HABITAT: The Walleye is found in a wide variety of coolwater habitats in lakes and streams. As its eyes are light sensitive, it is typically found in deeper waters during the day or, if in shallower waters, in dense aquatic vegetation.

STATUS: Walleye: G5; N5; S5.
Blue Pike: X^F.

Maximum Age: 29	Ontario Average	Ontario Record	World Record
Length:	42.0 cm (16.5 in)	107.0 cm (42.1 in)	107.0 cm (42.1 in)
Weight: Overall	0.7 kg (1.5 lbs)	10.7 kg (23.6 lbs)	11.3 kg (25.0 lbs)
Angling	–	10.1 kg (22.3 lbs)	11.3 kg (25.0 lbs)

YELLOW PERCH *Perca flavescens*

Perca: old Latin name for perch.
flavescens—flavidus: yellowish; refers to the background colour of the body.

The Yellow Perch is one of the few remaining commercially fished species in Ontario. The largest fishery is in Lake Erie, which represents one-third of the total catch and value of all commercial fisheries in Ontario.

DESCRIPTION: The Yellow Perch is a medium-sized, deep-bodied fish. It has small **ctenoid scales** (51–61 **lateral scales**). The mouth is large, and the upper jaw extends to below the middle of the eye. The teeth of the lower jaw are all about the same size, and there are no enlarged canines. There are 2 separate dorsal fins. The back is green to golden brown. The sides are yellow to green, with 6–8 wide dark bars. The belly is grey to white. Spawing males are more brightly coloured with orange or red pelvic and anal fins.

SIMILAR SPECIES: The Ruffe, Sauger, and Walleye lack prominent dark bars on the sides. The Ruffe has spots on the body and fins, and a single, distinctly notched dorsal fin. The Sauger and Walleye have large canine teeth in the lower jaw.

FEEDING: The Yellow Perch feeds on a wide variety of items, including crustaceans, small fishes, aquatic insects, worms, and molluscs. This species actively feeds during the winter and is often targeted by ice fishers.

REPRODUCTION: The Yellow Perch spawns in spring when the water temperature is above 6°C. Spawning usually occurs at night over vegetation or fallen trees in lakes and streams. Males move in large schools into shallow waters. Once the females arrive, each is pursued by up to 25 males, and eggs and sperm are released en masse. The female releases a gelatinous mass of eggs up to 2.4 m long, which is

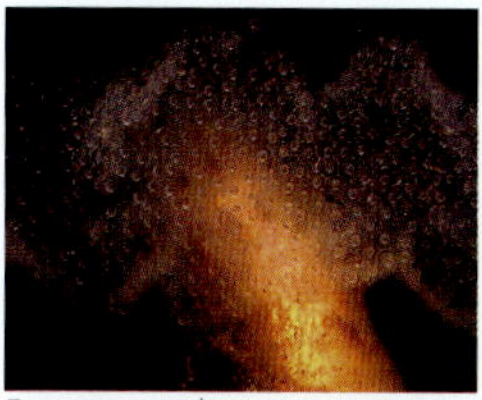

Eggs in a gelatinous mass

♂

adhesive and folded accordion-style. The strand may often be seen wrapped around vegetation or lying on the bottom. No parental care is given to the eggs or young.

HABITAT: The Yellow Perch can be found in a wide variety of water temperatures and habitats in lakes and slow-moving streams.

STATUS: G5; N5; S5.

Maximum Age: 11	Ontario Average	Ontario Record	World Record
Length:	18.0 cm (7.1 in)	40.0 cm (15.8 in)	50.0 cm (19.7 in)
Weight: Overall	<0.1 kg (0.1 lbs)	1.1 kg (2.5 lbs)	1.9 kg (4.2 lbs)
Angling	–	1.1 kg (2.5 lbs)	1.9 kg (4.2 lbs)

SCIAENIDAE
Drums and Croakers

Most members of this family are found in the Atlantic, Indian, and Pacific oceans. Only one species occurs in fresh water. Drums and croakers are bottom feeders and have a mouth that is overhung by the snout. They have conical teeth on the jaws and blunt **pharyngeal teeth** on each side of the throat for crushing molluscs. Some species have one or more small **barbels** on the chin. There is one long dorsal fin that has a deep notch between the spiny and soft rays. The pelvic fins are below the pectoral fins. The anal fin has two spines followed by soft rays. The **lateral line** extends to the end of the tail. Thick **ctenoid scales** cover the head and body.

Many species of fish produce sound to communicate fright responses, mating calls, and warnings to competitors. Fishes make sounds in a variety of ways. Some fishes, such as the grunt, grind their teeth. The aptly named drums and croakers create a drumming noise by rapidly flexing muscles against the **swim bladder**. Male drums and croakers produce sound during courtship. Croakers may also use sound in **turbid** water to initiate group feeding when prey is found. To hear sounds, fishes use both their **lateral line** and **inner ear** to detect vibrations.

There are 297 species worldwide, one of which occurs in Ontario. The Freshwater Drum is often referred to as "Sheepshead."

< Freshwater Drum

FRESHWATER DRUM *Aplodinotus grunniens*

Aplodinotus—*aplo*: single; *dinotos*: turned or rounded; refers to the single dorsal fin.
grunniens—*grunnio*: to grunt; refers to the grunting noises the **swim bladder** makes.

Fish ears have several bones known as **otoliths**. The Freshwater Drum has the largest **otoliths** of any freshwater fish in Ontario, measuring, on average, 25 mm in diameter. These **otoliths** are sometimes kept as lucky stones and have been used for jewellery and currency.

DESCRIPTION: The Freshwater Drum is a large, silvery, very deep-bodied fish, which is very thin from side to side. It has small **ctenoid scales** (48–53 **lateral scales**). The **lateral line** extends onto the tail. There is a single, long dorsal fin that is distinctly notched between the short and spiny, and long and soft-rayed sections (p. 24). The first pelvic ray is extended. The anal fin is small with 2 spines, the second spine distinctly enlarged. The back is dark green to brown, the sides are silvery, and the belly is white.

SIMILAR SPECIES: The Largemouth and Smallmouth basses, White Bass, and White Perch have 3 anal spines, and their **lateral line** does not extend onto the tail.

FEEDING: The Freshwater Drum feeds from the bottom on molluscs, crustaceans, aquatic insects, and fishes. Its large, molar-like **pharyngeal teeth** are well adapted for crushing mollusc shells, and there is evidence that it feeds on Zebra Mussels.

REPRODUCTION: The Freshwater Drum spawns in summer when the water temperature reaches 18°C. Males produce a drumming sound that

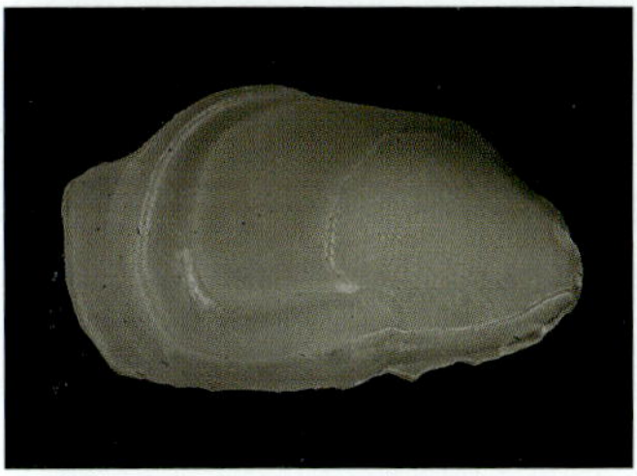

Otolith, with distinctive L-shaped groove

Pharyngeal tooth pad

likely attracts females. Schools of males and females form near the surface during spawning, and eggs and sperm are released. The fertilized eggs and young are left unguarded.

HABITAT: The Freshwater Drum prefers cool to warm waters of lakes and large, slow-moving streams.

STATUS: G5; N5; S5.

Maximum Age: 13	Ontario Average	Ontario Record	World Record
Length:	48.0 cm (18.9 in)	88.9 cm (35.0 in)	95.0 cm (37.4 in)
Weight: Overall	1.4 kg (3.0 lbs)	10.3 kg (22.6 lbs)	24.7 kg (54.5 lbs)
Angling	–	10.3 kg (22.6 lbs)	24.7 kg (54.5 lbs)

GOBIIDAE
Gobies

This family contains the greatest number of marine fish species and the shortest vertebrate (shorter than 6 mm) in the world. Gobies occur in fresh and salt waters, primarily in tropical and subtropical areas. They are small, typically less than 10 cm long. There are usually two dorsal fins—the first with sharp spines and the second with soft rays. The pelvic fins are fused together into a cup-like disc and are located below the pectoral fins. There are **cycloid** or **ctenoid scales** on the head and body, sometimes both types on the same fish.

In Ontario, the **invasive** Round Goby has spread rapidly throughout the Great Lakes and surrounding waters. This is because of several adaptations: its ability to survive in a wide range of habitats; its diverse diet; its aggressive behaviour; its ability to spawn up to four times in one growing season; and its parental care of the eggs, which ensures high hatching success. The Round Goby now inhabits much of the Great Lakes, with populations estimated in the billions. Its impact has been enormous, including **predation** on, and **competition** with, native species. A school of Round Goby can eat 4,000 Smallmouth Bass eggs in 15 minutes when bass nests are left unguarded. Conversely, the Round Goby has become a dominant food source for Smallmouth Bass and Burbot.

There are approximately 1,437 known species worldwide, of which two are found in Ontario.

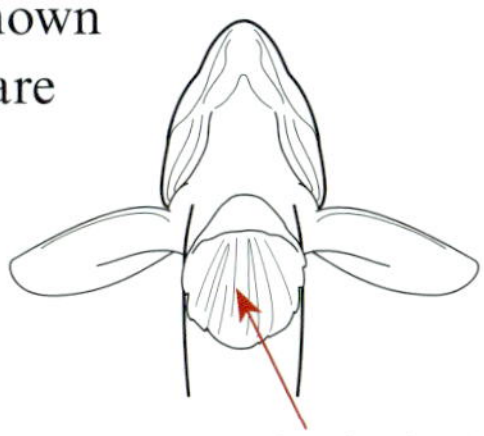

< Round Goby

FRESHWATER TUBENOSE GOBY *Proterorhinus semilunaris*

Proterorhinus—proteros: before; *rhinos*: snout; the snout overhangs the mouth.
semilunaris—semi: half; *lunaris*: of the moon.

Like the Round Goby, the Freshwater Tubenose Goby was introduced from Europe, probably in ballast water. Unlike the Round Goby, it has not spread as quickly and has little known impact on Great Lakes ecosystems. This is probably the result of its more specific habitat and prey requirements.

DESCRIPTION: The Freshwater Tubenose Goby is a small, slightly deep-bodied fish. It has large **ctenoid scales** (34–48 **lateral scales**). There are 2 distinct pairs of nostrils; the front pair extends as very long tubes. The pelvic fins are fused together into a single fin (p. 451). The back and sides are reddish brown to yellowish grey. The sides have irregular dark bars, blotches, or mottling. The belly is pale and may be mottled with brown.

SIMILAR SPECIES: In sculpins and darters, the pelvic fins are not fused together. The Round Goby has a dark spot on the first dorsal fin, and its front pair of nostrils extends as short tubes.

FEEDING: The Freshwater Tubenose Goby feeds mainly from the bottom on aquatic insects and small crustaceans and fishes.

REPRODUCTION: In Ontario, the Freshwater Tubenose Goby spawns in spring and summer in the shallows of stream mouths over sand and gravel. Both the male and female produce sounds during the spawning season, likely as part of courtship behaviour. Little is known of the spawning behaviour, but fertilized eggs have been found in nests under rocks and logs. The male guards the nest. This species is a **fractional spawner**, with up to three batches of eggs being laid by the female during the long spawning season.

HABITAT: The Freshwater Tubenose Goby prefers warm, heavily vegetated stream mouths.

STATUS: GNR; NNA; SNA.

Maximum Age: 2	Ontario Average	Ontario Record	World Record
Length:	5.0 cm (2.0 in)	8.5 cm (3.3 in)	11.5 cm (4.5 in)

ROUND GOBY *Neogobius melanostomus*

Neogobius—neo: new; *gobius*: a kind of goby.
melanostomus—melano: black; *stoma*: mouth.

The Round Goby is native to Europe and was first discovered in the Great Lakes in 1990. It was likely transported by ballast water of ocean-going vessels. Since its initial discovery in Lake St. Clair, the Round Goby has rapidly spread throughout the Great Lakes and their tributaries. This spread has likely been aided by the abundance of its preferred prey, Zebra and Quagga mussels, and by bait buckets.

DESCRIPTION: The Round Goby is a small, slightly deep-bodied fish. It has large **ctenoid scales** (44–55 **lateral scales**). There are 2 distinct pairs of nostrils; the front pair extends as short tubes that do not reach the upper lip. The pelvic fins are fused together into a single fin (p. 451). The back and sides are yellow to grey, with dark blotches. The belly is white to grey. The first dorsal fin has 2–3 dark stripes and a large distinct spot. There is also a spot at the base of the large pectoral fin. The spawning male is charcoal black with a white or yellow edge on the dorsal fin and tail.

SIMILAR SPECIES: In sculpins and darters, pelvic fins are separate, not fused together. The Tubenose Goby lacks a dark spot on the first dorsal fin, and its tubular front pair of nostrils are much longer.

FEEDING: The Round Goby feeds near the bottom on a wide variety of molluscs, aquatic insects, fish eggs, and small crustaceans and fishes. It is known to consume large numbers of Zebra Mussels. Unfortunately, the Round Goby probably cannot eat enough Zebra Mussels to control them. It is able to outcompete native fishes for food, partly because of its well-developed sensory system, which detects movement. This allows it to feed at night, which many native, bottom-dwelling species are not able to do.

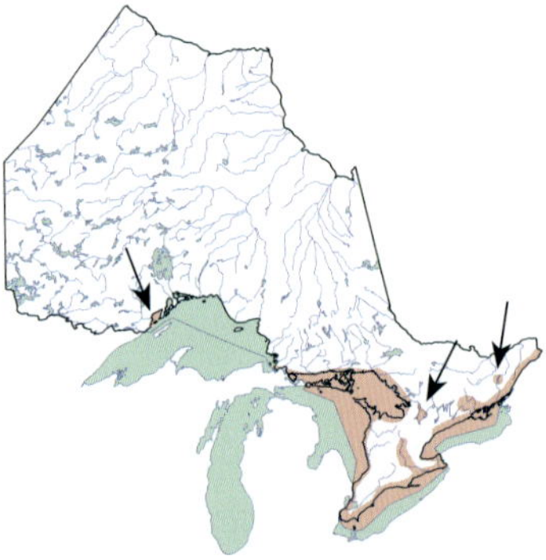

Round Goby eating zebra mussels

♂ Round Goby guarding his nest

Round Goby with eggs

REPRODUCTION: The Round Goby is a **fractional spawner**, reproducing from spring to fall when the water temperature is above 9°C. The male aggressively competes for prime nesting habitat in cavities under logs or rocks. The female is attracted to the nest cavity by the male and deposits eggs, one at a time, onto a hard surface in the nest. The male fertilizes the eggs and aggressively defends the eggs and young for 7–10 days after hatching. The female produces 80–600 eggs and often deposits them in several nests over the long spawning season. The male may guard up to 10,000 fertilized eggs in his nest cavity, and dies after the spawning season.

HABITAT: The Round Goby can be found in an incredibly wide variety of cool- to warmwater habitats in lakes and slow-moving streams. In the Great Lakes, it has been found from shallow beaches to depths of more than 30 m.

STATUS: G5; NNA; SNA.

Maximum Age: 6	Ontario Average	Ontario Record	World Record
Length:	7.5 cm (3.0 in)	24.4 cm (9.6 in)	30.0 cm (11.8 in)

FISHES THAT MAY OCCUR IN ONTARIO*

Species occasionally caught (likely to be seen again)

These species primarily originate from the aquarium and live-food trades and are illegally released into the wild. Other non-native species may disperse through canals into the Great Lakes. In the past, several species have been transported by ballast water and released into the Great Lakes (e.g., European Flounder); however, current ballast-water regulations reduce the risk of this happening in the future.

LEPISOSTEIDAE / GARS

FLORIDA GAR *Lepisosteus platyrhincus*

KNOWN LOCATIONS: Island Lake, York County (formerly Orangeville Reservoir). Undoubtedly an illegal release of an aquarium pet.

SIMILAR SPECIES: The Longnose Gar has a longer, narrower beak. The Spotted Gar has bony plates under the gill **membranes**.

* At the time of reprinting, a reproducing population of Kokanee, the freshwater form of Sockeye Salmon (*Oncorhynchus nerka*), was confirmed in central Ontario.

XENOCYPRIDIDAE / XENOCARPS

BIGHEAD CARP *Hypophthalmichthys nobilis*

KNOWN LOCATIONS: The Bighead Carp has been recorded in the Canadian waters of Lake Erie. Although this introduction did not result in an **established** population, Bighead Carp may invade Lake Michigan through the Chicago Shipping Canal (about 600 km from Ontario).

SIMILAR SPECIES: The Common Carp and Goldfish have a long dorsal fin of more than 12 rays and a strong, **serrated** spine at the front of the dorsal and anal fins. The Black and Grass carps have large scales (fewer than 40 **lateral scales** vs. more than 84). The Silver Carp lacks dark blotches on the back and has a long ventral **keel** that extends from the throat to the anus (vs. a short ventral **keel** that extends from the pelvic fins to the anus).

COBITIDAE / LOACHES

LOACH SPECIES *Misgurnus* spp.

KNOWN LOCATIONS: A loach was captured in Bond Lake, a spring-fed, kettle lake north of Richmond Hill in York Region and another in Hamilton Harbour. Undoubtedly illegal releases of aquarium pets.

SIMILAR SPECIES: No other Ontario fish has the combination of a long eel-like body with 10 short **barbels** around the mouth.

SERRASALMIDAE / PIRANHAS AND PACUS

PIRANHAS e.g., *Catoprion, Pygocentrus, Serrasalmus* species

KNOWN LOCATIONS: The Red Piranha (*Pygocentrus nattereri*) has been caught in various locations in southern Ontario. Undoubtedly illegal releases of aquarium pets.

SIMILAR SPECIES: There are no similar species **established** in Ontario. The Pirapatinga and other species of pacus have rounded, blunt teeth (vs. pointed, sharp).

PACUS e.g., *Colossoma, Myleus, Piaractus* species

KNOWN LOCATIONS: The Pirapatinga (*Piaractus brachypomus*) has been captured in various locations in southern Ontario. Undoubtedly illegal releases of aquarium pets.

SIMILAR SPECIES: There are no similar species **established** in Ontario. Piranhas have pointed, sharp teeth (vs. rounded, blunt).

LORICARIIDAE / SUCKERMOUTH CATFISHES

SUCKERMOUTH CATFISHES e.g., *Hypostomus, Panaque, Pterygoplichthys* species

KNOWN LOCATIONS: An Amazon Sailfin Catfish (*Pterygoplichthys pardalis*) was caught in Duffins Creek, and an unidentified suckermouth catfish (*Pterygoplichthys* sp.) was caught in Lake Erie. The Royal Panaque (*Panaque nigrolineatus*) has been reported caught in the Sydenham River. Undoubtedly illegal releases of aquarium pets.

SIMILAR SPECIES: There are no similar species **established** in Ontario.

SALMONIDAE / TROUTS AND SALMONS

ARCTIC CHAR *Salvelinus alpinus*

KNOWN LOCATIONS: Hudson Bay tributaries (strays), various locations in southern Ontario (introduced). Previously stocked for aquaculture and recreational purposes in southern Ontario.

SIMILAR SPECIES: The Lake Trout has a deeply forked tail (vs. slightly forked) and is covered by small, pale spots, none of which are red (vs. some red spots). The Brook Trout has wavy lines on the back and dorsal fin, and a black stripe behind the white leading edge of the pelvic and anal fins (vs. no black stripe).

POECILIIDAE / LIVEBEARERS

MOSQUITOFISH *Gambusia* species

KNOWN LOCATIONS: The Mosquitofish (*Gambusia affinis)* was stocked in a farm pond in southern Ontario in the 1940s. Although this population did not survive, mosquitofishes (*Gambusia* spp.) are currently being used in garden ponds, and it is quite possible that they may escape or be released into the wild.

SIMILAR SPECIES: The Blackstripe Topminnow and Banded Killifish have a dorsal fin **origin** over or slightly behind the anal fin **origin** (vs. far behind anal fin **origin**). The Banded Killifish has distinct bars (vs. no bars).

CICHLIDAE / CICHLIDS

CICHLIDS e.g., *Astronotus, Cichlasoma, Oreochromis, Parachromis* species

KNOWN LOCATIONS: Loiselle's Cichlid (*Parachromis loisellei*) and Red Oscar (*Astronotus ocellatus*) have been captured in various locations in southern Ontario. Tilapia have been caught in several locations in the Greater Toronto and Ottawa areas. They are most likely to be found in urban areas where they are sold in live-food markets. Other cichlids are undoubtedly illegal releases of aquarium pets.

SIMILAR SPECIES: Sunfishes have 2 nostrils on each side (vs. 1 nostril), and the **lateral line** is not broken (vs. **lateral line** broken into 2 parts: front part higher than posterior part). Darters, perches, and temperate basses usually have 2 dorsal fins (vs. 1).

PLEURONECTIDAE / RIGHT EYE FLOUNDERS

EUROPEAN FLOUNDER *Platichthys flesus*

KNOWN LOCATIONS: Lake Erie and Lake Superior. Undoubtedly a ballast-water release.

SIMILAR SPECIES: There are no similar species established in Ontario.

Occasionally caught (unlikely to be seen again)

POLYODONTIDAE / PADDLEFISHES

Paddlefish (*Polyodon spathula*)

ICTALURIDAE / NORTH AMERICAN CATFISHES

Blue Catfish (*Ictalurus furcatus*)

PIMELODIDAE / LONGWHISKERED CATFISHES

Bloch's Catfish (*Pimelodus blochii* complex)

PANGASIIDAE / SHARK CATFISHES

Striped Catfish (*Pangasianodon hypophthalmus*)

ESOCIDAE / PIKES AND MUDMINNOWS

Alaska Blackfish (*Dallia pectoralis*)

OSPHRONEMIDAE / GOURAMIES

Siamese Fighting Fish (*Betta splendens*)

POECILIIDAE / LIVEBEARERS

Guppy (*Poecilia reticulata*)

SALMONIDAE / TROUTS AND SALMONS

Arctic Grayling (*Thymallus arcticus*)
Cherry Salmon (*Oncorhynchus masou*)
Chum Salmon (*Oncorhynchus keta*)
Cutthroat Trout (*Oncorhynchus clarkii*)

POTENTIAL INVADERS

Not currently known (may become established)

ALOSIDAE / SHADS

BLUEBACK HERRING *Alosa aestivalis*

KNOWN LOCATIONS: The Blueback Herring has been found on the American side of Lake Ontario and the St. Lawrence River.

SIMILAR SPECIES: The Alewife has a grey-green back (vs. grey-blue to blue), and the eye diameter is usually greater than the snout length.

LEUCISCIDAE / MINNOWS

ALLEGHENY PEARL DACE *Margariscus margarita*

KNOWN LOCATIONS: The Allegheny Pearl Dace, and **hybrids** with Northern Pearl Dace, are found less than 50 km from Ontario in New York tributaries of eastern Lake Erie and eastern Lake Ontario.

SIMILAR SPECIES: The Finescale Dace has a larger mouth, the upper jaw extends backwards to below the front of the eye, and the **lateral line** is incomplete. The Creek Chub has a larger mouth, and individuals longer than 50 mm have a dark spot at the front base of the dorsal fin. The Lake Chub has a dorsal fin with a concave posterior edge, and a larger, visible **barbel** at the corners of the mouth, and the spawning male lacks a red stripe on the lower side. The Allegheny Pearl Dace is difficult to distinguish from the Northern Pearl Dace, which has finer scales (65–75 vs. 50–60 **lateral scales**).

BIGEYE CHUB *Hybopsis amblops*

KNOWN LOCATIONS: The Bigeye Chub is found about 15 km from Ontario in tributaries of the Niagara River in New York state.

SIMILAR SPECIES: The Bigeye Chub may be confused with the Bluntnose Minnow and **blackline shiners**, such as the Blacknose Shiner. The Bluntnose Minnow has smaller scales (42–50 vs. 33–38 **lateral scales**). **Blackline shiners** lack a **barbel** at the corners of the mouth. The Bigeye Chub may also be confused with the Silver Chub, which also has a **barbel**, but lacks a dark lateral stripe, and its tail is grey with a white bottom edge.

BIGMOUTH SHINER *Notropis dorsalis*

KNOWN LOCATIONS: The Bigmouth Shiner is found about 10 km from Ontario in tributaries of the Niagara River in New York state.

SIMILAR SPECIES: The Bigmouth Shiner is very difficult to distinguish from the Ghost, Mimic, River, and Sand shiners. The Ghost Shiner is much paler, often translucent in life. The River and Sand shiners have only 7 anal rays (vs. 8). The anterior lateral scales of the Mimic Shiner are more than twice as high as they are wide.

EASTERN BLACKNOSE DACE *Rhinichthys atratulus*

KNOWN LOCATIONS: The Eastern Blacknose Dace is found less than 1 km from Ontario in a small tributary of the St. Lawrence River in New York state near Cornwall, Ontario.

SIMILAR SPECIES: The Central Stoneroller lacks **barbels** and has larger scales (49–55 **lateral scales**), a continuous groove that separates the upper lip from the snout, and a mouth that is crescent-shaped when viewed from below. The Longnose Dace differs in having a longer snout that greatly overhangs the mouth, and its upper lip is much lower than the eye. The dark lateral stripe is usually not as prominent. The Western Blacknose Dace is very difficult to distinguish from the Eastern Blacknose Dace. The body of the western species tends to be more heavily spotted, and the mature males lack bright red pectoral fins.

SATINFIN SHINER *Cyprinella analostana*

KNOWN LOCATIONS: The Satinfin Shiner is found about 2 km from Ontario in two tributaries of the St. Lawrence River in New York state.

SIMILAR SPECIES: The Common and Striped shiners lack a black blotch on the posterior part of the dorsal fin, and their scale outlines do not form a distinct cross-hatched pattern on the body. The Satinfin Shiner is very difficult to distinguish from the Spotfin Shiner, which usually has 8 anal rays (vs. usually 9) and a dorsal fin that is not pigmented at the front (vs. scattered pigment).

SILVERJAW MINNOW *Notropis buccatus*

KNOWN LOCATIONS: The Silverjaw Minnow is found about 25 km from Ontario in western tributaries of Lake Erie in Michigan.

SIMILAR SPECIES: No other Ontario minnow has large **sensory canals** below the eye.

SOUTHERN REDBELLY DACE *Chrosomus erythrogaster*

KNOWN LOCATIONS: The Southern Redbelly Dace is found about 75 km from Ontario in western Lake Erie tributaries in Michigan.

SIMILAR SPECIES: The Northern Redbelly Dace is very similar, but differs in having a shorter snout and a more upturned mouth. If present, the red or yellow stripe below the mid-lateral black stripe is not as wide in the Northern Redbelly Dace.

SUCKERMOUTH MINNOW *Phenacobius mirabilis*

KNOWN LOCATIONS: The Suckermouth Minnow is found about 100 km from Ontario in western Lake Erie tributaries in Ohio.

SIMILAR SPECIES: Suckers have lips that have **plicae** and/or **papillae** (vs. lips that are wrinkled with 2 prominent fleshy lobes on each side). The Cutlip Minnow has a uniquely shaped **trilobed** lower jaw consisting of a central bony projection with a fleshy lobe on each side. The Longnose Dace also has a snout that greatly overhangs the mouth, but differs in having smaller scales (more than 60 **lateral scales** vs. fewer than 55).

WEED SHINER *Paranotropis texanus*

KNOWN LOCATIONS: The Weed Shiner is found about 50 km from Ontario in the Winnipeg River in Manitoba. Although it may have actually entered Manitoba through waterways in northwestern Ontario, the species has never been reported from Ontario.

SIMILAR SPECIES: Minnows with a black stripe extending onto the snout, other than **blackline shiners**, have smaller scales (more than 40 **lateral scales** vs. fewer than 40). The Weed Shiner is often difficult to distinguish from other **blackline shiners**. All of these shiners have a less prominent spot at the base of the tail. The Blacknose Shiner and Bridle Shiner also differ in having pale chins. The Pugnose Shiner has a very small, upturned mouth. The Weed Shiner is most similar in appearance to the Blackchin Shiner, which has a shorter, more pointed snout.

XENOCYPRIDIDAE / XENOCARPS

BLACK CARP *Mylopharyngodon piceus*

KNOWN LOCATIONS: The Black Carp may invade Lake Michigan through the Chicago Shipping Canal (about 600 km from Ontario) and then expand into the other Great Lakes.

SIMILAR SPECIES: The Common Carp and Goldfish have a long dorsal fin of more than 12 rays (vs. fewer than 12 rays) and a strong, **serrated** spine at the front of the dorsal and anal fins. The Bighead and Silver carps have very small scales (more than 84 **lateral scales** vs. fewer than 40). The Grass Carp is silver or pale grey and has **pharyngeal teeth** with prominent grooves (vs. club-like teeth without grooves), which cannot be seen without the **pharyngeal teeth** being removed.

SILVER CARP *Hypophthalmichthys molitrix*

KNOWN LOCATIONS: The Silver Carp may invade Lake Michigan through the Chicago Shipping Canal (about 600 km from Ontario) and then expand into the other Great Lakes.

SIMILAR SPECIES: The Common Carp and Goldfish have a long dorsal fin of more than 12 rays (vs. fewer than 12 rays) and a strong, **serrated** spine at the front of the dorsal and anal fins. The Black and Grass carps have large scales (fewer than 40 **lateral scales** vs. more than 84). The Bighead Carp has dark blotches on the back and a short ventral **keel** that extends from the pelvic fins to the anus (vs. a long ventral **keel** that extends from the throat to the anus).

COPPER REDHORSE *Moxostoma hubbsi*

KNOWN LOCATIONS: The Copper Redhorse is found about 70 km from Ontario in the Rivière des Mille Îles near Montreal, Quebec.

SIMILAR SPECIES: All other redhorses, except the Greater Redhorse, have 12–13 (vs. 15–16) scales around the narrowest part of the caudal peduncle. The Greater Redhorse has 12–13 (vs. 15–16) scales across the back in front of the dorsal fin from just above the **lateral line** on one side to just above the **lateral line** on the other.

EASTERN CREEK CHUBSUCKER *Erimyzon oblongus*

KNOWN LOCATIONS: The Eastern Creek Chubsucker is found less than 50 km from Ontario in New York tributaries of eastern Lake Ontario and the St. Lawrence River.

SIMILAR SPECIES: The Eastern Creek Chubsucker is difficult to distinguish from the Lake Chubsucker, which has smaller scales (39–45 vs. 34–38 **lateral scales**) and slightly more dorsal rays (11–13 vs. 9–11).

WESTERN CREEK CHUBSUCKER ***Erimyzon clavifrons***

KNOWN LOCATIONS: The Western Creek Chubsucker is found about 60–80 km from Ontario in tributaries of the western end of Lake Erie in Michigan.

SIMILAR SPECIES: The Western Creek Chubsucker is difficult to distinguish from the Lake Chubsucker, which has smaller scales (39–45 **lateral scales**, vs. 34–38) and slightly more dorsal rays (11–13, vs. 9–11).

ESOCIDAE / PIKES AND MUDMINNOWS

REDFIN PICKEREL ***Esox americanus americanus***

KNOWN LOCATIONS: The Redfin Pickerel is found about 125 km from Ontario in the St. Lawrence River in Quebec.

SIMILAR SPECIES: The Muskellunge and Northern Pike have partially scaled gill covers (vs. fully scaled) and a total of 10–18 **pores** on the underside of the lower jaw (vs. fewer than 10). The Chain Pickerel has 14–17 rays in each gill **membrane** (vs. 11–13). The Grass Pickerel has grey to yellow-green pelvic and anal fins (vs. red to orange).

APHREDODERIDAE / PIRATE PERCHES

PIRATE PERCH *Aphredoderus sayanus*

KNOWN LOCATIONS: The Pirate Perch is found less than 30 km from Ontario in New York tributaries of the eastern end of Lake Ontario, where it has recently expanded its range.

SIMILAR SPECIES: No other fish in Ontario has the anus situated in front of the pelvic fins and three spines in the dorsal fin.

CENTRARCHIDAE / SUNFISHES

REDBREAST SUNFISH *Lepomis auritus*

KNOWN LOCATIONS: The Redbreast Sunfish is found about 40 kilometers from Ontario in the Raquette River, a tributary of the St. Lawrence River in New York, where it has been introduced.

SIMILAR SPECIES: Other sunfishes, except the Bluegill, have pale edges to their **ear flap**. The Bluegill has a longer, more pointed, pectoral fin and a black blotch near the posterior base of the dorsal fin.

REDEAR SUNFISH *Lepomis microlophus*

KNOWN LOCATIONS: The Redear Sunfish is found about 80 km from Ontario in southwestern tributaries of Lake Erie in Ohio.

SIMILAR SPECIES: The Pumpkinseed is more colourful, has wavy blue stripes on the cheek, a more rounded snout, and shorter pectoral fins.

PERCIDAE / PERCHES AND DARTERS

ORANGETHROAT DARTER *Etheostoma spectabile*

KNOWN LOCATIONS: The Orangethroat Darter is found 1 km from Ontario in tributaries of the Detroit River in Michigan.

SIMILAR SPECIES: The Rainbow Darter has the deepest part of the body behind the dorsal fin **origin** (vs. deepest part of the body before or at the dorsal fin **origin**). The male Rainbow Darter has red markings on the anal fin and tail (vs. no red markings).

FURTHER INFORMATION

BOOKS

Bernatchez, L., and M. Giroux. 2012. *Les poissons d'eau douce du Québec et leur répartition dans l'est du Canada.* Broquet Inc., Saint-Constant, QC.

Coad, B., with H. Waszczuk (contributor), and I. Labignon (contributor). 1995. *Encyclopedia of Canadian Fishes.* Co-published by Canadian Museum of Nature and Canadian Sportfishing Productions Inc., Waterdown, ON.

Hubbs, C. L., K. F. Lagler, and G. R. Smith. 2004. *Fishes of the Great Lakes Region.* Revised Edition. University of Michigan Press, Ann Arbor, MI.

Page, L. M., and B. M. Burr. 2011. *Peterson Field Guide to Freshwater Fishes North of Mexico.* Second Edition. Houghton Mifflin Harcourt, Boston, MA.

Page, L. M., K. E. Bemis, T. E. Dowling, H. Espinosa-Pérez, L. T. Findley, C. R. Gilbert, K. E. Hartel, R. N. Lea, N. E. Mandrak, M. A. Neighbors, J. J. Schmitter-Soto, and H. J. Walker, Jr. 2023. *Common and Scientific Names of Fishes from the United States, Canada, and Mexico*, Eighth edition. American Fisheries Society, Special Publication 37, Bethesda, MD.

Scott, W. B., and E. J. Crossman. 1973. *Freshwater Fishes of Canada.* Fisheries Research Board of Canada Bulletin 184, Ottawa, ON.

Stewart, K. W., and D. A. Watkinson. 2004. *Freshwater Fishes of Manitoba.* University of Manitoba Press, Winnipeg, MB.

INTERNET SOURCES

Committee on the Status of Species at Risk in Canada (COSEWIC), cosewic.ca

Committee on the Status of Species at Risk in Ontario (COSSARO), cossaroagency.ca

FishBase (a comprehensive information system on all known fishes), fishbase.ca

Fisheries and Oceans Canada, dfo-mpo.gc.ca

Natural Heritage Information Centre, Ontario.ca/page/natural-heritage-information-centre

NatureServe Explorer (an online encyclopedia of life), explorer.natureserve.org

Ontario Endangered Species Act, ontario.ca/page/how-species-risk-are-protected

Ontario Federation of Anglers and Hunters, ofah.org

Ontario Freshwater Fish Life History Database, ontariofishes.ca

SARA Registry canada.ca/en/environment-climate-change/services/species-risk-public-registry.html

GLOSSARY

aestivate—hibernate in summer during poor environmental conditions (e.g., low oxygen).

ambush predator—a fish that hides and then captures its prey quickly by surprising it.

ammocoete—the young of lampreys before it transforms into an adult, also known as **larva**.

anadromous—living in an ocean and then migrating into fresh water to spawn.

anterior dorso-lateral—area between the **lateral line** and the middle of the back in front of the dorsal fin.

anti-tropical—distribution that includes higher northern and southern latitudes (i.e., temperate and polar), but excludes lower latitudes (i.e., tropical).

asymmetric—with two halves that are not exactly the same in shape and size (e.g., the tail of a sturgeon).

barbel—whisker-like, fleshy structures usually found near the mouth, chin, or snout.

bicuspid—teeth with two points known as "cusps," a condition used to distinguish between some lamprey species (p. 84).

blackline shiners—shiners in the **genus** *Notropis* with a black lateral stripe extending onto the snout, including Blackchin, Blacknose, Bridle, and Pugnose shiners.

carnivorous—feeding on animals.

cartilage—firm, flexible connective tissue that replaces bone in fishes such as lampreys and sturgeons.

catadromous—living in fresh waters and then migrating to the ocean to spawn.

char—an old term used in Europe for Arctic Char, a relative of Lake Trout and Brook Trout. Sometimes, all members of the *Salvelinus* **genus** are collectively referred to as char.

circumoral—around the opening of the mouth. Usually refers to location of those teeth immediately adjacent to the mouth opening in lampreys.

class—one in a series of ranks in a hierarchy used to classify living things. As an example, the classification for Lake Trout is Kingdom: Animalia; Phylum: Chordata; Class: Actinopterygii; **Order**: Salmoniformes; Family: Salmonidae; **Genus**: Salvelinus; Species: namaycush.

cobble—small pieces of rock (6.5–25 cm in diameter) found on the bottom of lakes and streams.

collapse—drastic decline in the number of individuals in a population, typically greater than a 90% reduction.

competition—interaction between individuals or species for resources (e.g., food, habitat), usually resulting in a winner and a loser.

crepuscular—exhibiting the greatest activity at dusk and dawn.

ctenoid scales—scales with minute, sharp projections, giving them a rough feel, typically found in species with spiny fins (p. 25).

cycloid scales—scales with smooth edges, typical of species without spiny fins (p. 25).

detritus—decaying matter from plants and animals.

ear flap—the small tab-shaped extension on the trailing edge of the gill cover in sunfishes.

elver—the third stage of the eel life cycle after hatching; it is a small pigmented eel that will grow into a young adult (*see also* **glass eel**, **leptocephalus**).

encrusted algae—plant-like organisms found attached to rocks.

esophagus—tube between the mouth and the stomach.

established—an introduced population that has reproduced for at least two generations.

extirpated—a species no longer occurring in part of its range (e.g., Ontario), but still found elsewhere.

eyelid—transparent **membrane** over sides of eye.

filamentous algae—plant-like organisms that grow in lakes and streams in clumps of long green strands.

filter feed—strain food out of the water.

fin membranes—the skin between the rays of the fin.

fractional spawner—an individual that releases its eggs in batches over an extended period of time.

fry—newly hatched fishes.

ganoid scales—heavy, bony, diamond-shaped, non-overlapping scales, typically found in gars.

genital papilla—short tube-like structure used to release eggs and sperm.

genus—name given to a group of closely-related species below the family level.

glass eel—the second stage of the eel life cycle after hatching; it is a small transparent eel that will then transform into an **elver** (*see also* **elver**, **leptocephalus**).

groundwater upwellings—underwater springs that seep through the bottoms of lakes and streams, often used by trout for spawning.

herbivorous—feeding on plants and algae.

hybrid—offspring resulting from the mating of parents from two different species.

hybridization—the act of mating with an individual of a different species.

hybridize—produce offspring with an individual of a different species.

ichthyologist—ichthyology is the study of fishes; ichthyologists study fishes.

inner ear—a series of small bones (*see also* **otoliths**) and canals found in the skull and used for hearing. Fishes lack an external (outer) ear.

invasive species—species not native to a region (e.g., Ontario), that has a negative impact on native species or ecosystems.

invertebrates—animals without backbones (e.g., insects, crayfishes).

keel—sharp ridge on the midline of the belly.

landlocked—species that are isolated in a lake and are prevented from migrating to the sea.

larva—life stage of a fish immediately after it hatches.

lateral line—series of **pore**-like openings to an underlying canal, found along the side of the body, typically from head to tail, and used to detect movement and vibration. Not to be confused with lateral stripe, which is a colour pattern.

lateral scales—the number of scales along the side of the fish from the head to the base of the tail (p. 23).

leptocephalus—the first stage of an eel life cycle after hatching; it is a transparent, ribbon-like individual not resembling an eel that will then transform into an elver (*see also* **elver**, **glass eel**).

leucistic—reduction in all pigments that give the animal colour.

membrane—thin layer of skin.

metamorphosis—the change from one life stage to another (e.g., from **ammocoete** to adult in lampreys).

niche—the relationship between a species and the environmental conditions required for its survival.

nuptial tubercles—hard bumps, usually small and sharp, on the head, body, and fins present during the spawning season.

omnivorous—feeding on a variety of food, including plants, animals, and **detritus**.

opportunists—individuals or species that feed on anything that is available.

order—one in a series of ranks in a

hierarchy used to classify living things. As an example, the classification for Lake Trout is Kingdom: Animalia; Phylum: Chordata; **Class**: Actinopterygii; **Order**: Salmoniformes; Family: Salmonidae; **Genus**: Salvelinus; Species: namaycush.

origin—where the front end of the fin attaches to the body.

otoliths—small bones in the **inner ear** that transform sound vibrations into nerve impulses (*see also* **inner ear**).

ovipositor—short tube-like structure used to lay eggs that extends from the body.

papillae—fleshy bumps, such as those found on the lips of some suckers (p. 223).

parr marks—vertical ovals or bars found on young (termed **parr**) salmon and trout.

pelagic—living in open water above the bottom.

periphyton—algae, bacteria, fungi, and small **invertebrates** that form a community on submerged surfaces in fresh water.

pharyngeal teeth—teeth found in the throat (p. 27).

phytoplankton—microscopic free-floating plants that live in water.

piscivorous—feeding on fishes.

plankton—microscopic free-floating plants, animals, and bacteria that live in water.

plicae—ridges, separated by grooves, found on the lips of fishes (e.g., suckers, p. 223).

pores—small holes in scales or skin typically associated with sensory organs such as the **lateral line**.

predation—preying on, or being preyed upon.

prickles—minute, sometimes curved, spines on the head and/or body.

protrusible—extendable; for example the lips of many fishes are loosely connected to the jaw and can be extended forward to aid in capturing prey.

redd—nest made by salmon and trout by creating a depression in streams, and sometimes lakes, using the tail.

riffles—shallow, fast-flowing areas of streams.

riparian—vegetation found on both sides of a stream, often shading it.

scutes—bony scales, often with sharp ridges, typically found on Lake Sturgeon.

sensory canal—a thin depression or tube-like structure found on the head and body of most fishes, usually with **pores**, and used to detect movement and vibration. The **lateral line** is the major sensory canal in fishes.

serrations—small barbs found on the fin spines of catfishes and carps (e.g., catfishes, p. 256).

sexual dimorphism—presence of different characteristics, often colour, in the two sexes of a species, usually related to spawning.

siltation—the build-up of fine sediments on the bottom of lakes and streams.

sister species—two species that are more closely related to each other than to any other species.

species pairs—two closely related species living in the same waterbody.

standard length—length of the fish from the snout to the base of the tail.

stitched—a colouration pattern where the **lateral line pores** are bordered above and below by dark dots or dashes, resembling a series of stitches.

substrates—the sediments found on the bottom of lakes and streams.

swim bladder—balloon-like structure in the body cavity used for buoyancy and sometimes for breathing and sound production.

tapetum lucidum—special reflective layer in the retina of the eye used to improve vision in low light conditions.

thermocline—the depth zone in a lake where the temperature drops at the greatest rate.

transverse grooves—thin, shallow

depressions perpendicular to deeper depressions found on the lips of some suckers (p. 224).

trilobed—having three lobes, such as the lower jaw in Cutlip Minnow (p. 154).

turbid—having a lot of fine suspended matter, giving water a muddy appearance.

turbidity—the amount of fine suspended matter in the water.

type specimen—a specimen used to originally describe the species.

unicuspid—teeth with a single point known as a "cusp," a condition used to distinguish between some lamprey species (p. 84).

urogenital papilla—short tube-like structure used to release eggs, sperm, and waste products.

Weberian apparatus—specialized bones connecting the **swim bladder** to the **inner ear** bones found only in minnows and their relatives (*see also* **inner ear**).

zooplankton—microscopic free-floating animals that live in water.

CHECKLIST OF ONTARIO FISHES

This list includes 176 fish species, three subspecies, and five **hybrids** that have been caught in the wild in Ontario. Species are native unless otherwise marked. Those species, subspecies, and **hybrids** that have been introduced and are successfully breeding in Ontario are marked with an (I,S) and those introduced, but unsuccessful at breeding, an (I,U) and those introduced, but with unknown breeding status, an (I, ?). Species with more than one designation (e.g., N and I,S) are native to part of Ontario, but introduced elsewhere. **Extirpated** species are marked with an (XP), and extinct species with an (X).

LAMPREYS

- ❑ American Brook Lamprey
- ❑ Chestnut Lamprey
- ❑ Northern Brook Lamprey
- ❑ Sea Lamprey (I,S)
- ❑ Silver Lamprey

STURGEONS

- ❑ Lake Sturgeon

PADDLEFISHES

- ❑ Paddlefish (XP)

GARS

- ❑ Florida Gar (I,U)
- ❑ Longnose Gar
- ❑ Spotted Gar

BOWFINS

- ❑ Emerald Bowfin

MOONEYES

- ❑ Goldeye
- ❑ Mooneye

FRESHWATER EELS

- ❑ American Eel (N and I,S)

SHADS

- ❑ Alewife (I,S)
- ❑ American Shad (N and I,U)

THREAD HERRINGS

- ❑ Gizzard Shad

CARPS

- ❑ Common Carp (I,S)
- ❑ Goldfish (I,S)

MINNOWS

- ❑ Blackchin Shiner
- ❑ Blacknose Shiner
- ❑ Bluntnose Minnow
- ❑ Brassy Minnow
- ❑ Bridle Shiner
- ❑ Central Stoneroller (N and I,S)
- ❑ Common Shiner
- ❑ Creek Chub
- ❑ Cutlip Minnow
- ❑ Eastern Silvery Minnow
- ❑ Emerald Shiner
- ❑ Fallfish
- ❑ Fathead Minnow
- ❑ Finescale Dace
- ❑ Ghost Shiner
- ❑ Golden Shiner
- ❑ Gravel Chub (XP)
- ❑ Hornyhead Chub (N and I,S)
- ❑ Lake Chub
- ❑ Longnose Dace
- ❑ Mimic Shiner
- ❑ Northern Pearl Dace
- ❑ Northern Redbelly Dace
- ❑ Pugnose Minnow
- ❑ Pugnose Shiner
- ❑ Redfin Shiner
- ❑ Redside Dace
- ❑ River Chub (N and I,S)
- ❑ River Shiner
- ❑ Rosyface Shiner
- ❑ Rudd (I,S)
- ❑ Sand Shiner
- ❑ Silver Chub

- ❑ Silver Shiner
- ❑ Spotfin Shiner (N and I,S)
- ❑ Spottail Shiner
- ❑ Striped Shiner (N and I,S)
- ❑ Western Blacknose Dace

TENCHES

- ❑ Tench (I,S)

XENOCARPS

- ❑ Bighead Carp (I,U)
- ❑ Grass Carp (I,U)

SUCKERS

- ❑ Bigmouth Buffalo (N and I,S)
- ❑ Black/Smallmouth Buffalo (I,S)
- ❑ Black Redhorse (N and I,?)
- ❑ Golden Redhorse
- ❑ Greater Redhorse
- ❑ Lake Chubsucker
- ❑ Longnose Sucker
- ❑ Northern Hog Sucker (N and I,?)
- ❑ Quillback
- ❑ River Redhorse
- ❑ Shorthead Redhorse
- ❑ Silver Redhorse
- ❑ Spotted Sucker
- ❑ White Sucker

LOACHES

- ❑ Loach (I,U)

PIRANHAS AND PACUS

- ❑ Pirapatinga (I,U)
- ❑ Red Piranha (I,U)

NORTH AMERICAN CATFISHES

- ❑ Black Bullhead (N and I,S)
- ❑ Blue Catfish (I,U)
- ❑ Brindled Madtom
- ❑ Brown Bullhead
- ❑ Channel Catfish
- ❑ Flathead Catfish (I,S)
- ❑ Margined Madtom (I,S)
- ❑ Northern Madtom
- ❑ Stonecat
- ❑ Tadpole Madtom
- ❑ Yellow Bullhead

LONG-WHISKERED CATFISHES

- ❑ Bloch's Catfish (I,U)

ARMORED CATFISHES

- ❑ Royal Panaque (I,U)
- ❑ Suckermouth Catfish (I,U)

SHARK CATFISHES

- ❑ Striped Catfish (I,U)

PIKES AND MUDMINNOWS

- ❑ Alaska Blackfish (I,U)
- ❑ Central Mudminnow
- ❑ Chain Pickerel (I,S)
- ❑ Grass Pickerel
- ❑ Muskellunge
- ❑ Northern Pike (N and I,S)
- ❑ Tiger Muskellunge (Pike-Muskellunge **hybrid**) (N and I,U)

SMELTS

- ❑ Rainbow Smelt (N and I,S)

TROUTS AND SALMONS

- ❑ Arctic Char (I,U)
- ❑ Arctic Grayling (I,U)
- ❑ Atlantic Salmon (XP and I,S)
- ❑ Aurora Trout (N and I,S)
- ❑ Blackfin Cisco
- ❑ Bloater
- ❑ Brook Trout (N and I,S)
- ❑ Brown Trout (I,S)
- ❑ Cherry Salmon (I,U)
- ❑ Chinook Salmon (I,S)
- ❑ Chum Salmon (I,U)
- ❑ Cisco
- ❑ Coho Salmon (I,S)
- ❑ Cutthroat Trout (I,U)
- ❑ Deepwater Cisco (X)
- ❑ Kiyi
- ❑ Lake Trout
- ❑ Lake Whitefish
- ❑ Nipigon Cisco
- ❑ Longjaw Cisco (X)
- ❑ Pink Salmon (I,S)
- ❑ Pygmy Whitefish
- ❑ Rainbow Trout (I,S)

❑ Round Whitefish
❑ Shortjaw Cisco
❑ Shortnose Cisco
❑ Sockeye Salmon (I,S)
❑ Splake (Brook–Lake Trout **hybrid**) (I,U)
❑ Tiger Trout (Brook–Brown Trout **hybrid**) (I,U)

TROUT-PERCHES

❑ Trout-perch

CODS

❑ Burbot

NEW WORLD SILVERSIDES

❑ Brook Silverside

TOPMINNOWS

❑ Banded Killifish
❑ Blackstripe Topminnow

LIVEBEARERS

❑ Guppy (I,U)
❑ Mosquitofish (I,U)

STICKLEBACKS

❑ Brook Stickleback
❑ Fourspine Stickleback (I,S)
❑ Ninespine Stickleback
❑ Threespine Stickleback (N and I,S)

SCULPINS

❑ Mottled Sculpin
❑ Slimy Sculpin
❑ Spoonhead Sculpin

FATHEAD SCULPINS

❑ Deepwater Sculpin

TEMPERATE BASSES

❑ White Bass
❑ White Perch (I,S)
❑ Wiper (White Bass–Striped Bass **hybrid**) (I,U)

SUNFISHES AND BASSES

❑ Black Crappie (N and I,S)
❑ Bluegill
❑ Green Sunfish (N and I,S)
❑ Largemouth Bass (N and I,S)
❑ Northern Sunfish
❑ Orangespotted Sunfish (I,S)
❑ Pumpkinseed
❑ Rock Bass
❑ Smallmouth Bass (N and I, S)
❑ Warmouth
❑ White Crappie

PERCHES AND DARTERS

❑ Blackside Darter (N and I,S)
❑ Blue Pike (X)
❑ Channel Darter
❑ Eastern Sand Darter
❑ Fantail Darter
❑ Greenside Darter (N and I,S)
❑ Iowa Darter
❑ Johnny Darter
❑ Least Darter
❑ Logperch
❑ Rainbow Darter (N and I, S)
❑ River Darter
❑ Ruffe (I,S)
❑ Sauger
❑ Saugeye (Sauger-Walleye **hybrid**) (I,U)
❑ Tessellated Darter
❑ Walleye
❑ Yellow Perch

DRUMS AND CROAKERS

❑ Freshwater Drum

CICHLIDS

❑ Loiselle's Cichlid (I,U)
❑ Red Oscar (I,U)
❑ Tilapia (I,U)

GOBIES

❑ Round Goby (I,S)
❑ Freshwater Tubenose Goby (I,S)

GOURAMIES

❑ Siamese Fighting Fish (I,U)

RIGHT EYE FLOUNDERS

❑ European Flounder (I,U)

INDEX TO COMMON AND SCIENTIFIC SPECIES NAMES

PHOTOGRAPHS AND ILLUSTRATIONS

Lower case letters adjacent to each page number refer to the position of the photograph or illustration on the page (a–j, top to bottom).

Illustrators

© Marianne Collins 23a, 23b, 23c, 24a, 24e, 24f, 25a (left), 25a (right), 25b (left), 25b (right), 25c (left), 25c (middle), 25c (right), 25d (left), 25d (middle), 25d (right), 26a, 26b, 26c (left), 26c (middle), 26c (right), 26d (left), 26d (right), 26e (left), 26e (right), 26f (left), 26f (middle), 26f (right), 27a (left), 27a (right), 27b (left), 27b (right), 27c (left), 27c (middle), 27c (right), 27d (left), 27d (middle), 28a (left), 29d (left), 30a (right), 30b (right), 30c (right), 31b (left), 33d (right), 33f (right), 34d (left), 34e (left), 35c, 36a (right), 36b (right), 37d (right), 48b (right), 48d (right), 48e (right), 50a (right), 52a (right), 52b (right), 52c (right), 84a (left), 84a (right), 84b (left), 84b (right), 84c, 85a, 85b, 85c, 107, 111a, 111b, 136a (left), 136a (middle), 136a (right), 136b, 136c, 136d, 136e, 136f, 136g (left), 136g (right), 137a (left), 137a (middle), 137a (right), 137b (left), 137b (right), 137c (left), 137c (right), 137d, 137e, 137f, 137g (left), 137g (right), 139b, 141b, 145b, 147b, 149c, 157, 187b, 191c, 211b, 211c, 223, 224a (left), 224c (right), 225a (left), 225a (right), 225b (left), 225b (middle), 225b (right), 225c (left), 225c (right), 225d (left), 225d (right), 256a, 256b, 256c, 256d, 256e (left), 256e (right), 280a, 280b, 280c, 281a, 299 (left), 299 (middle), 299 (right), 331d, 361 (left), 361 (middle), 361 (right), 369 (left), 369 (middle), 369 (right), 451

Ellen Edmonson, New York State Department of Environmental Conservation, 443b

© Julia Herr, 27d (right), 29e, 30d (right), 33b, 257b, 257c, 281b, 281c, 423a (right)

E. Holm, 32a (right)

Karen Klitz, Michigan Sea Grant, 24b, 24c, 24d, 28a (right), 28b, 29a, 29b, 29c, 29d (right), 30a (left), 30b (left), 30c (left), 30d (left), 31a, 31b (right), 31c, 31d, 32a (left), 32b (left), 32c, 33a, 33c, 33d (left), 33f (left), 34a, 34b, 34c, 34d (right), 34e (right),35a, 35b (left), 35b (right), 35d, 35e, 35f, 257g, 257h

Will Pridham all species and maps

© W. B. Scott and E. J. Crossman, Freshwater Fishes of Canada, 32b (right), 33e, 48a (right), 48c (right), 50b (right), 50c (right), 51a (right), 51b (right), 51c (right), 155b, 224a (middle), 224a (right), 224b (left), 224b (middle), 224b (right), 224c (left), 224c (middle), 257a, 257d, 257e, 257f, 257i, 257j

Tom Sheldon, Royal Military College, 13

© University of Michigan Press, 125, 317b, 323c, 327c, 331c

Paul Vecsei with permission from Great Lakes Fishery Commission, 304c, 306c

Photographers

Alamy Stock Photo, 53a, 96, 128, 214, 216, 217b, 217c, 218, 221a, 221b, 301a, 301b, 302a, 302b, 331a, 460b, 470b

David Arbour, 267a

Mac Armstrong, 123c

W. D. Bakowsky, Ontario Ministry of Natural Resources and Forestry, 14b (right), 15b (left), 15c (right)

Blaise Barette, 121b

M. C. Barnhart, 431c (right)

Louis Bernatchez, 46a, 284

Biopix.dk, 131b (right), 357a, 461

Alex Borbely, 302c, 329a

B. Boyle © ROM, 221c, 449c (left)

C. Brant, Great Lakes Fishery Commission, 93a

D. Brenner, University of Michigan School for Environment and Sustainability, 93c

Sam Brinker, 15c (left)

Richard T. Bryant & Wayne C. Starnes, 36d, 36f, 37b, 37d (left), 44a, 44c, 44d,

45b, 51c (left), 52d, 52e, 54b, 55c, 60a, 60c, 61b, 62a, 64a, 64d, 64e, 65a, 65d, 66a, 66b, 66c, 68b, 69c, 69d, 70b, 70d, 71b, 71c, 71d, 72a, 72c, 72d, 74a, 75a, 76c, 76d, 86, 102, 108a, 116, 120, 122, 126, 130, 132, 142a, 142b, 150, 184, 202, 204, 206, 210, 244, 258, 260, 264, 274, 276, 282, 348, 382, 387a, 389, 395, 396a, 399c, 401, 408, 409a, 410, 414, 426, 430, 432

Kathrine Burgsma, 131b

Noel Burkhead, U.S. Geological Survey, 58d, 59e, 61c, 65b, 65c, 68a, 68c, 70c, 73a, 74c, 152, 154, 192, 198, 268, 272, 386, 398, 416, 444

Jason Butler, 91b, 91c

W. H. Carrick, 45a, 55b, 59d, 174, 196, 376

© Patrice Ceisel, Visuals Unlimited, 309e

© Patrice Ceisel / Shedd AQ / SeaPics.com, 402b

Brian Coad, © Canadian Museum of Nature, 69a, 153b, 183b, 269a, 400, 405c, 425a

George Coker, 417a, 417b, 450, 455a

© Mark Conlin / SeaPics.com, 319c

Gordon Court, 239b, 327b

Jon Craig, © New Hampshire Fish and Game, 36e, 38c, 56b, 62d, 63d, 67d, 73c, 92, 146, 156, 160, 300, 344, 354, 355

Todd Crail, University of Toledo, 89b (left), 89b (right), 185c, 251a, 261a, 271a, 349b, 423a (left), 423b, 423c, 429b, 433a, 433b (right), 465a

John Cramer, 87b

Robert W. Criswell, 147a, 462b, 464b, 468b

Tim Daniel, Ohio Department of Natural Resources, 273c

Marion Daniels, Ontario Ministry of Natural Resources and Forestry, 39c

© Solomon David / www.PrimitiveFishes.com, 100, 106, 456

Alan Dextrase, Ontario Ministry of Natural Resources and Forestry, 151a, 169b, 173a, 177c, 179b, 197b, 205b, 207b, 273a, 340, 343b, 365b, 394b, 415a, 419a, 419b, 427a

© Reinhard Dirscherl / SeaPics.com, 101b (left), 101b (right), 278

Engbretson Underwater Photography, 222, 227a, 229b, 247a, 254, 259b, 267b, 289a, 289b, 289c, 292b, 292c, 321b, 384c, 387b, 388, 405b, 412, 425b, 443a, 445a (right), 445b, 445c, 446, 449a

William M. Estes, Sr., 161b

Fisheries and Oceans Canada, 52c (left), 101a (right), 228

D. Flescher, National Oceanic and Atmospheric Administration, 44b, 462a

M. Gautreau, 161c

R. Bruce Gebhardt, 57b, 151b, 227b, 235b, 263a, 269b, 360, 363a, 382, 399a, 421a, 425c, 435b, 449b, 469b

Bryce Gibson / Engbretson Underwater Photography, 193b

David Gilchrist, 445a (left)

Bill Glass, University of Windsor, 17b (right)

J. D. Grabarkiewicz, 421c, 435a

Glen Guthrie, Sahtu Renewable Resources Board, 47d, 292a, 365a

Ken Hammond, U.S. Department of Agriculture, 409b

Harbor Branch Oceanographic Institute, 117a

Kazutoshi Hiyeda Aqua Photo Studio, 42b, 67b, 67c, 296, 297a, 297b, 350, 356, 357b, 358

© E. Holm, ROM, 45c, 48c (left), 48e (left), 50b (left), 50c (left), 57c, 58b, 58e, 59a, 59c, 61a, 62b, 63a, 63b, 69b, 70a, 71a, 72b, 74b, 76a, 76b, 78b, 78c, 138, 148, 162, 163c, 165a, 172, 176, 177a, 181c, 183a, 183c, 186, 187a, 188, 189b, 190, 207c, 230, 232, 233c, 236, 240, 241c, 243c, 247b, 286, 392, 393b, 402a, 418, 433b (left), 440, 452, 454

Tiit Hunt / Wikimedia Commons, 437b

© Chris Huss / SeaPics.com, 41b, 315a, 319b (left)

Jennifer Idol / Engbretson Underwater Photography, 105b

Colin Iles, Fisheries and Oceans Canada, 49d, 75d, 420

Inspired Planet Productions (Yvonne Drebert and Zach Melnick), 307, 368, 371a, 371b

C. Jones, Natural Heritage Information Centre, 15d (left), 15d (right)

© 2007 Brian Jorg / www.brianjorg.com, 375c, 411a

David Jude, University of Michigan, 453b

E. R. Keeley, 319a, 325a, 339c

Lonnie King, Fisheries and Oceans Canada, 385

Fang Fang Kullander, 53c, 467a

Sean Landsman / Engbretson Underwater Photography, 117b, 118,

119, 123b, 125b, 294

Gregory Lashbrook, Gregory A. D., 95a, 95b, 99b, 99c (left), 99c (right), 99d, 131c, 241a, 271c, 273b, 332, 335b, 339a, 339b, 403a, 403b, 405a, 431c (left), 455b (left), 455b (middle), 455b (right)

Ted Lawrence, Great Lakes Fishery Commission, 82, 93b

Paul Lebeau, 80

Mike J. Leung, 235a

John Lyons, 43b, 45e, 47b, 54f, 63c, 73d, 75b, 166, 170, 287b, 326, 367c, 428, 436

John MacGregor, Kentucky Department of Fish and Wildlife Resources, 191b, 245a, 375b

Rob MacGregor and Nicki Butala, 310a, 310b, 310c, 311, 406a, 406b (left), 406b (right)

Madolyn Mandrak, 449c (right)

Nicholas Mandrak, University of Toronto, 37c, 104

Jim McCormac Photography, 127a

Dave McShaffrey, Marietta College, 143a

Gary Meszaros, 39a, 49c, 91a, 103b, 127b, 131a, 131b (left), 134, 153c, 159a, 163a (right), 169a, 179a, 185b, 197a, 201b, 205a, 207a, 209b, 211a, 213a, 237b, 241b, 249a, 261b, 271b, 275a, 283c, 309b, 335c, 343a, 347a, 347b, 349a, 353b, 372, 377a, 381a, 396b, 399b, 411b, 415b, 427b, 429a, 435c

Robert Michelson, Photography by Michelson Inc., 123a

© Larry Mishkar / SeaPics.com, 390c, 391a, 391b, 406c

Jeff Mondragon / mondragonphoto.com, 41d, 325b, 325c

© Jeff Mondragon / SeaPics.com, 319b (middle), 319b (right)

K. Moore, 15a (left), 15a (right)

Christopher Morey / Engbretson Underwater Photography, 124

© Fumitoshi Mori, Nature Production, 378, 384b

Andrew Muir, Great Lakes Fishery Commission, 304a, 304b, 305a

Nature's Images, Inc., 58c, 103a, 109a, 133a, 149a, 153a, 185a, 189a, 201a, 265c, 275b, 277a, 283b, 353c, 363b, 375a, 381c, 396c, 431a, 441b, 458a, 458b, 471a, 471b

Nebraskaland magazine, Nebraska Game and Parks Commission, 47c, 290a, 290b

Steven Noakes, 17a

Mike Oldham, NHIC Archives, 15b (right)

David Ostendorf, Missouri Department of Conservation, 39d, 49e, 56d, 237a, 313a, 463a

James F. Parnell, 155a, 161a, 441a, 464a

Todd Pearsons / Engbretson Underwater Photography, 359a

Jack Perks, 217a

Tony Pletcher, Bio-DITRL, 40b, 40c, 318

David Reicks, UIUC / IL-IN Sea Grant, 53e, 467b

Mont Richardson, 313b

William Roston, 191a

Brian Round, Fleming College, 17b (left)

Royal Alberta Museum, 49a, 49b, 163a (left), 163b, 175a, 175b, 177b, 181b, 239a, 253a, 253b, 335a, 367a, 367b

Sue Russell, 269c

Ryan Photographic, Dr. Paddy Ryan, 460a

© Atsushi Sakurai, Nature Production, 38a, 38d, 39b, 40d, 41c, 53b, 53d, 63e, 68d, 220, 298, 308, 309a, 312, 321c, 324, 383, 457a

Peter Sale, 309c, 309d

Konrad P. Schmidt, 87a, 89a, 103c, 139a, 141a, 145a, 159b, 165b, 167, 171, 173b, 173c, 179c, 181a, 195a, 195b, 203a, 203b, 209a, 213b, 231b, 243a, 243b, 277b, 283a, 359b, 359c, 394a, 421b, 439b, 463a, 463b, 470a

© D. R. Schrichte / SeaPics.com, 101a (left), 377b, 381b

Kate Schwartz, 453a

© Shedd Aquarium / www.fishphotos.org, 46b, 110, 123a, 259a, 265a, 287a, 327a, 336, 353a, 437a, 439a

Dave Smith, 105c

© Garold W. Sneegas, 48d (left), 105a, 143b, 149b, 229a, 233a, 250, 253c, 263b, 265b, 349c, 390a, 390b, 431b, 465b

Todd Stailey, Tennessee Aquarium, 99a

Shawn Staton, Fisheries and Oceans Canada, 14a (right)

Mark Sullivan, 114, 117c

D. A. Sutherland, Natural Heritage Information Centre, 14 (left)

Isaac Szabo / Engbretson Underwater Photography, 109b, 193a, 231a, 233b, 251b, 285a

Matthew R. Thomas, Kentucky Department of Fish and Wildlife Resources, 65e, 270

Uland Thomas, 42c, 47a, 51b (left), 56c, 60b, 64b, 234, 266, 285b, 342, 457b, 469a
Kenneth Tse, 108b, 169c, 249b
University of Michigan Museum of Zoology, 353d
Nathalie Vachon, Ministère des Forêts, de la Faune et des Parcs, 468a
Markku Varjo-Kuvaliiteri, 199a
Paul Vecsei, 209c, 239c, 245b, 317, 459b
Paul Vecsei / Engbretson Underwater Photography, ii, 315b, 321a, 323a, 323b, 331b
Viktor Vrbovsky / Engbretson Underwater Photography, 293
Doug Watkinson, 36a (left), 36b (left), 36c, 37a, 37e, 38b, 40a, 41a, 42a, 43a, 43c, 43d, 44e, 44f, 45d, 46c, 46d, 48a (left), 48b (left), 50a (left), 51a (left), 52a (left), 52b (left), 54a, 54c, 54d, 54e, 55a, 56a, 57a, 58a, 59b, 62c, 64c, 67a, 73b, 73e, 74d, 75c, 77a, 77b, 77c, 78a, 88, 90, 94, 98, 112, 113, 140, 144, 158, 164, 168, 178, 180, 182, 194, 200, 208, 212a, 212b, 226, 238, 242, 246, 248, 252, 262, 288, 291, 306a, 314, 316, 320, 322, 328, 329b, 330, 334, 338, 346, 352, 362, 364, 366, 370, 374, 404, 424, 434, 438, 442, 448, 466b
Andre Werner, 459a
Matt Windle, 199b
Brian Zimmerman, 393a

ACKNOWLEDGEMENTS

We wish to thank the many people who contributed to this book in so many ways. Mark Engstrom, former Deputy Director of Collections and Research, and Josh Basseches, Director and CEO, ROM, authorized the funds for the second edition. Special thanks go to members of the Fishes section of the Department of Natural History, ROM, for their guidance and encouragement, including Nathan Lujan and Margaret Crossman. We would especially like to acknowledge Brenna Wells for her many suggestions for improvements to the guide, for researching additional photographs for the second edition, and for her tireless efforts to document photographers. Margaret Zur patiently edited several versions of the manuscript.

We gratefully acknowledge Sheeza Sarfraz for managing the new edition. We are indebted to ROM graphic designer Tara Winterhalt for her redesign and to production designer Claire Milne for her work on all the new elements added in this edition.

We are grateful to Eric Berglund, Dustin Boczec, Brian Coad, George Coker, David Copplestone, Andrea Dunn, John Furlone, Bernard Lebeau, Jenna McGuire, Jamie Sanza, Nathan Staels, and Blair Wasylenko for correcting errors and providing new information for the second edition.

Many photographers contributed to this field guide, and we are especially grateful to those who generously donated their images, including David Arbour, Louis Bernatchez, Alex Borbely, C. Brant, D. Brenner, Kathrine Burgsma, Noel Burkhead, Jason Butler, Brian Coad, George Coker, Gordon Court, Todd Crail, Robert W. Criswell, Alan Dextrase, Yvonne Drebert, Bill Glass, Great Lakes Fishery Commission, Colin Iles, Ted Lawrence, Paul Lebeau, Mike Leung, John Lyons, Rob MacGregor and Nicki Butala, Madolyn Mandrak, Zach Melnick, Andrew Muir, Steven Noakes, David Ostendorf, Brian Round, Konrad Schmidt, Matt Thomas, Kenneth Tse, Doug Watkinson, Matt Windle, and Brian Zimmerman.

Very special thanks to our families for their continued patience, support, and encouragement.

ABOUT THE AUTHORS

Erling Holm is an Assistant Curator Emeritus of Fishes in the Department of Natural History, Royal Ontario Museum. With more than 46 years of experience, he is a recognized authority on the identification of Ontario's fishes. He has trained a couple of thousand fisheries biologists and other interested individuals at the Royal Ontario Museum's annual fish identification workshops. Erling has conducted dozens of expeditions to study the fish fauna of Ontario, Quebec, and South America. He has been an advisor to the Committee on the Status of Endangered Wildlife in Canada and has authored status reports on 12 rare freshwater fishes of Ontario.

Dr. Nicholas E. Mandrak is a Professor in the Department of Biological Sciences at the University of Toronto Scarborough, where he also directs a professional Master's program in Conservation and Biodiversity. He conducted graduate research on Ontario fishes at the University of Toronto and Royal Ontario Museum under the supervision of Dr. E. J. Crossman. Nick is a Research Associate with the ROM and the South Africa Institute for Aquatic Biodiversity and an Adjunct Professor at several Ontario universities. He has co-authored more than 300 scientific articles and reports, and several books on the biodiversity, biogeography, and conservation of Canadian freshwater fishes.

Mary E. Burridge is an Assistant Curator of Fishes in the Department of Natural History at the Royal Ontario Museum. With more than 35 years of experience, she has written over 35 scientific and popular articles, focusing on new species descriptions, Ontario's native species, invasives, habitat loss, and climate change. Mary has been involved in numerous field expeditions in Ontario, Southeast Asia, and South America. Mary is a team member of the ROM's Life in Crisis: Schad Gallery of Biodiversity and the popular Patrick and Barbara Keenan Family Gallery of Hands-on Biodiversity. She is also active in outreach programs, visiting schools and youth groups to advocate for Ontario's native biodiversity.

< School of ciscoes